Poet Of The Wrong Generation

A Fable Of Stardom's Rewards

LONNIE OSTROW

Harmony
River Press

POET OF THE WRONG GENERATION

www.harmonyriverpress.com

Author: Lonnie Ostrow
Cover Design and Art: Robert Sauber
Published in print by Harmony River Press; eBooks by Amazon KDP.
Poet Of The Wrong Generation is available on Amazon.com, though major book distributors (e.g. Ingram, Baker & Taylor, etc.). Please ask your local bookstore and library to stock it.

Isbns:
978-0-9974042-0-3 (Trade Paperback)
978-0-9974042-1-0 (Kindle Ebook)
Library Of Congress Control Number: 2016905424

First Edition: November 2016

Harmony
River Press

Songwriting Copyrights

We've Got Tonite
Written by Bob Seger
Copyright: 1976, Gear Publishing Company (ASCAP)
Used by permission.

Time
Words and Music by Eric Woolfson, Alan Parsons
Copyright © 1980, Woolfsongs Ltd., and Universal Music - Careers
All Rights Administered by Universal Music - Careers
International Copyright Secured All Rights Reserved
Reprinted by Permission of Hal Leonard Corporation

House Of The Rising Sun
Copyright: Unknown
Lyrics reprinted under the use of public domain

Prologue
A Poet's Lament

Johnny Elias stared at the photograph with bittersweet regret. Four suntanned faces smiled back at him; a precious memory from the best day he could ever remember. The blazing sunshine. One enormous stage. Soaring music. Scores of people dressed in summer clothes lined up for miles on the Great Lawn. A perfect day when all was right with the world. If only life could again be so invigorating. So free.

The snapshot was date-stamped August 15th, 1991: the day Johnny had keenly anticipated that whole summer. His last college summer. A fleeting moment when life seemed full of endless possibilities. A time when a ballad was a three-minute escape into someone else's melancholy. When friendships were real. When love was more than a crippling game of insincerity.

Johnny's eyes momentarily broke away from the framed photo and over to a heap in the center of the room. Twelve cardboard boxes contained mementos of the last few tumultuous years. The framed gold records. The press clippings. The fan mail. He drew a heavy sigh then refocused on his own bronzed face in the picture. How young he looked at twenty-one. His hair thicker. His smiling green eyes without a trace of sadness. He was so naively happy. So very much in love with the young woman whose shoulders his arm was draped around. *Ah, love... whatever that was.*

Johnny spotted his CDs and vinyl records stacked haphazardly against a wall. The Beatles. Paul Simon. Bob Dylan. Jim Croce. Joni Mitchell. Elvis

Costello. A plethora of songwriting legends, most of whom had reached their creative apex long before he was born. Back in 1991, this collection was Johnny's only meaningful possession inside his tiny Brooklyn apartment – the address he departed from on that celebrated August morning en route to Central Park.

Suddenly, another wave of glorious memories came flooding back. Megan's "borrowed" green blanket. A maze of revelers jockeying for prime position. The blistering sun setting perfectly behind the midtown skyline. The deafening roar of the crowd. A crowd in which he was just one anonymous voice, blending in, cheering on one of his boyhood heroes.

Anonymity, what a concept!

Of course, that was long before the impossible balancing act. The late night rehearsals. The early morning laryngitis. The amphetamine haze. The mounting expectations. The in-band politics. The covert enemies. The media bombardment. The endless demands.

Disillusionment.

Johnny's eyes shifted to the right hand side of the treasured snapshot. Andy Raymer was squinting through his studious, horn-rimmed spectacles, a Cheshire-cat grin etched on his face. Andy: his loyal partner-in-crime. His Cobble Hill High compadre, and later the man who would manage the madness that became his career.

A pained expression spread across Johnny's face. *Damn!* All that Andy had sacrificed! All those hours he sat in a lonely, cluttered guestroom, fanning the flames of his unlikely stardom. And for what? If only he had found a way to enjoy the ride… and the words of gratitude for everything Andy had done along the way.

It was on that brilliant summer day in the photograph when Andy improbably met the lovely woman to his left, Jacqui Spencer. Johnny smiled at the memory. The socially awkward Andy had never been much of a ladies-man. And yet look how comfortably he and Jacqui interacted, only hours after randomly meeting.

Jacqui, Johnny thought. *Andy's soul mate, but my own personal sounding board.* In fact, his spiritual advisor too. His perspective provider, and of course, the artist whose album cover would help launch one of the most legendary debuts in pop music history.

Ah, but a short-lived career, Johnny reminded himself. More like a two-year whirlwind that saw him evolve from a directionless, novice poet to a national megastar in a drumbeat. From a one-room Brooklyn hovel to a doorman building overlooking Central Park. From dingy nightclubs to theatrical euphoria. It was breathtaking. His ultimate rock and roll daydream. And yet nothing like he could ever have envisioned. Nothing at all!

The last pair of eyes in the photo that Johnny's were drawn to belonged to Megan Price. *Megan,* Johnny sighed. Sweet, fragile, complicated Megan. The first girl he ever loved. The only one he ever loved. The woman who embraced him for who he was, who shaped his impression of loving stability - and whose haunting betrayal inspired the painful, creative storm that would evolve as the musical soundtrack of a generation. If only she had the courage to stand up for what mattered most, how different things would have been... for both of them!

Johnny fell back in an easy chair, clutching the framed photo, closing his eyes. He could feel the warmth of that bright summer day. A symphony of boom boxes echoed across the Great Lawn through the corridors of his mind. The smell of freshly cut grass and cold beer filled his sinuses. And suddenly the years melted away. He was twenty-one again, racing ahead of his friends, hoping to score a prime viewing location for the massive free concert.

Long before the boisterous cheers. Before his infamous fall from grace. Long before he understood the consequences of success, the agony of betrayal, or the origins of lyrics and melodies.

Long before he became poet of the wrong generation.

The Concert In Central Park

August 15th, 1991

Johnny Elias raced into Central Park like a bullet fired from a well-oiled chamber. Along a narrow jogging path, he noticed the crowds gathering beneath a hazy sky for summer's biggest celebration.

Though the day was only approaching noon, it had already turned into a typical New York summer swelter. Johnny's white t-shirt had long been soaked with perspiration, causing his backpack to slide down his broad shoulders. Peeking back, he recognized that he'd actually gotten several paces ahead of Megan and Andy, who were lugging the picnic blanket and the cooler.

"Always running away from me, Johnny," Megan shouted, hoping he'd hear her through the crowd. When he spun back she added, teasingly, "Between me and the music, I guess there's no contest, huh?"

Johnny waited near the edge of the grass. The Great Lawn beckoned; and in the distance was a giant stage, framed by Manhattan's glistening skyscrapers. "Sorry!" he exclaimed as his companions caught up. "So what if we're seven hours early. We're seeing history tonight! Gotta nab the perfect spot."

"Johnny, this ain't some lame-ass job seminar!" shouted Andy above the surrounding excitement. "Long as we can hear the music, we're cool."

Johnny swallowed the last gulp of his lemonade, purchased moments earlier from a vending cart on 72nd Street. *What a field day for the heat!* he silently quoted. *The place is already jammed. Some must've slept here overnight.*

The threesome tiptoed through a maze of wicker baskets, sunbathers and pot-smokers, paying little notice to the surrounding flurry of activity. Along the way, Johnny scoped out a prime location between two blankets near the center aisle. His face lit up. "Guys, over here!"

"Look out!" Andy warned a second too late as a tri-colored beach ball bopped Johnny on the side of the head. No sooner had Andy gotten his words out that an errant Frisbee struck him square between the shoulder blades. Laughing, Megan set down her bundle on the unoccupied grass. She turned to a group of teens sprawled out next to them. "Hey, boys, this turf taken?"

Five youthful revelers feigned ignorance, carrying on a boisterous conversation as if in their own private luxury box. Megan repeated her question with greater vigor. She received only blank stares and negative vibes until one finally spoke up above a blaring radio. Michael Bolton's *Love Is a Wonderful Thing* clearly irritated Johnny's ears. "Oh, um… we're savin' it for someone, ya know. But those losers, they probably ain't gonna find us, so–"

"So, thanks," Johnny began, only to be cut off by another of the younger men. "But if they show, well, you'll have to piss off. First dibs, man. "

"Nice attitude," Johnny muttered softly. "Especially for some tuneless frat boys who probably can't name a song pre-1984."

Andy diplomatically intervened. "No problem. Too damn hot today. First round of Cokes is on me. And you guys can use our binoculars later if you want."

"Binoculars? Dude, we're like ten rows away," pointed out one of the five adolescents, wearing an M.C. Hammer tank top. "Make it a beer and our boys can watch from Harlem for all we care."

Megan removed a plush green blanket from a Bergdorf Goodman shopping bag and began unfolding it. Although the forecasted rain had yet to arrive, she noticed that the ground they were about to pitch camp on was damp. She stopped abruptly. "Hey, John, something spill here?"

Johnny bent down to inspect the grass. "Wouldn't know, Meg. It coulda rained last night. You didn't really expect to keep it clean, did you?"

Megan followed the trail of moisture in the grass to a leaky cooler thawing beneath the blazing sun. Reluctantly, she grabbed one end of the blanket and spread it out over the empty emerald patch. "Guys, try not to stain it, okay? Mom'll kick my ass."

"It's just a picnic blanket, no?" Andy chimed in.

"Hey, we're talkin' about a woman who sent her kids to etiquette classes before we knew how to walk!" Megan chuckled. "Actually, it's from the beach house. No footprints, okay?"

Johnny slipped the backpack off his shoulders; the sun's intensity toasting the back of his neck. Around him people were flying kites, unpacking picnics, and wilting in the humidity. It wasn't just young New Yorkers playing hooky, either. People of varying nationalities, professions, and ages had bought into the hype and converged upon Central Park.

A beat-up spiral notebook emerged from Johnny's backpack, and a pen from his faded denim shorts. All the nearby sights and sounds were soon preserved in rhyming verse. Johnny liked poetry. It often served as a temporary respite from the reality of his turbulent youth.

At twenty-one, Johnny Elias was two weeks shy of his senior year at Brooklyn Post College. An English major with an undecided future, he'd spent his last undergrad summer earning an hourly wage in a local library. Only recently had he begun to contemplate life after graduation.

"Hey, Johnny," Andy called out, startling his friend. "My folks are tossing their old kitchen table and chairs. I'm thinking maybe you could use 'em over at your place."

Johnny's look of irritation at the disruption quickly changed to gratitude as the offer sank in. "Cool. Thanks, man. I'll swing by this weekend. Some furniture would be great."

Johnny was the only child of an impoverished young widow who left him on the steps of Brooklyn's 76th precinct when he was just 16 months old – a mother he'd never meet again. His formative years had been spent in city public schools and an assortment of foster residences near the foot of the Brooklyn Bridge. Now, he was on his own for the first time.

"Speaking of weekend plans," Megan said, "there's a career expo up at Columbia a week from Sunday. Whadayasay we do brunch that day, then maybe pop in?"

"Sure Meg." Johnny shrugged before returning his attention to his notebook. "Long as we're together, I don't mind time-wasters."

It had been two and a half years since Johnny had literally fallen for Megan. It happened in Central Park's Wollman Rink on a bitter January afternoon. Both were skating alone. Johnny spotted a petite blonde crossing in front of him. Clumsily, he lost his edge and slammed into a sidewall. Megan extended a shivering hand. Johnny's fingers tingled through his shriveled gloves as though he had banged his elbow on the ice, though he had not. It was pure magic. Soon, the pair was clutching each other for warmth as they glided around the frozen oval.

For each of them, this first true love brought with it the common misconception of how it would last forever. They spent every possible moment together in blissful defiance of gravity.

Then came Johnny's first visit to the Price family's Fifth Avenue apartment: a sprawling four-bedroom showcase of antique furniture, colorful Persian carpets, and hand-blown Venetian glass collected from their numerous overseas trips. A total culture shock.

Beyond the intimidating museum-like existence of their home, Johnny perceived that it was Megan and her brother Zach who were on display; often decked out in the latest designer threads from their mother's weekend shopping sprees in Paris and Milan. This extravagance was hardly the life Johnny grew up knowing. But it was not a lifestyle he was after.

"Hey, John. Gotta free hand to rub sunblock on me?"

Megan Price curled up to Johnny, all five feet, two inches and 98 pounds of her. If not a stunning beauty, she was certainly attractive in most eyes. A touch of makeup helped to cover a few defects from a bicycle mishap at age ten. But it was her shoulder-length strawberry-blonde hair, coupled with a shining pair of blue eyes that provided the distinctive look Johnny was drawn to. That, and her surprising rejection of splendor and pretension.

On days like today – when her mother wasn't around – Megan dressed down in jean shorts, a t-shirt and comfortable white Keds. Johnny was tickled to watch her bask in the golden sunshine, snapping off yet another pink chewing-gum bubble against her lips.

"Okay, hon. I'm good. Half a tube's plenty!"

"Oh… sorry, Meg. I'm kinda writing something… fishing for a rhyme."

Johnny wasn't proficient on any instrument, or trained in musical notation. None of his foster parents ever splurged for formal lessons. But for as long as he could remember, he enjoyed composing lyrical stanzas influenced by the clever wordplay of the great singer/songwriters of yesteryear. In many ways, music and poetry had helped plug the emotional void for the family he never had. Lost in the pages of his notebook, he had resumed scribbling a few lines when reality pushed its way back into his consciousness.

"So, what was your lame excuse for ditching work?" Andy asked, nudging Johnny even as he slid his glasses up the bridge of his nose.

"I just told her the truth. For a librarian, she was pretty cool with it."

Andy laughed. "I called in sick around seven this morning. If he's pissed off, well, Labor Day's just around the corner." Then turning to Megan, Andy arched his eyebrows. "And how 'bout your boss, Ms. Price?"

Megan propped her sandals neatly on the blanket's edge. "Well, you know my deal. If Mom finds out I blew off work to hang with you guys... just told her I'd be shopping with girlfriends. I think she bought it."

Of the three friends, Megan certainly had the most demanding summer job: an internship at her mother's public relations agency, Price & McLennan. Just the day before, she'd been fielding calls at a temporary desk set up in the office of her mother's controversial young partner.

"Sheila McLennan's line… Sorry, she's on a conference call. Something I can help you with?"

Megan took down the number of a reporter from Sheila's persona-non-grata list, then flashed a smile across the room. "Hey, Sheila, that was the Page-Six lady, asking about your boyfriend again."

"Gossip vultures! Damn, you'd think the tabloids would prefer a naughty A-lister tidbit to my pathetic social life." Sheila pushed an impatient hand through her black hair. "Whatever you do, Megan, never date an aging rock star in the middle of an ugly divorce, ya hear?"

"No problem," Megan said empathically. "My boyfriend may look like a young Don Henley, but he's hardly the celebrity type. And with the way Mom has me chained here –"

"Hey, that's not a complaint I hear, is it?" Sheila interrupted.

"Cold calling from endless press lists; assembling these tedious clipping binders. Not exactly the thrill of a lifetime."

"Poor baby," Sheila said, her voice lightly sarcastic. "You're all of twenty-two. Got your foot in the door for a fabulous PR career. And you and Zach are what, three years from collecting on Grandma's trust account? Tough living baby girl."

Clueless Sheila, Megan thought. *Always putting a satirical spin on everything.* "Hey, for three glorious months here, I'm getting two elective credits at Barnard. And no disrespect, but hyping glitterati, it isn't my thing."

"Maybe not," Sheila laughed. "Then again, with Katherine Price hovering, that decision might not be yours to make."

Now Megan was thrilled to be away from the hectic office pace. She rolled across the blanket, cuddled up to Johnny and stroked his chiseled shoulders. "Hey, John, just look uptown! Betcha he draws more tonight than when he played with Garfunkel."

Johnny stared back on the growing compression. "No way! Simon and Garfunkel had half a million for their '81 reunion. This is big, but it's also gonna be live on HBO."

"Come off it, man." Andy was lying on his back, looking up at the Goodyear blimp. "New York's a big event town. Think the July Fourth fireworks; the Macy's parade. Folks show up from everywhere just to say they were here. Hell, the Philharmonic draws fifty thou and no one even knows their names!"

"Point taken," Johnny conceded. "Especially given the shortlist who've done it here before: Elton John. James Taylor. Diana Ross. The Beach Boys." He scrambled to his feet to stretch his legs and pointed at the big stage. "Andy, stand here a sec; just close your eyes. Can you imagine anything more mind-blowing than being up there, knowing all these people are here for you?"

"I know," Andy concurred, his eyes wide. "Amazing, right? Rock and roll Shangri-La!"

It was three o'clock. Concertgoers covered the sun-drenched lawn in every direction. Onstage, a small figure suddenly appeared at the center microphone and tapped it twice. "Testing, testing, one, two." In mock elation, much of the crowd gave the audio technician a sizable cheer. Moments later, the opening guitar strains of Creedence Clearwater Revival's *Up And Around The Bend* prompted the growing masses to expend their pent-up energy. A recording of CCR's entire greatest hits followed, touching off a party atmosphere.

Johnny and Megan leapt to their feet and danced beside much of the crowd. At one point, Johnny let loose, passionately shouting along with the rock anthem, *Fortunate Son*. When the last chords faded out, a scruffy stranger approached. He was wearing an NYPD baseball cap.

"Dude, I was gonna tell you to shut the hell up, but you actually don't suck!"

Johnny shrugged his shoulders. "Thanks, I guess." He squeezed Megan against his side. "Not too many better than Creedence."

"Amen, bro. My name's Jim Penetti. Also go by Jimbo." There was an obvious Bronx accent in his voice. "You guys from 'round here?"

"Yeah, we're natives," Megan confirmed. "Our buddy Andy was here with us too. Went to grab a few of those bootlegged t-shirts. Just don't arrest him, okay?"

Once the music stopped, all three sat down on the green blanket. Jimbo wiped the sweat off his forehead beneath the brim of his cap. He glanced at Johnny. "So, dude, I'm guessing you're not one of those pathetic fly-by-nights who just showed up to be counted?"

"Ooh, don't get me started." Johnny waved dismissively. "For those of us who are too young to have been at Woodstock... well this is probably the next best thing. At least for the few who still believe that music can save your mortal soul... or at least inspire it!"

Jim Penetti grinned. "So, Don McLean: I take it you're not sold on the synthesized stylings of New Kids on the Block and Technotronic?"

"Uh, no." Johnny smiled back lopsidedly. "The pop flavor of the month is total crap."

Penetti laughed. "Ah, so you're into the oldies then, like me."

"The oldies?" Johnny squinted at him. "That term's so lame! It's like ever since John Lennon died, every pop star's got a radio expiration-date of forty. Yet almost all of today's best music still comes from guys who've been around forever."

"My boyfriend, the throwback." Megan laughed. "Old fashioned values. Old-time music."

Jimbo nodded with a stubbly grin, then reached over and helped himself to a can of Miller Lite from Andy's cooler. He popped it open and took a swig. "So, you in a band, Johnny?"

"A band?" Johnny stared at him quizzically. "I don't play guitar; not much of a singer. But I can play *Frère Jacques* on any keyboard with two fingers!"

Jimbo's serious expression melted into laughter. "Come off it, man. You've got that longhaired thing goin' on. And that sweet voice; kinda reminds me of a white Smokey Robinson; maybe Jackie Wilson."

Johnny glanced at Megan. She was smiling at him in agreement, but Johnny still wasn't convinced. "Yeah, right, Meg. Someone's got a sick imagination. Hell, I've never even sung for an audience."

"Would ya maybe take a stab at it?" Jimbo raised an eyebrow.

"You mean join a band?"

"Not necessarily. You heard of The Lion's Gate? West 4th, near Bleecker?"

Johnny took a half-minute to jog his memory, then smiled and nodded as recognition dawned. "Right, that dungeon. It's like forty steps down. Tiny stage? Solid house-band?"

"Damn straight!" Jim confirmed. "Ever been there on a Wednesday night?"

"Wednesday? Can't remember."

"Dude, that's open mic night! The band lets anyone up to sing. Some kick-ass. Others totally bite. The scene's hilarious!"

Megan tugged on Johnny's t-shirt, her eyes growing wide. "What do ya say we check it out? Bet you'd blow 'em away."

"Who am I gonna blow away, Meg? The waitresses? All six weeknight desperados? Wouldn't wanna embarrass myself; not even for a pitiful crowd."

"John, this isn't about impressing people." She squeezed his hand. "Hey, you're always on my case about confidence. Here's a chance to prove you're really good at something. At least think about it!"

They covered common musical ground together for balance of the afternoon. Later, contact info would be exchanged, along with promises to be in touch sometime following the concert. It was six o 'clock when Jimbo departed. Megan turned to Johnny, mildly concerned.

"It's been ages since Andy wandered off! Think he's lost?"

Johnny stood up, scouring the mass of humanity. "Lost? If anyone's genius enough to navigate this maze..." He slid on his sunglasses. "But what about all those cops? Tell me they're not turning people away now that it's jammed?"

"John, this ain't prison," Megan reassured him. "People can pee, you know?"

"Yeah, probably," he said, then laughed. "But still, you gotta wonder where he's at."

Andy Raymer was a year older than Johnny, and his closest friend, going back to Johnny's junior year at Brooklyn's Cobble Hill High. Andy had forever been known as an effortless straight-A student. However, with academic success came the predictable banishment by those who could never simultaneously envision a corduroy and cardigan-wearing smart kid as "cool."

The unlikely friends met at a rehearsal for an informal student production of *Macbeth*. Touted as the unofficial poet laureate of Cobble Hill High, Johnny was assigned to re-write Shakespeare's tragedy in playful rhyming verse. Andy - the future valedictorian - was tabbed to narrate the modern adaptation:

The play we have studied is called Macbeth
A Medieval king in a spiral of death.
Macbeth becomes King; his majesty rough
And in the end - sweet revenge for Macduff.

While Johnny got to showcase his raw talents for an audience of his peers, it was Andy's reading of the lines that ignited the crowd's laughter, and soon thereafter a loyal alliance.

Now Megan's apprehension grew. "John, you think Andy decided to ditch us? I mean, maybe he felt like a third wheel."

"Not Andy Raymer. He's not the jealous type. Too bad he ain't here to see this." Johnny tackled Megan to the ground, raised her shirt above her navel and planted a sweaty kiss on her firm belly. Megan freed her hands and tickled Johnny's neck until he rolled away. She sat up giggling.

"So if Andy isn't envious, care to share why he practically moved into your old foster mom's apartment once you got him hooked on her old record collection?"

Johnny laughed. "Well, for a rich kid, the boy was seriously deprived. Never even heard of the Spoonful, ELO, or Dire Straits! Fortunately he knew enough about physics and algebra to help get me into college."

"And yet he's never had a girlfriend. Why not? I mean, he's smart... hardly hideous."

Johnny shrugged. "Um, awful luck, I guess."

"Oh, c'mon, John. What's the deal? Maybe we can help him."

"Can't." Johnny buried his face in his hands. "Andy'll kill me."

Megan glared at him. Johnny didn't stand a chance. "All right. But you'd better not repeat it. Ever. And you better not laugh."

"I promise." Megan nodded, stifling a giggle.

"Well, I wasn't there, but I heard it happened back in 8th grade; a Halloween bash. Andy always sat alone in a corner eating candy corn. Anyway, this one time, the girl hosting the party pitied him; asked him to dance. Turned out to be a slow song, *Almost Paradise* – you know, from that *Footloose* flick. Andy was terrified. Had no idea where to put his hands and —"

"He didn't!" Megan's eyes flew wide open. "Tell me he didn't grab her butt."

Johnny blushed in embarrassment. "Worse! For three whole minutes he swayed to the music, cupping the breasts of this thirteen year old, Fiona Farmington. She froze up. Everyone stopped and stared. Even the parents doubled over in hysterics. In some circles it's one of those legendary stories that just keeps going."

Megan grimaced. "No way! Poor Andy! Talk about a guy who could use a do-over!"

The scorching afternoon melted into a humid early evening. A welcome breeze blew through the eager crowd. A nearby radio was tuned to WNYR-FM, New York's classic rock station. Legendary DJ, Larry Jacobs was broadcasting from somewhere near the stage.

"Folks, we're just one hour away from show-time. The NYPD are already estimating this monster crowd at over a half-million. And people are still squeezing in to find a spot on the Great Lawn. Incredible!"

Imagine finding Andy in this lunacy? Johnny thought. *Hope he enjoys it from wherever he ended up.*

He was roused from his pessimism by a thinly veiled British accent calling him out of his reverie. "Johnny? Megan?"

Johnny sat abruptly upright. A dark-haired young woman, a stranger towered above him, dressed in cutoff green jeans and a black halter-top. "I'm Jacqui." She extended her hand politely. "Jacqui with a Q."

Megan stood to greet the slender foreigner. "Do we know you from somewhere?"

Jacqui smiled. "Actually, no. But I reckon I'll be seeing lots of you blokes tonight. Guess you could say I'm with Andy."

"Andy?" Johnny repeated, incredulous, then sighed. "Did he put you up to this?" That had to be it. "And where the hell's he been the past four hours?"

"Well, I'm not one to smooch and blab, but it's fair to say we've been getting acquainted."

Johnny and Megan exchanged confused looks. Jacqui sat down and joined them, uninvited.

"We met earlier, waiting in a queue for ice cream."

Johnny eyed her curiously. "Hmm, interesting. But how'd you know to find us here?"

Before she could answer, there was Andy, gingerly stepping over blankets and bodies, a plastic bag dangling from his left wrist. "What's up?" he asked, grinning. "Oh, I see you've met Jacqui. And Jacqui, I see you're pretty solid with directions."

Jacqui leaned forward and accepted a peck on the cheek from Andy. "Well, your description was spot on. Almost the bloody inquisition!"

Andy tossed a bootlegged concert t-shirt in Johnny's direction. "So I'm standing in line earlier, and we just… well, one thing to another and I… um I mean *we*, decided to hit the Natural History Museum. Found a quiet place in the Astronaut exhibit and…" His voice trailed off. Andy was nervously waiting for his best friend's approval.

"So you just assumed we had room for four?" Johnny asked innocently, staring down at the new t-shirt, triggering a quartet of laughter. "And Jacqui, lemme guess? You're a lifelong Paul Simon fanatic who flew transatlantic to be here, and just randomly hooked up with my pal?"

"Partial score," she answered, winking. "Actually, I'm here studying design. The concert's just a bonus."

Megan reached into Johnny's backpack and pulled out her trusted Nikon. She quickly snapped off a few shots of everything around her. Now, there was only one remaining on the roll. Eager to make a record for posterity, she handed her camera to a nearby fan, wearing a faded Paul Simon *One Trick Pony* t-shirt from a decade earlier. "Can I ask you to do the honors?"

Megan slid back over to her blanket. She threw her arms around Johnny, who secured the cap on his pen, and tucked his notebook beneath him. He huddled next to Andy and Jacqui, who were only too happy to lean in. "All together now," the volunteer urged. "One, two, three, say Garfunkel!"

Just before eleven o'clock, a lone electric guitar played the last haunting note of a slowed-down *The Sounds of Silence*. A rapturous ovation followed; the last of what were too many to count. There was a long moment of stasis, a sense of having participated in something magical. And then the lights came up. This 55-acre pocket of utopia appeared to be nothing more than a tattered lawn littered with bottles, paper and cigarette butts. More than half a million music fans all began pushing down narrow jogging paths, through constricted pedestrian exits. Getting out wasn't going to be easy.

Johnny lost sight of Andy and Jacqui through the crush of humanity. He hooked his fingers to Megan's belt loop, keeping her close to his side. It wasn't until they reached the subway stairwell at Columbus Circle that the two couples were reunited.

"Hey! Let's keep it going," Andy urged. "What do ya say we grab a pizza?"

"Damn. Wish I could," Johnny bemoaned, his voice shredded. "But I gotta be functional tomorrow. You know how tough Brooklyn librarians can be!"

"Same here." Megan grimaced. "Maybe tomorrow."

Andy smiled playfully. "Well then, Jacqui, looks like it's just us two." Jacqui winked back at him and corralled his hand in hers. Andy's grin turned sheepish. "Too bad our pathetic grown-up friends forgot what it's like to be young and reckless."

The couples bid good night and turned in opposite directions. But only steps apart, the still-giddy Andy spun back toward Johnny, shouting one last request. "Oh, hey, Wordsworth, care to give us your poetic take on the day from that notebook before we go?"

Johnny shook his head. "Still a work in progress."

"Then how 'bout a couple of lines?" Andy pressed on.

The look of encouragement on his friends' faces proved persuasive. Johnny flipped to the page where he'd been scribbling that afternoon. "All right, just a snippet. Then I really gotta fly." He leaned back against the steel railing at the top of the subway stairs, and began.

Yes we danced and we sang and we whistled and screamed
and we left our voices behind
Still we knew this is all we would ever share
somewhere in the back of our minds
So we traded life stories and craved precious shade
from the morning until it grew dark
But we swore in our lifetime we'd never forget the concert in Central Park

A rumbling D train drowned out the appreciative whooping from the departing Andy and Jacqui. Johnny stepped toward Megan. "Walk you back uptown, babe?"

"That's okay, John. Go get your train. Today was awesome. But if Mom sees you bringing me in… well, you know how she can be!"

Johnny nodded. Sensing Megan's anxiety, he wrapped his arms around her waist, initiating a soft bubblegum flavored kiss that was far too short for either of their liking.

"Call ya later," Megan promised, easing from his clutches. Then gracefully as possible, she lifted the bulky shopping bag with both hands and headed east toward Fifth Avenue. Johnny watched her disappear: Unofficially, his day had just ended.

Hers was just about to get interesting.

2

Shattered Afterglow

It was nearing midnight. Megan arrived in her building lobby on Fifth Avenue at 75th Street. Her ears were still ringing from the concert. She greeted the doorman on her way to the elevator.

"Hey, Walter. You happen to notice if my mom's home?"

The uniformed, gray-haired gentleman tipped his cap. "Yes, Ms. Price. I believe Mrs. Price arrived thirty minutes ago."

"Okay, thanks," she responded, thinking of how her mother usually retired straight to her bathtub on summer nights. Just as the elevator doors slid open, she opted to amend her strategy.

"Actually, I'll take the stairs, but thanks," she said to the nighttime attendant.

Megan was figuring that her safest bet was to walk to the third floor and go in through the kitchen entrance. From there, she could easily sneak down the hallway to her bedroom, stash the soiled blanket and change into pajamas. Taking the elevator would leave her right in the center of the apartment – no doubt a higher-risk scenario.

Megan glanced at the gold men's Cartier watch on her wrist. It was another fond reminder of her late father. *How'd Dad ever manage all those years?* she wondered. *Hope he's in a better place now.*

Since just prior to her seventeenth birthday, Megan's family had been comprised of just herself, her mom, and Zach, her brother, three years her junior. Her father, Alan Price had been a prominent upper West Side psychiatrist for three decades. But years of excess – hard drinking and chain smoking – had taken his youthfulness and ultimately his life at the age of fifty-three.

Abruptly widowed with two children, Megan's mother, Katherine Price, was forced to roll up her proverbial sleeves to reinvent her socialite trophy-wife existence.

And reinvent she did.

The radical transformation began with lavish dinner parties in her opulent Fifth Avenue residence. There, she invited several of her late husband's former patients, many of whom comprised the who's-who of the New York social scene. Katherine leveraged these friendships to build a small public relations firm that she originally ran from home. It didn't hurt that some of her husband's so-called 'friends' were from the world of politics, entertainment and real estate. But it wouldn't have mattered: Katherine was talented, relentless, even ruthless when necessary.

Reaching the third floor, Megan momentarily put down her shopping bag. She snatched the early Friday edition of the *New York Times* from the doorstep and examined the front page. Staring back at her: a black-and-white photo of Mayor Dinkins shaking hands with Paul Simon. Megan smiled. *Mom'll love this!*

Wasn't it just yesterday that David M. Dinkins – then the Manhattan borough president – stood in her living room discussing his plan to widen New York City's voter registration? And standing beside him, her mother, Katherine Price, whispering something about polishing his image to challenge a vulnerable Ed Koch for the Democratic nomination.

Megan's memory was actually from 1986, three years prior to Mr. Dinkins' improbable mayoral run. And amazingly, Katherine's advice proved prophetic. David Dinkins would go on to defeat Republican District

Attorney, Rudolph Giuliani by the smallest-ever margin to become the first African American to reside at Gracie Mansion.

His success was hers. Overnight, Katherine Price evolved from running a boutique agency into one of New York's premiere PR powerbrokers, serving as a consultant to the new mayor.

Megan didn't resent her mother's astounding professional transformation. But neither was she impressed by swanky dinners at the Waldorf and Broadway premieres, to which her mom routinely dragged her. And these days she really didn't want to spend all those hours with all her mother's colleagues and clients; Johnny was her world.

Now reaching for her keys, Megan made an effort not to jingle them and reveal her backdoor arrival. She lifted her bag, turned the lock and tiptoed into the dimly lit kitchen. It was immediately apparent that her decision to take the alternate route had backfired.

"Something happen to the elevator?" The voice had a cynical ring to it. Katherine Price was sitting in the dark at the kitchen table, sipping a cup of tea, still in a chic pinstriped pantsuit.

Megan clutched the plastic shopping bag handle to control her shaking. "Oh, hey, Mom. Still only two flights up."

"I'll bear this in mind next time you wait for the elevator." Katherine reached over and snapped on a light. She studied her daughter's suntanned face. "So where've you been all day, sweetheart?"

"Like I told you: bargain hunting with friends. I met Vera this morning. And after lunch we caught up with Emily down at Century 21." Megan figured the talk of shopping would please her mother. She treaded cautiously. "Don't know the last time you've been over there. The basement has this cool gift department. I'm thinking about opening a charge account and —"

"How interesting that Century's started bagging merchandise in Bergdorf bags," Katherine interjected, her voice sarcastic. "Unless Bergdorf quietly opened a downtown location that I'm unaware of."

"Actually, Mom, I took the bag this morning from the front closet. You know, something sturdy, just in case." Thinking quickly now.

"Oh, I see." Katherine lightened up. "So obviously you must've made out pretty well in spite of the deplorable outfit on your back. Let's see what you bought!"

This was what Megan had been afraid of. She dropped the newspaper on the table and made one last-ditch effort to avoid a fiery confrontation. "Mom, this stuff mostly isn't mine. I took home a few things for Emily. And my shoes are inside. I changed for the walk back. From Century's we all went to Vera's; caught the concert on TV. I came straight home when it ended."

Megan casually stepped past her mother at the table and turned left into the dark hallway leading to her bedroom. She hoped her explanation would prove satisfactory.

"Just one thing, dear," Katherine noted, as Megan edged by. "Your friend Vera called the office today around noon and again at four. She requested a call back each time. I grabbed your messages from the reception desk on my way out tonight."

Not looking back, and not responding, Megan quickly entered her room and closed the door behind her. She drew a deep breath. *I'm busted. But how to avoid an all-out detonation? I hate lying to her. If only she'd just let me grow up.*

Megan's heart was racing. She emptied the shopping bag and shoved the muddy blanket under her bed skirt. Next, she threw on a pair of pajamas and slid into comfy slippers. For good measure she put on her most innocent face and headed back to the kitchen.

"You didn't answer my question," Katherine reminded her, as her daughter walked over to the stainless-steel refrigerator.

Megan pulled out a water pitcher, poured herself a tall glass, then turned back to the table. "Didn't know you asked a question." She took a sip. "Ya know, mom, I'm certainly entitled to one day off this summer. I'm sure you'd agree I've earned it?"

Katherine's face reddened; her anger erupted. "Where to begin? Shall we first address your dishonesty, or your other failings?"

"Oh, long day today, huh? If anything's gotten messed up, I'll start early tomorrow. It's only one day."

Katherine pretended to shudder at her daughter's nonchalant deception. "I know damn well where you were, young lady. You and your friend Johnny were lounging all day in the park. No use denying it. The grass stains on your jeans are a dead giveaway."

Megan was flabbergasted by her mother's observations. Whatever anger Katherine was feeling, Megan had trumped her. "Gimme a break! So what if I did, Mom? I'm almost twenty-two. A workingwoman. You know, the place was jammed with tons of working people. What's the problem here?"

Katherine was glaring at her. "I'll tell you the problem. Just look at you! My only daughter has no standards! Here she is, walking around the city looking like a discount rack, wasting her time with a hopeless, vagabond hippy! And to top it off, she can't even be truthful about where she goes, or who she spends her time with."

Megan nodded furiously. "I see! So this is about Johnny again? Why not just come right out and say it? Wait, I know! Maybe it's 'coz he's done nothing wrong. I'd love to tell you that I just spent my best summer day outside with my boyfriend. But every time I mention him–"

Katherine pounded a fist on the oak tabletop. "Megan Price! I could swear we've had this conversation fifty times! That aimless friend of yours is dragging you down! He's headed nowhere fast. And you're being taken along for the ride. You do know, don't you, that it's our money he's after? Dollar signs are branded on his eyeballs every time he looks at you."

Megan felt like stomping her foot in rage, just like she'd done when she was a little girl. But wasn't her whole point now that she was grown-up? "Mom, you've got it all wrong. Johnny loves me. He never asks for anything other than my time. He's loyal, talented. And he has a sweetness that reminds me of Dad on a good day – you remember those – the days he didn't reek of tequila." It was a low blow, and she'd meant for it to hurt.

"Oh, how dare you?" Katherine spat out the words. "Your father was educated, a doctor, a man of the world. The only talents your aimless friend displays are parasitical. He wasn't even good enough for his own family, let alone ours!"

These arguments used to end in tears, in Megan storming off and slamming doors. It seemed these days that all interactions with her mother were arguments, though, and you couldn't spend all your time slamming doors, could you? Instead, she leaned back against the counter for support. A pair of fluorescent orange salad tongs shone back at her from the drain board – one of the many well-intended trinkets Johnny had given the family through the years. *How dare she call him a freeloader? If anything, he's always been too self-conscious, trying too hard to please everyone with money he doesn't have. And as for career plans, well he's still at college, after all.*

Megan took another sip of water. She refused to back down easily. Calmer now, she said, "Mother, your being ludicrous. Johnny's always been so polite, so thoughtful. He helps me keep it together. All your claims… they're totally outrageous."

Katherine reined in her anger, choosing a different tack. "Megan, honey, this isn't about anything he has or hasn't done. Johnny's a sweet boy. I don't blame him for his past. It's just… well let's not kid ourselves. You're so young. You've never had a serious relationship before. How can you possibly know if he's the one?"

"Because, he makes me happy," Megan answered emphatically. "Like those great shoes you bought me last fall in Italy. They're the most supportive and comfy pair I've ever owned. Why trade in a perfect fit?"

"If only life were like a pair of Valentino's." Katherine sighed theatrically. "But remember, no pair lasts forever. And hey, you've owned many before, so you do have a basis for comparison. Please, just think it through. How fair are you being to Johnny, or yourself by having no one to measure him against?"

Megan was tired. There was no use fighting on. Katherine Price always got her way. And confidence was hardly Megan's strong suit. But at least she knew how to end an argument: by partially placating her mother. "Fine. If it's really about diversity, I'll give it some thought," she said grudgingly, avoiding eye contact.

Katherine exhaled slowly. "I suppose that's really all I can ask; for you to keep an open mind. You're a real good catch, you know? And you have a way of life to uphold. Someone more appropriate is bound to come along, sweep you off your feet."

Megan knew full well that the final comment was entirely her mother's wishful thinking. She nodded as if to go along.

"I knew you'd see it my way." Katherine rose from her seat and strode over to the shiny granite countertop. She embraced her daughter with a sweaty hug. "I hate it when we fight this way. I only want what's best for you, for our family. You do understand?"

Megan poured another glass of water and downed it in one gulp. Her hands were shaking. After placing the glass in the sink, she walked slowly past the table and back down the corridor toward her bedroom. But as she reached the doorway, her mother shared a final observation.

"By the way hon, I'm sure you intend to have my blanket dry-cleaned, after heaven knows what it's been through today. It really serves no purpose collecting dust under your bed."

Johnny remained on a natural high in the days following the concert. Hardly did he notice that Megan had cancelled plans for Saturday night, or that Andy had yet to resurface since his discovery of Jacqui in Central Park.

Across the five boroughs, a prevailing afterglow from the concert visibly lingered. This extravaganza showcased New York at its best. Newspapers ran a bevy of features, declaring Paul Simon's show a great triumph. At office water coolers, on subways and everywhere people typically gathered, the concert in the Park was topic-A on everyone's lips.

And then just four days later, and in a single moment, everything changed.

It was a quarter past eleven on Monday night. Johnny was sitting on his bed, putting the finishing touches on the poem he'd started in Central Park when the phone rang. He figured it was Megan calling to say goodnight. "Hey babe! Just thinkin' of you."

"Johnny, its Andy. Should I be calling you sweetheart?"

"Andy... you've finally come up for air!" Johnny recovered. "How's that Englishwoman treating you?"

"Yeah, yeah, Jacqui's great. But that's not why I'm calling. Hey, you watching TV?"

"You know I can't concentrate with that damn thing on." Johnny stretched the coiled phone cord toward the center of the room. He reached to turn on his small black and white screen.

"Never mind your poetry. The whole city's totally flipped out. And it's practically just down the block."

On the late news broadcast, Johnny caught a glimpse of the pandemonium. A full-scale riot had broken out on the streets of Crown Heights, Brooklyn. Footage showed an angry mob of African-American teens hurling rocks and shouting obscenities at the local Jewish residents.

The mayhem had been touched off when a car in the entourage of the revered Lubabvitcher Rebbi accidentally struck and killed a young black child, Gavin Cato. In retaliation, a throng of rampaging youths chased down a rabbinical student from Australia, Yankel Rosenbaum. After beating him, one thug fatally stabbed the young man, right on the main thoroughfare of Eastern Parkway.

The vicious incident sparked four consecutive days of senseless violence. Cars were overturned, windows of homes shattered, garbage cans set ablaze, and people tormented for the crime of leaving their front door.

Right in the center of the storm was Mayor David Dinkins. He stood accused of ordering the police to pull back at the outset. Bold headlines harshly criticized the mayor for failing to do enough to calm the four-day fracas. All harmonious feelings following that magical day in Central Park became, suddenly, a distant memory.

Johnny watched the ugliness unfold on TV. Police sirens echoed nearby.

He tried to make sense of it all. How could two minority groups living as peaceful neighbors just one day turn combatants?

Memories flooded back to his days as a foster kid, floating from place-to-place. He'd lived with all kinds of people. The Weisman's, a traditional Jewish family with five kids, had taken him in for his third grade year. The Boyd's, an African American family of four had put him up for the summer of '82. All of them decent, caring folks with similar values, conflicts and goals, he recalled. He couldn't imagine any of them wielding knives and spewing malice toward each other on Brooklyn's streets. So why this eruption of violence in Crown Heights? And where was the city's leadership? Why wasn't this appalling episode immediately condemned? This could have just as easily been Brooklyn Heights, less than four miles away.

Johnny skimmed through the extensive newspaper reports all that week. He came across a photo of four Crown Heights children, none older than ten, engaged in an apparent confrontation. Two faces were white, the other two were black, but on the ground beside each was a silhouette of similar shape and tone. The words came immediately to mind: *Shadows of the same color.*

He couldn't get the phrase out of his head, and so Johnny locked himself away for an hour with a pen and notebook. What emerged was an expression of disgust for the angry clash, countered by aspirations for a more hopeful future.

The headlines screamed out war between the races
I thought we all were human last I checked
Cries of fury – venom-laden faces
Now where are our leaders we elect?
Must our children be exposed to hatred?
Bear witness to the violence in our streets?
Teaching them to fight against their neighbors
won't make their education more complete

(Refrain)
Tell me why must we fight each other
when our shadows are of the same color?
Don't lose sight, there's one sky above us
Confrontation won't ease our struggles

The headlines read that riots have erupted
Is hatred something we cannot resist?
If we can't learn to befriend one another
At least we can peacefully co-exist
Minorities petitioned through the ages
searching for acceptance and respect
Divisiveness won't strengthen our ambition
Just what should the majority expect?

The headlines read that peace had been accomplished
The words were sharp, but the date was faded
It must've been a headline in the future
Our conflicts all had long since been debated
The streets once filled with violence now are peaceful
There isn't any anger to avenge
The words on everybody's lips are justice
And justice here no longer means revenge
(Refrain–End)

When he finished writing, Johnny returned Andy's call, seeking feedback. Andy didn't disappoint him. "Wow! That's deep. It'd make for one hell of a timely hit if it were a song."

"A song?" Johnny replied cynically. "Words in song don't count anymore. Unless it's got a wild dance beat, or some sexy video, not a chance! But thanks."

"Seriously, Johnny, you should get that piece published somewhere! How 'bout the school paper? Or try the *Daily News* as a letter to the editor?"

"Andy, man, you're very optimistic. But I didn't write it for them, or for anyone else. It's just what I do for sanity in an insane world. Poetry's much cheaper than therapy!"

The day after he penned his Crown Heights rant, Johnny returned from a shift at the library and tried to phone Megan at the office. She was brusque. "John, can't talk right now. We're totally flooded with the mayor's riot crisis. I'd see you tonight if I could. But it'll probably have to wait till Sunday."

"Three more days," he grumbled. Already it had been a week. Though he had to admit: it did make sense that the Crown Heights hostilities were forcing the Price & McLennan staff to work overtime, but still... "Okay, Sunday it is," he said, trying to sound upbeat.

Sunday couldn't come quickly enough for Johnny. Although occasionally Megan traveled with her mother, this was the longest they'd gone apart while she was in town. His anticipation grew with each passing day.

Johnny arrived by subway from Brooklyn, jumping aboard an uptown bus just outside Penn Station. The Q-32 took him up Madison Avenue, past some of New York's most exclusive boutique shopping; a trip he had made frequently over the span of nearly three years. At 72nd Street he jumped off and walked along the bustling avenue. *Fifteen minutes to kill.* He ducked inside an accessories shop at the corner of 75th. He was casually browsing a display of costume jewelry when a particular piece caught his eye. A platinum blonde saleswoman quickly joined him and removed the necklace from a glass showcase.

"Ah, one of my favorites," she exclaimed, placing it on a black felt surface. "The fifty-inch tri-colored beaded necklace. Some women wear it double, or triple twisted. And it has a fourteen karat gold clasp."

Johnny gasped upon seeing a tag marked $150 on the underside. He started to back away when the saleswoman began her bargaining. "I can tell you have in mind someone special."

"I do," he answered, moving slowly. "But this one's out of my range."

"What if I offer you ten percent? I'll put it in a nice box; gift wrap it too."

"That's cool. But fifty bucks is my limit." Johnny inched toward the door. He was about to head off when the woman called him back again with a better offer.

"Young man, I have a similar piece in your budget if you'd like to see it."

Johnny returned to the glass counter. A virtual replica of the beaded necklace lay on the countertop, only half the length of the one he'd just viewed. "You say this one's fifty?" he asked. "Yeah, I'll take it!"

Johnny was already revved up to see Megan after ten days apart. Now, with a charming gift in tow, his enthusiasm shifted into overdrive – even if he'd just blown one month's pocket money. He raced around the corner and headed inside the venerable Fifth Avenue building.

"Hi, Walter." He waved to the regular doorman, getting a friendly nod in return. He strolled past the oval gold-framed mirrors in the lobby as he had done so many times before and pressed the elevator call button. It took a while for the old compartment to arrive. First the outer doors opened, followed by the inner metal gate. Johnny stepped in and exchanged brief pleasantries with the regular operator. He was tickled at his sense of belonging.

Johnny was met by Megan who was waiting in the vestibule of the lone third floor apartment. "Hey, Meg!" he said grinning, as he watched her reach anxiously behind to pull the front door shut. "Oh, so I guess we're leaving already?"

"We're heading down, José," she said to the attendant. Casually, she leaned over and kissed Johnny on the cheek.

At the lobby level, Megan grabbed a stick of gum from her pocket and deposited it in her mouth. Briskly, she escorted Johnny across to the park side of Fifth Avenue and a handful of blocks uptown. They stopped at the imposing steps of the Metropolitan Museum – the site in which they shared their first kiss on a frigid February morning. Megan sat on a granite stoop near the outdoor fountain and popped off one of her patented pink bubbles. "John, we need to talk."

"What about?" There was a short, awkward silence. "Something wrong?"

"No use trying to sugarcoat this, so here's the deal." She looked away from Johnny's worried reaction and waited as a city bus roared past the museum. "My mother's been on the warpath about us lately. It's nothing that you've done to tick her off, but—"

"But what?" he interrupted, eyeing her curiously. "I've always gotten on decently with her and Zach, or at least I thought so. Wait, this isn't about the beach blanket?"

Megan sighed. "Johnny, it's about the future. Our future. Mom has this idea that her upper class daughter needs to be making a bigger splash in the pool of her social circles. To her, this means I should be dating some guy from around here. Someone to impress her friends and clients."

Johnny felt his throat narrowing. "After three years, after everything… why now, Meg?"

"To be honest, this isn't the first time she's brought it up, you know? In our first year together, she was probably in denial. Dad was only gone a couple years. I was finally smiling again, and she was relieved that I didn't need to see a shrink. So she was cool with it. Then we hit eighteen months. She started asking questions when you weren't around."

"What kind of questions? And why not mention any of this till now?"

"Oh, she'd quiz me about your childhood, your career plans, your classes at school. At first, I thought she was just making conversation. Then I realized what she was fishing for. Her standard of living is… you know. Different."

"So what set her off now? I don't understand."

"Well, the night I came home from the concert, Mom went ballistic. Somehow she knew I was there with you. Had to make a few concessions to shut her up."

Johnny felt increasingly lightheaded. It was like he was standing at the edge of a precipice, lurching forward, unable to stop himself. He was still a school year away from graduation, an eternity from any meaningful job. Even if he were lucky enough to land an entry-level position out of college, would this really alter Katherine's perception of him, of his worthiness? *Probably not!* Not with his wandering Brooklyn background.

But what about Megan?

Deep down, Johnny believed that she wouldn't walk away from what she always claimed to be her happiest days. Not as long as it was still her decision to make. Plus, he well knew that she wasn't consumed with issues like family pedigree and earnings potential. She loved him for who he was... even in spite of who he was. If only she had the self-confidence to stand up to Katherine. He stared down at her Keds, then up to her faded blue jeans, hoping her casual attire was a subtle nod to her capacity to act independently. "So what now, Meg? You know, you're all I've got, right?"

Megan brushed a strand of hair off her face, then placed her hands on Johnny's knees. She was breathing heavily. "John, you remember what I told you that night we fell asleep on the beach at Coney Island? The night we first talked about my Dad and how lost I was back when he died?"

Johnny nodded in recognition. Megan continued.

"You know I can't imagine my life without you; don't even wanna think of it. You're the only one who understands me. Your face: it's the one I wanna wake up next to every morning... on the beach, at your place, wherever. You're my protector. My happiness. My strength. But for the sake of keeping the peace at home, I may need to see some other guys; go through the motions."

Johnny stared into Megan's blue eyes, shocked. "And what happens to us while this is going on? What'll be a few months from now when she still doesn't see things your way? Are you just going to let her split us apart?"

"Don't you worry," Megan said, her voice comforting. "We'll just need to be more discreet. And – John, it'd be best if you didn't call me during hours when she's around."

"For how long? I mean, can't you just get your own place; get the hell outta there? She can't possibly run your life this way forever, ya know!"

Megan flashed a look of uncertainty. "Hey, I'd move out in a heartbeat if I could. But remember, she doesn't pay me for working at the agency. Until I turn twenty-five, Mom still controls the purse strings; pays my tuition. And on your part-time library salary… well, we can't both get by on that. At least till I graduate, she'll never allow it."

Megan saw the raw disappointment on her boyfriend's face. It was a look she had rarely seen in their three years together. Some reassurance was surely in order. "John, I don't wanna lose you for all the money in the world – not even temporarily. Please say you won't leave me while this is happening?" She pushed her hands together in a pleading gesture.

Johnny put one arm around Megan and pulled her close. Gently, he touched her reddening cheek. "You didn't expect me to say I was giving up on us, did you? I mean, this whole deal… it sucks, but of course I trust you Meg… with everything. Always."

Megan squeezed Johnny's hand and exhaled a relieved sigh. Her head rested on his chest.

Johnny totally forgot about the necklace he'd purchased for Megan earlier. He only found the wrapped box inside his school bag when he arrived home. He tucked it away inside a drawer, then flipped the pages of his bedroom wall calendar over to the month of November. *Megan's birthday comes up on the fourth. Guess I've gotten my shopping done early this year.*

In an otherwise cheerless and confusing day, this would be his happiest thought.

IMMINENT DISTRACTIONS

Johnny began his senior year at Brooklyn Post coping with the sting of an unwanted separation.

Registration day landed him in the last of his required English major courses. With two elective credits still at his disposal, he enlisted in a contemporary music-history class that spanned the great twentieth-century composers, including the pop music era. It seemed interesting enough.

Johnny gradually familiarized himself with the names and faces of his newest collegiate classmates. Among them was a guy who stood out like a chaperone at a high school prom. Howard Greffen had a graying goatee, thinning brown hair, and always wore a pair of maroon tinted glasses. Some students ignored his odd presence. Others disrespectfully bestowed upon him the moniker of "Gramps." But appearances notwithstanding, it was his after-class activities that drew an entirely different observation.

The music department at Brooklyn Post was the university's smallest. Situated just above the auxiliary cafeteria, it was comprised of four full-sized classrooms, two small offices, and a back room that was hardly ever accessed by the students.

Behind the often-locked door was a small studio with soundproof cork walls. In the center stood a black upright piano. Following afternoon classes, Howard regularly borrowed a key from the receptionist. He would leave the door partially ajar and place his considerable skills on display via a wide array of musical styles. His fine playing was occasionally accompanied by an adequate vocal performance, limited in range, but certainly ample for this impromptu setting.

It was during the third informal recital that a handful of students gathered just outside the door. A bouncy interpretation of Elton John's *Philadelphia Freedom* inspired a round of applause. Unaware that he had an audience, Howard looked up, startled. When he finished his next song, a modern arrangement of *Who Will Buy My Sweet Red Roses* from the musical, *Oliver*, the crowd dispersed with the exception of two.

While Johnny stood in the doorway, Frank Traber — a music major doubling as a prototypical, longhaired, club scene guitarist — stepped forward. Frank's lingering presence had nothing to do, however, with any particular fascination with his colleague's performance. "So Howard, see you at O'Callaghan's in thirty. And let's be on time tonight." He snapped the waistband of his black spandex pants for emphasis.

"No worries." Howard stood from the bench. "And I suppose your drummer boy, Ian, will be completing our little trio? Hate to miss our weekly drunken all-request hour."

Once the musicians finalized their plans, Johnny approached the man at the piano, armed with curiosity and a compliment. "Hey, nice set. Who knew we had a real musician here in this department of all these wannabes?"

"Thanks," Howard replied, sliding his glasses up the bridge of his nose. "But I never figured it was my talent that made me stand out in a venue where everyone's half my age!"

Johnny shrugged. "So, I guess you left the door open for attention?"

"Actually, we're just above the cafeteria kitchen. Gets awfully warm in here."

"Ah, right." Hesitantly, Johnny jammed his hands in his pockets. "So, hey, I was wondering what someone so... accomplished is doing in college? Don't mean to pry or anything, but –"

"No offense taken." Howard chuckled. "Someone was bound to ask. Now what'd you say your name was?"

"It's Johnny. Johnny Elias."

Howard zipped his canvas school bag closed, then headed toward the stairs. "Well, Johnny Elias, I've gotta get to a paying gig on Montague Street. You're welcome to walk me to my car if you want."

Keeping pace through the parking lot, Johnny pressed on. "So you were about to tell me how you ended up here? You don't strike me as some retired guy taking classes for your sanity."

Howard smiled. "No, it's nothing like that. Actually, I haven't got time for the extended version, but in a nutshell, I'm back to get a degree. Musicology. When one musical career dried up, I figured I could maybe teach it someday."

"A career in music?" Johnny's eyes lit up. "Were you in a band, or something?"

"Actually, for nineteen years, guess you could say I was considered a hot property in the songwriting community. It's just… no one stays inspired forever."

Johnny was bursting with curiosity. They arrived at Howard's car, a light-blue, '83 Chevy Nova on its last legs. Howard slung a beat-up school-bag into the backseat. Feeling rushed, Johnny unloaded a cluster of rapid-fire questions: "So you wrote songs professionally. Ever record anything? We talkin' pop songs? Broadway? And how many did you write?"

"A little of everything." Howard shrugged. He eased into the driver's seat, shut the door, and twisted his key in the car's ignition. Almost as an afterthought he rolled down the window. "Listen, kid, why don't we pick this up after class, say, Wednesday?"

Johnny smiled. "Could we? I'd like that. Music's always what's gotten me by too."

Johnny's instinctive reaction was to call Megan as soon as he got home that evening. But he remembered her request not to ring the apartment while Katherine was around. Reluctantly, he put down the receiver. With any luck, he'd hear from her later.

Two weeks had passed since their inauspicious discussion outside the museum. And although their time apart was more superficial than a true separation, the strain of uncertainty had begun to wear on each of them.

Megan was privately enduring greater difficulty than what she openly exhibited. She had initially planned to end her internship at Price & McLennan once the new semester at Barnard was underway... until her mother offered her a $250 stipend for two afternoons a week. Determining that the extra cash would eventually help emancipate her from Katherine's clutches, she agreed to stay on. It wasn't until much later that Megan came to realize the sweet triumph this development proved to be for her mother. Between office responsibilities and schoolwork, she now had even less time for Johnny. And the noticeable satisfaction on Katherine's face since the night of her tirade was eerily troubling. Soon, her suspicions would prove to be entirely correct.

While Johnny sat at home in Brooklyn that Monday evening, Megan attended the opening of *Opal,* an off-Broadway musical. She was provided with a front row seat and told to come home with a full report. Just before the curtain went up, she found the empty chair beside her suddenly occupied by a gawking stranger.

Megan's eyes were fixed on the stage for the mediocre first half. She tried ignoring the man next to her, who appeared to be sizing her up. Then the lights came on for intermission. The young man popped in a Tic-Tac, slicked back his hair, and made his move.

"Hey, Blondie. How'd you manage to score a seat to the premiere?"

"Oh, um, I'm here on assignment," Megan muttered, folding her arms. "And you?" she asked, sounding more polite than sociable.

"Connections," he boasted, sliding his left arm behind her seat. "Guess you can say I know a few people."

"Me too." Megan pretended to jot something down on a yellow notepad.

Jonas Worthington, the thirty-four year-old heir to a chain of Broadway theaters, fancied himself a smooth talker. He also happened to be a prospective new client of Price & McLennan; it was no accident that he was there. "So what you doin' after the show?" He leaned in. "I think I could get us backstage; meet the cast. A smokin' blonde like you will get us anywhere."

Megan compressed her lips, convinced that her mother had set her up. Her real fear was that by ignoring him, she'd only set herself up for later trouble no matter how crude he was.

When she returned home near midnight, Megan again found her mother strategically awaiting her arrival, only this time in a far more pleasant disposition. "So how was the show, hon? You have fun tonight?" Katherine was lounging in the living room, wearing a red silk yukata, relaxed and comfortable.

"It was nothing special, really." Megan fumbled though her schoolbag for a textbook, adopting a nonchalant pose. "The music sucked. The scenery was pretty lame. Probably won't be running very long, but then again, I'm no theater critic."

Katherine reclined further back on her leather sofa. "Well, that's off-Broadway for you, dear. Though you're home much later than I expected. Anything else I should know about?"

If Megan had even the slightest doubt about how Jonas Worthington ended up next to her, her mother had just made it eminently clear that the encounter was anything but random. She decided not to make an issue of it. She wasn't going to win, anyway. Might as well make it entertaining, though. "Funny you should ask." Megan smiled. "There *was* a certain young man who happened to be sitting next to me."

Katherine couldn't hide her delight. Megan proceeded with caution. "Anyway his name's Jonas. Really sweet… even got us into the cast party." She yawned for effect. "The thing is, he's much older than me; not my type."

"Oh, well," Katherine sighed. "At least I'm glad to hear how receptive you are to meeting new people. It'll be so exciting for you as you broaden your horizons."

4

A Heartbreak and a Melody

Johnny slid out of his seat just as Wednesday's music class ended. He waited at the back of the classroom for the piano player who had so impressed him earlier that week. Once the room emptied of students, he caught a glimpse of Howard Greffen strolling toward him.

"Oh, hey there, kid," Howard greeted him; he had clearly forgotten Johnny's name. "I'm gonna go play for a bit. Still wanna join me?"

"Yeah, cool," Johnny nodded. "Long as you don't mind company."

They walked together down the hall. Howard reached for the wall switch, turning on the overhead fluorescents in the windowless room. "Pull up a seat," he offered, steadying himself on the rickety piano bench.

Johnny lugged a desk-chair to Howard's left, then leaned over to observe. "So, you got a setlist or something?"

Howard shrugged his lanky shoulders beneath a brown, plaid shirt. "Usually just whatever's on my mind. Hey, why don't you get us started? Pick any familiar piano-based song. I can probably figure it out."

"Me? Really? Well, I want it to be one you know the words to."

Howard glared at him. "I didn't figure you to be a sideline observer. Just pick something you can croon along with."

Johnny took a quick glance at the door. It remained fully shut. He turned back to Howard, nervous. "I'm not really much of a singer; wouldn't know where to begin."

"How 'bout something you've heard recently? I don't care if you're tone-deaf. You can't be any worse than me. Let's just get going."

Johnny contemplated for less than a minute. A familiar ballad popped into his head. "Okay... *We've Got Tonite*. Bob Seger's song. Heard it on the radio before class."

Howard didn't say a word; he just pressed his fingers on the keys and played the song's introduction from memory. He glanced over to Johnny and motioned with his head as if to signal that it was his turn. Tentatively Johnny joined in. "*I know it's late. I know you're weary. I know your plans don't include me.*"

As Howard played on, Johnny swayed side-to-side with the melody, gradually finding his vocal rhythm. With each verse, he grew more liberated, even letting loose on the song's rigid bridge. His rendition came off surprisingly solid.

"Not bad at all, kid. I've probably sung that one a hundred times, but never with all that range. Nice phrasing on the verses."

Johnny stared at the floor. "Thanks, I guess. Never really gave it a second thought."

"For a guy who says he can't sing, you've got a sweet high tenor. A little polishing and vocal exercises could do you wonders."

"But we were just messing around." Johnny waved his hand dismissively. "I mean, you're really nice to say that, but I only popped in here to finish our chat from the other day."

Howard looked the other way. "Never mind my sorry existence. No need to bore you with that. For the moment we've got a quiet room, a piano in tune and a fairly decent vocalist in here. Go ahead. Pick another one."

Johnny felt a jolt of confidence that had been missing in recent days. The surprising compliment was a major ego booster. "Okay," he agreed, eager to give it another go. "How 'bout *Jealous Guy*, John Lennon's song? Know it?"

Again without answering, Howard leaned forward and began to play. Before long, the two men were immersed in a banquet of pop music history. Though separated in age by almost twenty-five years, they managed to bridge the generational gap with their shared interests.

Howard was struck by Johnny's uncanny ability to effortlessly pull from memory the lyrics to songs from his own youth. And Johnny was mesmerized by Howard's slick, tuneful arrangements on music spanning four decades. The late afternoon morphed into evening. Each took turns, trying unsuccessfully to stump the other with obscure song references. This fleeting escape from real-life continued until they were eventually interrupted by a knock on the door. It was the night janitor, attempting to sweep the room.

On his way home, Johnny felt a rampant impulse to keep this momentum going. Howard's encouragement was rewarding; but to sing in front of an audience... that would be something totally different.

As he passed the subway entrance, it occurred to him that it was still reasonably early for a Wednesday night – amateur night at the Lion's Gate club. *Wonder if that Jimbo guy'll be there?* He found the decision easy to make. Johnny pulled a token from the pocket of his black Levis and headed into Manhattan, his adrenaline carrying him the whole way.

It was just after ten by the time he reached the popular nightspot. Johnny walked down the long narrow staircase into the cavernous, brick-walled basement, expecting a sparse mid-week crowd. To his surprise, the smoky room was more than half occupied. At two long tables toward the back sat a mixed group of college students. Many had come out to celebrate the twenty-first birthday of a pretty brunette named Helen. This became apparent when they stood up and drunkenly serenaded her as she got onstage to sing with the house band.

A nearby table of rowdy Australian tourists stood collectively to jeer the off-key performance of the Eagles's *Already Gone* as sung by the birthday girl. Some tossed ice cubes from their drinks. One heaved an empty beer can at the drum kit. *Tough crowd,* Johnny thought.

A six-dollar cover charge earned him a wobbly wooden chair near the left of the stage. Between songs, he noticed a short line forming right next to the keyboard player. One-at-a-time, the whiskey-breathed drummer intro-duced the amateur singers, along with their song selection.

Onstage, each nervous, or inebriated soul tried reciting a popular stan-dard in front of the six-piece band. Few performances were particularly good, though the crowd seemed amused by several. One guy called Sid, put forth such a dreadful rendition of Joe Cocker's *You Are So Beautiful*, that the band urged him to sing an equally heinous version of the timeless classic, *Mack The Knife*. Another woman, introduced as Sophie, brought the room to tears with a butchered version the Carpenter's *Close To You*. And a drunken young couple was booed to their wobbly foundation with a putrid take on Meatloaf's *Two Out Of Three Ain't Bad*.

The lack of quality in the amateur singers was not lost on Johnny. He scanned the vast musical library in his head, hoping to select a generally familiar tune for the informal crowd; a song that could impress, provid-ing he was up to the challenge. After narrowing down countless options, he got his courage up and headed to enlist for a turn on stage. *Can't be any worse than these guys.* When he reached the front of the line, the keyboard-ist leaned forward with a clipboard. "Name and request for the band?"

"Do you guys know *House of the Rising Sun*? The Animals version?"

"Who doesn't?" the man replied unflinchingly, penciling it in on the ledger. "And what'd you say your name was?"

"Johnny Elias," he pronounced. "How many ahead of me?"

"Let's see. Looks like you're third now. So hang out here. Be ready when we call you."

Johnny stood off to the right, watching the next two singers. His mouth felt increasingly dry and cottony. His heart began to flutter. A myriad of thoughts flooded his head: Stage presence. Style. Composure. Suddenly, he was revisiting every live, or televised performance he'd ever witnessed all rolled into one.

Immersed in his recollections, Johnny barely noticed a rather competent delivery of Elvis Presley's *Kentucky Rain* by a hefty southerner introduced as Bill. This was followed by a pleasant interpretation of 'Til Tuesday's *Voices Carry* by a shorthaired redhead. It wasn't until the room responded enthusiastically, that he shifted back into the present.

"Next up, a guy who calls himself Johnny Elias to do an oldie but a goodie." Johnny nervously staggered to stage level and maneuvered past the keyboard player toward the center microphone. The bright stage lights caused him to squint. He pulled the mic from a silver stand. His breathing grew heavy. His hands began to tremble with the bizarre thought of being electrocuted by the metal against his sweaty palms.

"You ready?" the lead guitarist asked. Seeing Johnny's nod, he shouted, "I'm gonna play the opening chords, then you come in singing. We don't have an organ, but the keyboards'll more than fill for it." Then turning to the drummer he announced, "Okay, on four!"

Before Johnny could blink twice, the guitarist was ably duplicating the familiar opening notes. Feeling breathless, Johnny did not start at the precise moment where he was supposed to join in. This drew a dirty look from the bespectacled bass player. Johnny sweated out a repeat of the chords, then recited the lyrics in lackluster fashion.

There is a house in New Orleans
They call the Rising Sun

Johnny focused in on the table of Australian tourists through the opening verse. They appeared to squirm as if he'd kicked at a stray puppy. Then the unthinkable occurred. A deafening screech resonated through the room. It caused the entire song to break down on the spot. "My mother was a tailor," Johnny continued to sing until he heard the drummer yell, "Stop, stop."

The audience booed half-heartedly, tossing ice cubes as they'd done for most inferior performances. A can of Guinness whizzed by Johnny's head. He blushed in embarrassment. *At least the others were able to finish their songs, however torturous it was on everyone!*

Johnny turned to the keyboardist on his way off the stage, primed to apologize. But before the words could leave his lips, a last second reprieve was granted.

"Let's try that one again. With a little passion! And please: don't grip the mic so tight. It's not a window ledge."

Johnny flashed a relieved smile. He was only too pleased to give it another go. This time, he jumped right in on cue, singing with a surprising degree of gusto.

Gradually, Johnny became oblivious to his surroundings. The lights. The stage. The audience. He didn't even hear the applause in response to his mostly on-key navigation of the powerful high notes in the chorus. It wasn't until the final chords that he could process the enthusiastic reception from the now won-over audience.

So this is adulation? he wondered.

It was good.

Johnny awoke the next morning remarkably energized. Everything wasn't perfect, however.

He found it odd that he hadn't received a call from Megan in three days. After grabbing the handset to see that his phone line was working, he tried her at the apartment. An answering machine with Katherine's voice picked up. *No way I'm leaving a message.* He rolled his shoulders and hung up.

It was with good reason that Megan couldn't be reached. Miles from New York City and forty degrees warmer, she was checking in at the Water Club Resort in San Juan, Puerto Rico. She should have been readying for medieval history class. Instead, she was on "special" assignment for Price & McLennan.

It had all happened so fast. On Wednesday night, Megan returned home to study for an English Literature exam. Reading until her eyelids were no longer cooperative, she turned in just after 2am. But it was only 4:42 on her bedside clock when she was awakened by a panicked voice. All Megan could remember clearly about that frantic early morning was how dark it was outside, and the hurried manner in which she dressed and stumbled out the door.

When they arrived downtown, Katherine rushed from the taxi into her office building. Only half-awake, Megan valiantly tried to keep pace. She looked on as her mother busied herself with frenetic phone calls about runway models and hiring a photographer on minimal notice. An hour later, Katherine turned to her daughter in supplication. "Honey, so sorry to do this to you, but I'm really in a jam."

"What is it?" Megan asked, her voice tired.

"It's Sheila. She had to rush her sister to the hospital last night. Some kind of blood disorder. Might be serious."

Megan shook her head. "Oh, sorry. But where do I come in? I've got classes today, a study group tonight, and a Monday midterm. My plate is full."

Katherine's voice grew more serious. "I know how hard you're studying. But we're not losing an account over a last-minute cancellation." She slid a manila folder across the desk. "You'll be covering for Sheila in San Juan this weekend at the Kinard-Giverny fashion show. I promise you won't have to work too hard. And you'll be back here come Monday with plenty of time to ace that exam."

Megan stared at her mother. Most of her schoolmates' parents were always on their cases about studying; hers was on her case *not* to. It didn't matter and she knew it. No matter what she said, she was going to be on that flight. Her mother always got what she wanted. Flipping through the folder in front of her, she felt a nervous twinge. "And when am I supposed to leave? I haven't even got my allergy pills. Should I run home now, get ready?"

"No, sweetheart," Katherine shook her head, polite in victory. "I'll figure it all out. And here: take our corporate Amex, buy whatever you need. By the time you get down there and check in, I'll have something arranged."

Now Megan unlocked her suite with the electronic key-card. Her spirits lifted as she caught a glimpse of the lovely ocean view from the balcony.

There were two bulky garment bags and a Gucci suitcase on the king-sized bed. A faxed note sat on top. Her mom's handwriting was instantly recognizable.

"*Hi, Hon. Hope you got some rest on the flight. Call me with any questions. Also, I've taken the liberty of buying you a few outfits. Sorry for the short notice. I know you'll do great.*"

Excited in spite of herself, Megan opened the packages. Four designer outfits lay on hangers in her petite size. Tucked inside a front pouch were two pairs of Valentino high heeled Slingbacks -- red and black. The suitcase contained everything from swimsuits to silk pajamas, plus a pair of Dior sunglasses. She laughed when coming across the lacy underwear. It was more revealing than anything she owned. Still, it was brand new and apparently ordered inconspicuously through the hotel concierge.

Knowing Mom, there's gotta be a catch, Megan surmised. This so-called emergency trip, probably just another of her manipulative schemes. But still, there are worse scenarios than spending a weekend in a tropical paradise with a brand new wardrobe!

Once settled in, she reached for the phone on her nightstand. *Gotta tell Johnny that I'm outta town, and why.* But as she dialed, it occurred that her mom would almost certainly see the itemized bill with a list of outgoing numbers dialed. *Or maybe I'll just find a payphone later,* she rationalized. *Much better that way.*

Johnny rushed to his apartment after his Thursday library shift. His answering machine light was flashing. Eager for the sound of Megan's voice, he was instead surprised to find a message from someone else.

Hey kid, just wanted to say it was fun hanging out the other day. If you have time, how 'bout again this weekend. Call me at home; let me know.

Putting Howard's invitation aside for a moment, Johnny's thoughts went impatiently to Megan. Why hadn't she called? Inside his small black phonebook was a folded page that contained Megan's school schedule and planned work-hours at Price & McLennan. Against his better judgment, Johnny dialed her office.

"Price, McLennan," a friendly voice answered.

"Megan Price, please."

"Just one moment. And who can I tell her is calling?"

"Tell her, Johnny," he said clearly.

He listened to the on-hold Muzak for two minutes. It felt like two hours. *What's keeping her?* He grew increasingly fidgety. The receptionist finally picked up again. "Transferring." Three more rings were followed by another friendly sounding woman.

"Megan Price's office."

Perplexed by the unfamiliar voice, and by the fact that Megan did not in fact have her own office, Johnny slid anxiously to the edge of his chair. "Is... is Megan there, please?"

"I'm sorry, sir. Ms. Price isn't here. Is there something I can assist you with?"

"Can you tell me when she'll be back? It's pretty important."

"Who again is this calling for her?" the sugary voice prodded.

"My name's Johnny. I'm... a friend of hers. I know she's usually in the office about now. You know where I can reach her?"

After a slight hesitation, the woman answered, her voice smooth. "I don't wish to get involved in Ms. Price's social calendar, but I do believe she and her boyfriend have taken off to a warmer climate. She's not expected back until next week."

Johnny winced, as if someone had punched him in the gut. Surely Megan would have told him if she were going out of town! And this boyfriend – what was she talking about? Megan and somebody else? He could feel his heart hammering in his chest. It took him a while to find his voice. "Um... d'ya have a number where I can reach her?"

"My apologies sir. Megan's trip is of a personal nature. I haven't been provided with contact information. Anything else I can help you with?"

"Just one more thing." He grabbed a pen with his free hand. "Can I ask who I'm speaking with? Megan never mentioned a new assistant."

"Actually, you're correct. Just handling some responsibilities in her absence." This elusive reply was followed by a beeping sound and then another female voice, this one muffled. "Sheila, Liz Smith on line two. Sheila, line two."

"Sheila? Is that your name?" Johnny's ears were ringing; it was hard to believe that no one could hear his pulse pounding as loudly as he could. He slammed down the phone.

How the hell could she do this to me? he thought bitterly. *If Megan wanted to end this, wouldn't she at least have the decency to tell me first?*

Johnny began restlessly pacing his narrow bedroom. Thoughts of Megan waking up in the embrace of another man on a sun-splashed beach left him feeling helpless and panicked. Someone else's hands caressing her silky blonde hair; exploring the curves of her body. It was too much to bear. After waiting hours for a silent telephone to ring, his mood swung from despair to anger. In a rare fit of rage, he kicked over the brown cardboard box serving as an end-table for his phone. He stepped over the dislodged receiver on his way out for some fresh air.

Megan again reviewed the assignment folder, lying facedown across her bed. Loose pages listed the names, contact numbers and an activity timeline for Friday's fashion show. It looked simple enough. And the entire program would only last forty-minutes, leaving more than enough time to relax poolside. *This can't be the whole deal,* she thought dazedly. *Must be some kinda trap.*

Frantically, Megan searched the suite for hidden bachelor number two. There was no such thing as being too careful, not where her mother was concerned. She even checked under the bed for a concealed recording device before concluding that perhaps she was being overly suspicious.

One hour passed. Megan felt overcome by a heavy sense of guilt – and a desire to hear Johnny's voice. She scrounged up all her available change, scurried to a payphone in the lobby, and dialed his number. Anticipating that he wasn't likely to be home, she planned to leave a detailed message. Instead, she repeatedly got a busy-signal.

Johnny never did manage to call in at the library to cancel his Friday rounds. When he returned to consciousness on his bedroom floor, he did so with a sense of uncharted emptiness. Weary and confused, his thoughts of Megan shifted from burning jealousy to sheer determination. He could still win her back, he reasoned. He was not going down without a fight.

Out of habit, out of need, Johnny reached for one of his spiral-bound notebooks. One answerless question after another took shape in the form of rhyming verse. But the inherent sadness now engulfing his thoughts initiated a new sensation; a feeling he could not articulate nor comprehend. Words of insecurity stained the paper. Johnny unearthed a sad, but haunting melody from within. At first, he questioned its authenticity. Was he simply borrowing one of the countless tunes he'd been exposed to in his lifetime? As he continued to write, it became apparent that in this moment of distraught confusion, he'd found inspiration to breathe life into his very first song.

This primitive ballad - packed with raw emotions - summarized his bare, vulnerable thoughts.

Has the world gone mad?
Or is it just you and I?
One moment we embrace
and in the next we cry
I am anchored by sweet memories that just won't die
Do you plan to forget me and cast my heart awry?
I hardly ever sleep at night - It's just so hard to do
'Coz every time I close my eyes my thoughts return to you

(Chorus)
I'm hoping you'll return to me
It just tears me up inside
I long that we will find a way
This yearning won't subside

How badly do you plan to hurt me?
Offer me a clue
I can't believe what's happened here
Our happiness askew
Have I done you wrong? – Is this worthy of repair?
You know how I adore you – it's beholden in my stare
I showered you with kindness
not a single drop was forced
Now I'm left here in confusion
Has our love just run its course?

You know I loved you madly and I thought you did the same
Now I ask for your return and not a place to put the blame
Was I wrong for trusting you? – Pull me from this dark malaise
Should I keep on loving you or have we gone our separate ways?

I'm searching high and low for answers I may never find
Maybe I should quit this fight or maybe I'm just blind
If indeed I've hurt you here is my apology
Baby please forgive me and return to loving me
(Chorus- End)

Johnny was astonished by what he'd just done. He scrambled for a portable cassette recorder, then sang the lyrics with a tape running to preserve this fragile creation. A half-dozen replays convinced him of its originality. He knew exactly what to do next.

The Greffen residence stood on the corner of Willow Street, just before a dead end near the Brooklyn-Queens Expressway. This peculiar red brick dwelling was a throwback to an era gone by, ironically, on a block of modern architecture. Two cement lions guarded the creaky front porch. Overgrown shrubbery and broken stained glass windows offered little curb appeal. This Brooklyn abode had clearly seen better days.

Johnny double-checked the address, then rang the bell with some trepidation.

"Oh, hey!" Howard appeared at the door. "Glad you found it. Come on in."

This landmark house had been built by Howard's grandfather in 1924 and remained in the family for three generations. Though updated with such modern conveniences as baseboard heating, the interior was kept dark and disorderly. Heavy black curtains were drawn over each window. Dust particles covered most of the surfaces. The smell of mothballs was overpowering. This place had the distinct feel of a haunted house, cobwebs, candelabras and all.

Howard escorted Johnny to the back parlor. He proudly showed off what was probably his most prized possession: a distressed wooden piano with exquisite hand-carved legs sitting against the back wall. "It's from 1926," he gloated. "Still plays like a charm."

Johnny was curious as to why Howard lived as he did. Surely a successful musician couldn't be living in more humble confines than the majority of the foster residences he'd resided in. These crumbling, dispassionate surroundings were in sharp contrast to his expectations. Momentarily, his initial songwriting attempt took a backseat to the depressing existence of his host. "Interesting place you've got here," he remarked, taking it all in. "Who's your decorator?" *The Addams family?* he mouthed silently.

Howard pointed to a broken grandfather clock in the corner. "Like this big guy, much of what you see has been around far longer than me. I always tell myself that I'll get around to fixing things, or throwing stuff out. Guess I'm just short on time."

An old velvet folding chair leaned upright against the piano. Howard unfolded it, patted away layers of dust, then motioned for Johnny to join him. "So you say you've tapped into the great beyond; joined the songwriting ranks. Let's see what you've come up with."

"Well, I'm sure someone of your musical ability won't be too impressed. It's just… things are falling apart with my girlfriend and me. I wrote something to try and win her back."

"Ah, inspiration." Howard nodded, then drew in a deep breath. "Good. Anyway, what makes you think I'm so extraordinary? From the get-go, I've been telling you my life's nothing special. Now that you see where I live, you oughta realize I've been brutally honest."

Johnny stared off into a corner of the room where a stack of tattered sheet music lay. Howard's evasiveness only fueled his curiosity. "But that's just what I don't get, Howard. With all respect, you've hardly told me anything about you till now. I mean, we've talked music for hours. Yet whenever I ask anything personal…." His voice trailed off.

Howard squirmed on his piano stool. "Kid, it's complicated. Sad, really. Not used to talking about it. I mean… you wouldn't understand."

"Try me," Johnny encouraged. "Hey, I'm a pretty good listener. No use keeping it bottled up, right?"

"Well, actually, it's been years since I've had anyone around here to judge me. Kinda prefer it that way. My splendid isolation, if you will."

"So you just keep everything to yourself? Doesn't sound all that splendid to me. Can't be too healthy either, you know?" Johnny looked up at Howard, his eyebrows arched. "Hey, I spent my whole life trusting strangers. Nine different foster families since I was two. Worked for me. Sorta. Maybe its time you start learning to trust somebody. Remember, I'm here to play you this song I wrote. Wouldn't be here if I didn't trust you. It's all about trust, right?"

Howard folded his arms and locked eyes with Johnny. An awkward minute passed. "It's just… well I'd rather people not know too much, you know?

And my life ain't the prettiest picture, so don't say I didn't warn you, ya hear?"

Johnny nodded. Howard leaned forward with his hands on his knees.

"So yeah, I started on this piano like forty years ago; wrote a few songs back when. Pop, rock, whatever. Early on I realized that carrying a tune versus becoming a recording artist were totally different. My voice is… well, limited. So I focused on songwriting. Even sold a few to record labels. No hits, mind you, but album cuts for some mainstream bands. And then fate intervened. I got *discovered* one night by an ad exec at some piano bar; wrote some TV jingles you've probably heard. A steady gig. Flexible too. Even got to teach at performing-arts camp each summer. It was pretty cool while it lasted."

In the early 1970s, Howard met the girl of his dreams, a spirited redhead named Suzanne, he boasted. They dated for a few years, then married happily. But wedded bliss was shattered by a string of family tragedies. It started with the death of his mother in a multi-car accident. His father succumbed to a broken heart just months later. And then there was Suzanne's courageous battle with breast cancer.

"They found a lump during a routine appointment. Must've been '82, just months after we moved back in here. Suzy had it removed, thought she beat it. A year later, it came back. The doctors had no choice… a double mastectomy. Man, she was brave; fought on for five years till finally… She was only forty-one."

Following her death, Howard's artistic inner voice went silent. He was seemingly never able to unlock whatever creative forces had enabled his success. Within a year, he quit his primary job at the ad agency, and simply let himself go.

Now, sitting at the old piano next to Johnny, Howard was beginning to see elements of his former self in the younger man. Though they'd only met weeks earlier, he was hardly surprised that Johnny now claimed to possess the ability to create music. But Johnny didn't share Howard's limitations: he also had the voice and the looks to perhaps achieve higher recognition. "So – lemme guess. You had your dreams shattered and felt inspired to let it all out?"

Johnny looked back at Howard with deeper appreciation. "Well… let's just say whatever pain I'm feeling, it's nothing compared to all the crap you've been through. I mean, this is gonna really sound trivial, but this girl; she's my whole world. Three years, you know? Now I'm feeling like I've been completely duped. It sucks! That the way it happens for everyone?"

"Actually, that's how most of us get into any kind of art. True inspiration, man! Without it we're just going through the motions. And heartbreak: that's the golden ticket." Howard paused to read Johnny's expression. "First time for you?"

Johnny nodded dejectedly. Howard smiled in acknowledgement. "I sympathize, kid. But one never has their feet firmly planted till they've experienced their first broken heart."

"Just wish it didn't have to be so damn bitter," Johnny countered.

Howard patted Johnny on the back. "No one can rationalize why something so positively beautiful comes from the depths of our pain. I guess that's what classifies art and artists among life's great ironies. Like Harry Nilsson once sang: there would never be a love song if folks were always happy."

Taking this as his cue, Johnny drew a deep breath, then shared his new composition, unaccompanied and from memory; his dejected voice quavering throughout. By the second verse, Howard gradually added the slow under-melody on piano and vocal harmony on the chorus. It went notably smoother than Johnny anticipated. A basic arrangement was captured on a simple tape recorder.

"A nice first effort," Howard remarked after hearing it back. "Kinda reminds me of something I wrote back in the day, when a two-timing Donna crushed my teenaged spirit. It's a simple tune you've got there, but it shows potential."

Howard watched a hint of a smile emerge from beneath Johnny's saddened exterior. He winked back at the young man across the room.

"So enough about me. Tell me about this girl who's turned you into such a tortured soul?"

Emotional Inventory

Megan found her row in business class. She lifted the plastic window shade and connected her seatbelt. Her unexpected trip to San Juan had been a relative success.

The Friday fashion show hadn't been much of an event. Aside from a brief allergy attack, nothing disastrous transpired. *Hardly the apparent emergency mom freaked over.*

As the flight began its decent into JFK, her thoughts returned to Johnny. Megan tried reaching him from a variety of payphones over the weekend. She found his line continuously engaged. By Sunday morning, she figured that she was only a few hours from home: *No urgent need to try again.*

Only now she was harboring second thoughts.

Megan arrived home to an empty apartment Sunday night. A note from her mother lay on the kitchen table. It was written in haste and somewhat illegibly, but she could make out the line about Zach and a restaurant. *Lucky me*, she thought. *My mini-vacation's just been extended.*

Another failed attempt to connect with Johnny by phone prompted her to dial up a car service. Despite weekend traffic on the FDR Drive, she arrived in Brooklyn by 8:30.

An unseasonably warm mid-October night proved fortuitous. At the front entrance of the six-story building she repeatedly buzzed Johnny's intercom. No response. Megan raced to a corner payphone. She tried Johnny's number every five minutes while keeping an eye out for his arrival. She even dialed Andy Raymer's house, unaware Andy now lived in a dorm at NYU. Her frustration mounted with each passing minute. Yet, she would wait all night if she had to.

It was twenty minutes to ten when Johnny finally rounded the corner. Not even a home cooked meal and a chat with his onetime foster mom, Caroline could ease his confusion. "Just relax. Don't let it consume you," she kept repeating to him. "True love doesn't just evaporate overnight. I'm sure there's a good explanation." Johnny was so caught up in finding one that he nearly walked right by Megan, who was waiting on his building doorstep.

"What gives? You don't even say hello?" Megan followed him inside.

Johnny took an emotional inventory, then turned toward her hesitantly.

Megan let her pocketbook fall to the floor. She threw her arms around him. Johnny just stayed still, his arms by his side. Megan wasn't picking up on his silent message. "Hope you're cool that I'm here just like this. I tried calling all weekend but I couldn't get through," she burbled.

Johnny remained silent. He unlocked his apartment door and stood aside for her to pass through in front of him. He didn't know whether Megan was here for a breakup conversation or to further her deception. Her suntanned face only lent further credence to the story he had heard from Price & McLennan. Unsure of where to begin, he instead allowed Megan to do most of the talking.

"Johnny, it was total insanity. On Thursday my mom wigged out about some event in Puerto Rico. Sent me to cover for her. No notice. No suitcase. Nothing."

"You know, you could've stood up to her… for once."

"It wasn't worth it. She's just… you know I can never win with her. And besides, it was only this one weekend. No big deal, right?"

"Yeah, well if you're never gonna get your way, you mind telling me what we're doing here still together? We both know she's never gonna change her mind about me."

Megan looked up to the ceiling and sighed. "Johnny, she'll come around. I won't give her a choice when it comes to us. Eventually she'll see that you're the one person who makes me happy. And I'm here now, aren't I?"

"Yeah, well you could've called," he countered, still not looking at her.

"I don't know what's wrong with your line," she said, defensive. "For two straight days I kept getting a busy signal. I mean, what the hell?"

He still wasn't looking at her. "Anything else happen down there I should know about?"

"What d'ya mean? I oversaw some stupid fashion show." Megan sat down at the foot of Johnny's second-hand daybed and removed her jacket. "Oh, and my mom arranged everything."

Johnny shot her an angry look from across the room. "Arranged what? Any special company escort you on your trip?"

Megan hesitated. "Okay, you're right. I think Mom might've tried to hook me up with some resort owner. But – don't look like that, okay? He bored me to death, and, anyway, I wouldn't even think of it. How can you think I would?" She took a moment to catch her breath, and to change tactics. "And where were *you* all weekend, while we're on the subject?"

Suddenly on the defensive, Johnny returned fire with a curious inquiry. "So who is Sheila from your mother's office?"

"Sheila? She's Mom's partner," Megan answered, taken aback. "Why'd you ask?"

"Oh, she answered your line Thursday when I called the office. Told me you were away for the weekend… with your boyfriend."

"Boyfriend!" Megan blurted out. "The only boyfriend I've ever had is looking right at me!" She paused, the words sinking in. "And you say it was Sheila you spoke to? Mom said that she had an emergency. That's why she sent me down there." She took a deep breath. "That lying bitch!"

The pieces slowly were coming together. Johnny felt foolish about having been deceived by Katherine; he was not certain that Megan was entirely truthful either. He sat down beside her on the bed with an air of apprehension. *If she's just back from a weekend with someone else, this could be a cover up.*

Megan, on the other hand, was seething. "I'll quit that place first thing tomorrow! Don't care what she has to say about it. How dare she do this to us?"

Johnny stood up, restless. "Meg, I really thought I'd lost you. You can't imagine how helpless I felt, not knowing."

"Oh, John, I'm so sorry. Really, I am. Don't even know what I'd have done if it were the other way around. Must've been horrible!"

Johnny starred over at the cassette on his nightstand. He reached out for it, dropped it in his stereo and pushed *play*. His song for Megan filled the room, and Megan's eyes filled with tears.

"I... I can't believe it. Did you write that... write it for me? It's beautiful. And you sing it so well! I only wish it had been for something happier. But I love it just the same."

Megan curled up against Johnny on the edge of his worn-out mattress. Johnny began to stroke Megan's hair. Soon, they were both asleep in each other's weary arms.

It was 3am when Megan awoke in a cold sweat. She jumped out of bed, startled.

"John! Look at the time. I'm a dead woman!"

Johnny leaped to his feet and instinctively helped Megan on with her jacket, which had been slung over a nearby chair. He stood by the door with his hands folded while Megan called a car service. *Katherine Price! Haunting us, even while we sleep!*

When Megan hung up the phone, Johnny reached for her hand and pulled her body against his, hoping to change her mind. "Meg, why not stay till morning at this point? She can't keep ruining our lives like this! When'll this finally stop? When can we officially be happy again?"

Megan threw her arms around Johnny's broad shoulders and brought her lips to his. Then gently, she pulled away. "Listen. At the end of the month, Mom's taking me to Paris for my birthday. It'll just be the two of us. While we're away, I'll set her straight. Just you wait and see!"

The Barnard cafeteria was hopping with activity at lunchtime. Megan paid the cashier for her yogurt and a lemonade, then carried her plastic tray around the room in search of an empty table. There was none. She'd nearly given up looking when a familiar voice called out.

"Hey Meg, take a load off." It was Vera Watson, Megan's classmate and alibi from the day of the Central Park concert. Megan gave a friendly, one-handed wave, then sat down across the table to join her.

"Oh, hey Vera. Thanks. Didn't think I'd find a spot. Jammed as always."

"Sure is." Vera was picking at a plate of Caesar salad with a side of French fries. She waited to finish chewing her food, then leaned forward, smiling. "So how're things with the boyfriend? You and Don Henley still hanging on?"

"You mean Johnny?" Megan replied, competing with the surrounding noise. "Yeah, hanging in there... sort of."

Vera dropped her fork on the table. Her lust for gossip superceded her appetite. "Meg, either you are, or aren't still together. There's no in-between on this. What's the deal?"

Megan sipped her lemonade through a straw, then sat fully upright, her face solemn. "Vera, I'm not leaving him. Not now, not ever. It's just: I've had to make a few sacrifices to shut my mom up. Nothing that I'm particularly proud of."

"Oooh! Pray tell." A wry smirk spread across Vera's face. She leaned in closer to the table and rested her chin on her cupped hands.

Megan shook her head. "It's not really like that. I mean, I speak to Johnny at least twice-a-day since that night at his place. I just haven't been telling him everything, you know? He's... real sensitive about these things. Don't wanna hurt him anymore."

"Hurt him how?" Vera asked, her eyes arching open wide. "What aren't you telling Johnny? Knowing you, it can't be all that terrible."

Megan took another sip of lemonade, then looked down at the table. "Well, for starters, I didn't quit my job at Mom's agency. I tried, but she wouldn't let me; wouldn't hear of it. Instead, she raised me fifty bucks a-week and gave me my own office. I could care less about the office, but I guess the money comes in handy."

"And that's so terrible?" Vera stared at Megan, puzzled. "By the look on you're face, I thought it was way juicier."

"Well, actually," Megan leaned forward and lowered her tone. "I also had to go out with a few guys – guys my mother thinks I should be with. I feel so guilty about it. Keep having to make excuses so Johnny won't suspect anything."

"Ah, now we're talking! A few studs on the side. How many you juggling?"

"Four," Megan answered. "Four in the last two weeks. Can't believe Mom would even think that I'd go for any of 'em. It's insanity. She doesn't know me at all!"

"Hmm. Sucks for you. But any of 'em I might like?"

"Honestly, no, Vera. They'd bore you to tears. These aren't college guys. They're all much older than us; all business and careers."

"Well, they can't be revolting, right?" Vera had slid to the edge of her chair. "Otherwise, she wouldn't have picked 'em for you. Your mother's way too image conscious."

Megan shrugged. "I don't know. I guess the first guy was okay looking. A pediatrician. He's 31 and opening a practice in midtown. Spent the whole night talking about babies and insurance plans. Totally lame."

Vera dabbed at the corner of her mouth with a napkin, then pretended to yawn. "Yeah, sounds like a real snoozefest. Oh well. What about the others?"

Megan nervously twirled her fingers through her hair. She was growing fidgety. "The second guy, he's the son of the UN diplomat from Australia.

Ian something or other. Cool accent. Zero personality. Just rugby and foreign politics."

"No way!" Vera exclaimed. "Must've been so cool… and yet, totally frustrating." She scratched her head in disbelief.

"It was." Megan nodded in agreement. "He's also like seven feet tall; nearly twice my size. If we ever posed for a picture, his head would probably get cut off in the shot." She laughed in spite of her predicament. "Oh, and the third guy: typical lawyer. Second year in Columbia and a complete wise-ass. His Dad's some hotshot defense attorney, or so he kept boasting… when he wasn't arguing with me about everything else including paying the bill."

"Ouch!" Vera shouted, smacking her tray for emphasis. "You sure these are your mother's choices we're talking about? Total handpicked losers."

"Well, except for the last guy," Megan corrected. "Gerry Ridgewell. Medical resident at Einstein. He's actually a friend of the family. His mom, Myrna, she was the decorator who redid our apartment years ago. His dad's a retired plastic surgeon, or something."

"Hmm. Off to a good start." Vera was leaning forward again. "So what about him?"

"Um, he's twenty-six. About six feet tall. Good build. Great hair. Oh, and he's got this little goatee; makes his face look much older."

"Sounds cute. Is he nice?"

"Are you kidding" Megan waved her hand dismissively. "I've known Gerry since we were kids. Yeah, he's okay. Never really had much to talk about growing up. He was kinda weird back then. But I guess these days… well, maybe."

"So where'd you guys go on your date?" Vera was again resting her chin on her hands.

"Actually, it was twice. But let's not call 'em dates. It's not like I'm into him, or anything."

"But you saw him two times," Vera's eyes were growing wider, "in under two weeks!"

"Um, sorta." Megan took another sip from her straw. "I think of him as... oh how would you say... a diversionary prop. Just an old friend to bide my time with so that Mom thinks I'm trying. I mean, he's sorta fun. Took me on a picnic in the park the first time. And last night he got us tickets for the Big Apple Circus at Lincoln Center. But it's not like I allowed myself to enjoy it. That would be out of the question."

"I dunno." Vera was bursting with curiosity. "Sounds to me like a guy I could totally fall for. If you're not interested, let him know I'm on the prowl."

"Actually, it's kinda tricky, Vera." Megan's face grew more serious. "I can't let Gerry know that I'm not really into him. Not yet, anyway. I need my Mom to think I gave him a fair shake, before I tell her that I'm going back to Johnny. This'll probably be enough to get her off my case. But in the meantime, I can't go setting Gerry up with my friends. Plus, I've already agreed to see him again when I get back from Paris next week."

"Ooh! Sneaky, sneaky!" Vera flashed a look of surprise. "So you're just gonna string him along for a while; make believe you like him. And how far do you let this go? I mean, I'm sure this guy has feelings too, no?"

"Well, okay. You're right. So I haven't given much thought to Gerry's deal. But for me, this is really about finding a way to make it work with Johnny. Gerry knows nothing about him. I plan to keep it that way." She took a final slurp of her lemonade. "But yeah, I see your point. Don't want to hurt Gerry either. Maybe just the once more and then I let him down easy."

With ample time on his hands, Johnny sought to keep momentum building on his first songwriting effort. He borrowed an old Casio keyboard from Howard and played out melodies from his mind that he believed to be original. A little refining allowed him to match them up with some of the poems he'd scribbled in notebooks and saved through the years. *Vapor Trail of Tears*, was written in January of '86 to commemorate the space shuttle *Challenger* astronauts. It became a soaring ballad. *More Than Friends, Less*

Than Lovers was penned based on a conversation he'd overheard between a bickering couple in the college cafeteria. It evolved as a jazzy waltz. Momentum indeed!

Within a matter of days, he believed he had six completed songs to his name.

Midterm exams came and went. Johnny headed out to celebrate with Andy and Jacqui at *The Back Fence,* an intimate folk-rock club near the NYU campus. Johnny was impressed with each of the acoustic performers who sung on a small triangular stage in the corner of the room. He was equally intrigued by how well Andy and his new girlfriend were still getting along.

Once, while Andy had stepped out to the men's room, Johnny found himself alone with Jacqui. He turned to her. "Hey, so I just wanted you to know that of all the women Andy's dated, you probably rate right up there in just about every category."

"Well, considering he's never had anyone before me..." she laughed, reaching for a handful of shelled peanuts. "So what does Andy say about me when I'm not around?"

"Not very nice things, I'm afraid," Johnny answered, deadpan, then chuckled. "But seriously, these days you're all he seems to talk about. Must be doing something right."

Jacqui blushed. "I have my ways. Maybe it just took an older woman's touch to unleash his potential. I am twenty-four." She flashed a crooked grin. "And as Andy knows, despite my share of train-wrecks, I've never been so content."

Johnny crushed a peanut shell in his hand. "Breakups, huh? So you've had a few. Mind sharing why things didn't last?" He met her eyes. "I'd really like to know."

"Ah, who knows? With one guy we always seemed to be doing the things *he* wanted to do. Another: entirely about convenience. It worked okay till we realized that neither of us had anything in common. Oh, and then there was the bloke just before I came to America. We simply grew apart; wasn't anyone's fault really. Happens sometimes, you know?"

"All too well these days," Johnny muttered. "Only in my case, it's neither of us waiving the white flag. A common enemy divides."

Jacqui's eyes were sympathetic. "Yeah, Andy's been saying. I feel horrible." She cracked open a peanut shell and popped a nut in her mouth. "You guys were visual bliss in Central Park. That girl, she's entirely chuffed with you. I saw the way she looked in your eyes. Women tend to notice these things. And her opinion's really the only one that matters. Cheer up, then. I'm right, you know."

Johnny flashed a hopeful grin. "Maybe so. But the thing is: I'm having major trust issues. It's like she's holding something back. And all these restrictions... I mean, she's probably the one thing I've ever cared about; can't imagine losing her. But her mom, she's just calculating enough to always stay one-step ahead. Plus, Megan's confidence is so fragile that Katherine can just breathe on her and she folds up like a camping tent."

Jacqui reached over and patted Johnny on the back. "Ah, the perils of first love. Listen, Johnny: if there's one thing you young people are in short supply of, its patience. You've got to give it some time; let it play out. May not get fixed overnight, but learn to live with the ups and downs."

The next performer plugged her guitar into the stage amplifier. Andy returned to the table. "Anyone miss me?"

Jacqui smiled up at him. Johnny tossed a peanut shell on the floor.

"Yeah, I figured you guys had plenty to talk about." Andy chuckled. "Hope you managed to solve the world's problems in my absence."

"I wish." Johnny smiled inwardly. "Guess we all can't be lucky as you these days."

6

We've Already Said Goodbye

The telephone rang just prior to seven a.m., startling Johnny out of a dream. He fumbled for the handset in a semi-conscious state. "The sky better be falling," he answered, attempting to clear the night's cobwebs.

"Bonjour, lover boy. Guess who just got home from Paris?"

"Monday morning already?" His tone softened when he heard Megan's voice. "Well I guess that means today's somebody's birthday."

"Oh, you remembered!" she shouted happily. "So aren't you gonna ask about my trip? It was kinda productive on all levels."

Johnny sat up in bed and stretched his free arm skyward. "Tell you what. I'm just about to wash up; get my day going. Can I call you back in ten?"

"Not a good idea," Megan whispered. "We just got in. Mom's here, unloading her stuff. Plus, I gotta leave for school. Better if we just talk now for a minute. I'll call you later when I get to a phone booth."

Johnny drew a heavy sigh. "So I guess Paris wasn't as successful as you say. If I can't even call the apartment on your birthday, when'll it ever —"

"No, no. It's not like that! Things are really better. It's just… I wouldn't wanna undo it all in the very minute we've come in the door. Johnny, I can't wait to tell you about the strides we made this weekend. You'll be so proud of me."

"So when do we get to catch up in person? You up to a big night out?"

"Tonight? Um, well I do have something… a doctor's appointment. You know, allergies. How 'bout tomorrow? I'll be a lot more refreshed and in the celebrating mood."

"Meg, I've never missed your birthday! We don't have to do anything special. Look, I just need to see you. These last few weeks have been brutal for me."

"Yeah, me too. It's just… I'm exhausted." She let out a yawn.

Johnny groaned in disappointment. Megan gave in. "All right, but it has to be late. Like nine or later, okay? I'll meet you down in the lobby. But I can't promise I'll be up to doing much."

Monday, November 4th was shaping up to be a promising day. Sunny and warm for mid-autumn, Johnny only needed a lightweight jacket. He locked his front door, then suddenly remembered Megan's beaded necklace, still sitting in his top dresser drawer. Excited, he headed back inside to grab the gift-wrapped box and tuck it in his schoolbag.

Johnny got the first of his mid-term grades that morning: a B+ in physics. No marks were posted in his Advanced Shakespeare class. But an animated discussion over *Troilus and Cressida* further enlivened his spirits. They were doubly enhanced following music history, when Johnny was flagged down by a friendly voice in the hallway. "Hey, kid. Heading over to the piano room. Care to join me?"

"Oh, hey, Howard. I'd really love to. But I got big plans tonight. Maybe Wednesday, if you've got time then."

"Actually, Wednesday I've got a paying gig. We can either do it now, or wait till next Monday."

"Then I suppose it needs to wait a week," Johnny moaned. "Hate to put you off, but today's Megan's birthday! Got a few stops to make along the way."

Johnny was feeling particularly upbeat after visiting the barbershop and the florist. Buoyed by his early morning phone call, he looked forward to some positive developments after weeks of maddening disruption.

He dressed carefully and sharply in his best pair of black slacks, a red button-down silk shirt, and a gray pinstriped jacket. Figuring he might cross paths with Katherine Price, he wanted to make a strong impression. From flawlessly styled hair to his new black loafers, not a detail was overlooked.

Johnny exited the subway ahead of schedule. His watch read only 8:04. Megan asked that he not drop by until nine. At the 32nd Street bus stop, he thought back with mild regret on the missed opportunity to work with Howard. But along the route of the M-32, his thoughts switched back to what he hoped would be a perfect evening.

Johnny got off at 72nd Street. He was still a good forty minutes early. Gingerly, he strolled up Madison Avenue, passing the boutique where he had purchased Megan's birthday gift a couple of months before. Around the corner, he almost headed straight inside Megan's building, just as he had done so many times before. Instead, he crossed over to the park side of Fifth Avenue. A green wooden bench directly across from the tall brownstone sat empty – one on which he and Megan often snuggled, watching the snow fall on winter days. Johnny set down his schoolbag and the bouquet that he'd been clutching all the way from Brooklyn.

He looked up at tall buildings on Fifth Avenue that comprise some of New York's most exclusive real estate. These high-rise mansions were the home to many of Manhattan's social elite, providing spectacular, unspoiled views of the Central Park greenery directly across the way.

Expensive cars and city buses paraded past his vantage point with head-lights aglow. Darkness had fallen on the Upper East Side. Johnny stared up at the third floor of Megan's building. There was a light on in the living room. He wondered briefly if Zach, or Katherine might be inside.

Johnny occasionally glanced at his watch. The minutes ticked by in slow motion. At 8:37 a motorbike roared by. At 8:44, a pizza delivery boy entered the lobby. By 8:50 he was on his way out, counting his cash. At 8:51, Johnny was startled by the sudden presence of a bearded homeless man in a shabby coat on his side of the street. Instinctively, he reached inside his pocket, and pulled a dollar from his wallet, holding it out for the taking.

"May all your dreams come true," the scruffy stranger chuckled in appreciation. "Just be careful what you dream of, ya hear?"

"Loud and clear," Johnny answered, though the man was already off and running.

Before long, nine o'clock had come and gone. Johnny could only wonder if the momentary distraction had caused him to miss Megan's arrival. Following a rare blink of his eyes, Johnny spied two taxis pull up at the curb across the street. An older couple exited from the first car. They disappeared slowly beneath the large red canopy. Only one passenger emerged from the second cab: a heavyset man in a trench coat carrying a brief case.

A third yellow cab pulled up right behind. Johnny peered down at his watch once again. It was 9:17. He rose to his feet as two figures stepped out from the backseat. The first appeared to be his beloved Megan. The second silhouette was harder to make out.

Once the taxi pulled away, Johnny got a clear view of the landscape. In the light beneath the canopy, he distinguished familiar strawberry-blonde hair hanging over the back of a dark overcoat. It was her. And although he did not recognize her formally dressed companion, Johnny noticed that he had taken her hand as they strolled inside the lobby.

It was then that all rational thought emptied from his consciousness. Curiosity was replaced with a burning jealous rage. An urgent inner voice implored him to flee this scene of perceived betrayal. Concurrently, a prevailing tone of vengeance shouted for confrontation. Fueled by a blast of adrenaline, Johnny grabbed his bag in one hand; the flowers in the other. His eyes locked in on the couple just inside the second set of doors. He ran ahead with reckless abandon.

Not watching peripherally, as was ingrained in him since childhood, he did not see the blue four-door Lincoln Continental speeding to beat the red light in the far left lane. He didn't even hear the screech of tires as the driver slammed on the breaks and attempted to swerve right.

Johnny did not know what hit him. He was separated from his senses, lying facedown on the asphalt. The smell of scorched rubber assaulted his sinuses. His schoolbag lay just inches from the curb. Never had his heart pounded harder. Johnny pushed himself up, first to his knees, then to a standing position. He dusted off his jacket and staggered to retrieve the bag, barely noticing the shooting pain down his left leg where the car had delivered a glancing blow.

"You all right?" a burly voice shouted at him. Johnny turned back to the center lane. Still confused, he simply nodded.

"What the hell were ya doin, crossing against the light, jackass?" Johnny did not answer. Instead, he watched the driver inspect the left front corner of his vehicle. There was no discernable damage. The man hopped back behind the wheel and continued down the avenue.

The entire incident had taken all of ninety seconds from the moment of impact until the driver sped away. It took another half-minute for Johnny to locate the floral arrangement, which had blown onto the sidewalk ahead of him. He hurried to the building entrance, grabbing the colorful bouquet on his way inside.

He was in shock, unconvinced as to whether any of this had actually just taken place.

Johnny sprinted through two sets of glass doors, straight toward the elevator. The inner gate had just been shut manually. The outer door began sliding closed. Megan's profile through the metal grating was unmistakable. Now he was certain as to what he'd witnessed.

The digital console on the wall lit up floor number two, then three. Johnny hit the call button repeatedly, causing it to ring intermittently but little else. As he stood there dejected, breathing hard, a familiar voice called to him.

"Sir, all visitors must be announced. May I please have your name and the apartment number you're going to?"

"Walter," Johnny cried out. "I'm Megan Price's boyfriend."

The doorman reached for the house phone on the wall. "Hi, I've got a gentleman here for Ms. Price." He took a half-minute to listen to the voice on the other end. Then calmly, he turned to Johnny. "Your name sir?"

Two unbearable minutes ticked by. The uniformed man finally hung up the receiver. An obvious stall tactic. "Sir, I think Ms. Price is readying for your visit. Please wait here a moment."

Johnny paced the lobby frantically. He sensed the need to harness control of his emotions. He could surely march in screaming, make a scene and depart. But what good would this accomplish? Alternatively, he could confront Megan in front of her date, creating an eyeful of negativity. *That'd make him think twice about her!*

Yet a third prospect would be to turn his anger on the person he believed to be the primary source of his bitterness. If Katherine were home, perhaps he'd get to finally unleash all his bottled-up fury on her. Johnny's normal mild-mannered demeanor was fast becoming a raging inferno. Not even he knew what he was capable of now.

Yet despite everything he believed he'd observed, he was not prepared to let go. Not yet. Breaking glass and erupting in a verbal rampage would irrevocably damage whatever was left of their relationship. *Perhaps there's some logical explanation*, he rationalized. *Maybe the guy is a relative, or an old family friend.* But then mentally replaying how the fancy gentleman had gripped her hand as they walked in-step... *wishful thinking.*

Answers were needed. He was determined to get Megan alone.

The elevator arrived up at the third floor. Johnny underwent a radical, stone-faced transformation. He dabbed at his sweaty face with the sleeve of his jacket, switched on a calm disposition and stepped off the rickety car, pretending he'd only just arrived. Awaiting him in the doorway stood a bizarrely pleasant Katherine Price.

"Johnny, what a nice surprise! You're looking rather debonair tonight." With a saccharine smile and a wave of her hand she motioned for him to follow. "Megan's just getting ready. Come join me in the living room."

Through the foyer, Johnny peered in all directions. He could detect no sign of Megan or her companion. Then came the astonishing tug on his wrist. Katherine was firmly escorting him through the elegant dining room, in the direction of the living room sofa. She pulled him down to sit beside her. "So Johnny, it's been a while. Nice haircut. How've you been?"

Johnny swallowed hard to stifle an ironic laugh. In nearly three years, Katherine had never been more demonstrative than offering a polite peck on the cheek for a hello or goodbye. She rarely shared more than basic talk about the weather. He couldn't even recall the last time she sought his opinion on a movie he and Megan were returning from. Suddenly, here she was, tossing compliments as if they were a salad in one of her precious Waterford bowls. Her exaggerated affability was rather disquieting.

In the background, Megan's voice could be faintly heard coming from down the hall, along with that of an unfamiliar male, who surely must have been her date. Within seconds, Johnny's suspicions were confirmed. An unmistakable booming sound echoed throughout the third floor apartment. It was the slamming of the kitchen door leading to the back stairway. *She must've snuck him out the service entrance. They probably don't realize that I know.*

Getting no response to her initial question, Katherine repeated it. She was sounding a lot less friendly.

"Sorry, Mrs. Price. It's just: how 'bout I go put these flowers in a vase?"

Katherine stared at the battered bouquet. "Oh, it's okay, honey. That's really sweet of you. I'll stick them in water once Megan's ready. Is there any special occasion?"

Johnny wondered if Katherine had forgotten her daughter's birthday. He answered delicately. "Well, I figured there weren't any flowers delivered while you guys were away. Also, with it being Megan's birthday and all..." His voice trailed off.

"You shouldn't have," she smiled, accepting the arrangement. "So tell me, what have you been up to at school?"

"School's been goin' great again this year. Just aced my midterms. And I've nearly finished all my core requirements. Next semester should be a breeze."

Another door slammed somewhere in the apartment. Again distracted, Johnny began peeking around a Tiffany lamp to see if Megan was on her way. Detecting nothing further, he shifted the small talk into something more purposeful. "So how're things down at the agency? Your partner, Sheila tells me it's quite busy."

"Work is quite absorbing, as I'm sure you can imagine." She ignored the latter half of his comment. "New accounts come in all the time. And of course the mayor keeps me busy as ever."

All throughout this conversation, Katherine appeared to be making steady, appraising eye contact with Johnny, scanning for any display of anger or jealously.

For Johnny, it took every ounce of strength in his facial muscles to maintain his neutral exterior. He was likely to break if this kept up much longer. Staring back at Katherine, he noticed a hint of sweat forming above her eyebrows. Given the comfortable indoor climate, he took minor satisfaction in her nervousness.

After another blink, Katherine's steely brown eyes pulled away from his and made contact with someone else entering the room. She didn't say anything, just shook her head as though indicating that she was unsure of what Johnny knew.

"Hey, John!" Megan called out before she even reached him. "Thanks for being so patient. Just got home from my appointment."

Johnny turned to face her. Standing up, he moved in her direction and planted a polite kiss on her cheek. "Happy birthday, Meg. Looking great, after what must've been a long day."

The reassurance on Megan's face spoke volumes. Johnny had passed the preliminary audition.

Katherine rose from the sofa. She displayed the flower bouquet. "I'll go put these in water. And Johnny, it was lovely to see you. Thanks for always being so thoughtful."

The clatter of high-heeled shoes on the parquet floor seemed to end abruptly. Johnny guessed that Katherine had not gone all the way to the kitchen as advertised. She'd almost certainly be eavesdropping from the hallway. He continued his award-worthy performance. "So how'd things go with the doctor?" Seeing Megan shiver as if she had gotten the chills, he refined, "You know, the after-school appointment. Was it routine, or is something bothering you?"

"Oh, everything's fine, really," Megan quivered. "I scheduled my allergy check-up long before Paris. Guess I could've changed it, but I wanted it out of the way."

"Too bad it had to be on your birthday," Johnny stepped toward her and corralled her hands in his. She was wearing a faint citrus perfume. "I was hoping to take you someplace nice. Now with the late hour and all, we'll just have to settle for dessert."

"Actually, I'd rather we did it another night," Megan pulled away. "Even birthday cake sticks to your frame when eaten just before bedtime!"

"Oh, I wasn't being literal," Johnny clarified. "Just wanted to put the icing on your big day. Since you're dressed, we could head down Fifth. Like we always do. It's not pollen season."

Megan again felt ice slithering through her nervous system. Not that Johnny gave her reason to be fearful, but if somehow he knew about her earlier activities... "Hold that thought." She walked toward the kitchen. "Just need to check on something."

Johnny listened in carefully. From down the hall, he heard Megan consult Katherine if she thought he was on to anything.

"I doubt it," Katherine murmured. "He never left my sight. I don't think he has a clue."

Megan let out a sigh of relief. "Thanks, Mom. This could've been a total disaster."

Johnny's resolve grew even stronger. He tiptoed over to the living room piano and began playing a slow, unfamiliar refrain. That's where Megan found him when she returned.

"So, you wanna head out, or what?" she asked, a key chain dangling from her hands.

Johnny got to his feet and limped toward her. A spasm shot up his left thigh from just above the knee where the car's bumper had grazed him - his first reminder that the near-collision outside had actually occurred. He grabbed his schoolbag, trying to block out both physical and emotional trauma. "I'm right with you, Meg."

Downstairs in the lobby, Johnny made a point of taking Megan's sweaty hand as they walked past the doorman. "Be back shortly, Walter," Megan said. Johnny just glared at him.

They walked briskly down the residential side of Fifth Avenue. Johnny was eager to get her as far from the Price's building as possible. Katherine would surely be watching them from the living room window. He continued to clutch Megan's jittery hand until they reached 65th Street.

"So, where're we going?" Megan asked with a mixture of concern and curiosity.

"Honestly, I just figured we'd keep walking a bit; maybe even cut across into the park… if it's okay with you."

"The park, at night?" she said, trepidation in her voice. "I don't know, John. Don't love being out there all alone after ten."

"But, Megan, you're here with me!" They hit the corner of 64th Street. A nostalgic thought crept in amid the sorrow. "Actually, I'd love to take a walk down memory lane. Let's see how well you remember our past."

Megan nodded reluctantly. "Um, okay, I suppose. But remember, I'm still on Paris time. It's practically tomorrow morning for me."

Johnny gripped her hand tighter and began crossing Fifth Avenue. His tone grew ambiguous. "You trust me, Meg?" Seeing her nod, he pressed on. "Have I ever given you reason to doubt me?"

Megan stared uneasily, her heart rate accelerating. "What do ya mean? I trust you more than anyone. You know that. Why'd you ask?"

"No reason." He pulled her gently inside the park entrance. "I'm just surprised you didn't mention your doctor's appointment till now. I got worried."

"Oh, it was nothing. Just getting an obligation off my calendar."

Johnny's eyes narrowed. "So tell me about Paris; about the big break-through with your mother? Amazing how hospitable she was tonight."

"Please, Johnny, tell me what's on your mind?" she replied anxiously. "And where're we headed?" The question was a clear *double entendre*.

"You must remember the day we met?" he asked.

"Of course," she exhaled a long breath with the words. "Never forget it all my life. Wollman Rink; that frozen afternoon. I couldn't keep warm for the life of me. And I couldn't keep my hands off you. Still can't." Megan's glassy eyes shined back at Johnny.

"Care to relive the moment? We are just blocks from there."

"Really? Can we?" She brightened at the words. Megan recaptured Johnny's hand. With an extra skip in her step, she led him past the locked gates of the children's zoo. Memories of their first encounter flashed through her thoughts. Johnny's tattered black overcoat. His lopsided smile. His long flow-ing hair being blown by the wind. But approaching the darkened, deserted oval, her delight faded to disappointment. "Oh, damn! What's today, the 4th? Sign says it opens November 12th. Maybe we should just turn back."

"Why?" he shrugged. "Where's your imagination? Can't you picture how happy we were, stumbling around the rink in such wicked weather? The way we held on so close that first time."

On a hill overlooking Wollman Rink, Megan dropped to the leaf-cov-ered grass. She pulled a slightly hobbled Johnny down to sit beside her. The autumn air was turning cooler. "You're so right, you know. Right about everything. That day was the turning point for me. And I've never once gone to bed unhappy since… no thanks to you of course." She patted his knee.

"So tell me again about Paris." Johnny's gaze was intense. "How'd you manage to sort everything out with your mother?"

Megan looked up at the pale moon through the thinning trees and inhaled deeply. "I think in time we're going to make it. Trust me, Johnny, I really do. Oh, and Mom doesn't have it in for you like I thought. Ultimately, she wants me to be happy."

"So no more of those surprise dates like that theater guy? And I can again call freely; drop by the apartment like old times?"

"Sooner than you think. I made it clear: No more meeting new guys. I really stood up to her this time; told her I only wanna be with you."

Megan's mind raced with guilty thoughts of the dates she had accepted over the past several weeks: The night at the opera with the diplomat's son. The picnic in the park with Gerry. Their dinner at the Plaza just hours ago. *Well, it's not like I wanted to go on any of 'em,* she reminded herself. *I only did it to win our eventual freedom.* "You do believe me, Johnny?" she asked him, her eyes widening.

Ignoring her question, Johnny countered with one of his own. "Lemme ask you something. Answer me honestly. Aside from that lame-ass off-Broadway premiere last month, have you been out with anyone else?"

"Johnny," she cried out, squeezing his right hand. "You know I tell you *everything.*" She studied his saddened green eyes. "Well, I told you about that loser resort owner in San Juan. But he was never a consideration. No one else is." She was biting her lip, looking anxiously at him. "I love you, Johnny. I'd never do anything to hurt you. You've got to tell me you believe me."

Johnny freed his arm and placed it around her shoulder in consolation. "I want to, Meg. I've wanted to believe in you till the day I die. Guess I just needed some honest reassurance." He staggered to an upright position, and again reached for her hand, pulling her up to her feet. "Looks like we've both had our share of excitement tonight. I should probably get you home."

It was just over a mile back to the apartment. Johnny hoped the distance would provide one last opportunity for redemption. However, sensing Megan's anxiety with her every gesture, he instead made halfhearted chitchat about the food in Paris and the changing weather.

Megan appeared visibly exhausted as they approached the building. She couldn't wait to get upstairs, undressed and under the covers. Yet more than anything, she needed some affection from Johnny to hang on to. "Wanna come up for a while?" she asked, suppressing a yawn.

"It's a bit late for me, too," he responded lethargically. "I should really be going."

"Sure you don't wanna come in for a proper farewell? Just for a minute?"

Johnny retreated a step. "You know how much I hate saying goodbye. Plus, I already feel guilty about keeping you out so late as is."

"But you have nothing to feel guilty about," she replied quickly.

You certainly do, Johnny thought, glaring back at her, hoping desperately she would come clean. He bit down on his tongue and nodded in her direction with a feeble smile.

Megan placed her hands beneath his jacket. Trembling, she leaned her head against his chest, hoping to feel a stroke of her hair, or his firm, familiar embrace. It never came; just a gentle pat on the shoulder. She pulled back to get one last glance of Johnny's face. It was virtually expressionless, save for the formation of an innocent tear in the corner of his left eye. "Call you later," she muttered, now stepping away toward the entrance.

No you won't, he thought bitterly, knowing her exhaustion and dishonesty would again betray her, as it had all evening.

Megan turned to open the heavy outer door to the building. In the glass reflection, she looked back to locate Johnny, recalling how he always watched her depart until she was out of view. Only this time he did not linger: Johnny Elias was gone.

It wasn't until Johnny limped up the subway staircase that he remembered the wrapped gift still in his school bag. It didn't even occur to him that he left without reiterating birthday wishes. The only thought weighing on his mind was the sharp devastation of heartbreak confirmed. It was as though someone had taken a razor and left a gaping hole in his chest where his heart used to be.

All he wanted to do was break down and sob, yet something intangible was holding him back. Once inside his apartment, he flung his jacket across the room. He pulled out the gift-wrapped box from his schoolbag and tore off the paper in disgust. The delicate lid was the first casualty. He reached for the tri-colored necklace and stared at it with regret. "Happy birthday, Megan," he said, his voice breaking on the words.

He tugged mightily on both ends of the circular strand. The cord tore at the center. A hundred multi-colored beads hit the hardwood floor, scattering in every direction. Johnny tried to let out an expressive scream. But the conflict of agony and anger rendered him incapable.

He couldn't stop replaying the evening in his mind, touching the raw pain again and again. All of Megan's crying pledges of allegiance had now proven appallingly insincere. *Absolutely worthless*, he thought repeatedly. Had the entire three-years together been filled with the same deceit?

Again he tried to let the tears flow, and still he couldn't. Some invisible dam was holding him back. Instead, another deep emotion came flowing from Johnny's throbbing heart. He reached for the closest spiral notebook, lifted the cap off a black felt-tip pen, and the words virtually wrote themselves. A sad, dirge-like melody evolved with each verse. One that he would never be able to forget.

I think the time has come for me to tell you what's been on my mind
I've been avoiding it but no longer can I keep it inside
I saw you out tonight with another man in my place
The end was in my sight but the truth is what I couldn't face

I gave you every chance to confess to me the things you'd done
But you still played the game telling me I'm still the only one
You said you loved me while you looked me straight in the eye
You tried to hide the truth. I'll never understand the reason why

(Chorus)
It's not that I don't love you
and my tears are yet to dry

But you can't go back and forth forever
and we've already said goodbye

I thought that life was all about searching for that perfect mate
Through all the storms we weathered I was hoping for a better fate
I never answered no. Always running to be by your side
I could have turned away but I hung with you every time you cried

I never will forget you
For the first love never dies
But you can't go back and forth forever
and we've already said goodbye

The tides have turned – The winds have changed
Feelings have been rearranged
We shared our hopes – We built our dreams
I guess life's never what it seems

And now the hour has come for me to tell you what's been on my mind
I've been lamenting it, but no longer can I keep it inside
You broke my heart tonight with another man in my place
It's no use holding back. Now it's something that we both must face

It's not that I don't love you
and my tears are yet to dry
But you can't go back and forth forever
and we've already said goodbye
I never will forget you
For the first love never dies
But you can't go back and forth forever
and we've already said... goodbye

Johnny's first true masterpiece had emerged from the depths of his pain. The complete heart-wrenching experience was cathartic, but entirely draining, leaving him exhausted beyond words. Within minutes of constructing the final verse, he was sound asleep; his weary head slumped over a notebook at the kitchen table.

7

FROZEN MOMENTS

Johnny felt surprisingly numb when he awoke the next morning. Hardly refreshed from only a few hours' sleep, he was astonished to detect in himself a measure of relief instead of full-tilt pain.

Rising to change his clothes, Johnny suffered his first uncomfortable reminder from the night before. His left thigh, which had been grazed by the bumper of a speeding car, was now acutely stiff and discolored. Just to change out his pants was a major struggle. *My black and blue badge of courage,* he thought, wincing.

Johnny threw on a fresh shirt. He could still hear in his inner ear the sad, expressive tune he'd composed in the waning hours of the night. Over and again he mouthed the words, thinking of the fastest, most effective way to share them with Megan. A pile of loose papers sat chaotically atop his makeshift desk. He located a page with the home number for Howard Greffen and dialed.

"Thanks for meeting me on such short notice." Johnny greeted Howard in the lobby of Brooklyn Post's music department. "This couldn't wait till next Monday."

Howard came dressed in mismatched sweatpants and a ratty sweatshirt that he'd probably worn to bed the night before. "You know I dig working with you. But waking me up early on my off day… this better be good."

With a cup of coffee in one hand and the borrowed key in the other, Howard headed to the piano room appearing half-awake. Johnny on the other hand – while limping heavily – felt surprisingly energized. In one hand he carried a portable tape recorder, and in the other, one of his trademark spiral bound notebooks.

"Hey, you okay, kid?" Howard asked, his eyes on Johnny's legs. "Thought you said something about breaking up with that girl, not breaking a leg!" He chuckled.

Johnny frowned, not amused. "Don't even ask. I think the song'll tell you everything. Well, except for the part about getting hit by a car. I made a creative decision not to include my idiocy."

Howard got comfortable on the piano stool. Johnny shut the door to the soundproofed room. Without further delay, he sang the lyrics a cappella in a melodious run-through. Howard sat stunned and amazed. "That almost justifies your early wake-up call. So I assume you're planning to send her a recording to break the news?"

"Howard, you know all those sad songs that ooze desperation? This one, it doesn't ask for anything. It's just the best way… maybe the only way I can tell her the game is over. I still love her, ya know. Always will. But like the song says: can't let this go on forever."

Howard had stood in those same painful shoes a myriad of times. He wanted to extend a hand of consolation. But all-at-once he was authentically impressed with the raw, poignant music he'd just heard. The song was touching, honest – even heartbreaking. It was everything a grand ballad should be. Yet the heaviness struck a vulnerable chord in him. Rather than

dredge up the sad memories it evoked, he tugged at his goatee and pecu-
liarly changed the subject.

"Have I ever told you my philosophy on great music?"

"No," Johnny said staring back in bewilderment. "I'm sure I'd remember
if you had."

"Yeah, when I was maybe a couple years younger than you are now,
someone told me that melody is the language of the soul. Didn't make much
sense at the time. But gradually I got fluent."

Johnny looked perplexed.

Howard pulled his stool closer. "No really, listen. While our bodies
communicate verbally and with physical expression, the spiritual side of
us uses melody to converse. Problem is, in this physical world, there aren't
too many blessed with the ability to get in touch with their soul. Sure, lots
of folks appreciate great music. But what you just did – reaching inside and
funneling out a melody – well that's rare, man. Like one in half a million,
maybe more."

Johnny stared at him in obvious awe. "You serious? So once you find a
way in, does it get easier going back there again? Like tapping a well; letting
the music flow?"

Howard patted Johnny on the back. "True inspiration, whether it's joy,
or pain, that's the key to unlocking the door between your mind and your
soul. When you're deeply inspired, the words and melody spurt out like a
volcanic eruption. Problem is, our lives are so damned complicated, and
inspiration's a fragile instrument. When it's gone, good luck ever getting
back in there again."

"But inspiration, you can find it in anything if you really concentrate,
right?" Johnny stepped forward. "I mean, you were prolific. Just 'coz you got
blindsided, that's not to say you can never go back; find your musical soul."

Howard turned away evasively. He appeared to shiver for a moment.
"Naw, never mind. We've been through that already. Too many sad memories. You oughta save your voice for the definitive take. Don't waste your

energy philosophizing with me. Now let's get your slice of spiritual magic on tape, shall we?"

Johnny felt conflicted: he wanted to continue the conversation and was equally eager to record his purposeful ballad. Certainly, Howard's decades of anguish wouldn't be undone with one discussion. This much he understood. Instead, Johnny swallowed hard and refocused. "Yeah, let's do it. But you and I, we'll pick this up another time." He handed Howard the portable cassette recorder. "Ready when you are."

"Not so fast, kid. First let's get the arrangement right. Then I've got something much better than this amateur equipment."

On the heels of three rehearsal takes, Howard stood from his piano bench and gestured for Johnny to follow him. "Oh, good, they haven't locked it." He grinned and opened the door to a small rectangular booth in the corner of the room. An overhead bulb revealed the out-of-date, but still-functional recording board. "I hear this baby's from '67. But I've seen it used before, so I know it works."

Howard detected a gleam in Johnny's eyes. He hit the power button and simultaneously adjusted input levels. "I wouldn't exactly call this a proper recording booth, but it beats the hell out of your device. You know, if you had a few bucks, there are real studios nearby where you can cut a proper demo. But for your purposes, I suppose this'll do."

A red light came on over the booth. Howard rushed back to the piano with Johnny close behind. "This room has great acoustics, so you'll get a true sound during playback." Then, announcing, "Take one," he swept his hands across the keys before playing an improvised intro.

Back at the console after two gut-wrenching attempts, Howard rewound the master tape. "Johnny, I think you nailed it on the first go-round. That's your keeper. I could really feel your pain. And wow, that song... made me all misty-eyed, and I don't even *know* this woman!"

"Thanks, man! Means a lot coming from you. And your arrangement is perfect." Johnny patted Howard on the back. "So, can I get a copy now?" he then asked, his adrenaline still running from the intensity of his singing. "I was hoping to take home a tape."

"Hell, yeah." Howard fidgeted with a few knobs on the control board. "If you have two blanks, I'll make a couple of copies."

"Actually, I bought three," he responded, rummaging through his jacket pocket. "Let's make one extra and then I'll be on my way."

Howard took all three. He transferred the original recording from the large magnetic master reel, then handed over the two requested copies. "Here's hoping this gets you what you want from it. I feel... privileged, I guess, being the first to hear it."

"Thanks," Johnny said hesitantly. "It means the world that you came running out this morning. You're the best."

Johnny tucked two cassettes into their plastic cases, then stuffed them inside the breast pocket of his shirt. He raised a hand and hobbled off in a hurry.

As Howard readied to leave the booth, he wiped the master tape clean, then ejected the third cassette from the machine, labeled it, and placed it inside his weathered school bag. He too was quite pleased to own a copy of this stunning new song.

Andy returned to his dormitory in the late afternoon. He checked his answering machine and found two urgent messages.

The first, from Jacqui, was concise, yet concerning.

"Andy, please phone me straight away. I'm at the flat and really must hear from you."

Knowing Jacqui wasn't usually one to be needy, Andy immediately sensed trouble and dialed her number. While the phone rang repeatedly on the other end, a second message continued to play through his answering machine speaker.

"Andy, it's Johnny. I'd rather tell you this in person, but anyway... things are completely over between Megan and me. Fill you in later, I guess."

The line at Jacqui's end continued to ring. Andy felt a sense of loss over Johnny's bad news. *Maybe sometimes these things unravel, then reemerge stronger*, he thought optimistically. *I'll have to call later, play cheerleader.*

After what seemed like an eternity, Jacqui answered her phone. Her voice sounded startled.

"Hello?"

"Jacqui, it's me. Everything okay? Your line just rang forever."

"Andy, I was on long distance with my mum; couldn't take the call waiting."

"Oh, sorry. It's just: you sounded totally bummed on your message."

There was a slight pause, during which he thought he could hear her moistening her lips, and then Jacqui began sobbing, her words coming through her tears like hiccups. "It's my dad, Andy. He's horribly ill. Gotta get home to see him."

Andy sighed. "I'm so sorry. How serious is it?"

"Mum says he's had a heart attack; needs a transplant. The thing is, he's sixty-one and at the back end of the donor list. Who knows if he'll live long enough to get one?"

Andy twisted the phone cord in his hand. "Want me to run over to your place? I'll do whatever I can. Just say the word."

"Sorry, Andy, but no. You really can't right now. I have to get myself on a flight tonight. I've already called the airlines; packed my cases."

Andy felt helpless. He took down Jacqui's contact information in England and offered his prayers for a positive resolution. "So, how long do you think you'll be gone?" His hand tightened around the receiver. "You suppose it'll be weeks? And what about FIT? You're in mid-semester."

"Don't you understand? I haven't got any idea about time, or school – or the rest of my life. I just need to see my dad." He could hear her take a deep, shuddering breath. "I know what I've told you about not being close with my parents, but they're the only ones I've got."

He listened to the empty line buzzing for a long time after she hung up the phone.

Within two hours, Jacqui Spencer had cleared out her belongings in three suitcases and was flying back home to England on a lonely one-way ticket.

Not even a good night's sleep in her own bed could cure Megan's residual confusion. She was still feeling uneasy over the events of the night before.

Her date with Gerald Ridgewell had gone about as well as anyone could wish for... unless of course one wasn't interested in dating him. They had gone out for a light supper at the Plaza Hotel. Once again, conversation was pleasant, although for the first time it became clear that Gerry was interested in sharing more than just entertaining dialogue.

After paying the bill, Gerry helped her on with her coat, hardly brushing her at all with his hands. Soon he was walking in step with her, sliding his arm across her back and resting it around her shoulders. As they approached the revolving doors he started talking about the extravagant suites upstairs. Megan was amused until Gerry half-heartedly asked if she was interested in seeing what one looked like. It was a remark that could very well have been innocuous... but she had the feeling that if she'd expressed even the slightest curiosity, he'd have been on his way to the check-in desk in an eye-blink.

Had she considered herself to be single, Megan might have allowed Gerry to charm her; but she had known, going in, that her heart remained elsewhere.

Soon they arrived at her building by taxi. Megan protested that she needed to rest after her flight and six-hour change in time zone, but Gerry wasn't taking no for an answer. "Okay, one cup of coffee," she agreed listlessly, and Gerry paid the driver.

They had only just sat down when the house-phone rang. It was Johnny, right on-time as always. Katherine couldn't allow Gerry to be exposed to any kind of confrontation – which she feared would certainly happen if he ran into Johnny. Instead, she stalled Johnny, then distracted him so that Gerry could be discreetly removed.

Megan hurried Gerry through his French roast and out the back door. She felt almost sorry for him, even if his insinuations at the hotel had been out of the question. She still didn't want to hurt his feelings. A woman's eternal quandary. "My mom has two high ranking officials coming up," she improvised. "It's unexpected; an emergency." Megan stumbled a bit over the words. "Sorry about this. They need complete privacy."

"Sounds awfully important." He snickered, rubbing his goatee. "No one's ever come up with such a creative excuse to get rid of me."

Megan engaged Gerry in small talk on the way down to the lobby. "I'll call you soon," she promised, not knowing whether or not she was telling the truth.

"Great," Gerry said, smiling. "Looking forward to it. Well, except for the abrupt ending." He placed his hands on her shoulders and pulled her close.

Megan resisted at first, but quickly realized that a polite kiss was the best way to get rid of him. Relieved, she watched him depart, raising his hand to hail a cab.

Back upstairs, she inadvertently allowed the back door to slam again. She hurriedly changed into clothes more appropriate for a doctor's appointment and slipped into the living-room.

All night, she worried that Johnny knew about her earlier date. His usually expressive face gave nothing away. Still, there were stages in their conversation when she wondered if he was going to call her bluff. At times he came dangerously close, though he never actually said the words.

Between fear of losing him and her physical exhaustion, Megan's memory of the previous night remained hazy. She recalled the way Johnny gripped her hand as they walked down Fifth Avenue. The choice to visit Wollman Rink convinced her further that he was every bit smitten with her as he'd ever been. Yet his abrupt departure left her feeling hollow.

Now, Megan found a stack of mail sitting just below the slot in the service door. She picked it up to casually sort through it. On top of the pile was a thick parcel addressed to her. Megan opened it eagerly. The initial packet contained an assortment of photos of her school friends, interspersed with images of unfamiliar teenage boys. Megan found herself smiling. The unidentified bare behinds mooning from car windows were probably captured by her brother during the weekend he borrowed her camera for a rebellious road trip.

The second role was far more satisfying. Central Park. A sweltering August afternoon. Miles of happy faces, and – of course – Johnny Elias. Tanned, relaxed and carefree, he appeared so much happier than she could recall seeing him look in recent weeks. And yet it seemed only minutes ago that he had been hoisting her up on his broad shoulders, feeling the music together.

Megan's smile widened when she got to the end of the pile. It was the picture of the four of them huddled together, grinning, anticipating, happy. Her eyes were drawn to Johnny, second from the left, smiling broadly as he pulled her against his side. To his right was Andy, sitting with one arm around Johnny's shoulder and a joyous, wide-eyed expression. And then came Jacqui, looking entirely as though she belonged, even though she had only just met them.

Megan felt the picture tugging at her heart. She and Johnny looked so idyllic together! If only she could step back into that magical day!

Instinctively, she reached for the phone. Four rings were followed by the sound of his prerecorded voice. She left a message. "Hey John, it's Meg. I'm home alone tonight, so please call me when you get in. And thanks for stopping by on my birthday last night. It meant the world to me. Talk to you later."

On the other side of the city, Johnny waited for Megan's voice to stop. He had no intention of picking up the phone. He'd said everything that there was to say in his song. It would only be a matter of time before she'd get his message.

The balance of that week was pretty much a blur. Johnny only showed up for a handful of classes and his library shifts. Even at school, his mind was elsewhere. Activities such as eating, studying, even shaving went by the wayside. He remained alone in his misery, taking refuge in sad songs behind locked doors.

Megan's betrayal delivered a sobering reality. Up till now, she was the most permanent fixture in his life. The one shoulder he felt comfortable to cry on; to expose his vulnerability. Only now, turning to her was hardly an option. All of those nights when he and Megan lay in each other's arms, talking about stability, about the way things were going to be someday.… The fantasy of marrying the first girl he ever loved, and making it last was now, Johnny admitted to himself, just that: a fantasy.

Johnny had never before considered the kind of pain that could inspire such tender lyrics to the ballads in which he was now immersed. He just assumed that clever songwriters captured a fictional moment and put it to a tune. But now, listening to *Walk Away Renee*, or *Don't Let The Sun Catch You Crying*, it was almost as if they were custom made to fit his own dreary sentiment.

To make matters worse, news of the sudden passing of Jacqui's father in England only further enhanced his sorrow. Andy was equally glum; he could find no consolation in talking to his best friend.

Instead, Johnny turned to his only other outlet for expression. He sat in his room writing a flood of sad songs, most of which were as depressing as he felt. Too many anguished sessions went by. He sensed he'd dug himself into a creative rut, so he decided to stop writing.

He was just waiting for the next source of inspiration to come his way.

By Thursday, Megan was growing increasingly worried. It had been three days since she last saw Johnny, and two since leaving a message for him at home. Unable to reach him directly, she clung to the assumption that he was perhaps still avoiding her mother.

That evening, she found herself home alone again, save for Rosa, the housekeeper who barely spoke a word of English. Megan grabbed a pile of mail from inside the back door. She dumped it on the kitchen counter before heading to her room to change out of her work clothes.

Megan sifted through a pile of catalogs and junk mail. She set her mother's envelopes aside in a neat stack. Next, she came across a belated birthday card sent by her aunt Sylvia, and another unusual packet addressed to her. This one had no return address.

The sealed manila envelope opened easily enough. Inside was a cassette tape and a neatly folded piece of paper. She felt tears forming in her eyes, sliding down to her chin. It couldn't be… She reached back inside the package for something else. Nothing.

The lyric sheet fell to the floor. The tape was from Johnny. Had it really only been a few weeks since he had played his song for her? She grabbed both the sheet and the cassette. A pile of textbooks fell over as she cleared space in front of her bedroom stereo. She paused briefly before hitting play, her stomach clenching. When she thought she was prepared, she put her headphones on and started the tape. Johnny's voice immediately filled her ears, her head, her being… and confirmed her worst fears.

It's not that I don't love you, he sang to her. She knew that, knew too how painful it must have been for him to discover such an agonizing betrayal. Indeed, he gave her every chance to admit her deceitfulness as the lyrics suggested.

If somehow I could go back and change it all, she thought. Every suspicion Johnny would not, or could not, convey on the night of her birthday was now clearly and hauntingly revealed.

Surely, she had never wished to betray him, if for even a moment. While her decision to conceal details of recent dates had badly backfired, she had only good intentions – to spare him from further suffering. Only now did it occur that being truthful was probably the only way to deal with it.

Megan clung to one line: how "the first love never dies." Curled up, trembling, on her bedroom carpet, she wondered doubtfully if this provided the slightest glimmer of hope. But listening to his eloquent goodbye, Megan had a fatalistic sense that her first and only love had irrevocably departed. *And worst of all,* she thought, *I have only myself to blame.*

8

New Foundations

Howard Greffen arrived at Highpeak Records headquarters on Manhattan's West 57th Street. He noticed straight away how drastically the place had changed since his last visit. Only one of the artist nameplates on the framed gold records that hung on the surrounding walls appeared familiar. The Gibson Twins: a folk acoustic duo from 1985. *What a senseless tragedy those kids turned out to be!* Howard thought. *So young; a damn shame they did themselves in.*

Howard muttered his name to the receptionist. He was handed a visitors badge, then waited patiently in the marble waiting room, his hands folded and eyes wandering. It had been at least nine years, he figured, since he'd last been there. Oh, how he loathed the music business.

In days gone by, Howard periodically popped in to offer his latest material. This was following a successful string of songwriting credits for three of the label's better-known artists. At his creative pinnacle, he was cranking out close to twenty-five songs a month.

Howard knew the key to getting any song noticed was to cut a clean demo tape. From there he'd hand it over to the executives and let them sit back and imagine someone from their stable of artists singing it in his or her own unique style.

Of course, as far as music royalties were concerned, it was always most lucrative to be both performer and songwriter. The opportunity to collect double royalties on a successful pop song wouldn't necessarily set someone up for life, but a major chart hit surely could go a long way in that direction.

For a writer like Howard, who had never scored a hit single, getting a track selected for a successful album was artistically rewarding. Plus, the added bonus of having his name affiliated with a mainstream star offered instant credibility.

The reality was that it had seemed a lifetime since Howard's last decent composition. When the occasional fifty-nine-cent royalty check arrived in the mail, he tried convincing himself that he at least remained on the perimeter of the industry. But in the ever-changing landscape of the music trade, most of the executives he'd dealt with were long gone. Only Ron Neswick, the transplanted Englishman and longtime VP of Highpeak Records remained in place. *Ron Neswick: not the most trusted man in my Rolodex. But hopefully still approachable.*

Howard was kept waiting for about fifteen minutes before the receptionist called to him. "Mr. Greffen, Mr. Neswick will see you now."

Howard strode toward a set of double doors, feeling uncomfortable as he walked by. If only he'd been able to find something better to wear than this ill-fitting brown polyester suit and hideous yellow necktie! At the end of a long hallway lined with framed album covers, he was met by his only surviving acquaintance in the industry.

"How the hell are you, Howard my friend?" Ron patted him on the shoulders. "What's it been, like ten years?"

"You know how it is with us creative types," Howard answered, trying to sound more relaxed than he felt. "One day we're writing our magnum opus; the next we can't even string three notes together. Lately, though, I've been feeling pretty good."

Ron ushered Howard inside his posh office, which held the permanent aroma of burnt cigars. They caught up on the declining state of the music business. Then the executive got down to business. "So, Howard, aside from reminiscing, what brings you my way?"

Howard took a deep breath, his eyes on the recent issues of *Rolling Stone* cluttering Ron's marble desktop. "Listen, we've known each other a long time. And I know you trust my judgment when it comes to having an ear for great music."

"I'd say you speak the truth. But – it has to be said – that applies to, oh let's say, '74 through '83." Ron laughed. "And we've already put out a compilation of that period, I'm afraid. But, seriously, what're you insinuating?"

Howard nodded. "Just getting your attention," he said. "Listen, I've got something you have to hear for yourself. It's really something – rivals the best material I've ever brought in here, or anywhere else, for that matter."

"Ah, so you're writing again?" Ron sounded surprised. "What've you got going on?" He grinned. "New... ahem, inspiration in your life?"

"No, no. It's not that at all," Howard said, waving dismissively. "Let's not waste any more time talking. I just want to play you this one demo. Then I'll answer any questions you've got."

Ron glanced condescendingly at the handwritten label. "Howard, you really think we're back in the eighties or something? You honestly didn't expect me to play this now, did you?" He tossed the cassette back on the desk. "Today's demos are done digitally; on CDs. Professionally. I can't remember the last time I listened to anything on tape."

Howard leaned forward, tugging at his goatee. "I'm not asking for a handout," he said seriously. "So I don't have the flash suit, or a state-of-the-art recording studio. But I've got the goods, Ron. Listen to it. You owe me that much."

Ron stared at Howard, tapping a pencil on his desktop as he thought. He turned to his left and pressed a button on his telephone. "Fern? Can you bring a cassette player in here, please?"

"Right away," said the receptionist's disembodied voice. Neither man said anything. The receptionist came in, slightly winded, and placed a stereo boom box on the desk, plugging it in unobtrusively before leaving.

"All right," said Ron. "Let's hear what's worth digging out the antiques for." The executive inserted the tape into the cassette compartment and hit play. What he heard at first was Howard's voice shouting instructions, followed by a piano warm-up. "This is what you wanted me to hear?"

"Just give it a chance. It's coming," Howard said nervously, wondering if he should say more. But even as he did, the piano intro began, followed by Johnny Elias's singing.

"Not bad," Ron said, nodding, after the first verse and chorus. "You actually hired a singer to record your vocals this time. Don't remember you doing that in the old days."

"Shhhh." Howard put his finger to his lips. "Just hear it out, okay?"

They both stayed silent, listening, letting the music fill the room around them. It was even more powerful than it had been back at the school.

Ron was looking at the wall; Howard was looking at Ron, trying to read his face. He sensed the other man's interest but didn't let his own face betray his excitement. *Man, how could he not like this one?* Howard thought. *And how cool will it be to tell Johnny that I've landed him an audition? The kid'll probably wet his pants!*

"That's it?" Ron hit stop and ejected the tape, nodding slowly. "Yeah, this one could work. A little unpolished, but very lyrical. Nice melody. Kinda reminds me of a Neil Young ballad." He tapped his fingers on the tape, thinking. "Ian Hunter, maybe."

"So you like it, then?" Howard asked. He finally allowed himself a smile.

"Well, I usually need to hear a song a few times before passing judgment. But I gotta admit: this one's pretty arresting. You've obviously found your creative forces again, Howard."

"Uh, well, okay. That's me on piano. You picked up on that. But it isn't my song."

Ron narrowed his eyes. "It isn't?"

"Actually, it's a kid I've been hanging out with. He's the singer and the songwriter both."

Ron leaned back. His swivel chair creaked. "So," he gestured, "does this wunderkind sing like that all the time?" he leaned forward abruptly. "He got any other material? Anything I can listen to now? It's not like he'd be the first to ever write a halfway decent song and nothing more."

"He's the real deal," Howard assured him. "A bit green, but the kid can sing. And he's penned a handful of decent tunes already. Listen, I can probably get him to cut a few proper demos if you're really that impressed."

Ron tilted back again. "Ah, now I see where you're coming from. You're shopping his demo around; see who'll bite first. Where else have you been?"

"It's not like that," Howard protested. "Honestly, he doesn't even know I came here. But, listen – I've discovered a rising talent. All he needs is someone to give him a shot." He met Ron's gaze. "I haven't been anywhere else with the tape, man. You're the first I've played it for."

Ron ran a hand over his thinning hair. "You know the deal, Howard. If I tell you how many demos knocked me off my chair… Bottom line is: one nice song does not a career make. If the kid wants to sell it, sure, I'll consider making an offer. A few grand'll probably make his eyeballs pop. And who knows? If he's really this great raw talent, we'll audition him." He put his elbows on the desk and looked at Howard. "What? Only one song to his name, you expected more?"

Howard squirmed uncomfortably. *Maybe I jumped the gun*, he thought. The truth was that he only knew of one other song Johnny had written, and he was pretty sure the kid didn't even play an instrument. On the plus side, Johnny possessed a strong voice and had written something striking. Then again, he had never indicated any desire to become a recording artist. Still, Howard had a feeling about Johnny… He took a deep breath. "Tell you what, Ron. I'm gonna record a few more with him and bring 'em by. If you're as taken with that material as you are with his first track, well, go ahead: audition him. And if you don't care for his other stuff, talk to him about selling this one. But I've gotta tell you, he's really attached to his work."

"Fair enough," Ron agreed. "I'll look forward to hearing it. But next time, use a twenty-first century medium, like a CD, okay?" He stood to walk Howard out. "Not to rush you, but with the industry what it is, I can't recall the last authentic singer-songwriter we've signed. Today it's all rap, techno and grunge. Frankly, I'd love to hear more from… what'd you say his name is?"

"Johnny Elias," Howard said, his voice confident. "He's a student at Brooklyn Post; highly presentable."

"Sounds promising enough," Ron answered, taking a cigar from his pocket and examining the tip. "In fact, if you don't mind, I'll hang on to this demo until you deliver the next material."

"Can't do that." Howard reached out for the cassette. "I think its best I hold on to it."

If Ron was disappointed, he was too smooth to let it show. "Fine, have it your way." He leaned against the doorjamb, lighting the cigar. "Come to think of it, I'm not in a hurry. Are you? Come on back in, Howard. I'll have another listen before you go."

Andy Raymer sat on Johnny's busted mattress, studying the walls of his friend's tiny bedroom. The familiar faces of his musical heroes stared back at him. He had come seeking words of comfort. "So, what now? Do I quit, or what?"

"I'm not exactly thinking straight these days myself." Johnny raised his voice so Andy could hear him over Donovan singing *Turquoise*. "I think I'd have tried to get over there if I were you. Your folks, they would've covered the airfare if they understood."

Andy shook his head and reached to lower the stereo volume. "I wouldn't have gotten a penny if they knew I'd be skipping classes. A semester at NYU Business costs way more than a round-trip to England. Plus I had an economics paper due, and a business-law test prep. If she lived nearby, yeah, I could see it, but Sheffield and back, that's two days in travel alone."

"Aw, c'mon, Andy. If I knew it meant that much to you, I would've written your paper."

"Yeah right," Andy said, his voice mocking. "With your head the way it is nowadays, I'd probably get a rant on the economics of wealthy controlling mothers in Manhattan."

Johnny winced. "That's a low blow. I don't remember saying anything disparaging about your deal."

Andy made eye contact from across the room. "Didn't mean for it to come out that way. It's just… there's no way my folks were gonna allow me to screw up a semester by jetting off for the funeral of the dad of some girl they've only met once. And what the hell do you know about macroeconomics anyway?"

"Apology accepted," Johnny sighed. "But at least in your case, the girl didn't run off with some Armani-wearing jackass, then lie about it to your face while crying that she loved you. Jacqui probably misses you like mad."

"Yeah, but with her dad passing on so suddenly, she probably feels guilty for being away all that time. Now I think she's trying to make up for it." He let out a long breath. "My fear is that she'll start forgetting New York; never come back."

Johnny stood from his creaky desk chair, approached Andy and patted him on the back. "Hang in there, pal. I'll bet in no time she'll be back over here corrupting you. That night at the Back Fence, she kept telling me you're the best guy she's ever met."

Andy broke a smile. "Who the hell knows? Maybe you're right. It's not like other women are knocking down my door. And in the spirit of optimism, maybe you and Megan'll patch things up. Stranger things've happened."

"No chance of that." Johnny grimaced. "Let's not forget that I was cheated on. I trusted her with my life. Just kills me to think about it. You know, she had the nerve to leave, like, a dozen messages since getting the tape in the mail! But I just ignore 'em. Too painful!"

Andy looked at Johnny with arms folded, beginning to understand his friend's anger. Still, a few details confused him. "Can't say I disagree with your breaking away cleanly. But what's this about a tape? Pretty sure you haven't mentioned one till now."

Johnny did not answer. Instead, he switched his stereo to tape-mode, popped in a cassette and hit play. He watched as Andy sat silent, totally captivated.

When the music died away, Andy shook his head. "Must've something to do with my frame of mind these days, but your songs made me all teary-eyed. Did you really mail 'em to Megan? Must've blown her mind."

"I played her the first one right here in this room. She came to apologize about San Juan. I was gullible enough to believe her. I wrote the second one the night all hell broke loose. From the tone of her messages… well, I'm sure she gets it now."

Still choked up, Andy cleared his throat. "Johnny, lemme ask you something: Are those the only two you've written with a tune? I mean, they're *really* good."

Johnny laughed. "Thanks. Actually I've got about twenty so far. Maybe a handful are decent, but if you don't mind, I'll let you be the judge."

Over the next hour, Johnny brought the scrawlings from his notebook to life. Andy sat mesmerized, hanging on every melodic verse. "I'd say you've got at least eight from my count that really work. And I love how you rocked up the Crown Heights poem."

"Oh, you mean *Shadows Of The Same Color*."

"Yeah, that one's intense. And so is that tribute to the Challenger astronauts."

"*Vapor Trail of Tears*," Johnny said, smiling.

Andy nodded. "At least the music's a nice distraction. If I were you, I'd try to get someone to listen to it. And if you want, I'll get 'em copyrighted for you."

Johnny squinted at him, curious. "Copyrighted? Are we getting a little ahead of ourselves?"

"Hey, don't underestimate your work. Never can be too careful about protecting originality. But in the meantime, you should at least mail the lyrics to yourself as a poor man's copyright. Just don't open the envelopes once they're postmarked. You don't want anyone ripping off your stuff."

9

Alternate Philosophy

Gerald Ridgewell strolled past the doorman to the gated elevator. A bundle of flowers was in one hand, his Gucci attaché case in the other. He always kept a spare suit in the doctor's lounge, so he was at least prepared to change out of his scrubs when he received the unexpected phone call.

It wasn't so much the fact of another date with Megan that surprised him, but rather who it was that called to arrange it. After completing his daily rounds at Roosevelt Hospital, Gerry discovered a message to call Katherine Price at her office, ASAP. With no other plans that evening, he was perfectly content to resume where he and Megan had left off.

Gerry was greeted by Zach Price, who was heading out on a date of his own. "You here for my sister?" Zach guessed, opening the front door. "She's in her room studying. I'll check if she's ready."

Zach took a step toward Megan's room, but then had a change of heart. "Actually, I gotta split. Don't wanna keep the ladies waiting." He grinned sheepishly. "Um – before I go, could I borrow a few of those flowers in your bunch? I'm sure Megan doesn't need 'em all."

Gerry didn't respond to the joke, so Zach sobered up and led him across the parquet floor through the dining room, pointing to Megan's door.

"Good luck tonight," Gerry finally found he had something to say. "And if you screw up, remember to name your first-born after me."

"Sure. Whatever!" Zach retorted before heading off to the elevator. Gerry seemed to have his own sense of humor.

At the other end of the hallway, Gerry considered knocking. Once Zach shut the front door behind himself, however, he decided to enter unannounced.

Megan gave a low scream when her bedroom door opened. She hadn't been expecting anyone, and she leapt up, her heart pounding. When she saw Gerry, she reached automatically for a bulky gray sweatshirt, pulling it on over her tank top. "How'd you get in here? Shouldn't you have at least called?"

"I could ask you the same thing." Gerry let the door close behind him. "You promised to call me after last time. I was hoping you weren't being little Ms two-faced."

"Yeah, you and everyone else these days," she muttered under her breath. Megan was surprised by the unusual harshness of Gerry's tone. "But how'd you get up here?"

"I caught a cab from the hospital. Then I rode up in the elevator. Oh, and your brother let me in as he was leaving. He's pretty cool." Gerry stepped toward Megan. He handed her the bouquet. "What's the matter, you don't like surprises?"

"Thanks for these… I guess." The color slowly returned to Megan's face. "It's just… this isn't the best time for me right now."

Gerry laughed. "Remember, I'm only a few years older than you. I haven't forgotten what it's like to balance school with a part-time job."

Confused, and hardly prepared for a night out, Megan crept into the kitchen. She stood alone, leaning against the counter, thinking of the most polite way of asking him to leave.

For starters, Gerry had shown up unannounced at a time when she felt emotionally frayed. She was also immersed in an English Literature assignment due later in the week. But the reality was that Megan didn't dislike

Gerry – in fact, she had enjoyed his company in the past. And while discussing her despondency with him was surely out of the question, perhaps he could at least take her mind off it for the first time in days.

Before she had the opportunity to render a verdict, Gerry arrived in the kitchen and came up behind her. "Megan, you look hungry. C'mon: I made us reservations at the Four Seasons. Go get changed so we can get there on time." Then with a wink, he added, "Not that I mind you in a tank top and shorts."

Megan experienced her first partial grin in days. She headed back to her room. In her haste, she didn't bother to pull out a pair of fancy shoes, opting instead for black Keds that went reasonably well with the black skirt and blouse, tights, and tweed jacket. When she reemerged from the bedroom, she discovered Gerry hunched over in the kitchen, helping himself to the contents of the fridge.

"Ready when you are," she announced, expecting to startle him with her silent arrival. She received no reaction. "What time did you say the reservations were for?"

"Seven-thirty," Gerry mumbled, quickly chewing a mouthful of red grapes. He let the refrigerator door shut, spun around and eyed her head-to-toe. "Looking great! You changed much faster than I expected."

Johnny ran into Howard on his way to music history class the next day. Still looking the part of a jilted boyfriend, with a scruffy face and saddened eyes, he found his friend in high spirits.

"What's doin', kid? You still limping around? I hope your vocal chords aren't affected."

"The infirmary tells me it's bruised pretty bad, but not broken or anything." Johnny's voice was flat. "Anyway, I'm gettin' around just fine. Why'd you ask?"

"Whadaya say after class you and I head back to my place, work up some arrangements? I know I promised to do it last week, but tonight I'm free if you aren't too busy."

"Sounds good, I guess." Johnny shrugged. "I've got the lyrics in my notebook and the tunes in my head. If you've got the time, I suppose we could."

Later that afternoon, the pair climbed into Howard's beat-up Chevy, clearing away old newspapers, empty coffee cups and a CVS pharmacy bag off the passenger seat before heading over to Howard's place.

In the first hour, Johnny sang the lyrics to four new songs while Howard deciphered the melodies. Carefully, they refined the arrangements through multiple rehearsal takes, until at last they were both satisfied. While Howard took a break to open his mail and discreetly swallow some prescription pills, Johnny made himself comfortable at the piano stool.

A few minutes passed. Howard quietly re-entered the room. He watched Johnny picking out the melody to *Return To Me*, using just his index fingers. Once his pupil had the notes sequenced correctly, Howard applauded good-humoredly. "Funny, that's how I learned to play on this very same piano. Good for you, figuring it out on your own." He grinned vividly. "You do realize, don't you, that eventually you'll have to use all ten?"

"So I've been told," Johnny admitted. Carolyn, my foster mom in high school used to play a little."

Howard pulled a chair next to the piano stool, and they began working on the keys together. It seemed only minutes before the grandfather clock was striking two o'clock, when the eager pupil sensed he'd overstayed his welcome.

"Oh, man, it's really late! Hope I haven't kept you from anything important, Howard."

"Listen, I've got nothing to do and all night to do it. I usually charge for lessons, you know, but I'm having too much fun, so consider it on the house... or at least till you collect your first royalty check."

Johnny nodded his thanks. "Hey, I really appreciate it. If I had any money, I'd –"

"No worries. Listen, kid, I've got enough in the tank to tackle another hour, long as you haven't got somewhere to go."

"At two in the morning? No chance of that." Johnny got his third wind and put his hands back on the ivory keys.

Howard listened for a few minutes, then, as Johnny was obviously tired, sat back. "Have you given any thought to what you'll do with all these songs you're writing? I'm talking about having 'em recorded someday, you know, that kind of thing. Maybe even you could do them... assuming a record company prefers your voice to one of their signed artists."

"Someone else do it?" Johnny was getting a headache from too little sleep. "I mean, they are my songs... my personal feelings. Don't think I'd want anyone else singing 'em."

"Ah, so you wanna be a pop star?" Howard responded. "Someone who records music and plays it on the road to adoring fans with lots of hard work and maybe a little luck?"

"In theory, who wouldn't wanna be one?" Johnny arched his eyebrows. "Not that I'd have a clue where to start. I mean, I'm just your average screwed up guy who's written a few tunes from the heart. Sometimes I feel like sharing them with the world. Then again, I can't imagine my decision making any difference, since the only ones who are ever gonna hear 'em are you and me."

Howard stood up from his chair and moved over to the couch, making himself more comfortable. "Listen, what if I told you I could arrange an audition with a record label here in New York? A chance to perform for executives who could choose to sign you up, or maybe buy your songs for someone else to record?"

"Get the hell outta here! I'm mean, we're just having fun with this. And anyway, who am I? Hardly popstar material." He rolled his eyes and laughed. "Especially in this glorious era of rapper boys, grunge bands and video vixens. Besides, you told me you haven't been involved in the industry for years."

"No, really, Johnny. If this is something you'd seriously consider, I can possibly help a little. But you've gotta be sincere so we don't waste our time." Howard slid his glasses up the bridge of his nose. "Don't get me wrong, I really enjoy hanging out with you. But in my opinion… well, I just need to know how you feel about going after it full-tilt."

"Howard, man… I'm really touched," Johnny looked away. "And yeah, I can be serious. Sure, I'm game if you're really that optimistic."

"Well, if you aren't too busy with schoolwork and your social life, I'm gonna give you a few assignments for your spare time. Don't look so scared, it's not a big deal. Just some vocal exercises and piano work that you can handle on any keyboard."

Johnny stood from the piano, his expression serious. "Sounds like I'd be a fool not to. But, okay, that's all great for me, but what do you get out of the deal? I'm not even sure what you'd charge for this kind of thing."

"Gratification, kid. Satisfaction in seeing someone with your raw talent making something of his life." Howard crossed his legs, putting his hands behind his head, the fingers laced. "Looking at you, I can't help but think of how much I flushed away. All that unfulfilled potential. But you – you have the voice, man. Plus your lyrics put me to shame. And your very first song turns out to be as impressive as anything I've penned in twenty-five years." He brought his arms down, uncrossed his legs and leaned forward. "Listen. For me it's a no-brainer. I've got no real career, no family, and too much empty time around here. That's why I went back to school; why I want to teach. And most of all, that's why I wanna see you succeed - to be able to say I played a hand in someone's future."

Johnny was thunderstruck. Once he regained his composure, he stepped toward Howard, a look of determination firmly etched on his face. "Howard, I'm gonna find a way to pay you back. Already you've done so much for me. And even if this doesn't lead anywhere, our friendship's done more for my confidence than I can tell you."

"That's a two-way street if ever I've driven one." Howard nodded. "Haven't felt this determined in forever." He yawned and stretched his gangly arms over his head. "Now it's really late, kid. But before I walk you out, let me start you off with a little pamphlet I give all my students. Some basic vocal dexterity training to tackle here-and-there."

Johnny's songwriting took on a heightened sense of purpose over the next several weeks. He often carried along a portable tape recorder in an effort to preserve any new tunes that popped into his head during the course of a day. On other days, when inspiration arrived, he dialed his home number and sang the melody into his answering machine, so that he wouldn't forget it before the day's end. It was all a welcomed distraction from his personal emptiness.

Slowly, Johnny began to climb out of the creative rut, which had restricted him to writing only vulnerable, weepy ballads.

At Howard's insistence - and with $400 borrowed from his onetime foster mom, Carolyn - Johnny booked time at a local recording studio to cut a few proper demo recordings. Frank Traber, Howard's occasional nightclub bandmate, lent his guitar playing on two of the songs. His friend Ian Klatt provided the drumming on another. And of course, Howard played piano behind Johnny's soaring vocals. It was all taking shape as the framework for a real studio band.

It was after one late-night recording session that Johnny found himself recalling a recent conversation with Howard about the dearth of quality in modern day songwriting. He pondered whether it was the music-buyers or music-makers that had diminished the vitality of lyrics.

Whatever happened to the likes of Dylan and Donovan: songwriters lauded for their wit and substance? Musical messages were once considered sacred. Nowadays… nothing more than an afterthought. But have we become too jaded to embrace songs of distinction?

Johnny lay across his bed. Though the room was pleasantly cool, he was sweating feverishly as he worked on a slow, anthem-like melody at a portable Casio keyboard. Feeling particularly isolated, he began creating a song about connection – an unofficial mantra for songwriters who shared his desire for a more receptive audience – an ode to the art of articulation.

When the world has got me down
it seems there's nowhere left to turn
When I've got no one to talk with,
no one sharing their concern
I wish that I could fly away
But I haven't got a cape
So I use my pen and paper
as the means for my escape

Then I put it to a tune
Shifting lyrics as I change it
And should they not fit at first
I'll endeavor to rearrange it
But when the words from deep inside me
don't garner fair contemplation
I'm the self appointed poet of the wrong generation

Ahhhhhhh

Pull a tune from out of nowhere
Change a poem to a song
And if it's captivating
all the world might sing along
But as the writer no one wants to see
their lyrics shunned and betrayed
since our writings articulate
how our feelings are conveyed

We will labor over stanzas
making sure they're all in place
While the tunes spill from the heart
like scalding teardrops down our face

And through the mists of time
when the songs we write are played
I hope our tunes will hold up strong
and the lyrics never fade

A soaring, wordless chorus followed the second, third and fourth verses; an anguished cry echoing both Johnny's lament for what pop music once was, and his hope for what could again be. And then came that line about the "self appointed poet": potentially brash enough to launch the persona of a determined crusader.

"Absolutely spellbinding!" Howard pumped his fist skyward when he heard Johnny debut the song at the upright piano in his back parlor. "And your playing wasn't half bad either. Talk about a tune with signature potential!"

By Howard's count, Johnny now had nine songs of exceptional quality. It was just a matter of time before he could share them for critical evaluation.

10

Spontaneous Developments

Megan Price still throbbed from the abrupt end to her romance. Gerald Ridgewell served as her distraction of the moment. She wasn't particularly enamored by any specific quality he possessed, but she took comfort in having someone around to fill the void of Johnny's absence.

Megan noticed a complete transformation in her mother's attitude from the days when Johnny had been a regular visitor. Here was Katherine, showering Gerry with theater tickets, restaurant vouchers, and a variety of entertainment perks. On at least two occasions, Katherine even took the opportunity to invite him to a family dinner.

All this special attention was entirely new. But while Megan saw through this thinly veiled attempt to keep her close to Gerry, she simply didn't have the resolve to oppose it. It was just too comfortable, especially after all the earlier tension she had endured.

Megan was still in love with Johnny. But she could not seem to recapture his attention or interest. She at first tried with pleading phone messages, leaving at least a dozen on his machine. She failed to get so much as a single return call. Next, she turned to writing emotional letters that eloquently bared her soul.

Johnny;

How many ways can I say that I screwed up? I hardly blame you for being furious. But it's all a terrible misunderstanding. You were and still are the only one I've ever loved. Since you sent me that song, my heart is as hollow as an orange with all the pulp squeezed out.

Getting more creative, Megan ordered flowers accompanied by apologetic cards. She sent balloons, a gourmet bakery basket, and a compilation tape of favorite songs from their years together. Yet, despite her fervent efforts, no replies were forthcoming.

One early morning, Megan awoke at a quarter-to-two, feeling desperate. She dressed quickly and snuck out of the apartment. A car service dropped her at Johnny's Brooklyn Heights building. She hoped a face-to-face meeting would resolve their differences.

In the end she just quietly dropped a small package in front of his door, then silently slipped away in the early morning darkness. Her lack of self-assuredness had again proved her greatest deficiency.

Johnny could barely listen to the expressive diatribes that filled his answering machine. Nothing Megan could say at this juncture would change his determination for it to be over ... and yet he was left with unanswered questions and a bevy of mixed emotions. Often, he pondered Megan's lies, how many more she had told that he didn't know about... and the three years of promises now unfulfilled. Everything around him was a painful reminder of her.

Staring at his bedroom ceiling one night, Johnny found himself recalling the day he'd moved into his apartment. How helpful Megan had been in aiding him to find this place; in helping him to move in. They had stood in this very room, painting the walls, talking about how the next big move would be the home they would someday share. *Another someday that'll never come!*

When the letters began arriving, Johnny was reluctant to open them. Eventually he did, but he just scanned the long paragraphs to see if she had broken any new ground on the subject of her betrayal. She had not. He filed them away in a shoebox. *Might even read 'em all someday,* he figured, *when this all isn't so excruciating.*

The parade of packages changed Johnny's mentality from apathetic to uncomfortable. He was trying so hard to forget the pain. Megan's constant bombardment only pushed him further away. Immune to her repetitions, he stopped taking notice of the attached cards, or even of the mix tape she'd made and tucked inside one of the packages. Wasting hundreds of dollars to buy back his feelings was in contrast to everything he had grown to love about her.

The only special delivery of Megan's barrage to which Johnny was receptive was the collection of photographs. Johnny had walked over an envelope sitting in front of his door one morning on his way out to school. He only noticed it upon his return. Of the two dozen snapshots inside, he was most partial to the last one on the roll – the same sentimental shot that Megan had wept over. Johnny swallowed hard. The picture offered a fond escape to a happier time.

Johnny debated picking up the phone. There was something about these frozen images that replaced bitterness with longing for the past; a longing for Megan. But before he could bring himself to lift the receiver, it occurred that this was simply a pathway to further anguish. All that deception from their last night together… He winced at the painful memory.

Johnny sat on his bed, studying the envelope in which the photos had arrived. It contained no postmark. Certainly this flat package would have fit inside his mailbox down in the lobby. *Could it've been Megan, and not a postman, who dropped it off?* Uneasily, he wondered if this was not the first – or last – surprise visit.

Howard Greffen practically skipped inside the offices of Highpeak records, carrying the goods he had promised to deliver. This time he was not kept waiting.

"So what've you got for me today?" Ron Neswick knew why Howard was there.

"I brought the demos from the kid we discussed last time. I know you'll want to hear 'em?"

"Oh, right!" Ron pretended he had forgotten. "Need me to run and get the tape player again?"

Howard laughed. "Suffice it to say that modern technology was used this time around."

Neswick snatched the two CD cases from Howard's hands. Each was labeled with five song titles. "So which should I play first?" he asked, ejecting a disc from the CD player beside his cluttered desk.

"Ron, the sequencing's hardly important. Just pop one in and have a listen."

Neswick chose to stand. He appeared absorbed in deep concentration as the sounds of *Shadows of the Same Color* filled his office. When it ended, he hit pause and went back to his seat. "You didn't tell me this kid had a conscious too? Evocative, yet instantly catchy. Hardly your prototypical protest singer."

"Why'd you stop it there? There's not a bad one on either disc."

Ron scribbled some notes on a yellow pad, then reached back to the CD player next to him. "So I take it he wrote that one about Crown Heights? An interesting subject for a pop song."

"That's the beauty of this kid's talent." Howard tugged at his goatee. "He's like nothing you've heard in decades. A poet first and a songwriter second. His lyrics carry a message."

"Sorta like Brooklyn's answer to Bob Dylan," Ron said, chuckling.

Poet of the Wrong Generation was the next song. Howard watched

Neswick's face, seeing the other man's captivation, abstaining from further comment until the first disc ended. Ron was now pacing the room. He stopped to jot down further remarks and gaze intently at the song titles.

"So when do I get to check out this kid's intangibles?" Ron spun around, tapping the plastic jewel case on his knuckles. "Before we make any offers, I wanna be sure he's presentable."

"Oh, he's sharp. Highly charismatic," Howard said. "And you haven't even heard the other songs yet." He watched Ron pick up the phone in the center of the table. "Who're you calling?"

"Jessica, René and Heidi, please join me in my office. Thank you!" Ron put down the receiver. He turned to Howard, smiling. "I want my team to hear this before you leave. But while we wait, tell me again when it was you said you could get this guy in here?"

Andy dropped by Johnny's apartment on a gray afternoon in late January, near the end of winter recess. Their camaraderie had never been more valued.

"This for me?" Johnny accepted a folder of paperwork, confirming his copyrights to the songs he'd written recently.

"Let's just say you're now free to circulate your tapes to anyone willing to listen. I'd even be thrilled to help you shop them around if you need some leads."

Johnny nodded appreciatively. "Thanks, man. To tell you the truth, I wouldn't know where to begin. Howard tells me he may have a few contacts from his past. But how realistic is any of it?" Johnny flipped through the folder of completed applications before turning his thoughts elsewhere. "So what do you hear from Jacqui these days? She planning a return anytime soon?"

Andy dropped his chin. "I hardly know what she's got in mind anymore. Some days, I get the feeling that she's totally over me. Can't seem to get a handle on her."

Johnny gaped at him. "You know, I used to believe my messed-up child-hood helped make me a pretty good judge of character – well, at least I thought so before the whole thing blew up with Megan. But all that aside, there's no way that Jacqui's feelings for you just flickered out."

"Ah, who the hell knows? Maybe you're right. I offered to fly over last week. She asked me not to come. It's been more than two months." He rolled his eyes. "Just wish there was something I could do. If only I had your skills, maybe I could change her mind."

Even as the words were leaving Andy's mouth, Johnny's imagination kicked into overdrive. "Okay, so, tell me: what is it you miss most about her?" He turned to a clean page in his notebook. "When you're alone with your thoughts, what comes to mind?"

"What're you, my shrink? Don't need your analysis, thank you very much."

"It'd be hopeless trying to figure out your complexities, man. But c'mon, trust me. Just play along."

"Yeah, whatever. But this better be going somewhere that doesn't result in my making an ass of myself. Thought I'd outgrown that long ago."

Andy let out enough poignant memories to fill three cluttered pages. There was the way he studied Jacqui's photos. The calendar he kept on his bedroom wall, marking the days since she had gone. The abrupt manner she hung up the phone before leaving for England. And his insecurity over his own worthiness for her.

Finally Andy was quiet. Johnny excused himself to the bathroom, tak-ing along his portable keyboard and the notebook he'd been scribbling in. Nearly thirty minutes later, he came back into his room to find Andy staring at the framed photo on the dresser.

"How come you never showed me this?" Andy asked. "Were you keep-ing it a secret?"

"Oh, that? It came from Megan. She left it off one day while I wasn't here. Kinda freaked me out." Johnny pointed to his closet. "I've got more stashed away somewhere in there. Even a few with you and Jacqui. You can have the snaps; I don't have any negatives."

Johnny dug out the rest of the roll from a tattered shoebox. He handed a few shots to Andy.

"Man, these are great! I'll bet sending a few of 'em to Sheffield oughta rekindle the missing spark. I can keep some, right?"

"Sure, go ahead." Johnny nodded. "And I've got something else here you may wanna send along with it." Johnny placed his notebook on his desk to the left of the keyboard for reference and began to play.

Jacqui – It's been too long since I last saw you
And Jacqui – I hate when we say goodbye
Somehow, with all the time that's come between us
I've had the same tear in my eyes

Jacqui – You came from so far away
And baby how I wish you'd have stayed
Your letters and your postcards keep me whole sometimes
But your spirit is with me everyday

Jacqui – Your pictures grace my albums
And somehow – How I wish they could come alive
I stare at them at night and I whisper to myself
counting days until you arrive

Jacqui – All the hours I think of you
And when the legend that is you is by my side
while half of me is deserving – wishing to be with you
the other half of me wants to hide

Your journey's long – Your stay was short
And begging is my last resort
But if you leave me I'll be lost
I'm pleading with my fingers crossed, my Jacqui (Oh dear Jacqui)

Your with me now – I won't let go
'Coz when your gone it haunts me so
So take these words – hear my plea
And promise that someday we'll be together (Oh dear Jacqui)

Jacqui – It's been too long since I last saw you
And Jacqui – I don't wanna say goodbye

As the last note faded, he turned to Andy with a wink. "So what d'ya think of our first collaboration? And more importantly: you think she'll like it?"

Andy snatched the notebook from Johnny's desk. He sat reading the lyrics in total bewilderment.

"I assume you'll want me to record that one?" Johnny asked playfully. "Guess I've never written a love song for someone who hadn't ripped my heart out. Actually felt pretty good!"

The telephone began to ring.

"Johnny, it's Howard. You got a minute?"

"Howard, man, just talking 'bout you! In fact, my friend Andy and I, we just finished a sweet little song about —"

"Listen, man, I'd love to hear it, but now's not the time. How'd you like to audition for a major record label? I'll explain the details later, but I need to know if you're free tomorrow."

"A record label? You're kidding, right?" Johnny shouted.

"This is no joke. The outfit I'm dealing with is called Highpeak Records. I'm sure you've heard of 'em. Please tell me you've got nothing better to do around noon-time?"

Johnny looked over at Andy and covered the phone. "Howard's booked me a big-time try-out tomorrow! You free to come along?"

"An audition! Where? With whom? You for real?" Andy looked up at Johnny's smiling face. At least one question had been answered. "Well, of course I'll go. It's not like I had any big plans."

Johnny turned his attention back to Howard. "So – you'll be there to play piano? Can't do it without you! Who else'll be joining us? We haven't really rehearsed…" His voice trailed off. He felt incoherent in his excitement.

"Don't worry. I'll round up the usual suspects. We can practice tonight at my place, just to polish up. But I know you'll do just fine."

"Howard, I can't believe this! You're amazing! Later, you've gotta tell me the details."

Johnny placed down the receiver. He flashed the widest of grins. "Andy, this could be huge. Dare I say it, but tomorrow I–"

"Whoa, let's not get ahead of ourselves," Andy cautioned. "Remember, it's an audition, not a coronation. Just keep things in perspective."

Johnny bit his lip. "Andy, that's exactly why I need you there, buddy. Plus, you're the business guy. No one I trust more. Thanks in advance for saying yes."

Johnny was looking forward to a much-needed run-through at Howard's place that evening. He had invited both Frank Traber with his guitar and Ian Klatt, Frank's local drumming buddy. Shortly before their arrival, Howard boiled a kettle of water and placed two porcelain mugs on the cluttered kitchen table. "So, kid, I'll bet you're a little curious as to how this audition came about."

"Just a little," Johnny steadied his hands. He was nervous.

Howard tore open an orange wrapper and twirled a teabag around his left pinky. "You remember the tape we cut at school? The song for your ex?"

"Kinda hard to forget that one." Johnny nodded in acknowledgement.

"Well, I have a little admission to make. That morning in the booth, I made an extra copy; played it for a few ears in the music biz. They *really* liked it. One thing led to another and…"

The teakettle whistled on the stove.

Johnny slowly descended from the cloudy perch where he'd spent the afternoon. His face turned a bright shade of red. "Can't believe you said nothing this whole time. That song particularly… it's just a little personal. I didn't expect it to have an audience."

"Listen, hold on a second." Howard raised his left hand like a stop sign. "This was done on the up-and-up. It's all about trust, remember?"

Johnny shook his head. "Don't get me wrong. I'm beyond thankful for everything you've done. It's just… you were shopping my music without my knowing."

"Listen, kid, sorry if I got a little overzealous. You know I'd never screw you over." Howard stood to remove the screeching kettle from the stove. "And I never left behind a single tape."

"So then why'd you wait till now to tell me?"

Howard's hands began to shudder. Some boiling water from the kettle spilled onto the kitchen floor. Johnny assumed it was nervousness.

"The only reason I kept quiet is: I didn't wanna set you up for an instant letdown. I've seen far too many talented people quit too easily. Wasn't about to let it happen with you."

Johnny grabbed a paper towel, then bent down to wipe up the spill. "So, these Highpeak people, they've never seen my face, or heard me sing a note. You must've played 'em everything."

"Johnny, sometimes, we make decisions from the heart – especially us songwriters. I have an old acquaintance who gives me the time of day. When he confirmed my original belief in you, I knew that a few more songs would totally blow him away. Now, he's basically convinced." Howard steadied his hands and poured some water in his mug. "All you need to do tomorrow is show up and look the part: The rest'll take care of itself."

11

Sealed and Delivered

Johnny awoke to a blustery winter morning. After a night of tossing and turning, he pulled open his cramped bedroom closet.

At first he reached for his only formal outfit – a navy blue blazer with gray slacks and a red silk tie. Then, gazing in the mirror, he recalled Howard's comment about looking the part. *It's a music audition, damn it.* Swiftly, he grabbed a black leather vest, a white denim shirt and a pair of black jeans – similar attire to what the lead singer wore in the recent movie musical, *The Commitments.*

He met up with Andy at the Hoyt Street station. Together they rode the C train to Manhattan's Columbus Circle. Through punishing wind and frigid temperatures, they soldiered two blocks south to Highpeak headquarters on West 57th.

Inside the lobby, Johnny was immediately overcome with a feeling of warmth. The comfortable interior climate was perfectly complimented by the soothing *Nocturne in E-flat* by Chopin, which played through overhead speakers. He looked to see if Howard had arrived. But with no sign of him in the marble waiting area, Johnny went straight to the receptionist. "Hi, I'm here to meet Ron Neswick."

A raven-haired young woman stood to greet him with a welcoming smile. "Mr. Elias, we've been expecting you. Can I get you something hot to drink?"

Johnny removed his overcoat, then turned back to Andy grinning. "You want anything?"

"Black coffee if it's not too much trouble."

"And I'd love a hot cocoa if you've got some."

The receptionist showed the way to an art deco conference room. Bronze gramophone sculptures and 1930s radios lined the surrounding shelves. A black-and-white checkerboard carpet complemented the framed art prints of Marilyn Monroe and Charlie Chaplin on the walls. A movie poster for *Some Like It Hot* caught Johnny's attention.

When the receptionist left, Andy deliberately cleared his throat. "Hot cocoa? Are we regressing? I figured you'd wanna make a more sophisticated impression."

"Well at least I'll drink it to warm up. It relaxes me. But you're no coffee man. You plan to stare at the cup till it turns cold?"

"Touché!" Andy smiled. "At least I didn't ask her to waste any milk on me."

The receptionist reentered the room. She placed down the steaming mugs, then handed an outline page to Johnny. "Here you go, Mr. Elias. Ron Neswick and our New York staff are on their way. Some of our West-Coast team also happen to be in town. One is Ed McCauley, VP of artist development. The other is Faye Aurichio. She handles our label's marketing and design."

What's with the large delegation? Johnny wondered. *Howard said this was a simple try-out.* Then he realized the significance of the empty chair to his left and his heart accelerated to a gallop. *And where the hell is Howard? How can he be late to a meeting he arranged?* Johnny's piano playing skills had vastly improved. But his confidence was not at the point of auditioning solo. Feeling fidgety, he sipped his cocoa and stared at the Elvis wall clock, its swiveling hips doubling as a pendulum.

Nearly ten minutes passed. A well-dressed man with dark hair and a waxed moustache popped his head into the room, briefly surveying the occupants. "Which one of you is Johnny Elias?" he asked. His voice had a hint of a French-Canadian accent.

Johnny leaned forward. The man walked over and extended a hand. "René Fontenot. I work closely with Mr. Neswick. Your demos, they have us all really excited."

"Thanks, thank you." Johnny grinned nervously. "Any particular tune that stands out?"

"Well, from where I sit you've got at least three cuts with radio potential. Commercial viability. That's my primary responsibility. Songs like yours make my job pretty easy."

Next to enter were two highly attractive younger women in matching dark pantsuits. "Hi, I'm Jessica," announced the first woman, a brown-haired beauty of no more than thirty. "Assistant VP of East Coast marketing."

"And I'm Heidi Ellison!" trilled the second woman, a redhead, drowning in a bottle of Calvin Klein's Escape. "PR liaison for our New York based artists."

Ron Neswick arrived a few minutes later with an entourage. To his left was a tanned, older man in a blue pinstriped suit. And on his right was an equally tanned but much younger woman who simply called herself Faye. *Must be the left-coast contingent,* Johnny conjectured. He watched them banter cordially around the black Formica table.

Shaking hands with Ron for the first time, Johnny made a point of making one more introduction. "Mr. Neswick, this is Andy Raymer... my adviser for today. Hope it's cool that he's here?"

"Sure, no problem," Ron said, shrugging. He reached across for Andy's hand. "I see you've already made yourself comfortable."

The proceedings evolved into something of a team interview. The questions came from all sides: *So tell us how long you've been writing your music? What instruments do you play? Do you perform with a regular band? What artists are you most influenced by?*

At first Johnny felt overwhelmed by the attention. But one-word answers soon expanded into a cappella performances and narratives about the meaning behind his songs. Although it was not what he expected, he managed to engage the whole room with his charm.

Ninety minutes of animated discussion gradually shifted from questioning to a comprehensive presentation. Johnny nodded pleasantly as each executive extolled his or her area of expertise. Andy took careful notes. Halfway through, the receptionist was summoned to take a lunch order. She walked around the table handing out paper menus from a Chinese take-out, *It's Only Wok and Roll*.

"I'm okay," Johnny waved her off. "You guys go ahead without me."

"Really," Ron insisted. "We'll probably be here a while. And besides, this place is quite superb. Even got authentic Thai-food." Proudly, he rubbed his rotund figure.

Johnny was tickled by all the attention to his music. It hardly now occurred to him that Howard and Frank had still not turned up. However unexpected, he was perfectly content to be wined-and-dined by a room full of executives.

Andy had yet to complete his masters degree. However, observing the hard-sell tone and enthusiastic body language, it was clear to him that this clever sales pitch was never going to be an audition. It would almost certainly conclude with some kind of an offer to lure his friend aboard. And with his escalating business acumen, Andy was determined to make certain that Johnny agreed to nothing, until it was reviewed by a savvy professional.

Half eaten egg rolls and broken fortune cookies soon littered the conference table. After dessert, Johnny met individually with various team members. He found each Highpeak department head personable, though not everyone's professional efforts captured his fancy.

He was hardly enamored with the design work of Faye Aurichio. Looking through her portfolio of CD covers, Johnny perceived them overly airbrushed and formulaic. These glorified publicity shots bore little resemblance to the classics he was raised on in Carolyn Green's basement. He also found Heidi Ellison's tone a bit loud and flirty. And the stench of her fragrance made him sneeze. *She's overwhelming. If she has this prickly affect on me, imagine how the media must feel?* he scribbled in his notes.

The bustling conference room gradually emptied until just three remained. Ron Neswick got up to shut the door. He began his closing statement like the seasoned attorney that he was.

"So now that we've gotten to know each other, I think it's fair to say that we here at Highpeak are rather impressed with your talents. As you can see, we have quite a capable lineup in place to promote up-and-comers like yourself. And although you're just entering the development stages, we believe you have the potential for a solid, if not dazzling future."

Johnny fought to conceal a smile. "Thanks. I'm really flattered. And your presentation; now I know why you guys've been so —"

"So in a nutshell," Ron interrupted, "we're prepared to have you record your first album with our label. I hold here in my hand a contract with your name on it and today's date. We feel confident you'll find it to be more than competitive. I'm asking that you please sign two executable copies before heading out today."

Johnny received a thick manila folder across the table. He removed one stack of papers for himself, then handed a duplicate set to Andy.

"Sir, may we have a minute?" Andy asked politely.

"Uh, no problem." Ron shrugged. He stepped out, letting the door close behind him.

Johnny was beaming like a giddy adolescent. Thoughts of cheering crowds and hit singles danced inside his head. "Andy, Highpeak Records is gonna pay *me* to record *my* songs! Hey, man, pinch me before I wake up back in another Brooklyn foster home!"

"Shhh," Andy gestured, scurrying to the other side of the room. He inspected a telephone at the far end of the conference table. The red speakerphone light was illuminated. He quickly hit the mute button and made his way back to where Johnny was sitting. "I thought someone might be listening in. And I'm still not comfortable talking here. So let's keep a lid on the celebration, take the unsigned contracts, go home and review them."

Johnny squinted curiously. "Don't know if I follow. How 'bout at least a brief explanation before Ron Neswick comes back in here. I mean, could things've gone any better?"

"Just trust me. This could be an amazing opportunity. But don't sell yourself short either. And rule number one in business school: never sign anything before your lawyer sees it first. From here on, just shut up and let me do the talking."

It had been several weeks since Megan had last showed up at Johnny's door. She was sure he would have at least called with some reaction to the set of photos. Instead, she was left to continually reabsorb his last message: a heart-wrenching ballad that told her goodbye.

Down deep, Megan believed that Johnny had never stopped loving her. And in truth, she was correct. But without a reply to her letters, gifts and cards of apology, her faith in him rapidly began to fade.

More than anything, the convenience of a relationship with Gerry afforded Megan the opportunity to relax. The strain between Megan and her mother had disappeared. And in a remarkable turnabout, she witnessed Katherine's tolerance of disposable flatware and casual clothing – subliminal statements of rare contentment.

While Megan enjoyed Gerry's company, she had also uncovered aspects of his character that were less than flattering. Front and center was a nasty temper that flared up in two separate incidents.

The first came during a dinner date at the renowned Rainbow Room, high above Rockefeller Center. A waiter inadvertently delivered the wrong entrées to their table. He immediately apologized and hurried to bring out the correct order. Not content to let the matter drop, Gerry asked to have his Veal Marsala returned to the kitchen for reheating three times.

Then the bill came. Gerry called over the maitre d' and handed him a credit card.

"Listen, I'll pay for the food and wine, but I'll be damned if you make me pay a cent of gratuity to that mixed-up sonofabitch waiter." A frenzied argument ensued. A blushing Megan slipped out to the main elevator and headed home alone.

It happened again one week later. Gerry lost his composure inside an uptown parking garage when an attendant took ten minutes to drive up with his sleek new Jaguar. Once the car reached the exit ramp, he began a detailed inspection of the exterior, looking more for trouble than any new blemish. "Hey, what's this?" He pointed at a light scratch on the right fender. "You dumbasses think you were gonna get away with this?" A shouting match ensued. Megan shamefacedly ducked inside the front passenger door. She turned up the radio to drown out the commotion.

Though Gerry never turned his fury against her, Megan felt privately apprehensive. And while she accepted his profuse apologies after each incident, she found the tantrums hard to forget.

From rage to the outrageous, the relationship took yet another peculiar turn during a Sunday dinner around the Price's dining room table. Gerry and Katherine engaged in a boisterous debate about city politics. The soft-spoken Megan found herself unable to get a word in for over an hour. Instead, she held a quieter talk with Zach and his girlfriend-of-the-month.

"Can you believe those two?" Zach pointed in his mother's direction. "I mean, does anyone really care what ads they run in the subway? Like someone would ever call 1-800 MD Tusch!"

As they laughed together, Katherine tapped her knife on a wine glass to grab everyone's full attention. "So, Gerry, the kids and I are heading out to Hawaii next month for a little winter vacation. If your schedule allows, Megan and I were hoping you might be able to join us?"

"Hawaii. You serious? I don't know what to say, Mrs. Price!"

Before any objections could be raised, privately or otherwise, Gerry had already blocked off the time in his date book. Megan swallowed hard, saying nothing. *What's the point?* She thought to herself. *Never gonna get my way anyway. Might as well not wreck the delicate harmony, right?*

To her surprise, six days in Maui provided Megan some sorely needed time to clear her head. Tropical weather and breathtaking scenery enabled her to warm up to Gerry in ways she had been unable to do back in the New York City winter.

Together, they strolled down Maluaka beach on the afternoon of their arrival. Megan felt Gerry drape one arm affectionately across her bare shoulders. "Hey, Meg, I've never asked you this before, but I assume you plan to stay in New York once you wrap your degree?"

"Well, one never knows what life has in store," she said, chuckling, "though I'll probably stick around." Then, pondering his intentions, she straightened her posture. "Why'd you ask?"

"Oh, it's nothing really. It's just that with my residency ending soon, I'm thinking about buying a place on the West Side. Think you'll be able to help me?"

Not considering the consequences of her answer, Megan grinned innocently. "I know a realtor through Mom's agency. When we get back to town, I'll make a few calls."

Gerry squeezed her snugly against his side. He kissed her reddening cheek as they walked on. "Ya know, I'm incredibly lucky to have someone like you. Buying a place, that's huge! Good to know you'll be with me every step of the way."

"So – are you thinking Broadway, Columbus, maybe Amsterdam? The West Side's a great neighborhood for young professionals."

"Actually, it's gotta be Central Park West. Since coming around so often to your place, I'd love to get a similar layout on the other side of the park. It's so cool looking down at the tiny people below."

Megan allowed her guard to slowly fall as the vacation evolved. One afternoon she went snorkeling with Gerry deep in the Pacific. The next day, they hiked up a dormant volcano, collecting exotic lava rocks. At a traditional beach luau that same evening, Megan found herself hesitantly cuddling up to him on the sand, savoring a picturesque sunset. Soon, she was submitting to his advances, kissing him with eyes closed, allowing his frisky hands to wander -- trying in vain to fight off thoughts of Johnny. If not romantic, it was the warmest feeling she'd experienced since that memorable summer day in Central Park.

Then came the grand finale.

They were all summoned by Katherine to a candlelit banquet in a bamboo hut with a spectacular ocean view. There was a wonderful aroma of Pacific-Asian cuisine. Red orchids decorated the table and a trio of local musicians serenaded the party with Hawaiian music.

Katherine poured everyone a glass of sparkling pink champagne, then opened the dinner conversation by asking everyone to share aloud their favorite part of the vacation.

"What's with that?" Zach asked in derision. "Since when did family meals become some lame confessional?"

"Zachary," she chided him. "I thought it would be nice to reminisce, while our memories are still fresh."

"Fine, well then I'll start. Since I was on my own this past week, no one'll know if I'm lying or not." He paused to sip from his champagne flute. "Let's start with the drinking. Oh, man! No one carded me anywhere. Talk about tropical Margaritaville! A close second would have to be seeing Mom in that dreadful coconut bra on Kaanapali beach. Guess we won't be finding those pictures magneted on the fridge anytime soon!"

When the laughter died down, Megan volunteered to go next. "I'd have to say it was swimming under that Blue Angel waterfall on Tuesday. There's nothing more relaxing than that cool water rushing down on you after lying out in the sun. Absolute tranquility!"

Katherine smiled at Megan's inviting description. She reached to clear a vase of orchids from her view. "For me, I'm struggling to settle on any one memory. I know I made these rules, but I'll bend them just a bit." She leaned closer to the table. "My fondest recollection is being surrounded in this paradise by the people who mean the most to me. Sitting here tonight at this festive table might be the most precious time of all."

A collective "awww" was the response. Katherine blushed. "So, Gerry, dear, we haven't heard from you yet. It's your turn to go next."

"Well, only if I must, Mrs. Price." Seeing the eager look on Katherine's face, he unfolded his arms, and slowly exhaled. "I'm also having a hard time picking only one." He turned to Megan and smiled boldly. "How could I ever forget those long walks on the beach? Holding your hand at sunset…" His voice trailed off."

"Yeah, and what about after sunset?" Zach blurted out. "What else did –"

"Zachary!" Katherine shouted. "Let Gerry finish. And keep your rudeness to yourself."

Gerry was flustered. He gazed round the table, seeking facial reactions. Zach flashed a smile of apology, then covered his face with a linen napkin. Katherine nodded approvingly, raising her glass in his direction. Megan's face showed little emotion as he turned back to face her.

Gerry rose from his chair. Nearby waves could be heard crashing on the beach. Nervously, he reached for Megan's sweaty hands. "You know, the past week's been unreal. I've been hoping all along that it would never end. Too bad nothing does. That said, with your permission, I'd at least like to keep it going a little longer."

He released one of Megan's hands and reached into his pocket. A small blue jewelry box emerged. Inside, a sparkling, pear-shaped diamond ring took Megan by complete surprise.

"Megan Price, I want you to marry me." He watched her jaw drop. "I want to spend the rest of my life with you."

12

Working On A Mystery

"**J**ohnny, you heard what they told us today. This deal's in line with what other new recording artists get in their first contract. It's pretty much standard fare, though there may be some wiggle room."

"You mean the songwriting-royalties?" Johnny's eyes glazed over at the business details.

"That's altogether a separate issue." Andy sifted through some papers on Johnny's desk. "Songwriting royalties are paid on top of standard artist royalties in separate quarterly payments. The lawyers'll help you set up a separate publishing deal for your songs. And that percentage'll be paid based on sales, broadcast frequency and so on. I know this all sounds complicated, but you'll catch on quickly once your album is released."

"Legal costs? Publishing fees? I don't have that kind of money to throw around."

"Not yet!" Andy exclaimed. "But as soon as you sign the contract, you'll have close to a six-figure advance coming your way. You don't get to keep it all, but it's surely enough to get you a bit more space for your music collection, if you catch my drift."

Johnny gaped at him in astonishment. It was only now seeping in that life was about to take a radical turn from his volatile, tightfisted youth. If he wanted to, he could actually buy an apartment, a nice car, or even take an extended vacation without worrying about every dime spent.

Since the age of twelve, Johnny had often worked in his spare time to compensate for the lack of any significant allowance from his assortment of foster parents. Memories flooded back to long Sunday afternoons in the coat-check closet at the Imperial Terrace banquet hall. Then came the after-school job, handing out flyers to disinterested passersby on Atlantic Avenue. His summer résumé included lifeguard, waiter, and now library assistant.

It had been less than a year since Johnny finally earned enough part-time money to move into his tiny apartment. He often envisioned a best-case scenario of finding a steady job out of school and working his way up the corporate ladder. Now, in just a handful of weeks, he was suddenly on the cusp of something far greater than anything he could have imagined.

Johnny sat on the floor, sifting through a pile of his favorite vinyl cases–many of which he'd "borrowed" from Carolyn Green's basement record collection. Fleetwood Mac's *Rumors*. The Who's *Tommy*. The Beatles *Sgt. Pepper*. "Too bad they don't design 'em like they used to," he muttered. Thinking back on the Highpeak meeting, his primary issues of concern suddenly shot to the forefront. "Andy, man, I know this probably sounds greedy and all with everything going on, but those Highpeak album covers: mostly hideous! And their music videos… just an extension of the lame-ass cover shots. I mean, where's the imagination? How 'bout individuality? You don't suppose they'd allow a first-timer some artistic jurisdiction, do ya?"

"Score another for having not signed the contract last week," Andy slapped his knees. "You're not getting creative control, but if they want you badly enough, they'll likely offer some leeway. Still, you do have to remember: as the new guy, you can't be making too many demands. Until you've proven something, you might have to live with the generic alternative."

Andy marked down Johnny's thoughts next to his Highpeak meeting notes. "Aside from those points, is there anything else you'd like me to negotiate on your behalf?"

"Actually, yeah, there's one off the top of my head." Johnny's eyes narrowed. "As a novice to this whole process, I need to know what your cut'll be as my representative?"

"Oh, c'mon," Andy laughed out loud. "Look, I'm thrilled to help you get this deal. But you're gonna need a real manager if things take off. All I've got is one semester of grad school under my belt. I don't know the first thing about managing a recording artist."

"And like I know the first thing about being one?" Johnny snickered. "I figure we'll learn together as we go along. Plus, if I'm paying lawyers to deal with legalities, and accountants to handle the money, why can't I count on you to spearhead my business side of things?"

Andy laughed heartily. "Coz you can't afford my services. If you wanna be the first client at Raymer Management, you're gonna need a whole lot more than what the advance is paying. And you'd better pray that someone out there buys the music, or it's back to Brooklyn for you."

"So I'll take that as a yes," Johnny said, grinning. "And as part of your first payment, I've got a certain little song to record for your elusive friend overseas."

It had been several days since Johnny had heard from Howard. Up until now, he'd been mostly curious as to his friend's recent whereabouts. By now, his curiosity had turned into genuine concern. He frequently tried calling Howard's home during intersession. He even twice swung by the old house on Willow Street, hoping to share his good news in person. But finding no signs of life, Johnny headed off, entirely perplexed.

Following the second attempt, he dug up a number for Frank Traber and dialed.

"Oh, hey, Johnny. I was hoping you could tell me the same thing. Haven't heard from the geezer since rehearsals that night at his place."

"But weren't you also supposed to play at the Highpeak audition? What the hell happened to you guys?"

"Sorry, man. I honestly don't know what went down. I got to Howard's around eleven that day. He never came to the door. When I got home, he'd left some hazy message about having someplace to go. Haven't heard from him since. Even missed a paying gig at O'Callahan's."

The two men arrived at Howard's home later that afternoon. The mailbox was overflowing with envelopes. Frank suggested either breaking in or calling the police.

Johnny had another idea.

"Sorry to trouble you, ma'am, but I was wondering if you'd recently seen one of your neighbors, Howard Greffen?"

"Who're you guys, detectives or something?" The elderly neighbor stared back at Johnny and Frank through her screen door. "He rarely ever comes out since his wife died. But, no, I haven't seen him come or go in a while."

"Actually, we're really just concerned friends," Frank explained. "He sorta disappeared on us last week."

"Disappeared, eh?" the woman rubbed her chin. "Well, I don't know if this'll help, but I've got somewhere an old set of emergency keys for that house. The late Mrs. Greffen gave 'em to me years ago. You're welcome to try if I can find them."

Johnny figured Howard was not likely to have changed the lock – or much else in the home. With a key ring in one hand and Frank in tow, he marched up the front steps and, his hand on the latch, turned the key in the lock. The door opened easily.

In his previous visits, Johnny had only been on the ground floor, spending most of his time in the dusty back parlor. He found that familiar room exactly as he remembered on the night of the rehearsal. Even Howard's scribbled notes for *Poet of the Wrong Generation* were still lying atop the old piano. While Frank checked the kitchen, Johnny headed to a part of the house he'd never been. "Frankie, I'm running up to the bedrooms. Holler if you find anything."

Johnny flicked a switch at the top of the tall staircase. An old chandelier illuminated a creaky wooden door to his right. It was halfway open. Johnny knocked, then entered the master suite. There were empty brown boxes, weathered nightstands and a king-sized bed with only one side disturbed by activity. The powder blue quilt and clashing blue linens appeared to be from the 1970s, as did the tarnished polka dot drapes.

Oddly, the closet doors were wide open. A collection of dated men's suits hung on the right side. A full compliment of women's gowns and neatly organized shoes were visible on the left. Johnny guessed that they once comprised Suzanne Greffen's wardrobe. *It's like someone's expecting her to return to find things exactly as they were*, he thought, the sadness of it striking him.

In the far corner, Johnny plugged in an old lamp with a surprisingly working bulb. A dusty picture frame lay atop a nearby six-drawer dresser, a photo tucked inside. Wiping off the filth with his sleeve, he immediately recognized a younger Howard on the left, minus the goatee and with a thicker head of hair. In the center, he figured, was a smiling redheaded Suzanne, just as Howard had described her in eloquent detail. But to her right appeared the cheerful face of an unfamiliar boy about seven or eight years old.

Upon closer inspection, two things were eminently clear. Firstly, this was a professional studio portrait – the kind families would sit for. The other was the eye-catching facial resemblance of the boy to Howard Greffen.

"Who's the kid? He never mentioned a child to me," Johnny murmured.

A long narrow hallway led Johnny to another neglected bedroom. This one was empty, save for a rocking chair, a disorderly bookcase and a folded playpen. Next, he checked a bathroom, two cluttered hall closets and finally a third bedroom at the end of the corridor.

A faint mildewy smell greeted Johnny's entrance. The light switch wasn't working, so he cleared a few collapsed cardboard boxes from the windowsill, until just enough light from outside streetlamps illuminated the floating specs of dust. Now, his suspicions were further piqued.

Posters of one-time New York Yankees pitcher Dave Righetti, and New York Giants Quarterback Phil Simms hung on the walls. Both were stars in the 1980s, corroborating his theory that this was hardly Howard's childhood room. Sitting on a dresser were two hockey pucks, a second-place

Little League trophy, and an autographed baseball with a Brooklyn Dodgers logo. Johnny lifted it from its display and read the inscription.

To Josh: Keep your eye on the ball. Best wishes, Duke Snider # 4.

Oh man! He really has a kid, or at least had one, he thought.

Johnny walked slowly and thoughtfully down the stairs, curious as to what – if anything – Frank had uncovered. He heard the guitarist fumbling in the basement. "Hey, any sign of life down there?"

"Nothing yet, Johnny. Just some really old furniture and piles of junk. Like a scene out of *Citizen Kane*. Hang on. Be up in a minute."

Johnny pondered the merits of divulging his discoveries as he reached the kitchen. But could Frank be trusted, given the sensitive nature of his findings? He determined it was best to say nothing at all.

An empty cereal box lay on the table next to a half-eaten bowl of soggy flakes and the pair of tea mugs from the last time he was there. Beside them, he uncovered a folder with random papers from a doctor's office. And to the left, a prescription bottle of pills labeled "Trazodone" next to three unused syringes.

Frank nonchalantly reentered the room. "That stale basement was a dead-end. I'm not sure where to look next, but —"

"Did it occur to you to check the kitchen table?" Johnny interrupted. "And if so, did you happen to notice these needles and meds lying around?" Frank shook his head. Johnny inspected the pages carefully. "Did Howard ever mention anything about being a diabetic?"

A confused look spread over Frank's face. "No. Never. But now that you mention it, there were a few times when he raced outside between sets at O'Callaghan's. Always thought he was heading out for a smoke… till I once saw him back there with a needle in his arm. Didn't ask questions; didn't wanna know. But till now it never occurred to me that he might be sick."

"Good evening, Doctor Aaronstein's office."

"Um, hi, I'm calling to inquire about one of your patients. His name's Howard Greffen."

"Greffen… let's see… Howard… Why? Who wants to know?"

"Well, could you tell me if he's seen the doctor recently? No one's heard from him in nearly a week and —"

"Sir, I'm sorry. This office can only release medical information to a spouse, or the next of kin," the evening receptionist explained.

Next of kin? Johnny thought fearfully. *Is Howard Dead?* "Can you at least tell me if he's been by in the past week?"

"Again, sir, we can't divulge sensitive information to a non-family member."

Johnny clenched his fist in frustration. Then he played his trump card. "Listen, my dad would want me to know if something happened to him. You gotta tell me where he is?"

For a moment, the line went silent. "And what'd you say your name is?"

"Uh… Josh. Josh Greffen. I'm his son."

"Josh… let's see… Josh… oh, right, my apologies. You should've identified yourself in the first place." The woman punched up Howard's computerized profile. "Well… says here your dad came in unscheduled last week, complaining of dizziness. Neglected his insulin for some time. Dangerously low blood sugar levels, possibly caused by antidepressant intake. Pulse rate was high; sweating profusely. He got to our office, then slipped into a diabetic coma. We rushed him to Methodist Hospital. That's where you'll find him now."

Johnny spotted an older woman lying in the near bed inside room 304. A black-and-white episode of the *Lone Ranger* blared at an earsplitting level. Moving past her, he caught a glimpse of Howard, apparently sleeping and turned on one side. A few tubes and monitors were connected to him.

Johnny sat watching Howard breathe peacefully on his own for close to an hour. Then his friend awoke.

It took Howard a minute to regain his bearings. He rubbed his eyes and blinked rapidly to improve his focus. Then he reached for his colorful glasses on the nightstand. "How the hell did ya find me here, kid?"

"Howard, you scared the living piss outta me! Never told me you were diabetic," Johnny whispered.

"Never told anyone 'bout a lot of things." Howard moved the hospital bed to a sitting position. "Anyway, just a scare. The happy pills they were giving me must've screwed up my diabetes. Probably be free from here in a day or two."

"Well, that's a relief," Johnny sighed. "When I heard the word *coma* I freaked. Thought you were a goner."

Howard laughed. "Well as you can see, I'm fine. Just need to start taking my shots; taking better care of myself." He smiled and reached for Johnny's hand. "Hey, thanks for tracking me down. At least I got one visitor up here. Nice to have somebody who cares."

Johnny was touched. He was also overcome by a sudden urge to quiz Howard about his bout with depression and his alleged family mystery – at least, until common sense prevailed. *Hardly the time to initiate that awkwardness.* And he didn't want Howard to know where he'd been snooping, even if well-intended.

Slowly, Howard leaned toward the bed rail, smiling. "So tell me, kid, how does it feel to be inked by a record label? Sorry I missed the big audition. I'm sure you rocked it on your own."

"Oh, you gotta be kidding me! You mean, you knew all along it was a sure thing? And here I kept worrying about when you were gonna show up. Only the suits never asked me to play anything. Obviously, you did some sales job."

"Actually, you did all the heavy lifting. It was your music that had Neswick sold. His label hasn't developed any half-decent singer-songwriters in eons. Maybe not since those Gibson boys did themselves in back in '87. Poor bastards."

"The Gibson Twins?" Johnny squinted back at Howard. "Oh, right. That acoustic duo from Boston. The ones who OD'd on tour. They were with Highpeak?"

"Sure were." Howard nodded in the affirmative. "I don't think Neswick and his cronies have ever gotten over that one; certainly haven't replaced their talent. I think your hard luck, good-guy image coupled with your songwriting skills is one reason they've been so quick to jump on you. Sometimes, it's just about timing."

"Timing and connections," Johnny countered. "If you hadn't known these people, there'd be nothing to talk about. But now, if you can believe it, I've got an album to record. So you'd better be on the mend, damn it, taking your meds properly, 'coz I doubt I can do it without you."

13

Harmonious Acceleration

Rehearsals resumed in Howard's den just four days later. While running through the new songs, Johnny and Howard worked up a tender, piano driven recording of *Jacqui*, written for Andy's still-distant girlfriend.

Johnny took the tape over to Andy's house, where he was met on the front stoop with a potpourri of information.

"Oh, hey, boss. I've got lot's to share, so listen up."

"Oh, right." Johnny rubbed his brow. "How'd the meeting with Highpeak go?"

"Well, the good news is: you'll get most of the album advance just as soon as you turn in the signed contracts. The bad news: you're hardly in a position to take on creative control of cover art, videos and the like. They'll be calling the shots, though that doesn't mean you won't have input. I was able to negotiate a measure of final approval."

"Final approval, eh? Well, thanks for getting that much out of 'em. Can't say I'm surprised. I guess for now I'll just have to let the music speak for itself."

Recording time for Johnny's debut album was originally estimated at ten weeks. The sessions were booked at the Blue Line Studios on Manhattan's Upper West Side. Johnny calculated that he could handle classes during the day and record in the evening, while completing coursework in transit.

Then came a cluster of lengthy weekday sessions. He was forced to take a series of incompletes, putting his degree on temporary hold. Weighing the big-picture of a music career versus the short-term academic disruption, he believed it was a gamble worth taking.

On day one in the studio, Johnny was awestruck by his surroundings. He ran excitedly back and forth between the control room and the recording booth, caressing knobs, levers, amplifiers and microphones.

At that point, Joe Rivera strutted in.

"So, Mr. Elias, first time inside a recording studio?"

Johnny froze in his tracks, one hand on a mixing board. "Oh, hi. Yeah, I've cut a few demos. Just never in a place like this."

"Well, lemme explain a few things off the bat so we're clear." Joe Rivera stood six feet tall, dressed in a navy-blue Armani suit. He ran a hand slowly across his graying, wind-blown hair, then held up his index finger and pointed it in Johnny's direction. "Rule number one: All this equipment you see here, it's worth a wee bit more than you'll probably earn in the next decade. So don't be touching anything unless you're told to do so."

Johnny nodded and put down a wireless headset. "Sorry. I can handle that."

"Rule number two: Yeah, you're the songwriter, but in my sessions your songs belong to me. If I want your opinion, I'll ask it. Are we clear?"

"Um, yeah. I'm cool with that. I just hope you're somewhat open to my input. It's your production, but my name that goes on the cover."

Joe loosened his tie and removed his suit jacket. "Finally, they tell me you've got thirteen songs to record. Neswick wants twelve on the album, plus one bonus track. So anything else you write going forward, save it for your sophomore effort... providing you get that far."

Joe Rivera held a reputation as an industry legend. He had first made a name for himself back in the late 70s, recording orchestras for Highpeak's classical division. Graduating to the 80s pop scene, he maintained an ear for classical elements. Joe knew exactly where to add the hint of a string arrangement, or a choral harmony. His presence brought instant credibility.

Johnny was flattered to be provided with a first-rate producer and a handful of talented studio musicians. Yet, the experience of working with a room full of strangers left him apprehensive at the outset.

"Hey, cut. What the hell was that?" Joe shouted from behind the console after take-one on the tile track. "Elias, we're making a record here! Get your hands out of your pockets, stop the posing, and turn your lungs inside out, damn it. Powerful material like this deserves your best performance."

It took a good week of on-the-job learning, but Johnny would slowly adapt. Further reassuring for him was occasionally having Howard around as a piano-playing security blanket. Along with Frank - who would show up, guitar in hand between spring classes for the majority of sessions - it was their familiar presence, which put Johnny at ease.

By the third week, Johnny worked up the courage to offer a few suggestions of his own. His first was to bring in a children's choir to sing backup on the final chorus of *Shadows Of The Same Color*. The combined sweetness of forty innocent voices echoing Johnny's anti-violence lyrics proved a potent affirmation to the song's prevailing sentiment.

"Nice touch, Elias!" Joe remarked after playback. "Makes it sound epic and righteous all at once. A little Pink Floydian."

Another of Johnny's requests was to multi-track his lead vocal on the wordless chorus of *Poet Of The Wrong Generation*. This echo effect – one he'd remembered from a Simon & Garfunkel song - paired with Howard's backing vocals resulted in a gorgeous four part harmony that cascaded across the audio landscape like a silvery star shower against a nighttime sky.

Johnny delighted in hearing his lyrics and melodies come to life so vividly. Raw piano demos became full-scale recordings with textured harmonies. He was blown away by how impressive they now played in stereo, with a slick arrangement and multi-layered vocals. Johnny placed his complete trust in Joe, who in turn rewarded him with a sonic tour de force.

Progressively, Joe's hard-line approach lessened, as the pair formed a collaborative, artistic bond.

"Hey, Elias, I've gotta confess, driving home each night to Jersey, I find myself humming your tunes. They've got a great lyrical quality about 'em. For a rookie, you've got a knack for crafting one helluva pop song and delivering it big time."

In April, nearing the album's completion, Johnny received an unexpected in-studio visitor. Moments after overdubbing a double-tracked harmony, he caught a glimpse of a tan suit and tie waiting outside the control room. Johnny put down his headphones and emerged from the soundproof booth. "Hey, I didn't know the corporate guys ever ventured over here."

"Actually, Johnny, I come with some excellent news." René Fontenot was smiling proudly beneath his moustache. He settled down on a red leather couch in the lobby area. "We absolutely love what we are hearing so far from your sessions. A whole lot of heart and catchiness, to be sure. We're thinking about moving up the release date from mid-September to late June."

"Late June! I know we're ahead of schedule, but that's just around the corner."

"Precisely," René answered, popping the tabs on his brief case. "We figure everything in cycles of promotion. If the album comes out in mid-July, we first want to get an advance single on the radio. Even while the record's finishing touches are being added, we can certainly have the first song out there, and in stores."

René reached into his black attaché case. He pulled out a square art board about the size of a 45-record slipcase and held it up for display. "Your thoughts?"

Johnny studied the piece as though it were a final exam. It was simple, yet compelling and inoffensive. A grainy sepia photograph showed a generic young man and woman walking in opposite directions down an otherwise empty city street. Beneath the photo appeared Johnny's name, and the title, *We've Already Said Goodbye.*

René leaned forward. "We've respected your wishes to keep you off the cover. And we've kept it pretty literal in the spirit of the lyrics."

Not considering any personal ramifications, Johnny pulled a pen from his pocket. "Sure, I'll sign off on this one. But I hope this isn't also the cover for my album."

"This is only for the single," René agreed. "Mr. Neswick's been so, how would you say... haunted by this tune that he picked it personally."

"And when did you say it'll be out, again?"

"I can't promise any airplay, of course, but radio will have it by the first week of June. That means we're also going to need your album title ASAP. Oh, and we do have a video to shoot. Though I imagine we'll be hiring actors, since you've curiously asked not to appear, per your contract."

"Very cool," Johnny nodded approvingly. "I'm not looking to be difficult. It's just, as a fan it's always been my philosophy to keep the art separated from the artist."

René placed the art board back in his case, then flashed a puzzled look. "And what exactly do you mean by that? Aren't you all one in the same; artists and their music?"

"No, not really." Johnny was tucking the pen back in his pocket. "It's like, take Bob Dylan. Greatest songwriter ever. But personally... well the guy's had his share of demons. Addictions. Affairs. Accidents. Things I wish I never knew about. I admire his records to no end. But to emulate his personal life; his values... no thanks, man. That's not what I'm about."

René nodded as if he understood. "So you'd rather people just enjoy the music without delving too deep into your character?"

"Yeah, that's part of it." Johnny glanced at his watch, then stood from the couch and looked back into the control room. "There's something to be said for keeping a level of dignity, or at least privacy, you know? A layer of separation."

René stood up and lifted his briefcase. "Hmmm. I suppose. I just hope you aren't saying this as a man with something to hide."

Johnny laughed aloud. "No, no. I don't mean me." He held up two fingers toward Joe Rivera, who was waiting for him at the mixing board with a stern face and arms folded. "All I'm trying to say is: I just think it's better for musicians to let their music do the talking and keep their private lives private. Or at least as much as possible. So thanks for understanding and for respecting my wishes on this. Honestly, you won't regret it."

14

Beautiful Nightmares

Katherine Price was a bundle of energy as she left the office for a big June weekend. She'd been waiting for this moment for as long as she could remember. In the back of the limousine, she pulled out her notes for the engagement party, checking off items that still required confirmation for Sunday's festivities.

Of course, the caterer was preselected, along with a florist and an elite string quartet. Katherine would have preferred to hold the party at a fancy hall or restaurant – as she had initially proposed. But due to Megan's wishes to keep it "meaningful," she was open to compromise.

Katherine had been compiling a guest list since long before word became official. Now she was both delighted and relieved in knowing her guests would soon be arriving to celebrate.

On that final night of the family's Hawaiian vacation, Megan had not provided Gerry with an answer. She did not put on the ring, nor did she accept his proposal. Instead, she sat stunned by the request for a few moments before excusing herself from the table. It had all happened too fast. She needed time to think things over.

Back in New York, she spent hours trying to reach Johnny by phone. She rationalized that if she knew for sure that he'd moved on with his life, she could perhaps accept Gerry's offer with a clearer conscience... or at least once she really got to know him. But if there was a way to somehow win back Johnny's affections – well, she thought that she might be prepared, finally, to risk her mother's tantrums.

After weeks of agonizing alone with her dilemma, Megan invited Vera Watson up to the apartment one afternoon while Katherine was at work. They sat in the living room, trying to dissect the matter objectively.

"Vera, this whole ordeal, it's total insanity. I mean, how can I commit to marrying a guy I don't love? Yeah, Gerry's been okay to me, but Johnny still means everything. And I know he needs me too. I'm just so confused; feeling so pressured by everyone."

"I hear you, Meg." Vera was reclining on Katherine's favorite sofa with her worn-out Reeboks up on the marble coffee table. "But you do *like* Gerry, right? Your Mom certainly does, which you know is huge. Plus, you guys've been hanging out constantly. And don't get me started on the whole attraction thing again."

Megan was chewing nervously on a stick of Trident, facing Vera from a matching upright recliner. "Yeah, I *like* Gerry... as a friend. I have since we were kids. And okay, so he's grown up to be pretty good looking, but—"

"But nothing, Meg. You saw what he looked like in a tux that night he came to pick you up at school. All of us were salivating. If he weren't a doctor, he could be a model, even a game show host. That boy's a hottie." Vera reached forward to the coffee table and snatched two chocolate truffles off a tray next to her feet.

Megan allowed the hint of a smile to permeate her troubled face. "Maybe so. But looks aren't everything, you know? And besides, I'm just as attracted to Johnny. But never mind that. It's my life we're talking about. My future. I'm in love with Johnny, not Gerry, or anyone else. I just don't know what's happened to him. He doesn't answer his phone; no machine. Just rings forever. Seems to have dropped out of school too. And he's never home anymore. Five times I've dropped by his place, only nobody's there. I just don't know what to do next."

Vera popped one of the chocolates into her mouth and did her best to chew it inconspicuously. "Mmmm, raspberry cream. These are deadly." She met Megan's eyes. "Well anyway, have you considered letting him go? I know how you feel about Johnny. But he's obviously not an option anymore. This just doesn't sound like a phase where he needs a little time. Megan, I think he's moved on. Maybe literally."

Megan's gaze dropped to the floor. She sighed. "It's just so not like him. No one knows Johnny like I do. He's not the kind of guy who can just let go. Must be something else going on."

"Well speaking of goings on, what's with Gerry's apartment hunting? Any luck yet?"

Megan looked up from the recliner to find Vera unwrapping another truffle. "Actually, I think I may have just found him something. It's on Central Park West between 81st and 82nd. A bit pricey for him at this stage; needs some major decorating. But the place has everything." Her eyes lit up. "A new kitchen, three big bedrooms, and this amazing terrace with an awesome view."

"Ohmigod!" Vera squealed. "Sounds so perfect for you guys. So, you gonna go for it?"

Megan's eyes grew wide with surprise. "Vera, it's for him, not for us. And yeah, Gerry's putting in a bid this week. Says he's got a way to come up with the money. A loan or something."

"Way cool! Your own little love-nest. So, you gonna help him play house?" She chuckled. "All he needs is for you to say yes already. Then you can get the hell out of this stuffy joint like you've been moaning about forever. Still don't know what you're waiting for?"

Megan shook her head. "Yeah, Mom's been mostly impossible since Dad died. Probably longer. I'll help Gerry decorate; get set up, whatever. But a love-nest? Minor issue: I'm not in love with the guy. And he's not nearly Mr. Perfect as you make him out to be."

Vera shot Megan a scolding look across the table. "Now hold on! You told me that Gerry's been growing on you. He's gorgeous. He's a doctor. He's buying a little palace for you guys across the park. Hello! What's not to love? A man like that sure as hell won't wait around forever."

"So I should just settle, even while the guy I love is still out there? Vera, you're sounding like my mom." Megan was growing agitated. "I'm sorry, but no, I… I won't do it."

"Then why not at least tell the guy yes for now and ask for a lengthy engagement, you know? This way, you'll have plenty of time to back out in case the sparks don't fly later… or in the event that your wounded white knight comes back from being M.I.A."

Megan sighed. "Ah, who the hell knows? Maybe you're onto something. Maybe your way'll buy me some time to get things sorted out. Now pass me one of those truffles, will you? I could use a chocolate fix too."

The day of her party, Megan emerged from her room in a sparkling black sequined gown, high-heeled shoes and a stunning pearl necklace. She looked radiant – aside from a persistent runny nose – as she greeted the early-arriving guests. Gradually, the apartment filled with names and faces, most of whom she didn't recognize. And even with air conditioning on full-blast, the swarm of bodies caused a layer of internal humidity.

Rather than making the rounds with Gerry at her side, Megan gravitated to the kitchen. She stood sweating in the doorway, conversing with the wait staff. Occasionally, she pilfered a warm hors d' oeuvre or a glass of sparkling champagne from the silver trays as they went by.

"Hey, ain't this supposed to be your bash?" a tuxedoed waiter asked her on the way out."

"Something like that," Megan muttered from behind a cocktail napkin. "At least that's what I'm told."

Megan eventually resurfaced to hold court in the far corner of the living room when Vera arrived with her mother. Gerry, meanwhile, stuck close to Katherine. He paraded around the noisy apartment, embracing his future mother-in-law's closest associates.

At one point, the fêted couple did meet up in the claustrophobic dining room. Megan smiled politely and accepted gifts, trying her best to overlook Gerry's suddenly voracious appetite. As he stood munching on canapés, Megan wiped lipstick off her face after every pretentious double-kiss. This lengthy meet-and-greet session continued, until the fashionably late arrival of Gerry's parents.

"Ah, there's our fairytale princess!" Myrna Ridgewell cried, stepping off the elevator.

Megan extended her arms to embrace her future mother-in-law. "At last, someone I know." She smiled proudly. "So good to see you." But as Megan's hands came together, all color drained from her face. *The ring. How could've I forgotten?* Inevitably, someone would notice the absence of the most crucial component of her attire. She politely excused herself and maneuvered past the harp player into her air-conditioned sanctuary.

Megan checked herself in the mirror. First, she fixed her eye shadow and streaking mascara. Her engagement ring stared at her from atop her dresser. She slipped it on, feeling the weight of her obligation. There were at least a hundred guests crammed into the apartment. Megan figured no one would notice if her brief respite was to be extended just a few minutes longer. To drown out the noise, she switched on her nightstand radio. The familiar voice of Casey Kasem, conducting his weekly Sunday countdown was instantly recognizable.

Falling four notches this week to thirty-six, that was Eddie Money with, I'll Get By. Next: a newcomer to the Top-Forty. Hailing from Brooklyn, New York, this is the first single for Johnny Elias. Making his chart debut this week at number thirty-five, here's his heartfelt ballad: We've Already Said Goodbye.

Megan at first believed it to be someone's cruel joke. A lump of panic arose in her throat. Her trembling hands checked the cassette tray to verify if this was a prank recording. It was not. Her knees began to buckle. She collapsed across her four-poster bed. This very personal song, which had once served notice to the end of her fairytale, now generically belonged to the masses.

"How can it be? This can't be happening," she sobbed repeatedly as the song played on. The noise outside her room left her cries unheard as guests continued to file in, celebrating what should have been one of the her proudest days.

Johnny judiciously invested every dollar from his album advance on necessary expenditures. He established a music publishing company that he optimistically named *New Heights Music.* He also hired a recommended accounting firm and a part-time, independent PR rep, Jerry Goodman. The latter was deemed necessary due to Johnny's lack of confidence in Heidi Ellison and Highpeak's publicity staff.

After legal fees, some needed clothes and a new record collection for Carolyn Green – to replace the one he had generously "borrowed" from - Johnny still retained a fair sum for his own interests. At Andy's behest, he agreed that placing a down payment on real estate was likely to be his most practical investment.

"Johnny, you're mostly in the city these days making this record. Time to set your sights on upgrading this glorified Brooklyn closet for something more spacious; more conveniently located."

"Yeah, I figured I'd probably have to move. It's just… I've been here in Brooklyn my whole life. Kinda have mixed feelings about leaving it behind. And the city always seemed like a better place to visit than to live, I think."

The East Side was hardly an option; no desire to reside in a neighbor-hood where he might cross paths with Katherine Price and her family. Instead, he plunked down a deposit on a two-bedroom co-op in a pre-war building on Central Park West and 91st Street. Johnny was pleased to have a third optional bedroom/den, which he'd convert into a makeshift office. And he adored the limited view of Central Park from his fourth floor liv-ing room.

The recording sessions wrapped up two weeks earlier than estimated. This provided Johnny some rare downtime to rest his tired voice and pre-pare for the awaiting storm of promotion. It was one night during this period, while listening to the finished product with friends, that he was convinced of his forthcoming album title.

"I'd go with *Poet of the Wrong Generation*," Howard remarked candidly between sips of tea. "Yeah, that's a great song; brilliant harmonies. But as a title it also gives you a bold identity."

"I second that emotion," Andy cut in. "So many great albums get named after killer cuts. Supertramp's *Breakfast In America*. *The Stranger* by Billy Joel. Lennon's *Imagine*. All provocative, yet they happen to correspond with key songs."

Johnny presented his title concept to René Fontenot at Highpeak's offices. He was pleased to learn that René too was leaning in the same direction.

"I just like the symbolism of it," René agreed, twiddling with his waxed moustache. "For me, it conjures up the image of a talented orator, preaching to the wrong crowd; a genuine artist, among pretenders. We'll have cover sketches in a couple of days. Then it's on to production."

15

DON'T LOOK BACK

It had been an emotionally draining six months for Jacqui Spencer. The sudden death of her father in Sheffield had put everything into perspective.

Jacqui had issued her declaration of independence from parental guidance when she was just seventeen. The subsequent years found her coping with academic uncertainty and a string of misguided relationships. Then, along came Andy Raymer. Her chance encounter that summer's day with Andy was the furthest thing from her mind. In fact, upon her enrollment at the *Fashion Institute of Technology*, she had sworn off men and other distractions in favor of finding a career in graphic design. *All the more reason*, Jacqui thought, that their meeting was *an event of destiny*.

In Andy, Jacqui discovered a role model when it came to schoolwork dedication. She closely observed his flawless example, applying herself with renewed commitment. Together they made a superb pairing – completing one another like the answer to a riddle long misunderstood.

But when she got the call that shocking afternoon, everything around her was suddenly dwarfed by the seriousness of this imminent situation. There was no time for contingency plans.

The guilt Jacqui felt in not reaching her father in time was torturous.

The man who had raised her from infancy to adolescence was suddenly gone. And she never even got the chance to say thank you, or goodbye.

Jacqui grew accustomed to the awkward task of sleeping on her father's side of the bed, until her mother could finally make it through to morning without sobbing. She often wished that Andy had flown over during this difficult period. Publicly, she communicated it would be best for him to stay in New York. Any interruption of his studies would only prove detrimental in the long run, she figured.

By the fifth month, Jacqui was equally inclined to shelve transatlantic aspirations. Her extended stay felt nostalgically therapeutic. No matter how she adored Andy, and the notion of forging a career in design, the lures of a simpler life in Sheffield grew more appealing… until one late spring day when the overseas parcel arrived in her letterbox.

Johnny led Andy on a grand tour of his new space. Just days away from the release of his anticipated first single, the host was unmistakably walking on air. The jovial pair strolled through the empty living room. A loud buzzer sounded, prompting Johnny to locate the intercom. "Must be my first delivery," he guessed, buzzing in the movers.

"Johnny, you haven't even painted yet. What could you possibly have coming up here?"

"Only the centerpiece of my evolution," he said, grinning proudly.

A four-man crew carefully wheeled in the shiny black mahogany sections off the service elevator. Johnny and Andy stood by watching as it was meticulously assembled.

"So what do you think of my new baby grand?" Johnny beamed. "Never thought I'd be able to afford one of these… let alone to play one."

Andy ran a hand across the glossy Steinway logo. "Sure is a beaut. I guess as investments go, this is something you were gonna need. But doesn't it come with something to sit on?"

"It's on the truck," one of the deliverymen explained. "I'll get it when I catch my breath."

Johnny tipped each of the men, then anxiously returned to press the ivory keys for the first time. But before he could get comfortable, the buzzer again went off. *Must be the guy with my bench.* He hurried to the front of the apartment, leaving Andy behind to marvel. When he opened the front door, he stood astounded to see Jacqui Spencer on the other side.

"Hope I'm not disrupting anything," she whispered in the doorway. "You gonna invite me in?"

"When did you get into town? And… and how'd you manage to find us here?" Johnny asked, as if he'd just seen a ghost.

"Just my decorator's intuition." Jacqui stepped inside the empty foyer. A warm embrace followed. "Someone told me you could use a bit of help sprucing up the new digs. Figured I owed you a favor after that lovely song."

Johnny looked over his shoulder to see if Andy had followed. He had not. The surprise remained intact. "Does Andy know? He didn't mention anything about you coming back."

"He hasn't a clue. But his dad told me I could probably find you guys here. Now lead me to your so-called songwriting partner."

Before Johnny could turn around, his friend rushed by him, taking the most direct route to a precious reunion. Andy gathered Jacqui in his arms and twirled her around like a rag doll. Lovingly, he kissed her for several minutes, before finally taking a breath. "You back, or just visiting?" He gently returned her feet to the floor.

"I'm here to stay." She pushed a strand of hair from his face and kissed his forehead. "After those photos and hearing that song, I have all the evidence I need. So let's not ever be apart for another wretched day, you hear?"

Johnny stood, hands-on-hips, admiring the touching scene. "All right you lovebirds, any more gooeyness and you're gonna drool on the carpets I haven't yet installed."

Soon they were back in the living room. Johnny took Jacqui by the hand, proudly showing off his new piano. "Andy's been really careful about where I spend every nickel. But after all, what's a musician without his instrument?"

"It's gorgeous," she agreed, sitting down on the unpolished hardwood floor. "Hey, long as we're here, I'd love for the collaborators to perform the song you wrote for me."

Johnny sat at the bench and played the opening notes, then motioned toward his cohort. Andy butchered the first verse in an embarrassing falsetto. At least he got the words right. When his laughter died down, Johnny joined in for the balance, making it a reasonable duet.

Jacqui stood applauding upon completion. "My apologies for not getting choked up. All those months away… I'm kinda cried out. Even if it weren't for me, it's really lovely. And you, Mr. Johnny Elias, are a star in the making."

Johnny blushed. "Thanks. Glad you like it. I really only wrote it to help put things right with you guys. But long as I've got you here, I could really use a favor in return."

Jacqui nodded her complete approval, then stood up from the shiny floor.

Johnny marched his friends into the bare kitchen, pulled a blank piece of paper from one of the drawers, then placed it on the counter. "So Jacqui, I've got this concept in my head, but absolutely no ability to draw it out. Maybe if I describe it you could draft something rough?"

Jacqui headed to the apartment entrance. She hurried back seconds later with a canvas travel bag slung over her left shoulder, and a set of color sketching pencils in her hands. "Us FIT girls always come prepared for any emergency," she said, winking.

Just over an hour later, the three of them were taken aback by how skillfully the design had evolved. Jacqui sketched the figure of a loner sitting beneath a flowering oak tree by the bank of a flowing stream. In his hands, one could see the solitary figure writing in a notebook that rested on his lap. On the other side of the narrow water, she drew a neglected cemetery, complete with broken headstones and tall weeds growing haphazardly. The graveyard on the right was sketched in black on white, with shades of gray. The left side, including the loner beneath the tree, was drawn in vibrant colors. This dreamlike rendition roughly resembled the style of nineteenth-century painter, Sir John Everett Millais and his famous rendering of Shakespeare's Ophelia. Only Jacqui's attempt paid closer attention to intricate detail of the subject and his surroundings. And at the bottom right hand corner, she hid her initials in the deep grass.

Much later, the record company had its say. "I'm almost ashamed to say it, but this kicks the sod out of what our team came up with," Ron Neswick said, holding the page up to the light. "After seeing this, I won't even bother showing you what I've got in the folder."

Johnny was surprised by his reaction. "So you'll use this as a guideline or something?"

"Aside from some color adjustments, we just need to drop-in the typeface for your name and the album title. I think what you've brought in is a keeper."

Ron extinguished a half-smoked cigar in his ashtray. Satisfied to have the cover resolved, he outlined the forthcoming schedule. "I know René already told you about our choice for the single. Discs should be in-house by next week. I also know you've got your own outside PR guy. We'll try to accommodate him. But it's paramount that you make yourself available for every opportunity. Day. Night. Weekend. Whatever. Ya hear?"

Johnny nodded. Ron continued.

"We've got a small fortune invested in your music, Mr. Elias. So take nothing for granted and fasten your seatbelt. Should be one helluva ride."

The first time Johnny heard *We've Already Said Goodbye* on the radio, he was sitting in the driver's seat of a U-haul van between Brooklyn and Manhattan. He had enlisted the aid of Andy and Jacqui to help pack up his limited belongings and come along for the ride.

Andy fiddled with the reception while crossing the Brooklyn Bridge. He managed to lock in a top-40 station, just as the last verse was being played.

"Ohmigod, that's you!" Jacqui blurted out in total amazement. "Someone's playing your song! And it sounds bloody fantastic."

"Turn it up," Johnny ordered. A euphoric sense of pride erupted in his chest. Pure, instant gratification! All the effort and agony behind his album, behind his entire life to date was starting to pay dividends. He began to sing along with his own voice. But just as excitement sunk in, he broke into a cold sweat.

Megan! How will she feel, hearing it over the airwaves? What if the song picks up momentum; starts getting regular airplay? I mean, I should only be so lucky, but... It was never his intention to torture Megan by releasing this track as the lead single. In fact, the selection wasn't his choice at all. *Maybe she at least deserves a heads-up. Would be kinda nice to hear her voice.*

Switching lanes, his thoughts next veered to Katherine Price. *And to think she warned Megan that I'd never be good enough to become a part of her family? All her foolish naysaying prophesies...* Suddenly, here was his song playing on the radio for all of New York to hear – validation that he was anything but underachieving.

And yet, as this grin of satisfaction enveloped his face, a soberingly ironic notion arose. If it hadn't been for Katherine's scheming, almost certainly there'd never have been *We've Already Said Goodbye*, or perhaps any of the stirring compositions on his soon-to-be-released collection. *How remarkably different things might have turned out.* But now Brooklyn was fading in the rearview mirror. Johnny knew well that turning back was not an option.

16

Opening Impressions

Jerry Goodman's PR office held a look of organized chaos. This Brooklyn "boutique" agency consisted of five busy cubicles, a small conference table, and stacks of newspapers and magazines piled everywhere. While Jerry's account reps worked the phones, calling all of the area's FM stations to place requests for *We've Already Said Goodbye*, Johnny and Andy strategized with Jerry at the cluttered conference table.

"It's an interesting challenge, gentlemen," Jerry said while loosening a colorful Green Lantern superhero necktie over a Levi's denim shirt. "How do we get the masses to request a song on the radio when they don't yet know it exists?"

"Yet," Andy repeated for emphasis, then flashed a confident smile. "But they will, soon enough." He spun around and pointed to a nearby fax machine. "Your team can also fax requests to the stations, not just make calls. It might be more impactful seeing the song title on paper."

"Long as we don't overdo it. Too many from the same sender will set off red flags with station managers." Jerry reached for a can of Coke from a nearby mini-fridge, popped open the tab, then offered one each to Andy and Johnny.

"Oh, no thanks." Johnny shook his head side-to-side. "Too early in the morning for soda."

"Never too early for caffeine." Jerry laughed, took a swig from the can, then stared down at the list he had prepared on his notepad. "Look, I can create some exposure for Johnny. I know people at ballparks, hockey arenas, county fairs. I can book him as the anthem singer in a bunch of places. They'll announce his name over the PA system."

"Okay, maybe." Andy shrugged then looked over at Johnny who appeared unmoved. He turned back to Jerry. "Look, any exposure is good. We'll take it. But there's got to be a creative way to get the radio folks to play the single."

"We can certainly set up some local CD signings when the disc comes out." Jerry pointed in Johnny's direction and smiled. "I know the gal who does bookings for Tower Records. That's a pretty big opportunity."

"Yeah, it's probably worthwhile, but also somewhat predictable." Andy paused in mid-thought as the office receptionist loudly paged one of Jerry's staffers over the intercom. "Plus, it's not like too many people are gonna line up for autographs if they don't know who Johnny is. I was looking for something maybe a bit more creative."

"For whatever it's worth," Johnny leaned forward and raised his voice above a symphony of ringing phones, "I got an idea. Might be a little out there; could cost a few bucks, but…" His voice trailed off.

Jerry put down his can of Coke, then picked up a pen and flipped over to a fresh page on his notepad. "Great. Lay it on me, brother."

"Just remember the budget we talked about." Andy shot a look of caution in Johnny's direction. "No sky-writing planes, or Times Square billboards."

"No, it's nothing insane. I was just thinking… so some of the best memories I have of discovering new music are those days when someone would bring a tape player to the beach and blast out an album. Good or bad, the music was unavoidable."

Jerry Goodman scribbled down a few words on the blank page. "So you want to pick up a couple of boom boxes and play your song around town?"

"Yeah, that's the idea. Only I was thinking of getting maybe a couple dozen of 'em; get some volunteers to go round playing them in parks, subway stations, on the Staten Island Ferry, the Coney Island boardwalk, whatever. Just play the song everywhere until people start to recognize it. Let everyone think it's popular... until it actually is."

Andy was rocking back and forth in his chair, a smile spreading across his face. "Now there's one we hadn't talked about before. So we subtly ingrain the tune into public consciousness. Might actually work, given how catchy your song is. And the cost probably isn't horrible. We'd just need to loop the song on a tape, then hire people to go round playing it."

"Well, that's where I could really deliver," Jerry chimed in, his eyebrows raised in excitement. "My brother, Richie is head of his fraternity at LaGuardia. You know, the community college. Give those guys some beer money and we can have this whole city humming along!"

Within days, three stations in the metropolitan area had placed the song in semi-regular rotation. And with repeated airplay, artificial requests turned into real ones. For the first full week in release, *We've Already Said Goodbye* registered on the national singles chart at a respectable # 76. Extended airplay spurred on a few well-placed New York newspaper articles about the hometown foster-child making good. Momentum was building.

Johnny hit the road to sing the national anthem at major and minor league baseball stadiums in Philadelphia, Baltimore, Albany and Trenton. Then came an assortment of street fairs and morning drive radio shows during which he got to perform the single.

Underscored by a significant jump in airplay, the song climbed to # 44 in week two, just outside the coveted Top-40. To keep the arrow pointing up, Johnny performed mini-concerts on local college campuses accompanied by Howard on piano. Andy, meanwhile, instructed his handpicked PR team to blitz VH-1 for national video exposure. Johnny's blatant absence in the promotional clip only seemed to add intrigue for those of a curious mind.

Perhaps the biggest break came when Cara Skyler, a popular light-music DJ, offered a glowing on-air commentary of the ballad. "*Makes me cry every time I hear that one. That was We've Already Said Goodbye by newcomer Johnny Elias. Like Neil Diamond and Barbra Streisand, he's one of ours, a Brooklyn kid, and obviously one to keep your eye on.*"

By the third week of release, the single had snuck into the national Top-40 at number 35. "That's Casey's territory," Andy reminded, after taking the call from René Fontenot. "Just keep your feet on the ground and keep reaching for the stars," he playfully imitated the popular radio countdown host. "Not too shabby for your first record!"

We've Already Said Goodbye peaked at # 18 a couple of weeks later, then slowly began to slip backward, causing Johnny to wonder privately if the air had left the balloon. But in reality, a stronger debut couldn't have been expected from even the most optimistic believers. It proved a stunning prologue to a dazzling new album, set for rush-release that very week.

Even as the first single was cooling down, things were only beginning to heat up in the Highpeak war-room. The highly respectable showing was more than casually noted by executives on both coasts. In fact, during a sluggish period for the venerable label, this chart debut was one of the most commercially impressive by any of their artists, new or old.

Ron Neswick - anticipating strong critical review - ordered an extra four hundred promotional copies for media distribution. Next, he summoned his top honchos for a crucial strategy meeting to ensure that this "can't-miss" album wouldn't miss its mark.

"On today's docket, a few items concerning the Elias record. To start with, we've gotta get him in front of the record-buying public to spawn maximum exposure."

"Anyone got an idea as to what kind of a live act he is?" René Fontenot cut in. "From what I recall, I don't think he's exactly road-tested."

"Well then let's get him some experience," Ron replied, lighting up a cigar. "A safe bet is to book him as an opener for a summer headliner. If he sucks, no one'll really care. And if he rocks, he'll make a few fans every night."

"I'm on it," Jessica Frazier volunteered. "I'll call Cantor Productions this afternoon."

"The second issue isn't so much a question of whether to release another single from the album, but rather which one to choose. Any suggestions?"

"I say we continue to build his identity with a second power ballad. I'm thinking along the lines of *Jacqui*, or the title track," René offered.

Ed McCauley ran his fingers through silvery hair. "René, we're talking a follow-up single. A harder-edged track is more likely to reach another potential segment of listeners. That Crown Heights track is pretty edgy?"

Ron snuffed out his cigar in a guitar-shaped ashtray. "How 'bout a compromise? Given his mainstream potential, why not prepare two different singles and release 'em to varied radio formats?"

"An expensive solution," Ed McCauley said, wincing. "We're talking production of two videos, not to mention packaging for both songs."

"Yeah, but given how surprisingly well the first one's done – and the fact that his album advance was a bargain – I wouldn't hesitate." René nodded. "Let's call it a worthwhile gamble."

Ron pulled a folder from the pile in front of him. "Lastly on Elias, I've got here a request from a Meteor Productions in Hollywood. They're looking for a closing credits song to use in some romantic comedy. What's that jazzy, playful one he has about the bickering couple?"

René flashed a knowing smile. "*More Than Friends, Less Than Lovers*. I think we have consensus likeability for that one."

Ed MacCaully leaned back in his chair. "That's fine with me, assuming there's a soundtrack to generate another royalty stream. I hate giving anything away for free."

"Ed, if nothing else, it's free advertising." Ron signed the top paper inside his folder. "Now let's keep our fingers crossed that America still has an appetite for a folky throwback. I have a good feeling about this one."

One could hardly blame Katherine Price for failing to notice Johnny Elias's modest pop-chart success. Katherine was highly savvy when it came to keeping up with cultural trends. But between early preparation for Mayor Dinkins' '93 reelection campaign, and a massive celebration for twelve hundred of her nearest and dearest, it was easy to see how a modest chart hit by Megan's former flame had eluded her radar screen.

Fourteen-hour workdays were followed by coming home to sort through potential guest lists, dressmakers and videographers. Katherine barely managed to get it all done. Yet amid the chaos, it was not lost on her that Megan had hardly been herself since the engagement party. *Probably typical pre-wedding jitters*, Katherine guessed, *or maybe not*. Either way, she was perfectly content to ask no questions and let it all pass.

For Megan, there were moments when she felt as though she were being offered up as a mail-order bride for her mother's amusement. She was still not in love with Gerry, nor the idea of a publicity stunt wedding for another roomful of strangers. It was bad enough that her one true love had been unreachable all these desperate months. Now, as she endeavored to move on, the constant reminders were inescapable... especially the song of her ultimate grief, playing regularly on the radio.

Megan did feel genuine happiness in knowing that Johnny had finally caught his lucky break. She had always believed in his talent, never wavering in her opinion. If only somehow Katherine could see how far he'd evolved. Perhaps, this could pave the way for them to live happily ever after as it was supposed to be. Of course, this was assuming Johnny would return to her life, and take her back – something Megan knew was probably a long shot.

One evening, while moving some of her clothing into Gerry's new West Side digs, Megan found herself alone, and in need of reassurance. She dialed Johnny's Brooklyn apartment from the kitchen telephone.

A computerized message stated that his number was no longer in service. No further information was available. Megan slumped in her chair.

After trying directory assistance and again coming away empty-handed, Megan took a ride out to Brooklyn, in a final, last-ditch effort. *Maybe with his newfound popularity he changed to an unlisted number?* she wondered, sitting alone in the back of a taxi.

In the building vestibule, Johnny's name was missing from the intercom directory. A woman was coming out; Megan grabbed the door behind her and slipped into the lobby. She ran up to Johnny's floor, not waiting for the elevator, her feet pounding the stairs. Breathing hard, she hammered on Johnny's door. "Johnny, please let me in."

After an eternity, it opened on its chain. An elderly Chinese woman peered out. "Nobody here but me," she said, nodding. "Nobody but me."

On the ride home, Megan cried.

As the summer of '92 heated up, Johnny's life was becoming a whirlwind of activity. Six-hour daily rehearsals and heavy media training left him no time, or desire to instigate any semblance of a social life. With his heart still on the mend, he knew it was probably for the best.

Johnny polished his stage routine with Howard and Frank, drummer Ian Klatt, and Art Tillman, a bassist recruited through Highpeak. Out of familiarity, he booked *The Lion's Gate* during daytime hours as their rehearsal base – the basement club in Greenwich Village where he first sung for an audience. Frank had recently graduated from Brooklyn Post. Howard was off for the summer. The quintet were all delighted to find a steady paying gig; a six-week amphitheater tour as the opening act for the classic rock-band, REO Speedwagon.

Meanwhile, Ron Neswick's decision to send out extra advance album copies began paying immediate dividends. In the days leading up to the release date, Johnny was suddenly inundated with interview requests. Despite his rookie status, the demand for his time mirrored that of some the industry's established veterans.

Andy had been officially hired for the summer to oversee Johnny's business affairs. Out of loyalty, he passed on a prime internship at Merrill Lynch to instead work full-time out of Johnny's home office. Juggling a schedule that ranged from chaotic to turbulent, he managed to squeeze every booking into two solid weeks leading up to Johnny's departure for the concert tour. And even then, the requests kept on coming.

Poet of the Wrong Generation was officially released in the US on Tuesday, July 14th. It was met almost immediately with across-the-board acclaim – save for the usual handful of cynics. Out west, the LA Times raved, *"About as sincere and vulnerable as songwriting gets. Such mature lyricism and storytelling is virtually nonexistent in today's musical landscape."*

In San Francisco, one reviewer called it, *"A sure contender for best new artist of the year, if not best album as well. From the inventive cover to the evocative lyrics, this new classic exemplifies what musical craftsmanship can aspire to be."*

And in Chicago, a music editor simply offered, *"In an era when pop music could use a jolt of heightened literacy and dimension, young Mr. Elias is Johnny-on-the-spot."*

Back home, three of the four daily papers ran four-star reviews, calling the album, *"timely," "fresh"* and *"astoundingly mature."* Appraising his heartfelt ballads, the NY Post dubbed Johnny a *"master of melancholy."* Only the Daily News questioned the album's tone, referring to some of the music as, *"sappy, yet occasionally uplifting."*

Of particular interest out east was the Crown Heights-inspired anthem, *Shadows of the Same Color.* Reviewers picked up on the not-so-subtle meaning behind the song as a catalyst to stir up controversy. This attention garnered significant airplay, which led to brisk early sales.

Poet of the Wrong Generation impressively entered the Hot-200 album chart at number 42. For an artist with no prior following, it was clear the public was paying attention.

The first two weeks on tour proved a good learning experience for Johnny and the band. Like most unknown opening acts, the guys couldn't tell if it was their playing, or a lack of audience expectations, that brought about only halfhearted applause. Howard believed that the performances were actually reasonable; so he proceeded to break each one down in an intricate analysis.

"You just never know from night to night who's gonna show up. Arenas are really no different from small-time pubs. Some of 'em wanna be entertained. Others come to get drunk while we provide the soundtrack. If we can just detach ourselves from the surroundings; make every song meaningful, it'll all fall into place."

Johnny's initial shy reaction to the applause for his music gradually dissipated. Only without an instrument to play, he found his greatest challenge to be what to do with his hands while singing. Clutching a wireless microphone and gesturing to the crowd were two frequent options. Sometimes he felt more like an awkward cheerleader than a serious performer.

Initial indifference gave way to solid recognition for *We've Already Said Goodbye*. Johnny found an emotional connection with audiences through their warm response to his heartbreaking ballad. Each night, he targeted a random audience member and sang the words in his/her direction to portray sincerity. In Baton Rouge, he reached into the front row and pulled a curvaceous redhead onstage to sing a few lines from his modest radio hit. The predictably enthusiastic response prompted him to repeat this practice in Mobile, Charleston and Jacksonville.

By week three, Johnny's opening sets received bigger crowds and surprisingly sustained ovations. In Tallahassee, he handed his sunglasses to a wheelchair bound woman in the third row. In Orlando, the band was called out for an encore. Four NASA astronauts in attendance from nearby Cape Canaveral came onstage to sing the chorus on *Vapor Trail Of Tears*. Every night was another step forward.

"Like a soaring butterfly emerging from its cocoon," Howard assessed Johnny's evolution.

But the budding musical chemistry was abruptly interrupted one night following a show in Tampa, Florida, when Ron Neswick urgently summoned the band back to New York.

17

It Had To Be You

Megan Ridgewell stepped out of a steaming shower, grabbed a plush terry-cloth bathrobe and headed into her newly furnished bedroom. After the wedding event of the season and a four-day honeymoon on the island of Nevis, she and Gerry had just spent their first night back in New York. Finally, a moment to regroup.

The festivities at the *Plaza* Hotel were clearly something to behold. Megan and Gerry were married on Saturday August 15th, 1992 in front of more than a thousand guests. Their wedding had all the hallmarks people had come to expect from a Katherine Price event. From celebrities to spectacle, Katherine spared no expense to make this a day she'd never forget. Now Megan sat by her bedroom window, staring out at Central Park in silent reflection.

"Meg, quit staring outside already. This ain't the movies. He's not coming to rescue you."

Megan turned around quickly to find Vera Watson – her maid of honor – entering the bridal suite. Megan's face was flush with embarrassment. "I just don't know how I'm gonna go through with this. Can't believe we're actually here already."

"Well we are, so deal with it," Vera replied, while checking her fiery red lip-gloss in the mirror. "And it's going to be amazing. Have you seen who's out there?"

"Gee, lemme guess." Megan leaned forward to adjust her cumbersome headpiece. "Politicians. Celebrities. My Mom's big-name clients. As if any of 'em matter to me."

"Oh, c'mon. Lighten up, Meg. I just ran into Donald Trump on my way up here. Man, is he tall in real-life! Jackie Mason was yakking it up with Tony Bennett down at the cocktail reception. Oh, and your dress designer was in heavy conversation with that divorce lawyer, Raul Felder. Guess her marriage ain't doing too well."

"You mean Michelle LaRux," Megan clarified. "Yeah, she did some job on my gown. Damn thing's so stiff, I'm hoping I can sneak out of it and let it walk down the aisle without me. Like anyone'll notice!"

Vera laughed. "Well I know someone who will. There's a bunch of photographers from the *New York Times* Magazine waiting down by the elevators to snap your picture. How cool is that?"

"It's ridiculous, Vera. Gerry's folks already hired a photographer. The rest is overkill. How many shots do we really need? This is just my mother's idea of free publicity. Another way to show off how wonderful she is."

"Oh, Meg. This isn't just about her. You look totally gorgeous. Your hair; your gown… to die for. Gerry too. Oh and do you know about the horse drawn carriage out on Central Park South to whisk you guys away later? Girl, I'd trade places with you in a heartbeat if I could."

Wouldn't that be nice, Megan thought to herself. *Maybe Vera and I should swap places. Lord knows she's infatuated with Gerry. And if somehow I could get out of this…*

There was a knock on the door. "Ms. Price, you almost ready?" It was the party planner. "Time for pre-ceremony pictures. And then it's showtime."

Megan sat silently, staring down at her lacy shoes. Vera jumped up to open the door.

"Yeah, we'll be right down. Just give us a few more minutes." Then turning to Megan she prodded, "Hey Cinderella, almost time for your fairytale happily-ever-after."

"Whose fairytale? Not mine for sure." Megan's hands were becoming jittery. Her heart fluttered like a captured bird. "If only I could sneak outta here, I'd be on the next flight out to wherever Johnny is playing, recording, whatever. Somehow, someway, he'd take me back. I know he would. Then again, I'm sure if I did, Mom would hunt us down and have us both executed on national TV."

Vera laughed until she saw the tears starting to drip down on Megan's face. "Oh, no, don't cry now." She patted Megan's back. You'll ruin your make-up." She reached for some tissues and dabbed at Megan's cheeks. "Sweetie, do you know how lucky you are? I mean, how many brides can say they got to marry a prince like Gerry in a palace like this? Ya know, I even heard your mother asking Mayor Dinkins if he'd walk you down the aisle; give you away."

"She did?" Megan sat abruptly upright. "No chance in hell! I'm not doing it. Don't even know the man."

"Oh, don't worry." Vera was perfectly calm. "Dinkins was really nice about it, but he took a pass. So it'll just be you and your—"

"Megan Price, they're waiting for us, damn it!" The door had flown open and Katherine entered, furious. "No time for senseless chit-chat. We've got pictures and a ceremony to get to." She reached for Megan's hands and pulled her up from her white wicker chair to her feet. "If we keep things moving on schedule, Tony Bennett promised to serenade you guys with a song for your first dance. Otherwise, he's got a flight to catch for Vegas. Now come on already, let's go."

I'm so doomed! Megan thought as she was being led to the elevator. *Like I've ever stood a chance against her at anything. Not now. Not ever.*

Now back in the city, Megan's tranquil morning was unceremoniously interrupted with the ringing of her apartment door buzzer. "Gerry, can you please get that?" she shouted from the bedroom, fastening the belt at the front of her bathrobe.

"I'm busy with my stuff. Can you?" he yelled back from another part of the large apartment.

"I'm not dressed!" she called out. The buzzer rang unanswered twice more. Megan stepped into a pair of slippers and stomped to the front door. Through the peephole, she saw a man in a bellhop's uniform, a hand-truck of gift-wrapped boxes behind him. "Come in," she said, gesturing, her eyes widening as two more carts and two uniformed attendants followed behind him.

"Gerry, the presents are here from the *Plaza*."

"Hey, I'll catch up," Gerry shouted from the kitchen through a mouthful of food.

Megan directed the men to the living room, then gestured for them to stack the endless boxes against the wall on either side of the fireplace. After helping pile up nearly three hundred packages, Megan hurriedly headed off to her bedroom. She returned with a wad of cash, handing each a fifty-dollar bill.

Gerry emerged from the kitchen once the bellhops departed. There was a hint of jam on the corners of his mouth. Telltale crumbs lay scattered on his neatly tailored dress shirt. "What was that about?" he asked, swallowing his last bite of toast.

Megan took Gerry by the hand and led him to the fireplace. "Does this answer your question?"

"Oh right. Forgot about these." He brushed crumbs from his shirt onto the new living room rug. "How'd they manage to get 'em all up here?"

"Never mind that," Megan groaned, her frustration mounting. "Let's just get comfy and open these together?"

Gerry's eyes widened. "I'd love to. But you know I've got work today."

"Oh, but the hospital gave you a week for our honeymoon! Just 'cause we got back a day early doesn't mean you have to go in! Let's open everything on the right side. We'll do the rest when you get home for dinner."

"Sorry, babe. I really promised them a full shift. Can't back out now. But you go ahead. Put things wherever you want. Just make a list so I can figure out who bought what." Gerry politely kissed his new bride on the cheek, grabbed his workbag from a nearby closet and stepped out to the elevator.

Disappointed, Megan headed back to her bedroom. She threw on an oversized gray sweatshirt before returning to unwrap the mountain of gifts by herself. Just like the four days in Nevis, she was again alone with her reflections. Only this time it was not by choice.

That whole honeymoon week, while Gerry frolicked on the beach, snorkeling and parasailing, Megan chose to lay in the sun, punishing herself for allowing this to happen. And no matter how hard she tried, she was unable to resist conjuring up constant thoughts of Johnny Elias. Just as she had done throughout the wedding ceremony - even as she lay in bed with Gerry - Megan often wondered if Johnny was aware that she'd dated Gerry, let alone married him.

A forest of decorative paper soon lay on the floor. Crystal vases, silverware, linens and champagne flutes emerged from decorative boxes. At first, each wrapped package brought with it a sense of anticipation. But after three hours of repetitive activity, Megan grew numb to the process. She'd always envisioned this special moment to be a shared experience; now, instead, she had only herself to impress.

Megan was unfamiliar with the majority of the names on the cards. Halfway through, she stopped maintaining the list. Gerry likely didn't care anyway. A clock on top of the fireplace mantel struck noon. She decided to give it another half-hour.

After putting a silver candelabra in the new china cabinet, Megan reached for the top of the next stack. She pulled down a medium-sized heavy box with a white envelope stuck to one side of the gold wrapping paper. Only her name was written on it.

Megan slid out a generic wedding card. A small piece of stationary was tucked inside from the Holiday Inn of Branson, Missouri. On it, a note scrawled in a familiar handwriting.

Dear Meg:

As you read this, I presume you're now a married woman, so congratulations, I guess.

I first want to apologize for not alerting you about the release of my album last month. Since my music took off, I haven't had a minute to catch my breath. By now you may have heard it on the radio. I hope you're not offended. Guess you could say I couldn't have done it without you.

I learned about your wedding from my accountant, who your mother must've invited. Admittedly, this was quite a surprise. But your happiness is all I ever wished for during our years together, for whatever wishes are worth.

Figuring the massive wedding that your mother always wanted for you, I was at a loss for what I could get you that wouldn't come in triplicate. I picked up this little trinket while touring. With my best wishes for happiness and good health – Johnny

Megan feverishly tore open the shiny paper. Inside she found a handcrafted music box in the shape of a piano, made from washed white maple. A tiny metal key easily unlocked the top panel. The sound of Beethoven's *Moonlight Sonata* filled the room. Megan taped the note to the bottom of the music box, then cradled the cherished gift in both arms against her chest and carried it off to her bedroom. She placed it in the top drawer of her nightstand.

Oh Johnny, she thought wishfully. *If only you knew...*

Johnny arrived at the lobby of Highpeak headquarters on West 57th after the abrupt end to a run of successful concerts.

"Mr. Elias, I'm afraid I have some good news for you." Ron Neswick was grinning. "For starters, I've just been informed that your album has jumped into next week's top-20. They say it's charting at eighteen. We're going ahead with plans to rush-release a second single. But maybe best of all: you've nabbed the cover of next week's *Billboard* magazine. Get a load of this!"

Johnny reached out for a grainy faxed page. As he read, a smile spread across his face.

"*Whoever said musical poetry is a dying art form better hold off on the eulogy. Enter Johnny Elias, AKA the Poet of the Wrong Generation. This hard-bitten New York City kid – in the spirit of Paul 'Rhymin' Simon – is something of a revelation. His twelve-track debut blends lyrically-driven songwriting with topical themes and soaring melodies. It is, amazingly, one of the most captivating introductory efforts this side of the 70s.*"

Johnny put down the page and looked up at Ron with a straight face. "Paul Simon's a Queens boy. I'm from Brooklyn. Can't they get their facts straight?" He grinned vividly, his heart pounding with delight. "So I guess this means they like it? But did you really pull us off the tour just to show me something that could've easily been faxed?"

"Johnny, warm-up gigs are nice. Today: welcome to the big-time. You're getting a boatload of local ink for your underdog story. We need to exploit this further." Ron flipped the pages of a date book. "As of tomorrow, you'll be Heidi's top priority; the full media rounds. Also, we're gonna need you to start performing the title track everywhere. If we can turn this into a hit, we've got ourselves a blockbuster. Kick-ass reviews like this must be fully taken advantage of!"

Later that afternoon, Johnny headed back to his new apartment for the first time in weeks. He found Andy working behind his desk; the very spot where he had last seen his trusted friend.

"Hey, boss, we've got about a hundred things to review. Hope you've got some time to sit and concentrate."

Johnny made himself comfortable in a faux leather chair facing his desk. He reached into his pocket and handed Andy a folded photocopy of the *Billboard* review. "You happen to see this? Maybe I underestimated Highpeak's muscle."

Andy glanced at the opening paragraph. He grinned. "Yeah. This may be the best of a boxful that've come in so far. But I knew about this one days ago. Our PR guy, Jerry got it placed through an editor he knows. Like most of 'em, Highpeak had nothing to do with it. But yeah, it's really impressive." Andy pointed to a box in the corner of the room. "If you have time, or the need for an ego boost, there's, like, thirty articles inside. May not be a bad one in the bunch."

Andy's to-do list included a discussion of bills to be paid, a sunglasses endorsement offer, and the first pile of autograph requests. When Johnny's hand tired from signing his name, Andy reared back with a glorious smile. "Listen, John. As I explained when you first signed the contract, there'd be the potential to earn a few bucks. Obviously you know, your album's been selling. Royalties aren't far behind. And after doing the calculations, here's what it all totals up to."

A six-figure number jumped off the paper. Johnny jubilantly pumped his fist in the air. "Whoa, baby! That's way more than I got from the advance. I just… it doesn't seem real!"

"And the way things are going, this is only the tip of the iceberg. Between the finances and non-stop requests, someone's bound to have their hands full for a long time around here."

Johnny's smile died. He slid to the edge of his chair. "Wait. What d'ya mean, someone? I thought we were in this together, for the long haul."

"Johnny, I specifically told you that I could do this through the summer. It's been educational and… amazing. But once school starts up in three weeks, you need to find someone to do this full-time. Can't exactly do it between classes."

Another manager, Johnny thought anxiously. He began pacing the room. "Andy, if this is about money… Hey, look how far we've come already. Why not take off a semester; see where it takes us?"

Andy held up two digits. "First of all, I'm not you. No one can blame you for dropping out. Recording an album, that's the opportunity of a lifetime. And you can always go back for the last few credits. But I'm registered in grad school. They're holding a place for me. If I pull out and things go to hell, I could really set myself back."

"And your second reason?" Johnny asked.

"You should know better than anyone that if I drop out, my folks'll disown me. I mean, my mom's a lifelong academic! And my dad's been footing the bill. How'll I break the news that I'm giving up an MBA to oversee my friend's pop-star career?"

"We could pay them back," Johnny offered impulsively. "At the rate money's coming in, I could probably repay your entire tuition bill in a few weeks, right?"

Andy crumpled a page from the junk-mail pile and tossed it in his garbage basket. "It's not just the money. Hey, I'm an only child. If I don't cross the finish line, I'll be a total failure in their eyes, no matter how much I'm paid. Without that framed piece of paper, I may as well never go home again."

Johnny spun back in Andy's direction. "Then move in with me! You've already made the second bedroom your own. There's plenty of space here for the rest of your stuff. And if you need me to, I'll have a chat with your folks. Andy, I can't do this without you, buddy!"

Andy scowled silently. Johnny took a moment to reevaluate how best to convey his position without sounding selfish.

"Listen, neither of us could've anticipated this. But just look where we are! I've gone from being some foster kid at Brooklyn Post to magazine covers overnight! And where would I be without you? Sure, it's overwhelming." He sat down across the desk from his friend and met Andy's eyes. "But I'm starting to be compared to the artists we grew up listening to. This is no longer a summer hobby. Andy, I trust you implicitly. You're my best friend in the world. I'm begging you, man." He took a deep breath. "At least think it over before turning me down."

The Jones Beach amphitheater in Wantagh, Long Island had long been a popular concert venue. From May through September, the beachside stage attracted almost every major touring artist – and consistent sell-out crowds.

The execs at Highpeak saw the summer concert season winding down. Now it was time to test Johnny's box-office appeal. With all the prime dates booked far in advance, Highpeak gambled on a mid-week night in late September. They needn't have worried.

All eight thousand seats were sold out within three days. This prompted promoters to add an immediate second concert, for which the tickets were quickly snapped up. If this was any barometer of an emerging artist's growing popularity, it was not lost on anyone.

Johnny's spring tour had been just a six-song opening act. Now, he and the band needed to prepare a full ninety-minute headliner set; so they sweated it out at *The Lion's Gate* every afternoon, adding songs to their repertoire. It was early one evening between spirited rehearsals that René Fontenot called with the news that the *Poet* album had cracked the top ten. Simultaneously, the single of the same name had hit number 16.

"That's awesome!" Ian Klatt burst out, delighted for his front man. "This calls for an all-night rave-up!"

Johnny raced over to the far corner of the club, where the bartender was just setting up for the evening rush. He proceeded to buy drinks for everyone. Ian toasted their success over a round of beer. "Here's to our golden boy, Johnny, without whom we'd all be out lookin' for real jobs!"

Frank Traber popped the cork on a bottle of Korbel champagne. "To immortality and things that legends are made of: fast cars, red guitars and a little spending cash."

The celebration soon turned raucous; suds and bubbles everywhere. Johnny kept the drinks coming – to everyone's delight. Before long, he grew concerned, seeing Howard put down a few too many. Quietly, he took him aside. "I probably should've thought of this earlier, but are diabetics allowed alcohol? Don't need you getting sick on me again."

"I'm fine," Howard responded, though his bleary eyes and tequila breath told a different story. "Never had a drinking problem. And I hardly ever break the rules since the hospital. But if ya can't celebrate the good times, rare as they are, is life even worth living?"

Johnny understood Howard's perspective. "Just don't overdo it," he warned.

"Thanks, kid. Appreciate your concern." Howard raised a margarita to his lips and took a swallow. "Listen, did I ever tell you why I love you like I do?"

Johnny's eyes widened. "Well, you've always told me you wanted to be a part of something big. That was always good enough for me. Plus we seemed to hit it off going back to the piano-room at school. I just figured you liked hanging with me."

"It's not just your talent." Howard's voice had taken on the gravity of the seriously inebriated. "It's more like a comfort level. You only get it once you've made a connection, you know? It's all about connection." He paused to take another sip. "Sometimes I think of you as my friend. But occasionally… I feel you're like the son I never had."

Johnny put down his own drink. "Howard, man, don't you already have a son?" He tried to sound as non-intrusive as possible. "I thought you and Suzanne had a boy together. There's a picture of him somewhere in your house."

Howard nearly fell backward off his stool, his arms flailing for stability. Once he regained his balance, he scowled at Johnny. "If there's one thing I'm certain of, it's that I've never mentioned that boy in all the years since he's been gone. And sure as hell, I have no pictures lying around to haunt me."

Johnny tried to backtrack. "Look, I didn't mean to piss you off. I didn't think–"

"That's right," Howard raised his voice. "You didn't think at all, did you? Exactly how long've you known? Huh? Here I've trusted you all this time, only to find out you've been digging round my past. What else haven't you been telling me?"

"Howard, it's not what you think. I didn't mean to pry. It's just, that week you were in the hospital, you just vanished, man. I was desperate to do anything to help."

As the words came out, Johnny realized that he shouldn't have been snooping… certainly that he should never have brought it up.

"And you kept it to yourself all this time?" Howard asked, still aggrieved. "How could you possibly have kept a straight face around me, knowing I kept it hidden – that I wanted it hidden?"

"I never said anything 'coz I didn't know a lot. Other than a couple of photos –"

"All right, fine," Howard sighed. He shook his head. "So it wasn't done with malice." He wiped a buildup of saliva from his lips, then took another sip from the frothy margarita. "Yeah, I had a son. Suzy named him Josh after her granddad. Slight resemblance, I guess. Anyway, the whole parenthood thing… some people are born with those instincts, but not me. We were never close. He was always playing ball from the first day he could walk. I could never get him into music. Not for a minute. Imagine a boy of mine like that!"

Johnny shook his head silently.

"In junior high," Howard continued, "Josh turned into a jock; made the baseball team. Lacrosse too. I tried to show some interest, but my heart was never in it, ya know?"

"I hear ya," Johnny replied. "My childhood, it was all over the map; no place to call home. No real family either. Constant moving around. And I didn't always get on well with authority figures. Though I'm still not clear on why you never mention your kid."

Howard took another sip. "First of all, when Suzy got sick, Josh just clung to her everywhere she went. Doctor's offices; support groups. He insisted on being there to hold her hand. When things improved, he lightened up. Then Suzy took a turn for the worse. He'd lock himself in his room for days at a time, only coming out to pee, or to spend a few minutes with his mom in her moments of strength."

Howard placed his half-empty glass down on the table and dabbed at a few tears with a paper napkin. "When Suzanne died, Josh was inconsolable. Believe me, I tried everything. I wrote him a song; brought him to ball games. Nothing worked. We'd go days without talking." He took a deep breath, steadying himself. "I think he blamed me for her getting sick and all."

Johnny looked over his shoulder to make sure the others weren't listening in. Ian was dousing himself with a bottle of Corona by the foot of the stage. Frank and Art were tossing lime wedges at him, giggling. Satisfied that they were oblivious, he turned back to console Howard. "I'm sure he didn't. He was just trying to make sense of it. And he was in pain." Johnny winced for emphasis. "So – where is he now? He's gotta have figured out by now it wasn't your fault."

"No clue." Howard stared into his glass, his voice hollow. "One day during his second year of high school, he just never made it home. Took his schoolbag, his wallet, a change of clothes. That's it. I called the cops. We searched everywhere. For months I met with investigators, his friends, the counselors at school. No one even knew he was depressed. It was probably all my fault." Another shuddering breath. "I did everything, man. Followed false leads, filed reports, circulated his picture. Eventually the cops stopped calling. And then I worried myself sick. Clinical depression they called it. Three weeks psych evaluation."

"Oh, that's just horrible." Johnny waited a moment before continuing. He could feel Howard's pain coming off him, in waves. "So that's why you've been taking that medicine; why you talk like you don't have a family."

Howard still wasn't looking at him. "If only you knew what I've been through. Some days it's hard to just get out of bed, you know? Much less hope anything. All those years... I prayed for Suzy to get better. And then I was doing it all over again, except then it was for my boy to come home. To just one day walk in my door." He shook his head. "And then, after a while, you stop. Stop hoping. Stop praying. And then... you came along." He looked up at Johnny. "And I felt like I had the chance to do it right; to help you where I couldn't help Josh."

Johnny put his arm around Howard's shoulders and pressed his head against the older man's. "Howard, you know I never make promises I can't keep. Long as we're in this together, I'm gonna make it my mission to help bring you closure. Really, I swear, I'll never let you down: On this you can be sure."

18

PROMISING NEWCOMER

Katherine Price was experiencing the natural letdown that sets in after a major event. She returned to work with renewed focus: one eye on the upcoming mayoral re-election campaign, the other honed in on business expansion. She had never put in longer hours.

One particularly late night, Katherine took a break from paperwork to order up a Waldorf salad. In the conference room she flipped through the channels on her overhead TV. *Nothing but talking heads and pitiful game shows*, she thought. When she arrived at VH-1, Katherine's eyes narrowed. A brief interview clip was followed by a music video. *Nice song*, she thought, recalling the tune from the radio. Until now, she had never given a thought to the performer's identity.

Then she saw his face.

Katherine reached for the nearest phone and summoned her equally hardworking partner on the intercom. "Sheila, you familiar with this new song: *Poet of the Wrong Generation*?"

"Yeah, great track, isn't it?" Sheila responded. "They say a kid from Brooklyn sings it."

"Do you know his name?" Katherine asked.

"I don't, off hand. But one of the receptionists was playing the CD this morning. Maybe she left it at her desk."

Within minutes, Shelia was in the conference room. She slid the jewel case across the table. "Here it is. Artsy cover too, don't you think?"

"It's colorful," Katherine muttered, flipping through the liner notes.

"Well, from what I've heard, it's a killer disc." Sheila glanced up and saw Katherine's face. "What's wrong? This a potential new account or something?"

"No," Katherine grunted. "This *kid* from Brooklyn; he's Megan's ex-boyfriend. You remember Johnny Elias, don't you?"

"No. Get outta town! This guy's your Johnny? What're the odds?"

"Not exactly mine," Katherine countered. "Not the term I'd have used. Don't get me wrong, he wasn't a terrible kid. But he was hardly right for my daughter. Your classic, abandoned, longhaired underachiever."

"Well, he sure has come a long way," Sheila smiled. "Not exactly underachieving anymore. Kinda hot too!"

Katherine glared at her, not responding. "Enough, Sheila. Let's not discuss this any further. But as of tomorrow, I'm adding his name to our clipping service. Every article on Johnny Elias should be left in my in-box. I'd like to keep up with his progress… to monitor how my motivation has paid off."

Andy Raymer couldn't find enough hours to fit it all in. Johnny's debut album and two singles were holding steadily on the charts. Media interest was continuing to build. The requests for interviews and appearances now exceeded available hours on the daily schedule. And with the homecoming concert fast approaching, Andy turned to his handpicked PR rep for a solution.

"Sounds like you're running a three-ring media circus," Jerry Goodman gestured circularly inside his second floor walk-up office on Coney Island

Avenue. He guided Andy through his reception area to the tiny conference table. "Who knew he'd hit it big this quickly?"

Andy dropped a stack of folders on the oval table. "You might say that. I mean, there's popular, and then there's ridiculous. But how to keep everybody happy?"

"Guess that depends on your definition. We know there isn't time for all the one-on-ones. That's a given. But for the sake of hype and efficiency, you might want to think about calling a formal press conference. You know, like a politician on the campaign trail."

Andy stared out the window. A city bus roared by. "But where? And for that matter, when and how?"

"Why not do it the afternoon of the Jones Beach concert?"

"Where? Onstage? In the parking lot? We're talking like a hundred media credentials."

Jerry straightened his Superman necktie, then pulled out his local Yellow Pages. He found a schematic of the amphitheater in the back section. "Actually, I was thinking we might erect a large hospitality tent right alongside the backstage area. Before the first show, we'll have Johnny do a structured Q&A; maybe a photo-op. I'll prep him with talking-points. That should keep 'em satisfied."

The concert was scheduled for eight o'clock. The band arrived early for a full rehearsal. After an hour for hair and wardrobe, the musicians entered the tent for a series of publicity shots. Then Johnny headed back to the dressing room for a briefing with Highpeak's Heidi Ellison.

"Stay relaxed, that's crucial!" she shouted, her perfume overwhelming, her breath reeking of onions.

Johnny stood up. "You've told me that three or four times. I get it, okay? Anything else?"

"Just be yourself," Heidi said nervously. "Stay relaxed, and be yourself."

He couldn't wait to get away from her. The advice was superfluous; he was looking forward to real questions.

With just minutes before the press conference, Ron Neswick and René Fontenot popped into the small dressing area unannounced. They were flanked by someone Johnny didn't know; a gray-haired man in an impeccable pinstriped suit, and the gusto of a man half his age.

"Oh, hey, Johnny," Ron led the charge. "Great sound-check earlier. That's only the second time I've heard you guys play. You've really got this material down."

"And we love your take on that old Hollies song, *The Air That I Breathe*," René added. "Between the Poet songs and five covers, should make for a killer set."

Johnny looked at his trio of uninvited guests. "Thanks. "So what brings you guys back here?"

"Funny you should ask," René chuckled. He gestured for Johnny and the other men to sit down, each finding his own chair. "To begin with, this here's Herb Cantor, chairman of Cantor Productions, the premiere concert promoters in North America."

"Cool to meet you, Mr. Cantor." Johnny nodded respectfully. "You stop in to see our show tonight?"

"Please call me Herb, Johnny. And yes, I'm here to keep a close eye. I've been talking to your friends over at Highpeak. We all agree that an autumn tour of theaters is the way to go. Especially with your album burning up the charts."

"A tour of my own! Damn!" Johnny's imagination shifted into high gear. *Concert t-shirts with my name on front. Fancy hotels. A luxury tour bus for me and the guys.* He grinned in spite of himself. "So when do you expect to start sending us out?"

"As soon as we get the green light, really. I'm figuring on booking venues tomorrow, putting tickets out there in a week or so and then getting you onstage for about fifty dates by the third week of October."

"Fifty dates! You really think that many cities wanna hear me?"

"I don't think so." Herb slapped the table for emphasis. "I know it! With the ink and airplay you've been getting, you can easily pack three to five thousand seats nightly."

"Well, if you're that confident, then yeah, I'm on board! I'll have to let the band know, make sure their all available. But if the dates check out, and the dollars are right, I –"

"Don't you worry about the money," Ron cut him off. He leaned back and took a puff on an expensive Cuban cigar. "When it comes to first-rate concert productions, Cantor is tops in every respect. And knowing most of the guys as I do, I can't imagine any of your bandmates passing on a chance to tour America. Can you?"

Johnny rubbed his forehead. *Howard,* he thought anxiously. *He'll never do it during school; gotta finish his degree.* Convincing Andy to leave NYU early was one thing. In fact, Johnny considered him irreplaceable. Plus Andy was still young, his future wide open. And he was being well-compensated for his duties, however long they lasted. Howard, on the other hand was on a mission of another kind. Teaching was his focus, his future, something Johnny knew well.

"Just leave it to me. I'll work it out. I mean, most of us would probably kill for this. But Howard… I only have him on loan tonight and tomorrow. We may need a new piano player if we play those fifty dates."

"You do mean *when* you play 'em," René asserted, tugging on his moustache. "The timing couldn't be any better. The radio play; the exposure you're getting with that big movie song. If ever there was a time to capitalize –"

"Gentlemen, count me in. I can't wait to go out there. Just send Andy Raymer the paperwork. He'll probably murder me if I sign it without his blessing."

"Well, it sounds like we're all set!" Herb Cantor exclaimed. "I'll have the deal memo and contracts to your management by tomorrow." He reached out and firmly shook everyone's hand. When the door slammed behind him, Ron took another toke of his cigar and exhaled.

"Johnny, you do realize that Cantor Productions is huge?"

Johnny coughed from the smoke. "Honestly, it's all a little overwhelming. But the idea of headlining shows around the country... just wow."

"Keeping with that note of optimism," René chimed in, "we have some additional paperwork for your consideration."

"Based on your album's performance so far, we feel strongly about keeping you at Highpeak for a while," Ron added in tag-team fashion. "Rather than simply picking up our contractual option for your second record, we've come up with something a bit more enticing."

"Are we talking about a whole new deal?" Johnny asked, curious.

René handed Johnny a clear cellophane envelope across the table. "You've become a valued property. We want to solidify our successful relationship long into the future."

"Guys, this is awesome." Johnny glanced down at his watch. "But you do understand that I won't have a minute to look over the small print now. In case you're forgetting, I've got a press conference five minutes ago, followed by a really big gig."

"Understood." Ron pointed his cigar in Johnny's direction. "But I do want you to at least know what we're prepared to do for you. Namely: a hefty advance that dwarfs your original contract. A bigger promo budget too."

"Sounds great." Johnny fought to conceal a broadening grin. "So what am I in for?"

"In a nutshell, you'll be recording three albums for us over the next five years, plus there's a best-of compilation. The next one's due by April, which gives you seven months to get your material together. You are still writing, no?"

Johnny quickly grew analytical. *That dreaded second album!* The material for Poet was culled from a lifetime of inspiration. Since then, he'd only written three songs that he considered worthwhile. The sudden thought of pushing himself against a deadline for a follow-up caused him to pace nervously.

"Guys, just like I told Mr. Cantor, I'll need my people to look things over. In theory, I can be ready by the spring. But first things first. I've got a room full of media waiting."

"One last thing," Ron insisted, as Johnny threw on his jacket in front of the mirror. "At the press conference, we'll be announcing your new deal with us, and the upcoming national tour. I figured I'd give you the courtesy of knowing."

"Whoa! Guys, one thing at a time. You wanna say that the tour's almost set? Fine. But let's keep the contract thing in check till everyone's had a chance to review it. We can always announce it once everything's signed."

Johnny left Ron and René behind in his dressing area. He walked out to the rear of the media tent where his bandmates stood ready to enter.

"Everything okay?" Howard asked. He was standing in blue jeans and a black sports jacket. "They've been waiting for us in there."

"All's fine," Johnny addressed the group. "Just a heads up. Looks like we may be playing more than just these two local gigs. Details to follow."

A satisfied look appeared on three of the four faces: Frank beneath a black top hat, in a rainbow colored jacket and skintight black leather pants. Ian wore a camouflage army shirt over green sweatpants. And Art, in a white leisure suit. Johnny continued walking up a ramp to the side entrance when Howard tapped him on the shoulder. "It all sounds great, kid. But you know I can't be hitting the road with school in session."

"Yeah, I know. Priorities. And as much as I'm gonna miss you, don't you dare let anyone twist your arm. I'll figure something out."

Johnny was surprised by the informality of the temporary pressroom. There were TV camera risers, a section of still photographers, and a handful of reporters positioned by microphones. Others congregated around buffet-tables in the back. Large red banners with the Highpeak logo hung above a laminated poster of the *Poet* album cover. Johnny was led to a podium out front by Heidi Ellison, her perfume preceding her as always. This touched off a polite round of applause, and the popping of flashbulbs. Heidi grabbed the microphone for a brief introduction.

"Ladies and gentlemen, thank you all for coming out this evening. Highpeak recording artist Johnny Elias will tonight be making his first-major New York area concert appearance. This triumphant homecoming takes place while his album ranks in the national top-ten and his latest hit single resides in the top-twelve."

Heidi instructed the reporters to ask only one question each, then she turned the floor over to the press. The popping of flash bulbs resumed.

"Are you nervous to be playing in front of your hometown fans?" asked one bespectacled newspaperwoman. "Do you feel a special connection, having grown up here?" asked another.

Johnny answered a series of opening puff-piece questions. He seemed primarily reserved, until finally getting a few that required some real thought.

"Was *Shadow's of the Same Color* written to embarrass Mayor Dinkins?" an older male reporter asked, holding out a tape recorder.

"Actually, I wrote that one when all hell broke loose in Crown Heights. Remember, I'm from Brooklyn. The riots happened right near my home. Out of disgust over the incident, but with optimism for a peaceful future, I came up with the words to that song."

"What about *Jacqui*?" asked a smiling female radio reporter. "Who's that ballad written for? Any romantic implications?"

Johnny casually looked behind him. Andy and Jacqui stood together off to the side next to Jerry Goodman. They all looked amused and Jacqui winked at him. Johnny spun back to the microphone. "Jacqui Spencer designed my album cover. She also happens to be my manager's girlfriend. I wrote that one when she was going through a tough spell. But it's all good now."

Johnny looked back over at Jacqui. "Would you all like to meet her?" Considerable encouragement came from the press corps. Johnny motioned in Jacqui's direction, urging her to step out into the spotlight.

As she neared the podium, Jacqui subtly waved her hand at Johnny. A new diamond ring sparkled beneath the stage lights. Jacqui stopped to pose alongside the album cover replica. "We'll talk later," she whispered in Johnny's ear. When the flashbulbs stopped, the barrage of questions resumed.

"Johnny, do you really consider yourself the poet of the wrong generation; and if so, why?"

Johnny feigned being stumped. He cleared his throat for comic effect. "Honestly, I'm just a music fan; a guy who happened to write a few songs with something to say. It's just… I firmly believe that for far too long, we've been putting up with second-rate music. Just last summer I was in Central Park watching all those people harmonize with Paul Simon's poetry. My generation, they seem perfectly happy to settle for less. It's as if somewhere around the mid-eighties, someone flicked a switch and drained all the harmony; all the cleverness. Radio's dominated these days by novelty songs, mindless techno-beat, and melody-less rap. Maybe it's all harmless. But'll anyone be singing along with it twenty years from now?"

Johnny took a sip of water from a plastic cup. He studied the faces staring back at him. "I don't intend to group everyone together. Some good ones are still out there. But honestly, ask yourselves when the last time a pop song by a new artist left a lasting impression? I don't know if my generation is simply deprived or disinterested in meaningful music. Good melodies. Great storytelling. But if my songs can help change that perception, I'll be satisfied to have done my part."

The sound of a few hands clapping sparked a surprising round of applause among the usually impartial media. Johnny squirmed uncomfortably at the well-intended sentiment. And then the interrogation resumed.

"Hey, Johnny, all the girls want to know: do you currently have a girlfriend? If so, who is she?" asked a female gossip columnist.

"Knew that one was coming," he responded, his voice playful. He paused, though, and took a nervous sip from his cup. "These days I'm still getting over having my heart obliterated not long ago; the story behind some of my songs. Also: traveling so often, it isn't easy finding time for a serious relationship."

Before he could say more, Heidi Ellison interrupted, having been discreetly handed a piece of paper from René Fontenot. "Ladies and gentleman: I'm pleased to reveal that Johnny's two New York shows will be kicking off his first full American concert tour! Details are being finalized as I speak. Look for more info in the coming days about cities and ticket prices."

"Opportunistic bastards," Johnny muttered away from the microphone. *At least they didn't announce the new recording deal before that was signed. Talk about antsy.*

Johnny fielded a few more questions about his upbringing (foster care was rough), his favorite TV show (David Letterman) and his musical influences (too many to name 'em all). A warm round of applause accompanied his exit. Heidi Ellison escorted him from the tent.

"Wow! You really kicked ass out there. They totally embraced you." She massaged his shoulders. "For your first press conference, I'd say you left a helluva impression."

Johnny threw a backstage celebration after the second of back-to-back sold-out concerts. It had been an incredible homecoming: two electrifying performances lapped up by highly receptive audiences – shows played to crowds who had paid to hear his material, exclusively. The days of being a no-name opening act were now history.

For Johnny, the most dizzying moments occurred when the lights went down and he and the band first stepped out onstage. The joyous hometown ovation was unnerving, and yet everything he hoped it would be. The opening night adulation caught him a bit unexpectedly, causing his eyes to momentarily well up. The stage was literally shaking. For the second show, though better prepared, he enjoyed a similarly emotional response. Beyond the cheers, what most impressed him was the fans' familiarity with his lyrics. During a few precious intervals, Johnny would skip a line and turn the mic in the direction of the audience. He hoped to hear perhaps several dozen voices singing along. To his amazement: the boisterous echo of several hundred.

Now, with his ears still ringing from the encore, Johnny collected himself from the delirium and burst triumphantly into the reception room. First he greeted Carolyn Green, his onetime foster mom who had never before seen him perform in person. She was beaming. "Johnny, you've always been my little superstar. Guess your rooting section's just gotten a little bigger! I couldn't be prouder."

Next, he made a beeline to Andy and Jacqui. They were holding hands and wearing matching smiles of contentment.

"I think tonight was even better than last!" Andy exclaimed. "Maybe my deferring a semester wasn't the worst decision of my life. Given what I went through with my folks, you're making me look better by the day."

Johnny chuckled. "Funny, but I would've said that about you two with the way things've been going; springing your engagement on me like that yesterday."

"Oh, you enjoyed that, did you?" Jacqui punched Johnny in the shoulder. "I certainly didn't expect you to parade me out there in front of forty photographers in a sweatshirt and dungarees!"

"Fair enough," he concurred in a raspy voice. "But I think that photo-op may've opened a few eyes. In fact, I know you got two faxes on my desk, requesting your design talents."

Jacqui laughed. "Yeah, Andy mentioned that too. Funny thing is: I was actually studying to design adverts and such. Never dreamed of album covers as a career – not that I'm complaining!"

"Speaking of albums," Andy cut in, "we need to talk about that contract old Neswick handed you yesterday. The numbers, they're mind-blowing. But are you prepared to rush back into the studio in a few months? It seems they wanna push you right back out on the market with new product, whether or not you're ready."

"Hold that thought." Johnny stepped away from his friends. "I need to tell the others about the tour proposal while I have 'em all in the same room."

In a semi-quiet corner, Johnny rounded up the members of his band. "So, listen up. I know this is short notice. Highpeak's talking about us taking this show out to theaters across America."

"When?" Frank quizzed between sips of a blue cosmopolitan.

"They want us to start in about a month. We're talkin' serious paydays to do this almost every night in another city till New Year's. Just wanted to be sure you're all up for it?"

Art, Frank and Ian slapped high fives until their hands hurt.

Equally expected was Howard's response.

"Boys, I'm awfully sorry. I'm really committed to finishing my music degree. But I know you'll do just fine without the geezer."

"But we're just hitting our stride," Art said, frowning. "You're like our musical director. What about chemistry?"

"Hey, really wish I could. But I'm on another mission. This stuff's only play. At least for me."

Quietly, Howard stepped aside to check his glucose level. Johnny walked off to offer Howard his reassurance. It was Frank who helped restore the positive vibes.

"Guys, we've come this far together. And we do have a month to work someone in." A devilish smile overtook his face. "Besides, I've got this friend; great keyboard player. Good back-up singer too. And she's pretty darn hot as well."

"A babe in our boy's club?" Art remarked playfully.

"Well, she'd better be as hot as you say, or she has no shot, no matter how she plays!" Ian laughed.

"Not to worry," Frank assured, "as Jimi would say, she's a sweet little heartbreaker."

19

STORM CLOUDS HOVER

Megan Ridgewell's brief honeymoon seemed to have ended before it ever truly began. Now that she lived with Gerry all the time, it was as if she'd been provided a front-row seat to all his shortcomings. Her recollections of the handsome, well-dressed, spontaneous romantic were quickly replaced with an ill-tempered, selfish, overeating rich-boy, lacking in maturity or patience. The flower bouquets and fancy evenings from early on had been replaced with monotony and callousness.

Their first month of marriage found Megan setting up their home, handling the dry-cleaning, and writing out several hundred thank-you cards. A typical night had her loading the dishwasher, alone in the kitchen, while Gerry occupied himself in the bedroom with one hand in his pants and the other around the TV remote. She often felt as though she'd gone from her mother's domineering captivity to servitude in the house of her dispassionate husband.

To her credit, Megan tried at first to overlook her unhappiness. She figured things would improve once Gerry got a regular hospital shift. Always dressing up for him and putting dinner on the table, she'd usually end up holding one-way conversations while he wolfed down carefully prepared meals with indifference.

Megan planned her first dinner party at the new apartment in an effort to jump-start things a little. She hoped it would stimulate her husband to rediscover his social charms. Megan prepared all his declared favorites – Salisbury steak, sweet potato pie, and warm apple cobbler – and set the dining room with new china and a tablecloth from their wedding gifts. Nevertheless, despite the invitation of twelve guests, including six of his best friends from medical school, Gerry managed to show up hours late – stinking of alcohol – missing all but dessert and farewell greetings.

"Sorry, everyone! We had a hit-and-run victim who nearly lost a leg. Bad timing, I know."

Megan relayed her bitterness to whichever of her friends would listen. But when it came to her mother, she knew her complaints would only fall on deaf ears. Instead, she invited Katherine up to the apartment one evening to observe firsthand.

Gerry arrived home two hours later than expected. He went straight for the kitchen, ignoring the warm appetizers on the dining room table. Instead, he helped himself to a Rolling Rock six-pack while phoning a friend. It was only when Katherine went to interrupt her son-in-law's long-distance banter that he briefly emerged. But as soon as he pulled up a chair at the head of the table, his pager went off, sending him scurrying back to the kitchen.

"He's such a good doctor," Katherine praised him tentatively as she and Megan waited – to no avail – for his return. "I'm so impressed by his dedication to his patients, even on private time."

Graduating from untimely arrivals, Gerry next began to regularly skip coming home altogether. He'd tell Megan he'd been assigned a double-shift to compensate for understaffing. Yet when she tried reaching him at the hospital on two such occasions, she was taken aback to find that he wasn't on duty. Even calls to his pager went unreturned.

Megan figured she could live with disinterest. She was prepared to lower her expectations for the marriage. But one late summer night everything turned altogether ugly.

Katherine Price's annual Labor Day blowouts had become the talk of East Hampton. On the final weekend of every summer, she'd invite a mix of the biggest names in politics, fashion and media to her lavish summer home for an outdoor luncheon extravaganza. The big *Farewell to the Summer of '92* bash was no exception.

Once all 170 guests and most of the catering staff had come and gone, Megan and Gerry were charged with the responsibility of locking up for the season. It was Megan's idea that she and Gerry extend their summer with a spontaneous, romantic overnight.

"No way!" Gerry grunted through a mouthful of leftover pastry. "What? Suddenly you're trying to be nice to me after practically ignoring me all summer! Besides, I've got work early tomorrow. Can't miss a shift right after the holiday weekend."

Megan began rubbing Gerry's shoulders and gently kissed the back of his neck. "Even if we can't take off tomorrow, let's make a special night of it. We've got the Jacuzzi to ourselves; all those unopened champagne bottles. What d'ya say you and I create a few memorable high notes to end our first summer on?"

Gerry abruptly swallowed his food with a glass of chardonnay, then brushed Megan aside. "So now you just think that you can put on your little seductress act and everything'll be fine? You're kidding, right? Like you really care. As if you take me seriously."

"But, Gerry!" she protested, "I do take you seriously. I married you, didn't I? Sat with you all afternoon. And I wasn't gonna keep you from missing work tomorrow. Why should spending the night here mess you up?" Megan stepped toward him again, only to be shoved more forcefully, this time down to the kitchen floor. Too astonished to speak, she pulled herself up to her knees leaning on a cabinet handle. She took a deep breath and tried to talk normally. "It's like ever since our honeymoon, you've totally lost interest."

"Not true," he shouted defensively. "It's the other way around. I work like a fiend to support our lifestyle, so you can throw your parties; buy your pretty clothes. And have you ever once said thanks? Do you ever show me any real affection? Your heart's never into it. You're the one who shows no interest! It's like you're saving it for someone else."

"Someone else?" Megan's faced flushed of color. "How am I supposed to love someone who's never around? And let's not forget: I don't need your financial support. You only choose to work all those hours as an excuse to spend time away from me. Most nights you're coming home drunk; pigging out on our leftovers. Whatever happened to the sweet, handsome guy I dated? I'm finding it hard to believe that this is the same guy I married!"

Gerry's face turned a bright shade of red. Furiously, he reached behind him for whatever he could find and flung it across the room. A half-full wine glass whizzed by Megan's head. It narrowly missed her before smashing against the far wall. Tiny crystal fragments showered the tile floor. Gerry reached back for another. A frightened Megan covered her face.

"You want excitement?" Gerry smashed another crystal flute on the marble countertop. "I'll show you everything right here up close." He bent down and shoved a kneeling Megan backward, causing her head to smack against the cold, marble surface. "So what if I drink a little after work! Don't you know my job saves lives?" he shouted, towering over her. "And now, suddenly, you want to play nice; to pretend you understand the pressure I'm under?"

Megan cowered beside a pile of shattered glass. Gerry slowly regained composure, just as an apprehensive waitress approached the room with a dustpan.

"And just what the hell are you staring at?" he yelled, confronting her in the doorway. Getting no response, he seized her by the arm, tearing her sleeve at the seam. "This is a private matter between me and my wife! Mind your business, and let us finish!"

"Oh, it's finished, all right." Megan stood up and shook the sharp debris from her flowery dress. She strode past Gerry, grabbed her suitcase in the hallway and headed straight out the front door; never once looking back.

All along the cab ride home, Megan tried calming her nerves. An uncontrollable trembling had replaced her intense anger as the shock of Gerry's outburst set in. Refuting her advances was one thing. She even grew accustomed to frequent verbal tirades when he was irritable. But throwing glasses and physical abuse now tested her fortitude beyond even her range of tolerance.

Megan leaned against the passenger window, feeling fragile. She understood that this day's events were clear signals that her marriage – while barely begun – was already on the verge of ruin. Oh God, she thought anxiously. *Can things get any worse?*

Megan's fragility had turned to queasiness when she returned to the apartment. This wasn't one of her allergic reactions. She attributed her discomfort to the heated argument… or perhaps a concussion from her head hitting the floor. Two extra-strength painkillers went down easily with a glass of water. She then double-locked both the front door and the door to her bedroom.

When she awoke the next morning, Megan found no sign of Gerry. She thought back on his tantrum and began to feel guilty over having provoked him with her comments. Maybe I was too pushy, she rationalized. *Maybe he's right. My heart hasn't exactly been into it.*

Beyond the confusion, Megan's lightheadedness from the night before remained. She dressed hurriedly, hailed a cab and showed up without an appointment at the office of Doctor Max Abromowitz.

When Katherine's physician heard that Megan Price injured her head in a fall, he bypassed a scheduled appointment to see her at once. He personally administered a series of exams in an attempt to rule out a traumatic injury.

"Ms. Price. Although I won't have all the results back till tomorrow, I don't believe your symptoms are consistent with a concussion."

"Well, that's a relief," Megan sighed, rubbing the bump on the back of her head.

"However, I would suggest you take it easy for the next few days. And

I'd highly recommend that you set up an appointment with your OBGYN. Your urine test strongly indicates that you might be pregnant."

Johnny considered taking over the piano duties for the upcoming tour. His skills had progressed from the hobby level to being more than competent. Nonetheless, the idea of having the star stuck behind an oversized mahogany box for the complete performance was a legitimate concern for promoters. Plus, Johnny was gradually finding his niche as a vibrant front man. The most logical scenario was to hold auditions for Howard's replacement.

Johnny and the band sat through an afternoon at *The Lion's Gate*, evaluating an eclectic group of candidates. None of them were particularly impressive: A classically trained concert pianist. A synthesizer technician. A Liberace impersonator. He and the guys were prepared to call it a day when in walked twenty-five-year-old Lauren Minton.

Lauren's tall, shapely figure was crammed inside a three-piece suit and suede boots. It made her look like a cross between a fashion model and Julie Andrews in *Victor Victoria*. She possessed a slender frame, flowing brown hair and matching eyes; the kind of woman who always drew a second glance, even on days when she didn't look her best. Lauren wasn't one to flaunt her beauty. But there was something about the way she carried herself that had men turning in her direction.

Lauren took a seat at the piano. She waited for Ian to stop whistling before directing her comments to Johnny. "Don't take this the wrong way, but I'm really a big fan. I've pretty much got down all the songs from your *Poet* album. Any in particular you'd like me to play?"

Perfect renditions of *Jacqui* and *Return to Me* followed; Lauren's fingers dancing effortlessly across the keys.

Johnny conferred with the guys, then took Lauren aside to discuss the tour's details. Musically, she had certainly passed the audition. Now it was time to determine if she fit in with the group.

"So, tell me how you feel about touring the country in a band of four guys?" Johnny asked, placing two frosted mugs and a pitcher of cold beer on the table. "And what else can you tell me about your concert resume?"

"Well, I don't know what Frank's told you, but we met one night after my band finished a set, just before his was about to head on. Truthfully, I've never played live for a really big crowd, though I have done the club scene forever. Keyboards. Piano. I've also sung both lead and harmony since I was seventeen."

"And what about the all-guy part?" Johnny asked again, pouring the beer into the mugs. "You okay with that?"

"If you're asking if men intimidate me, no. Except for my soon-to-be ex-husband, I get on fine with every guy I've ever known. As long as we mesh musically, I'm cool."

Johnny figured the next question was valid, if only because Lauren raised the subject herself. "Well, your qualifications... pretty impressive. Though you seem really young to be getting divorced. If you're cool with me asking: how long were you married?"

Lauren laughed. "If you've got nothing better to do tonight, I suppose I could bore you with my saga. But in a nutshell, we all do things at a young age that we go on to regret. At nineteen, some girls get foolish tattoos or piercings. I ended up with a rotten husband. In hindsight, it's the stupidest thing I could've done. Though I've gotta say, the experience forced me to grow up pretty quickly."

"I kinda know what you mean," Johnny said, shrugging. "Relationships never seem to come with a rulebook. Instead, we're raised on radio and all those love songs with happy endings. Its like real life doesn't really kick in till we've been blindsided by heartbreak."

"Nicely put." Lauren raised a frosty glass toward Johnny. "Only, when you decide to make it legal, it's not just the cheating that weighs you down. Talk about learning the hard way! I'll be damn' sure to never act impulsively again when it comes to new opportunities."

"Can't say I blame you." Johnny nodded. "But then again, I'm not in a position to offer you much time to decide on joining our road show. We've only got a few weeks to rehearse before the first gig in Cincinnati."

"Is that an offer I'm detecting?" Lauren grinned. "Coz you know, if that was a business proposal – long as the specifics work out – you've got yourself a piano player!"

The weeks of rehearsals flew by quickly. Lauren Minton was going to be a capable onstage replacement for Howard Greffen. But Johnny was going to miss the battle-tested wisdom of his venerable mentor. Wishing to soak up a final session before going on tour, Johnny got the urge to return to Brooklyn. He found Howard in a whimsical frame of mind.

"What brings you to this neck of the woods?" Howard ushered Johnny inside. "I had you pegged as one who never looked back on anything, including the old neighborhood."

"Forget the man who changed my life? I figured you'd gimme more credit than that."

Howard smiled. "Well, it's not everyday a pop star shows up at your door. Glad to see your feet still touch the ground." He laughed. "But seriously, how you doin'?"

In the back parlor, Johnny hit the ground running with a detailed update on his flourishing career. "So the band's doing great. The contract extension just kicked in. And Highpeak's releasing *Jacqui* as the next single. It all seems a little too good to be true."

"Kid, I couldn't be happier for you. With your talent and work ethic, it was only a matter of time. It was all you."

Johnny flashed a look of surprise. "Howard, I'd be nowhere without you. When we met, I was a total novice. Even if I can never thank you properly, I do wanna give something back."

"Oh, c'mon." Howard jammed his hands in his pockets. "You know I'm just a simple guy, content with his lot, and too busy with school to worry about trivialities."

"Howard, you're gonna be a teacher. In the spirit of something you once told me, I want you to *look the part*. And with your permission, I also wanna spend a few bucks on you; fix up your place."

"Listen kid, you honestly owe me nothing. I got paid to play on your record. That covered a few bills. But really, the only things in my life I want changed, you honestly have no control over. I'm just pleased as piss that you're in such a good place, you know?"

Howard reached to clear a mound of sheet music from a rickety end table. A loud beeping sound from outside prompted Johnny to tug at his host's shirtsleeve. "Oh, hey, to be continued on that. First, I want you to open your pre-graduation gifts."

Parked out in the driveway, Howard discovered a shinny new black four-door Chevy Corsica. Tears of gratitude sprang to his eyes.

"This should replace the old clunker with all those coffee cups on the front seat that I wasn't supposed to notice." Johnny winked. He took the keys from the delivery driver and opened the trunk. An assortment of supplies sat inside, including a monogrammed, leather-bound daybook, a silver Mont Blanc pen, and a Samsonite briefcase. "So, professor, what do ya think?"

Howard gasped. "I… don't know what to say. It's all a little too perfect for me." He slid into the driver's seat and gripped the leather steering wheel. "You do know that if I'm going to accept this, I at least need to clutter it up to officially make it mine."

After a test-drive, Johnny led Howard back inside the house. It didn't take long for him to revisit their earlier conversation. "In speaking of the past and all the things I cannot change, I was curious about something you told me a while back."

"What about?" Howard shrugged, dropping his new car keys in his pocket.

"You once mentioned that you wrote a song for your son. You said it was in the days after Suzanne passed away. I was wondering if you ever played it for him?"

Howard didn't meet his eyes. "I don't get it. Why of all things... after all your thoughtfulness? What does one have to do with the other?"

"First tell me about the song. How'd Josh react? I can't imagine even the most music-hating adolescent not being moved by a song written for him."

"If you must know, I don't honestly remember. It was one of those mornings when he and I weren't really communicating. I played it here in this room. He probably got up and walked away after a few lines. Never got to see his face."

"So it's possible he was touched by it?" Johnny's eyes grew wider.

"Anything's possible. But why does any of this matter now? He's been gone for years."

"Howard, if it isn't too painful, I want you to play me that song right here at your piano. You still remember how it goes?"

No longer asking questions, Howard sat down at the piano. He found himself caught up in a distant memory. "There are some songs you never forget the words to no matter how hard you try." He placed his fingers on the ivory keys. Tenderly, he delivered a heartfelt rendition of the cheerful ballad, once composed to raise the spirits of a shell-shocked fourteen-year-old.

Oh dear boy the sun is shining, and its Thursday afternoon
There is breakfast on the table and the flowers are in bloom
All these hours you've been sleeping, lying face down in your bed
Do you care to share with Daddy all the thoughts inside your head?

Oh dear boy a warm wind's blowing straight across the southern plains
Can we head outside to have a catch and toss away our pain?
I am not adept at magic, as you now know all too well
But with springtime here upon us it has cast a hopeful spell

(Chorus)
For every obstacle in life there is a reason
For every fallen leaf below there is a season
For every question that we'll never find the answers we search for
There lies a locked door straight ahead to place your keys in
A new beginning waits beyond tomorrow's door

The frost that glazed upon our windows now has melted from the glass
Slowly seeping through the soil it irrigates our newborn grass
The icy walkway to our door no longer threatens our path
And the wicked wind that blew our minds has lost its evil wrath

Oh dear boy I hate to wake you but I need your company
As I watch you toss-and-turn I call your name out quietly
Though I make no promises on how this new day will play out
Somehow together we'll get by beyond the shadow of a doubt

(Chorus)

Oh dear boy the sun is shining and its Thursday afternoon
Breakfast waits upon the table. Lovely flowers are in bloom
All the while as you've been sleeping I have written you this song
If it's not too much to ask for, can you help me sing along?

For too long this quiet's deafening, my heart still weighs a ton
All I seek is conversation from a father to a son
There's a new day now upon us, let's not linger in the past
Won't you take a look around? Opportunities are vast
(Chorus – End)

When the last note faded, Johnny hurried over to the piano, a tear in his eye. "That was beautiful… as moving as I expected it to be." He placed an arm around Howard's shoulders. "Howard, can I record it for you? I wanna get it out there, release it for all the world to hear." He sat down on the bench next to his mentor. "If your son's anywhere out there, he's bound to know you haven't forgotten him. It's the least I can do."

20

CAGED IN

Katherine Price nearly knocked over a receptionist on her way out of the office. Frantically, she hailed a cab on lower Broadway and climbed inside. "Central Park West and 81st. Hurry!" she barked, prepaying the cabbie with a rumpled twenty-dollar bill.

Delayed in city traffic, Katherine jumped out three blocks shy of her destination, electing to run the remaining distance. She bolted past Megan's familiar doorman and scurried into an elevator, hitting twenty-three and the door-close buttons simultaneously. When the doors slid open on the twenty-third floor, what she saw was worse than she ever could have imagined.

When Megan discovered she was pregnant, she felt obliged to track Gerry down and welcome him back unconditionally. It didn't matter who was at fault in their problems up till now. She only cared to patch up any differences for the benefit of their unborn child.

Gerry was tickled at the idea of fatherhood. His initial excitement was clear to see. Even his attitude toward Megan improved vastly. Some days, he'd leave work early and bring home root beer and ginger snaps to help remedy Megan's perpetual morning sickness. He even microwaved lasagna for dinner one night when she was too exhausted.

It was not to last long.

Gerry's temper, which had lain dormant since the Labor Day incident, slowly reawakened. His inability to help Megan get past her constant nausea grew increasingly frustrating. He'd often storm out for hours at a time. Then came the sleepless nights, and Megan's rapid weight gain on her previously slender frame.

"Do you really need all these new clothes?" he'd ask rhetorically when she arrived home with bags of maternity outfits. "In med school they say this doesn't happen till the third trimester. Why are you getting so fat now?"

The child had been conceived around the time of their honeymoon, making Megan three months pregnant as of mid October. The waiting and physical changes to his wife's body proved more than Gerry was equipped to handle. Coupled with his outlook - which had swung rapidly from excitement to fear - he again turned verbally abusive.

Then came the current eruption.

It happened one morning after a particularly restless night. Gerry was awakened abruptly by a beeping pager on his nightstand. Instantly, he realized he was two hours late for his hospital shift. He began running in circles in a cold sweat. "Megan, get your ass out of bed, damn it. Why the hell didn't you set the alarm?"

Megan rolled out from under her quilt. She couldn't be much help, stopped by an immediate feeling of queasiness.

Where the hell are my shoes?" Gerry hollered, frantically tearing apart the bedroom. "And where'd you stash my black belt?" All he could find was Megan crouched on the bathroom floor, her arms tightly wrapped around the toilet bowl. Gerry's fragile stability snapped like an autumn twig. In one motion he reached down and violently heaved one of Megan's shoes across the room. It ricocheted off the bathroom door and caught her on the left side of her head. The two-inch heel caused a sharp crimson gash just above Megan's left ear.

Gerry expected his wife to come crawling back into the bedroom. Instead, he watched her remain eerily motionless. Her lack of reaction only added to his disgust. Gerry hurled a picture frame from Megan's nightstand. It narrowly missed her back and smashed against the bathtub. Still no reaction. He was now sweating profusely, his rage in full bloom. Gerry wound up and put his left fist through a mirrored closet door. The vigorous punch easily shattered the glass, causing his knuckles to bleed steadily as he ran toward her. "See what you've done to me, bitch? Look what you've done?" he cried hysterically, waving his bloody fist near her face.

The sight of a sobbing Megan knelt over the toilet only further infuriated him. "Get up, you spoiled princess!" He moved around her in a raging semi-circle. "Quit being so damn' useless!"

"Just calm down," she yelled back, her voice magnified by the echo of the bathroom walls. "I'm dizzy. I'm pregnant. Gimme a minute."

"How remarkably convenient," Gerry snarled, wiping his bleeding hand on the back of her ivory robe. "Your pathetic act don't fool anyone." Gerry yanked his wife from behind by her hair, then shoved her back into the bedroom. Megan stumbled, collapsing in the center of their bed. "You're not going back to sleep now," Gerry roared. "Now get up, bitch. Find my other shoe."

Megan struggled to a sitting position. Gerry reared back and struck her forehead solidly with the top of his injured left hand, connecting just above her left eye. He watched with indifference as she fell backward, landing hard on her mattress.

For several minutes, a terrified Megan lay still, with one hand shielding her battered face, bracing for the next blow. Warm blood trickled down her cheek. Slowly, she peeked around her fingers. She saw Gerry picking a jagged shard out of his hand. Megan was tempted to run for help. Instead, she found in herself a moment of startling resolve. She pushed herself back up to a sitting position.

"Yeah, it sure takes a lot of courage to hit a pregnant woman, doesn't it, you bastard?"

Gerry froze. Megan reached for the telephone on her nightstand. "I don't care if you find your shoes, your belt, or step in front of a speeding bus. Just get the hell out of *my* house, or I'll have the cops drag your ass outta here and lock you up like the rabid animal you've become!"

Megan began dialing 911. A stunned Gerry recomposed himself and scampered half-dressed out into the hallway, leaving a trail of blood behind him. When the front door slammed, Megan returned the phone to its cradle, having predetermined not to follow through. Instead, she allowed her rage to boil over. She began with some of Gerry's most cherished possessions. A Rolex watch. His framed diplomas. A computer monitor. One by one she smashed them against a wall in the hallway until satisfied that he was out of her life… permanently.

By the time Katherine arrived, it was hard to believe what had happened. She placed a cold compress on her daughter's swollen left eye, while simultaneously administering a damp towel to the gash on the side of Megan's head. "Did he really do this to you?" she asked, the last sparks of her denial igniting. "Please tell me this is all a terrible misunderstanding, or one of your allergic reactions?"

"Mother, this is as much your fault as his," Megan said, trembling. "It was always you who wanted him in our family. You forced him on me from the beginning. The only reason I didn't call the cops today was so you could be the first to see his handiwork. You know: when he originally attacked me after your Labor Day party, I had only the hired help as my witness. This time, I wanted you to see this with your own eyes."

Katherine cradled her daughter's head. "I'm so sorry, baby. I had no idea he was capable of hurting you. And I know you do love him. Don't you?" she asked in an unfamiliar, yet caring tone.

Megan was appalled by Katherine's last remark. She lifted her swollen face from the bloodied towel and unleashed her escalating fury. "Mother, there's only one guy I've ever loved. And right now, he just happens to be one of the most successful singers in America. You do remember Johnny Elias, don't you?"

"Andy, you shoulda heard the crowd last night! Every song went down great!" Johnny was on the telephone in his Cincinnati hotel room, his voice scratchy. "And Lauren: fit right in. Her harmony's gorgeous, angelic. For opening night she dressed in a white tux; just wowed 'em."

"Nice. Sounds like a helluva show. And speaking of things impressive, somebody seems rather sweet on that keyboard chick. I'm starting to wonder if your interest in her is more than just professional."

"Honestly, Andy, she's off limits. Even if I was into her, she's in the middle of a messy split. And secondly, we've got this unwritten rule: no flirting with her during the tour. So even without a gig nearly every night, I doubt we'd have anything to talk about beyond music."

"Well, in other matters close to your heart, your album's still holding in the top-fifteen. And the *Jacqui* single: number eleven. It's your fastest seller to date, which you know I'm a bit partial to anyway. Oh, and the title track still hangs in the Top-Forty, making you the only one with two chart entries. I guess someone out there still appreciates quality songwriting after all."

"Man! Can you believe this, Andy? I mean, who'd ever dare dream this up? Crazy, huh? Especially from where I come… and with all the crap radio churns out these days."

"Actually, I can. I deposit all your checks."

"Right," Johnny laughed. "Still doesn't feel real for me. Too far fetched."

"Yeah, well, what's that line Paul Simon once sang about every generation throwing a hero up the pop charts? What's to say you can't be the guy for this era? Your music's pretty damn brilliant!"

"Nah, no way! Not me. Not really. And the critics, they all seem to agree that I'm way more folky than contemporary. But I like the way you think."

"Yeah, well tell that to the folks at Worldwide Pants. They called to book you on Letterman when you're back in the city. And that's just the beginning. There's enough here to keep me busy straight to next October, if I only allow for a five-minute vacation."

"Sounds to me like you're lovin' every minute. But do remember to take a break from time to time so that famous girlfriend of yours doesn't come out here to hunt me down."

"Jacqui's fine with it, believe you me. She's already turned in first drafts for her next cover design." Andy paused to check his date book. "Speaking of new album projects, have you written anything recently? You kinda agreed to have at least ten songs for the early part of next year."

Johnny nervously cleared his throat. "To be honest, I haven't had a whole lotta writing time. Rehearsals and promo have me totally preoccupied. I do have three or four I'm feeling good about. But anyway, thanks for the reminder."

Andy looked down at the tour schedule. "So tomorrow it's Indy, followed by Pittsburgh, then Philly. We'll touch base along the way. Just be sure to say hi to your friend Lauren for me."

21

Road To Somewhere

A twenty-four-seat chartered *Greyhound* departed Louisville station, heading south for Memphis just after midnight. This was not the customized luxury tour bus Johnny envisioned with his name splashed across the side, or video monitors at each seat. Then again, life on the road was hardly as he'd pictured it to be.

Johnny watched the small towns roll by in slow motion through tinted windows. This was the first time he'd really gotten to see America outside of New York City. Sometimes, he would stare for hours, hardly believing what he now did for a living – or that his lyrical songs had found such a vast audience in this era of rap, techno and grunge. The long rides were his refuge from the cramped dressing rooms, the sore throats, the autograph hounds, the sleep deprivation, and the suddenly mounting expectations.

Johnny's meteoric rise to prominence was in stark contrast with his humble upbringing, or his personal emptiness since Megan's betrayal. There were nights when scores of young wannabe groupies hung out by the stage door, lifting their shirts, making their presence well known. But for the sensitive, twenty-two year-old rising pop star, the thought of meaningless encounters with bodies and faces he'd never again see held as much appeal as another greasy fast-food run.

Further complicating matters was the constant travel: hardly conducive for a stable relationship. Stability. It was really all he ever craved. The idea of meeting someone on the road seemed impractical for a young man whose heart remained in New York... and still burdened with the long-distance memory of a now married and pregnant Megan Ridgewell.

"Yo, Frankie, turn that up. We can hardly hear you," a familiar voice shouted from the back of the bus.

"Ian, you moron, I'm not plugged in. How 'bout *you* keep it down?"

Three rows behind Johnny, Frank Traber was strumming his new cherry-red Stratocaster. The archetypal longhaired lead guitarist – an avid Jimi Hendrix disciple – was fiercely dedicated to honing his considerable skills. It wasn't uncommon to hear strains of *The Wind Cries Mary* from his usual seat – or from under his hotel room door at four in the morning.

"Hey, Artie, name the only singer to record a duet with both Freddie Mercury and John Lennon?" The loud voice was again Ian Klatt's through a rolled-up magazine.

Ian held court from the back row on every trip. The tall, baldheaded, leather-clad drummer was the life of the party onstage and off. He found the undisciplined touring life his personal never-ending carnival. Ian's rock-steady drumming and general effervescence kept everyone upbeat most of the time... so long as his constant carousing wasn't overly disruptive.

"Oh, I don't know, Ian. Was it Elton John? I remember him doing *Whatever Gets You Through the Night* with Lennon," Art Tillman answered halfheartedly, trying to get some sleep.

"Errrr! Sorry, Artie. Wrong answer. Thanks for playing."

"Artie" was the seasoned veteran of the group. Years earlier, he'd played a tour of state fairs with his first band, The Anestisiacs. The forty-year-old bassist was the only group member hired by Highpeak. His generally reserved demeanor sometimes caused his mates to privately wonder if he was planted for the sake of reporting back to Ron Neswick. However, Art's lack of sociability was outweighed by his overall professionalism. This kept the others from harboring any lasting resentment.

"Wait, I know." Lauren chimed in. "David Bowie, right? He did *Fame* with Lennon, and *Under Pressure* with Queen. That was an easy one!"

"Bingo!" Ian's voice reverberated across the bus. "Dude, you're awesome. Next stop, I owe you a burrito."

"She's not a dude, Ian." Frank deadpanned, not looking back. "Treat the lady with a little respect."

As the newcomer to the band, Lauren Minton blended in flawlessly. She was perfectly content to sit around drinking beer and participate in marathon rock and roll trivia games. Lauren was especially grateful to Frank for getting her the audition, although she periodically questioned his true motivations.

Hey, Johnny," Lauren called out to the front of the bus. "We gonna get to hit Graceland when we're in Memphis? Always wanted to see the King's digs."

"Yeah, sure," Johnny replied, turning back to face her. "I figured we'd all go after soundcheck tomorrow morning. Never been there either. None of us have."

On off-days, Johnny and the band usually picked a sightseeing destination where the five musicians could bond and look back on their stage conquests. At first, these day-trips proved beneficial in building off-stage chemistry. But by the eighth or ninth city, the repetitious excursions grew progressively tired. Between early wakeup calls, daily rehearsals, and smoke-filled bus rides, there wasn't much glamour in living out of a suitcase aside from the musical companionship and the shows themselves.

One late night in Charlotte, North Carolina, Johnny got bored of in-room movies. He headed downstairs to the hotel bar, in hopes of finding a better offer. What he found was his new keyboard player, sitting alone – except for the bartender who was clearly trying to charm her.

Johnny smiled at the site of her shoulder-length brown hair, and suede cowboy boots. He quietly approached. "Lauren," he said, pulling up the adjacent stool. "Glad I'm not the only insomniac down here looking for some company."

"Oh, hey, Johnny." She waved at him, then downed a shot of bourbon and placed it on the glossy mahogany. "Guess even Charlotte can be a quiet town at this hour."

Johnny requested a light-beer from the bartender. Lauren ordered a Jim Beam refill, then turned to Johnny with a hollow expression. "So what should we talk about?"

"Well, by the look on your face, I guess the divorce thing is still a mess?"

"You could say that," Lauren agreed, her voice flat.

"So the lowlife figures that with your steady income from the tour, he's somehow entitled to a percentage of this too?"

"Johnny, in many ways the whole thing's really my fault. I'm the moron who agreed to marry him. And my stubbornness is what kept us hanging on for as long as we did. Even after he moved on to somebody else, I somehow had this crazy idea we'd patch things up. Who knew the jackass would pin the whole thing on me, screw up the next two years of my life?"

"Is that how long it took you to get over him? I mean, does it really take years?"

"It's probably different with everyone." Her fingers fidgeted with a toothpick on the counter. "People like you and me probably invest everything. That leaves us vulnerable. Others only put in just enough to say they know what suffering is. When you think about it, it's entirely about commitment. Well, that and maybe how much you're willing to leave yourself exposed."

The philosophy of derailed relationships was a subject in which each was well versed. Lauren's story sounded like a good country/western song. Johnny couldn't avoid noticing the loveliness of her face beneath her sadness. Even the delicate lines on her forehead held an alluring vulnerability.

Lauren ordered a third refill. Johnny moved on to another common ground. "So tell me: what is it about my songs that grabbed you? It's funny how well you know my music, yet I never asked how you got into it."

Lauren put down her drink and grinned sheepishly. "Remember: you're asking a fan. My opinion's not totally objective."

"Objectivity's totally overrated." Johnny laughed. "Let's hear it anyway."

"Well, I was always a sucker for a sweet melody and a handsome face. There's something about the way your tunes match up with those eloquent words… like they belong together."

"So it was my tunes that first struck you?" He raised his eyebrows. "Or was it something about the lyrics?"

"Actually, it was neither." She began to blush. "Even before I heard one note, I saw you being interviewed on *Entertainment Tonight*. I was smitten. Didn't realize you were a songwriter at that point. Though I must admit: your album's what clinched it for me."

A steady rain fell against a skylight above them. Johnny began whistling an old familiar refrain. Lauren added her beautiful high harmony to the chorus. Only it was the wrong chorus. Johnny chuckled aloud. "Right band. Wrong song!"

"What do ya mean? *Have You Ever Seen The Rain* by CCR? That's a classic!"

"Actually, Creedence had two rain songs. The one I started was *Who'll Stop The Rain*. A subtle difference."

The remaining color drained from Lauren's face. "Oh right. Guess I got 'em crossed." She giggled. "So, you gonna report me to the song police?"

Johnny patted Lauren on the back. "Nah, don't worry. This'll be our dirty little secret."

It was 4am. Johnny decided it was best to head upstairs for a few hours of rest. A morning bus ride to Atlanta loomed. Lauren placed her arm around Johnny's shoulders for support as they staggered to the elevator. Johnny didn't mind the attention.

"Wanna stop by my room for a bit?" Lauren asked, gripping his sleeve for balance.

Johnny steadied Lauren on her feet. "Tell me you didn't leave the key down at the bar?" He patted her jacket pocket.

"It's in one of my pockets," she murmured with eyelids half-open. "If only I had the energy to find where I put 'em."

Hesitantly, Johnny placed his hands on her narrow thighs, feeling for the key in the front of her jeans. He located it on the left side and reached inside her pocket. A tingling sensation shot up Lauren's spine. Impulsively, she pulled Johnny closer, and his arms closed naturally around her in response.

Johnny allowed the spontaneous hug to linger. The hint of jasmine perfume on her neck was intoxicating. Instinctively, he caressed the small of her back. Then he pulled gently away to open the door. *Oh mercy, give me strength.* Johnny summoned every ounce of self-restraint to fight the attraction. *She's technically still married, right? And she's wasted; hardly the way to start something meaningful,* he soundly rationalized. *Not to mention Frank and his politics.*

He flicked on the lights inside her doorway. "That was really nice – the conversation and the cuddling. But I think I'd better head off for a bit of shut-eye. I'll order you a wake-up call for around seven-thirty."

Lauren sighed softly. Johnny helped her over to the bed, set her down, and pulled off each of her boots. He covered her with a thin blanket and switched off the bedside light. "Goodnight," he whispered, slowly moving to the door. "We should do this again sometime. Sober, perhaps."

"I'd like that," she responded sleepily. "Thanks for everything."

Johnny was the first to board the Atlanta-bound bus the next morning. He stretched out in a quiet window seat near the front, hoping to catch a precious hour of sleep.

Then the rest of the band began settling in on the 24-seater. Each retreated to the farthest corners to ensure a degree of privacy. All: except Lauren. Boarding last, she opted for the aisle seat next to Johnny, where she promptly dozed off on his shoulder.

The performance onstage that night was as tight as any Johnny could remember, with the exception of a single uncharacteristic moment. They were playing *We've Already Said Goodbye*, the last song before the encore. Johnny flashed a subtle grin in the direction of the piano just prior to belting out the dramatic last high note. The usually flawless Lauren was temporarily distracted. She botched a note in her high harmony, before quickly recovering with an embarrassed smile. Her miniscule blunder was hardly detected by the sold-out audience. It didn't go altogether unnoticed.

"What the hell was that note you hit up there?" Frank grumbled backstage during the post concert buffet. "If I didn't know otherwise, I'd suspect something was going on between you and our resident celebrity."

"It was nothing," she downplayed the *faux pas*. "I guess the emotion of that song gets me choked up sometimes. It won't happen again."

"Better not," Frank insisted. "You know our fraternization policy. Since you established these ground rules, I expect you to uphold 'em – just like the rest of us."

The hectic tour schedule eased for two days in Atlanta before a trip down to Florida. All five bandmates were slated to explore the Coca-Cola factory after rehearsals the first afternoon, hoping for a taste of Americana. But Art was battling a heavy cold. Ian overslept. Johnny, Frank and Lauren were left to make the trip on their own.

Lauren made every conscious effort to keep her distance from Johnny throughout the day. She fought her instincts to gravitate toward him, to complete his sentences, to harmonize with his spontaneous singing. But whether it was the way she made eyes at Johnny or laughed at his jokes, it was clear to Frank that Lauren was progressively growing more attached.

The threesome encountered a large funhouse of flavors near the end of the visit. Hundreds of sodas could be sampled at an assortment of self-serve fountains. Lauren excitedly filled small disposable cups with exotic varieties, tasting one after another, before sharing them with Johnny.

Frank also took pleasure in such strange concoctions as watermelon mist from Korea, leeche nut cola from China, and a carbonated tangerine beverage from Argentina. A half-hour of fizzy fun elapsed. But where were his elusive friends? Nowhere in the vicinity. Then he spotted Johnny and Lauren emerging in-step from a gift shop, wearing matching Coke floppy hats and carrying identical souvenir bags. They were whistling along with a classic jingle from 1979.

"Ah, the lovebirds!" Frank yelled across the crowded room. He was seething when he caught up to them. "Just great: the group leader and the rule maker. Mize well make it public so the rest of us can deal with it. Sneaking around's only gonna build resentment."

Johnny folded his arms. "Frank, it's not like that. There's nothing to declare to you or anyone else."

"Sonofabitch," Frank countered with a look of disgust. "Cozy bus ride naps; your little stage flirtation. Now this. It's so damn obvious! Just look at the two of you in matching outfits."

"Frank, Johnny's telling the truth." Lauren removed her souvenir hat and tucked it in a shopping bag. "We've both been down a long tough road. Unless you've been there yourself, you couldn't possibly understand."

"Well, my eyes certainly work well enough," Frank snapped. "What a joke that you guys go round pretending it isn't happening! We still have another couple-dozen shows to play. The last thing this band needs is infighting over incest." He waggled a finger in Johnny's face. "Hook-ups are always death on any group. Fleetwood Mac. The Mamas and the Pappas. Go look it up."

Johnny clenched his teeth and stepped toward Frank. "You know, last I checked, I invited you on tour to be my lead guitarist, not my chaperone."

Frank grabbed Johnny by the collar and shoved him to the floor. Johnny bounced back up and took a wild swing at Frank, narrowly missing his chin. Lauren quickly stepped between them, her arms spread apart. "Knock it off. Both of you, damn it! We're all on the same side here, aren't we?"

"Well, considering three-fifths of this band are here 'coz of me, I'd say this jackass at least owes me the decency of playing by the rules," Frank fired back. "We're on too good of a run for him to suddenly need a new guitarist and drummer."

Awkward silence at rehearsals the next day spoke volumes. An equally silent bus ride back to the hotel followed. Johnny, Lauren, Frank, Art, and Ian all disembarked in separate directions to pack for the morning trip down to Florida.

Johnny was unable to fall asleep by 2am. Insomnia was just one side effect of a pill he'd recently, and reluctantly started taking to boost his onstage energy. "Black Beauties," Ian had called them, though they were actually black and blue – a highly addictive prescription medication. "Totally harmless. Pop 'em like Skittles," he boasted. Johnny wasn't so sure. But after twenty-six shows and a perpetually raspy voice, he finally caved in.

Drug taking was something Johnny always swore he'd never do. He had seen what drugs had done to so many rock & roll heroes. Janis Joplin. Jimi Hendrix. Jim Morrison. Elvis Presley. All of them gone before their time due to chemical experimentation. Johnny wasn't going to become another casualty. He prided himself on being "clean-cut." Drugs were for misfits; for the kids who smoked pot under the stairwell at school. But *this is kinda like cold medicine, he rationalized. Nothing hazardous like cocaine or LSD. Just a boost for physical exhaustion.*

Now he sat up in bed, his bloodshot eyes staring blankly at the shadows on the walls. Finding little comfort in this tedious exercise, he reached for the telephone and called Lauren's room. "Mind if I stop by for a minute?" he asked.

Lauren stood in her doorway, a pair of pink silk pajamas clinging to her shapely figure. When Johnny arrived down the hall, Lauren quietly let the door close behind him. She strode past the queen-sized bed and over to a table situated by the far window. "Have a seat," she offered, muting the TV with a remote. "Listen, Johnny, how do I say this?" She grabbed his hands and leaned in toward him. "Like I've told you before, it took me a long time to grow into my shoes, so to speak. But these days... well, I'm fairly confident in knowing what I want. And simply put: I think I'm really falling for you."

Johnny smiled. "Believe me, it's a two-way street."

"But, Johnny, what you can't possibly fathom is how incredibly lucky I feel. I mean, I joined this band as a fan of your music. Never expected this to happen." She pushed an errant strand of hair from her forehead. "Thing is, easy as it would be for me to dive in headfirst, I'm still really scared of the consequences." She frowned, seeing no reaction on Johnny's face. "What's the matter? Hope you aren't freaked out with anything I've said."

Johnny leaned in closer to Lauren and brushed a hand against her cheek. "Actually, I'm quite flattered. It's just... well, these days it gets a little lonely waking up every morning in another city, but always in a big empty bed. I mean, I wouldn't wanna wake up next to just anyone, you know. That's not what I'm about. But since we've gotten close, well my heart's been racing, my imagination's been working overtime and still..." His voice trailed off.

Lauren stood from her chair. She slid over to Johnny, put one arm around him, and planted a kiss on his cheek. "It's amazing how comfortable I've allowed myself to get with you. I mean, a divorce like mine can make anyone pretty mistrusting. But for the sake of this tour, and against my gut instinct, well, I think we're gonna have to cool down till the shows wrap up next month."

Johnny sighed. "So I guess it's like we're trapped inside that Tom Petty song." He stood up and moved toward the door. "*The waiting is the hardest part.*"

Lauren laughed. "We're only talking another few weeks. If by then we haven't grown tired of each other..."

Just steps from the door, Lauren caught up to Johnny. She brushed disheveled hair off her face, then lost herself in the moment.

Johnny hardly had a second to breathe. He closed his eyes. Lauren's peppermint lips pressed against his. They seemed to blend as perfectly as their onstage voices. Johnny braced his back against the wall. The dark room was spinning. So much for the pledge made seconds earlier. He ran his hands down the curve of her back, pulling her closer.

Softly, their mouths interlocked. Lauren stroked the back of Johnny's long brown hair. Johnny's fingers wandered up the sides of Lauren's silky pajama top until they lingered on the back of her neck. Her bare skin felt warm, inviting. Several minutes of kissing and caressing flew by. Then Lauren stepped back and filled her lungs with much-needed oxygen. "Well, if that qualifies as coming attractions, we certainly have much to look forward to! Now get outta here before we keep each other up the rest of the night. If Frank sees us with matching bags under our eyes in the morning, he's likely to strangle us with his guitar strings."

It was the Friday after Thanksgiving. Katherine Price rifled through Shelia McLennan's Rolodex, hoping to find a particular contact number from the music industry. After a string of unsuccessful attempts to reach people on the unofficial holiday, she finally connected.

"Good morning, Highpeak Records," the live voice answered on the other end.

"Oh, hi, this is Olivia Santos with MTV. I was wondering if you could please connect me with the business rep for Johnny Elias?"

Katherine sat on-hold for more than a minute, serenaded by *We've Already Said Goodbye*. She nervously fumbled with a box of paperclips, until the voice returned to the line.

"I'm sorry, Ms. Santos, but Heidi Ellison and our PR staff aren't in today. I can provide you with the number for Mr. Elias's personal management if you'd like."

Katherine took down the seven digits and smiled. "If it would be all right, can you also please let me know where I can direct a package for his consideration?"

The temporary receptionist unknowingly disclosed Johnny's apartment address. She didn't stop there. "Just for your general info, Mr. Elias is currently on a North American tour. Last show is scheduled for San Francisco, December 21st."

"Much appreciated," Katherine praised. "You've been a splendid help."

Andy continued to oversee Johnny's business affairs from inside his friend's crammed home office. The workload was inordinate, so he hired a second staff member.

Risa Sheppard, a twenty-six-year-old executive assistant, had been lured away from her post at a TV network. Out of the gate, she helped organize the ever-growing press clippings, media bookings and fan mail. Her productivity enabled Andy to concentrate on more pressing matters.

Over the first two-thirds of the tour, Andy saw the volume of media requests double in number. Pop radio, light music formats and even a few alternative outlets sought recorded station-IDs, morning interviews, and signed items for various contests. It seemed the only mainstream radio genre that hadn't caught on to Johnny's music with regularity were classic rock stations -- the format that Johnny grew up worshiping. Presumably, it was Johnny's heavy dose of folky tunes and piano ballads that had him branded as something less than a full-fledged rocker.

Andy addressed this situation in an early morning briefing, after the band arrived in Houston. "John, look, I know how badly you wanna be taken seriously by that audience. Ya know: a few of those stations have played your title track. I believe they're receptive. They just need an appealing, flat-out rocker; something to justify more airplay. Something edgier."

"I hear where you're coming from, buddy. And a few of my new ones, they're a bit more biting. It's just… when I'm feeling inspired, it's usually those sad, melodic tunes that tend to come out." Johnny reached for a spiral notebook from his overnight bag. "In fact, today I was working on one with someone in mind. All it needs is a proper chorus."

"Well, great to hear you're feeling inspired again. Coz' I just know when you get out to L.A., Highpeak's West Coast contingent will be riding your ass. Neswick's cronies are checking in weekly to see where you're holding on the next record. Getting really impatient."

Impatient? Johnny thought. "How d'ya figure? Poet's only just getting started."

22

A Lonely View

The tour wound down to a precious few dates. Johnny's long, lonely nights were spent laying awake, scribbling potential new song lyrics and fighting the temptation to dial Lauren's extension for an invitation down the hall. *Two more weeks of solitary confinement. Just two more!*

During rare downtime, Johnny often paired up with the local media escort on his afternoon trips. He was fully conscious of his bandmates' perceptions – especially Frank's. Great effort was required to fight the urge to flash a knowing glance, or share a deserving compliment when Lauren looked or played her best.

For her part, Lauren occupied her free time holed up in hotel rooms, talking to her attorney back in New York. Like Johnny, she also found it difficult to keep her distance. But all those demands on his time... *Best to stay out of his way, and let him fulfill his commitments,* she figured.

One night, after an electrifying show in scorching Phoenix, Arizona, Johnny and the band left the theater later than usual. A radio obligation was the culprit. Then came the swarm of autograph seekers, blocking the path between the rear exit and the waiting van. Johnny obliged all requests. For over forty minutes, he put his name to CD covers, concert programs, and ticket stubs. Frank, Ian and Art posed for some photos, then pushed through the crush of bodies and into an air-conditioned Dodge Caravan. Lauren also mingled with a few fans, then proudly stood by, watching Johnny scribble his name on item after item for the increasingly adoring public.

Toward the end of the line, Johnny encountered a set of barely dressed identical twins. Their shapely physiques were revealed beneath sheer halter-tops and hip-hugging shorts. The young bleached-blonde women began flirting as soon as they were close enough to make contact. Johnny didn't mind the attention. "And what're your names?" he asked.

"I'm June. And this is my sister Ashly. If you're free tonight we'd love to show you around all our favorite hotspots," offered the more vocal twin in a breathy, provocative tone.

"That's awfully kind of you." Johnny flashed his trademark lopsided smile. "The thing is, I already had plans here in Phoenix. I can sign something if you'd like."

The quieter girl pulled a Sharpie from her sock and stepped forward. "We didn't really bring anything. But if you wouldn't mind, we'd like for you to sign across our —"

"I'd be happy to sign your shoulders," Johnny interjected, "so long as you promise me you won't hold out from bathing again. I hear the novelty of an autograph isn't worth the long-term filth, if ya know what I mean."

The twins each pretended to roll up non-existent sleeves. Johnny signed best wishes and his signature in black ink. When he looked up, Lauren was halfway to the van.

Two nights later: a raucous reception at a Reno, Nevada casino. Just prior to the encore, a trio of overly enthusiastic teenaged fans tossed their bras onstage amid a handful of bouquets. Frank had bent down near the stage amplifiers to toss a pick in the crowd. A red undergarment flew over his head. It landed directly on top of Lauren's piano. Johnny turned from the center mic stand to identify the overthrown projectile. Art nearly dropped his bass from laughing. "It's like a Tom Jones crowd, only younger!" he howled. Ian stepped out from behind his drum kit to inspect the size. Then he threw it back. The crowd roared. Only Lauren seemed un-amused.

Johnny's popularity was growing with every sold-out show. So too were the raised expectations, the sleep deprivation through shifting time zones, and his need for amphetamines. The recent weeks had been a difficult stretch. Detecting the band's frustrations and occasional homesickness, Johnny sought to soothe everyone's ego by concluding the final leg of the memorable cross-country trek on a high note. He nixed the original plan for the band to stay at the Sheraton Gateway near LAX airport. Instead, Johnny personally splurged for each to get his or her own suite at the luxurious Beverly Wilshire.

King-sized beds. Marble bathrooms. An unspoiled view of Rodeo Drive. This generosity constituted a serious upgrade from the motel chains they'd routinely stayed at. But before anyone could unpack – or appreciate their posh surroundings - the bandmates were taken aback by an invitation slipped under their doors.

Please join Highpeak Records this evening for a cocktail reception
8pm
The Veranda Suite Patio
10th floor, Wilshire Wing
Access via private staircase

Johnny expected a penthouse full of suits and gowns in the former bachelor pad of actor Warren Beatty. Instead, he and the group – minus a hung-over Ian – walked into an unannounced meet-and-greet session with three-dozen delirious radio contest winners from a Top-40 station.

"What the hell's this?" Frank grumbled. "I wasted a night off for some gawking yahoos who don't even know my name. C'mon, we're outta here."

Art threw up his calloused hands and followed Frank and Lauren back to the staircase. "I see we're not needed."

"Guys," Johnny urged diplomatically. "We can't afford to piss off the

Highpeak honchos. At least I can't. Please, let's just smile and hang around for half-an-hour."

Begrudgingly, they did so.

At 5:30 the next morning, it was a surprise early wake-up call that startled everyone. Ed McCauley's secretary, delivered orders for a series of previously unplanned interviews at three LA radio stations, and one in nearby Anaheim. Johnny popped another pill and finessed his way through the repetitive Q & A sessions. His exhausted band-mates sat around yawning.

By 1:45, it was sound-check time over at the Greek Theater. Uneasiness within the group was again renewed as they rehearsed the usual hits. Art was spouting off about a lack of sleep; Frank threw a tantrum over a dented amplifier. Johnny felt the need to do something to change the mood. A playful impersonation of the Big Bopper's 1950s novelty hit, *Chantilly Lace* sprung to mind. His improvised diversion and accompanying Duck Walk inspired Frank to brake into a blistering jam of Jimi Hendrix's *Foxy Lady*. Art began strumming the theme from The Pink Panther on bass. And Ian did his best impression of Animal, the *Muppet Show* drummer.

The cheery exchange should have led to a laid-back afternoon. Instead, awaiting them backstage in the dank, stuffy dressing room stood legendary concert promoter Herb Cantor.

"Good afternoon, gentlemen. Oh, and Ms. Lauren too. Glad to be catching y'all together with some excellent news." Getting minimal reaction, Herb raised his voice a notch. "I'm sure by now you've all heard that you're one of this season's top five grossing shows. And those reviews… not too shabby for a bunch of first-timers."

Halfhearted applause materialized from the road-weary musicians. Herb loosened his tie, then strode up to Johnny in the center of the room. "I don't know if you're aware, but the demand for tickets… unprecedented, really, for such a new artist. If you stayed out another six months, playing larger venues, you'd still be selling out nightly."

"Mr. Cantor, nice to meet you again. And thanks for all you've done," Johnny said noncommittally.

"No need to thank me, Johnny. It's you who's conquered the masses. I'm just here to tell you that Mr. Neswick's green lighted me to add a few more dates, while interest is at its peak."

Johnny gasped, then took a quick peek around the room, fearing a group revolt. "No disrespect, Mr. Cantor, but I think we're all looking forward to heading east for the holidays and some home cooking."

"Precisely what I had in mind," Herb countered, punching the air for punctuation. "I'm also aware you have a second album to record in the coming months. But that shouldn't stop you from playing a few extra nights for the hometown fans."

Scanning the room again, Johnny got a mixed reaction. Surprisingly, Frank and Ian conveyed matching semi-pleased grins. Another week of shows meant another week's pay. Art Tillman held a look of tired reservation, knowing the finish line, which was so near, was now being extended by a week or longer. As for Lauren, she seemed indifferent at first, but then appeared to grow agitated as the news sank in.

"*The Beacon Theater*. Five shows right after New Year's. By the time you've had a week to relax, you'll all be ready for action in front of the noisiest crowds to date. And best of all, you can commute from home, while earning your biggest payday thus far."

"Count me in," Frank shouted from his changing stall. "The Beacon's a cool venue. And in this economy, I'd rather stay an employed musician than become an out-of-work college grad."

"How 'bout the rest of you?" Johnny asked, his head spinning round as if on a swivel. "Any objections?"

"If these are the last shows for now, I'll live with it," Art grumbled. "Though New York's hardly home for me."

"Hell, I won't be the dumb-ass who says no!" Ian shouted in mock frustration. "Guess I'm up for a few more paydays if everyone else is."

Johnny turned to Lauren. The glare on her face revealed her sudden uneasiness. "You okay, or does it impact some pre-arranged plans?"

Lauren stood frozen. "I think you already know how I feel about it. I won't lose my spot in the band by skipping a few gigs. But all things equal, I'd rather have the downtime."

The morning after a mostly impressive LA show, Johnny endured a last-minute grilling by Ed McCauley at Highpeak's West Coast offices over the progress of his next album.

"Four songs! Elias, that's just not acceptable. We're thrilled by the tour success, but you need to invent at least a dozen tunes ready to record by March. Time to reprioritize your downtime; get yourself writing with a purpose."

"I'm honestly giving it my all. Between interviews, travel and the gigs, my days and nights are pretty much jammed." Johnny wiped the sweat from his forehead with a local radio station giveaway washcloth. "I just can't force inspiration. Songwriting: it needs to be inspired or it doesn't work. You guys need to be more patient and lay off the pressure."

He caught up with the band at LAX and joined them in taking a chartered Lear Jet up to San Francisco.

To keep morale high, Johnny again oversaw an upgrade of accommodations. This time, the band checked into the Grand Hyatt, with its breathtaking views of San Francisco Bay. He also threw a private, end-of-the-tour party at the hotel restaurant, hours after they arrived. It seemed everyone had now embraced the idea of extending the tour. All that is, except for Lauren who quietly picked at a plate of nachos. She continued keeping her distance from Johnny, and precious thoughts to herself.

The final scheduled show proved to be the tour's most lackluster. Flat harmonies, two false starts and clumsy solos littered an inconsistent set. Ian's supply of pills had run out the night before, leaving the band lethargic and sober. Though the audience seemed not to notice, there were times when Johnny could detect how his bandmates were thinking ahead to the break.

Back at the hotel, a fax awaited Johnny under his door. It was in Andy's handwriting.

Amazing news, boss. Just heard from Billboard mag. The Poet album's been certified platinum. That's a million units sold! And you're still top five on the charts! Maybe you oughta re-think the whole "wrong generation" thing, eh?

Rather than calling around to share the good news, Johnny instead stuck to his plan. He showered quickly, changed into jeans and headed to the hotel's top floor revolving restaurant. *A relaxing setting for an important discussion*, he figured.

Johnny arrived upstairs just after midnight. Ten nervous minutes ticked by, a folded paper concealed in his hand. Lauren was late. Fortunately, the lovely panoramic view on a clear night kindled a spark of inspiration. He pulled out a pen and began filling in words between the printed stanzas. He was so preoccupied that he didn't even notice Lauren standing beside him.

She tapped him gently on the shoulder. "So what you working on?" Lauren's voice was the most relaxed he'd heard from her in weeks. "Looks like you're in another dimension."

"Oh, it's nothing, really." He placed the cap on his pen. "Just couldn't resist the urge to put an idea on paper before you got here." He smiled. "By the way, someone's lookin' great tonight."

They quietly sat down at a candle-lit table for two up against one of the large windows. A lone pianist played an Andrew Lloyd Weber medley in the background.

"I've been a bit worried about you," Johnny admitted. "It hasn't been easy, putting us on hold these past few weeks. Then again, it seems you've got a lot more on your mind."

"You could say that," she acknowledged, gazing out toward Fisherman's Wharf. "I guess the good news is that my divorce should be final by the time we get home. My lawyer has all the paperwork. Only needs my initials."

"Congratulations!" Johnny placed his hands on top of hers. "You must be feeling a sense of relief now that it's official."

"Relief, yeah, but the finality of the whole thing; pretty sad."

Johnny clutched her hands tighter. "Certainly understandable. But now that this is all behind you, I imagine you're also feeling hopeful at the same time."

"I guess," she replied in a voice mildly unconvincing. "I've learned more about myself by spending a half-dozen unhappy years with a man who turned out to be everything I didn't want. Yeah, I'm thankful, in some distorted way."

"And you also should know that wherever you're going from here, you've weathered the storm gracefully. So let me be the first to welcome you to a sunny new beginning."

Lauren stared out of the window with wide eyes. There was an awkward silence. "The Golden Gate and the Bay Bridge are so much bigger than I imagined, seeing 'em from up here. It's like having a view from the top of the world."

Johnny laughed. "Funny, but… that's exactly what I thought when I first got upstairs. Those exact words, they helped me wrap a song I've been writing about you these past few weeks."

"You didn't!" Her face lit up. "But how? I'm just your typical screwed-up, distrusting, piano-girl. Can't possibly be much fodder for more than a throwaway line or two, can it?"

"Why don't I play it for you first? You can decide if it's up to your standard."

Lauren flashed a surprised look. "I didn't know you played much piano. Isn't that why I'm in this band?"

"Lauren, there's a lot you'll soon learn about me." He took her by the hand and led her to the center of the round room. They waited for the tuxedoed player to complete his vanilla rendition of *Memory*.

Lauren sat down at the closest empty table. Johnny unfolded the lyric sheet and propped it up in front of him for guidance. After feeling out the keys on the piano, he began his upbeat ballad.

I once believed love came to everyone; that it was not so hard to find
Now I have seen the world through different eyes – It's hard to keep
an open mind
I know that you've been hurt before, and I have been there just the same
At times I thought that I'd lost everything to those who played love as a
game
But now the game I play is sincerity and the rules are give and take
I'm only out to fall in love with you, not to have your heart to break

(Chorus)
And if I showed you a view from the top of the world
would you chance your heart with me?
If I showed you the way, can I get you to say
that it all was meant to be?
If I took your past and changed it to a distant memory
Would you join in my climb to the top of the world?
And could you fall in love with me?

Some spend a lifetime searching for love that'll never come their way
And some will pass on opportunity that they will wish they could replay
Now could this be the break we've waited for? Only tomorrow
knows for sure
All the smiles we've shared from moment one would seem too
heartfelt to ignore
You know we may be on the verge of what we've put off all this time
And so to turn our backs right now is not a shame but more a crime
(Chorus repeats)

Better days will surely lie ahead but who'll be lying by your side
I'd like to think that I could wait forever but a man must have his pride
So ask yourself if I could be the one who you thought you'd never find

*I may not wear armor or ride a horse, but I could bring you peace of
mind*
And if I had the ideal words to say or the precise route to go
I'd give it everything I have to win your heart and let you know
(Chorus – End)

A few random diners enthusiastically clapped. Lauren was overcome
with emotion. Johnny stood from the bench and caressed her shoulders.
Then he reached for a napkin and dabbed at her tear-streaked cheeks.

"I'm sorry," Lauren managed to say when words returned to her. "No
one's ever been so thoughtful. I just… I don't know what to say."

"Tell me you and I have a chance. Now that the tour's ending, we have
no façade to maintain, not for Frank, not for anyone. Please tell me we're
both thinking alike?"

In her heart, Lauren badly wanted to allow herself to be swept away in
Johnny's warmth. But in her clearest thoughts, a deep conflict had taken
root since sharing that kiss in her hotel room back in Atlanta.

From a fan to a bandmate, and now a potential love-interest, Lauren
progressively saw Johnny in a different light. No matter how sweet natured
he'd proven to be, he was after all a beloved pop star, his fanbase growing by
the day. The notion of emerging from a disloyal relationship into one where
she would potentially share her new man with the world seemed a heavy
load to bear.

"Johnny, you need to know that you're probably the most understanding guy I've ever met. And those beautiful words you've written, they've
touched my soul." She straightened her back and blew her nose into a paper
napkin. "But this isn't easy. Even three weeks ago I'd have just gone for it.
The thing is: I can't afford to make the same mistake twice."

"Huh?" Johnny shook his head. "Do you mean loyalty?"

"I'm just speaking common sense, Johnny. I mean, rock stars, fidelity…
a precarious combo."

Johnny snatched the lyric sheet off the piano, then turned back to face Lauren. "Lemme tell you something about loyalty. My Dad died when I was just a year old, or so I was told. My mother was apparently too depressed, too poor to raise me. So she left me at a police station one night. Never saw her again. Don't even remember her face. But somewhere through all the hardships; the foster homes, I promised myself that I'd never be like her. I'd only be loyal to the ones I love." He drew a deep breath. "So now I've become this so-called star. I've made my best friend my manager. With the band, I usually put their interests first. Lauren: I'm faithful to everyone in my life. Why compare me to someone who's screwed you over so bad?"

"Okay. Point taken. So it's nothing you've done to me, or to anyone. But look at you. You're a handsome star coming into your prime. You've got women tossing lingerie onstage; all those groupies waiting in hotel lobbies. Tell me, how can I again put myself through the same ordeal with a clear conscience, knowing the temptation that waits for you around every corner?"

Stung by her words, Johnny took a step back. "Lauren, do you really think I'm the cheating type? I'm still coping with being burned by the only girl I've ever loved. Haven't been with anyone else since. Why would I ever put anyone through that, knowing what it's like to be on the receiving end? As my song says, I'm only out to fall in love with you. Why on earth would I break your heart?"

Lauren staggered back to their original table by the window and leaned trembling against the railing. Even as Johnny caught up and brushed a hand across her back, she remained tentative.

"Johnny, you're really sweet. A sincere guy. I also understand you're not asking for a lifetime commitment. Just gimme some time to get home, get settled and think it all through. Okay?"

Johnny wanted to plead his case further. Instead, he swallowed hard and stood motionless, staring into the San Franciscan night. When he turned to say goodnight, he found that he was alone.

23

SURPRISE, SURPRISE

Johnny felt like something of a stranger in his own home. He had slept only a handful of nights in the apartment prior to the concert tour. The still-unfamiliar surroundings offered little comfort. After setting down his bags, Johnny headed into the spare bedroom designated as the home office.

"Oh, you must be Johnny!" A young woman he didn't know rose to greet him. She was short and petite with brown curly hair. "Saw your picture in *Newsweek*." She extended a hand. "I'm Risa, Andy's assistant. We've spoken on the phone, but it's really cool to actually meet you in person."

"Same here," he uttered in a low, raspy voice, visually noting some of the changes made in the time since he'd been away. "I hardly recognize this place."

"That's 'coz I've taken the liberty to organize things. I'm happy to show you the new filing system if you'd like."

"Thanks, Risa. Actually, I need to get hold of Andy now. Know where I can find him?"

"Oh, Andy must've forgotten to tell you: he and Jacqui drove up to Niagara Falls. Said they'd be back sometime tomorrow. Anything I can help with?"

"Thanks. That's okay." Johnny stifled a yawn. "Well, you seem to have things in hand. I'll leave you to your work."

Johnny wandered the rooms trying to get re-acclimated. He gulped down a can of Diet 7-Up in the refurbished kitchen. The dining room was cluttered with Jacqui's art supplies. He was pleased to find his bedroom the one space entirely undisturbed. From his shelves of old record albums to the methodical wall of CDs, nothing appeared to have been altered.

An old, comfy sweatshirt lay folded beside his pillow. Johnny slipped it on, then sat on the edge of his bed in silent reflection. Although he could practically still hear the sound of cheering from the night before, it was Lauren's abrupt departure that lingered in his thoughts. He could not shake the glum perception of coming home alone and empty-handed, despite his musical triumph.

Sporadic amphetamine usage had wreaked havoc with Johnny's sleep patterns. But having gone cold turkey when the supply dried up, he was now helpless to fight the inevitable slumber. He reached over to his night-stand and grabbed the framed photo of that perfect day in Central Park. The bittersweet memory had a calming affect. Soon, he drifted into tranquility with all the lights on.

Less than three hours after passing out on top of the bedspread, a disori-ented Johnny was roused from his sleep. He got to his feet and scurried to the intercom panel at the end of the corridor. Halfway along, he recognized that the intermittent buzzing was actually coming from his front door. Johnny checked his watch. 7:45pm. Correctly, he figured that Risa had gone for the night, so he lumbered to the entrance, unlocked the bottom latch, and turned the knob.

Perhaps at first believing it to be a delusion, Johnny rubbed his eyes at the sight of a pregnant and beleaguered-looking Megan Price.

"Johnny," she gasped at the sight of his face. "If it's okay, can I please come in?"

Johnny was at a loss for words. He stared tensely at her altered physical appearance, then escorted her by the hand over to the living room sofa. Clearly their time apart had taken a toll on Megan's youthful face. The lines around her eyes were telltale signs of her tribulations.

Rather than sit next to Megan, Johnny sank into a matching beige recliner facing her. A glass coffee table served as a partition. Unsure of where to begin, he blurted out, "So how'd you find me?" followed by a more civil, "And how are you?"

"I'm okay, I suppose," she replied unsteadily. "Managing the best I can." Megan chewed frantically on a piece of gum, analyzing the modernly designed room. "Nice place you've got here. Feels cozy, like a real home. Did you decorate yourself?"

"You remember Jacqui Spencer, Andy's girlfriend? She's become a pretty successful designer. When I moved in, she was nice enough to lend a hand."

Megan smiled. "Glad to hear those two stuck together. Even on the beach blanket, I really believed they made a good pair."

Johnny was still confused as to how she had managed to arrive at his door. He rubbed his forehead and his bleary eyes. "I can't imagine you came up here to reminisce about old friends. But you still haven't told me how you found out where I live."

Megan's smile quickly evaporated. "Believe me when I tell you that finding your place was the easy part. Summoning the courage to show my face was hard enough."

"But you obviously managed to overcome your fears, not to mention my doorman, on the very night I get home from a long tour. Must've done a whole lot more than some soul searching to find my address and itinerary."

"Johnny, do you know how often I've shown up at your door? Even going back to Brooklyn, I tried so many times, hoping to say I'm sorry in person. I called you endlessly, mailed apologetic letters. And what about the snapshots of us in Central Park? Didn't you get any of it?"

"Yeah, I got everything. Those pictures brought back some great memories. Times I wish were still here. But your letters, they were just a reminder of the agony you put me through."

"But I swear, I never meant to hurt you," Megan cried out, fighting back the tears. "The men I dated, just a tedious exercise to please my mother! I could've told you about a half-dozen guys back then. But I saw the toll it was taking on you."

"So instead, you lied to me?" His voice was bitter. "I can't accept the way you kept a straight face when you swore there was no one else. And then you go on to marry one of 'em, just months later. You must've been terribly broken up about losing me."

Megan's fragile composure quickly unraveled. She used the sleeve of her cashmere sweater to absorb the teardrops, wiping away much of her make-up in the process.

Johnny felt suddenly guilty for unleashing so much fury at once. He grabbed a box of tissues, then sat beside Megan on the sofa. "Sorry. Didn't mean to be so harsh. I never liked seeing you cry. There something I can get you? Maybe a warm towel; something to drink?"

"No, nothing," Megan sobbed, dabbing at her face with a crumpled tissue. "I deserve nothing, and I want nothing other than to say how sorry I am. Johnny, you need to know that I've been through some terrible times since we split. I got pushed into a horrible marriage with a man I never loved. And he abused me in every way imaginable."

"That bastard!" Johnny blurted out, clenching both fists. "He hurt you? I'll kill that vile sonofabitch."

Megan waved her hand dismissively. "It's okay now. He's out of my life. But you know, all along I somehow believed it was justly deserved. No matter how much I suffered, I suppose it paled in comparison to what I put you through. All those beautiful songs you wrote, wracked with such sadness... Guess you'll never truly be able to forgive me for that."

To Johnny, the sight of a fragile, tormented Megan weeping before him proved a difficult vision to bear. He could feel his heart breaking all over again. *How grueling this apology must be for her.* No matter her circumstances, this was still the first love of his life. "Meg," he said softly, lifting her chin. "Obviously we've both been through a lot. Why don't you fill me in on everything? I wanna understand how you've ended up here like this."

Megan blew her nose and wiped the tears off her pale cheeks. "If only I had a rewind button back to that day after the concert in the park..."

Her tale of anguish was almost too much to bear. Megan spent hours telling Johnny about the men she dated, her engagement to Gerald Ridgewell and their disastrous marriage. When she had brought him up to the present, Johnny leaned forward, saddened and tired, but full of curiosity.

"So this Gerry... is that beast behind bars?"

"Well, I thought about pressing charges. But the truth is, he really needs help. Sending him to prison was no long-term solution. Instead, I showed up at his parents' door with my mother. Apparently they always knew he had anger-management issues. They figured it would somehow work itself out. It did, all right – on me! After they saw me bloodied like that, they had him sent away to a facility. I figure the divorce'll be final once he's out. He'll never come near me again."

"But what happens when he's released? Do you need protection? What's to prevent him from hurting you when he gets out?"

"In a word: Mother. My mom threatened to destroy not only his life, but also the reputation of anyone associated with their family. Next thing I knew, the Ridgewells skipped town. The apartment's in my name now. It hasn't been easy, but I've been coping the best I can."

Johnny stood up and hurried to the kitchen. He filled a pitcher with chilled spring water, grabbed two glasses from the cupboard and rested them on a Lucite tray. When he returned to the living room, he found Megan exactly as he'd left her. "Figured you could use something cold to drink. I know I sure can."

Johnny settled back into the recliner opposite the sofa. Megan regrouped and began asking questions. "So tell me, how've you been? There's been plenty about you in the papers. But how're you really doing?"

"You mean personally?" Johnny rubbed his bloodshot eyes.

"Yes and no." She nervously twirled a strand of her long blonde hair. "I wanna know how you're feeling overall. But sure, I'm a bit curious about your happiness."

Uncertain of the angle Megan was playing, Johnny hesitated. The hint of a smile formed around his mouth. "I suppose I've been all right. Too busy with performing and writing to focus on anyone else. It's been a whirlwind since I signed the recording contract. And I've hardly been in any one place long enough to focus on anything but the music."

"So then your being uninvolved presently has nothing to do with me?"

"If you're asking if I'm still having issues over the way things ended, hell yeah. You weren't just my girlfriend. You were my support system. My reason to believe that life could actually mean something besides endless transition. Yeah, I have my moments where I'm unwilling, or unable, to trust other women. But most of all, I didn't just suddenly lower my standards because you decided to move on."

"Of course, I know you wouldn't do that. I was only hoping you'd found a way to get past the pain."

"Hasn't been easy," he admitted softly. "But with everything going on... well life has been an incredible distraction." Johnny intensified eye contact. Quickly, he changed the subject. "So what were you hoping to accomplish by coming up here? Is this just about our breakup, or –"

"Johnny," she gasped. "Ever since you mailed me that song, I haven't been able to live with myself. Honestly, I had no expectations for tonight. I just needed to redeem myself in your eyes. Well, that and to let you know that you were, and still are the only guy I've ever loved."

Johnny reclined backwards, measuring his words carefully. "Wow! I'm... touched that you still feel that way. And it's cool to find that you're pretty much the same girl I grew to adore. But that was fourteen months ago. The boy you walked away from - the one scribbling in a poetry notebook - he's become a man with this crazy career. Fans, constant travel, demands..."

"And yet, I still see through it all. John, no one knows you better than me. Sure, you're tired now; out of sync. But you're still the same grounded, passionate guy I've always been so fond of." Megan leaned forward. "As much as life has changed, we're still those two people who shared all those daydreams together. A future of stability. Just maybe, I was hoping to find forgiveness in your heart, and possibly a chance to again be part of your life."

Johnny could hardly believe what he'd just heard. The explanation and apology were genuinely appreciated, but what else was she driving at? If Megan had simply come to express regret, receive his pardon and move on, he was perfectly prepared to grant her wish. However, if it was reconciliation she came seeking... Even as he'd never quite gotten over her absence, he was hardly prepared to take her back as though time had stood still all these months: not to mention the ongoing presence of the person most responsible for driving a wedge between them.

Johnny downed the water in his glass with one swallow. "Please don't take this the wrong way, Meg. It's just... I don't understand your intentions, showing up like this. I mean, look at you. You're hurting. You're pregnant. And understandably, you're feeling fragile. Who could blame you after all you've been through? If you want my friendship, you know I'm always here for you. But if it's miracles you were expecting –"

"I didn't know what to expect," Megan confessed. "I was hoping we could start again, by getting to know each other. We live only ten blocks apart. It would help me to know that you aren't opposed to the very idea of me in your life."

Johnny tilted his head toward the floor and nervously exhaled. "Of course, yeah. I'm cool with us reconnecting. I suppose you'll be needing my number."

Megan watched Johnny reach for some paper on the coffee table. "Actually, if all of my mom's info is correct, I should already have it," she volunteered.

"What'd you say?" Johnny dropped the notepad to the floor. "Your mother has my address?"

"That's not exactly what I –"

"And what else does she know about me, aside from where I live and my daily agenda?"

"No, no, it isn't like that," Megan trembled, instantly realizing her error. "After I was battered so badly that day, I told her you were the only person who mattered. She was so well intended, going out of her way to find you. But honestly, this has nothing to do with her."

"So I see not much has changed since we've been apart. And here I was about to welcome back your friendship, only to learn that Katherine Price is still pulling the strings. Is it now okay in her eyes for us to be associated, in light of my success? Do I now rate on her list of acceptable suitors for her daughter? Somehow I just knew this was all too good to believe."

Megan backpedaled in retreat. "I had no way of finding you without her help. But I swear everything's different now. I live alone, here on the West Side. I have my degree, and I don't work for her anymore. We only speak once or twice a week, and even that's just a pregnancy update. Please believe me. I'm beyond her control."

"But you also said that it was your mother who fixed things between you and that abusive degenerate. Didn't you say how she threatened to destroy his family? How can I believe that she isn't lurking behind some door, waiting to pounce, devour my carcass and spit me out? All that time she tried to split us up. And now she finds it convenient to track me down, sending you up here to say all the right things. How do I know she didn't script your apology like she did for Dinkins after Crown Heights?"

"Johnny!" Megan cried out in total exasperation. "I can't fault you for hating her. But I simply can't divorce a parent like a bad husband. And her effort to find you was from the heart: She did it for me."

Johnny slowly exhaled, his feet now firmly on the ground. Even if she were telling the truth, the sobering reminder of a conniving Katherine Price was enough to make his skin slither sideways. "Megan, I need some time to clear my head," he explained, not wishing to send her away in tears. "Just got back from touring. I'm sleep deprived; totally out of sorts. This has been a nice surprise. But I could really use a solid hibernation in my own bed. If it'd be all right, let's pick this up some other time."

Megan rose slowly from the sofa. She had the hollow feeling of having just failed in her only opportunity to get close to Johnny again. There was so much more to say. She wished to continue the conversation. Yet it was nearing midnight, and she too was wearing down.

"Well, thanks for letting me in and for being so understanding," she said as he escorted her to the door. "And yeah, I'd really like it if we could meet up again sometime soon." She reached into her coat pockets for a piece of paper. A wrapped stick of chewing gum and a Benadryl caplet was all she could find. On the inside of the gum wrapper, Megan jotted down her address and phone number. She hoped they were not being written needlessly.

Megan fumbled in her handbag for the keys outside her twenty-third-floor apartment. After turning the latch, she tiptoed inside and gently closed the door so as not to disturb her neighbors at this late hour. A crystal chandelier hung over the dining room table. Megan hit the light switch and kicked off her shoes on her way to the bedroom.

The long, emotional conversation had left her noticeably dry-mouthed. Quietly, she changed into pajamas and headed toward the darkened kitchen for a drink. As she approached, she was momentarily startled by the distinctive sound of silverware making contact with a solid object. Instinctively, Megan thought about snatching a blunt object for protection. But hearing nothing further, she thought better of it. *Something must've shifted in the drain board*, she surmised.

Overhead track lighting formed an oval shape on the kitchen ceiling. When Megan hit the button just inside the doorway, her suspicions of an intruder were confirmed.

"You were out much longer than I expected." Katherine Price shielded her eyes at the table. She took a sip from a steamy mug. "So, how'd it go with Johnny?"

Megan braced herself against the granite countertop. "Mother... how'd you get in here? You nearly scared me into early labor!"

Katherine stood from her seat, revealing a rumpled black Versace pant-suit. "I'm sorry. I came by to make sure everything went well tonight. I didn't want you to be alone in the event your visit went badly."

"But how'd you get inside? And why sit in the dark like that? I nearly grabbed a poker from the fireplace!"

"First of all, dear, you're forgetting that I have a set of keys. I let myself in. As owner of this apartment I've had them since the closing."

A look of pure astonishment engulfed Megan's face. Katherine paused to consider the impact of her revelation. "I guess now's as good a time as any for you to know who bought this pad for you and Gerry. But getting back to tonight: I was lying awake on your sofa for hours. Came in here for a cup of tea. The lights bothered me, so I shut them; didn't mean to alarm you."

"Mom, you didn't need to do this. You're obviously welcome to crash in the guestroom. I can barely keep my eyes open."

"So I take it things didn't go well with your rock-star Romeo?" Katherine frowned. "From your flushed appearance, it sure looks like you've been crying."

"Things went fine. I'll talk to you about it in the morning." With heavy lids drooping over glassy pupils, she stepped out of the kitchen. "Don't stay up too late, Mom."

Megan pulled up the duvet and slid comfortably under the top-sheet on one side of her lonely king-size bed. She reached for the wooden music box atop her nightstand. Once the tiny handle was between her fingers, she gave a gentle twist. The calming strains of Beethoven's *Moonlight Sonata* filled the room. But quickly as she nodded off, momentary peace was interrupted by the sound of her bedroom door being pushed open against the wall.

"We weren't finished talking," Katherine said coldly, finding a place on the empty side of the bed. "I didn't wait around all night to watch you fall asleep."

Megan slowly propped herself up against the headboard, shielding her face from the overhead light that her mother had snapped on seconds earlier. It took a minute to regain her senses, but when she did, Megan grew sharply agitated. "Why'd you wake me? I'd told you we'd talk in the morning."

"Well, I, for one couldn't sleep, not knowing what happened over there."

"I already told you things went well," Megan answered in a cranky voice. "He invited me inside. I apologized for the way things fell apart last year and he accepted. We spent a couple of hours catching up. Then he called me a cab. We decided it was best to pick things up another time."

"So he intends to see you again?" Katherine eyebrows descended. "And he expressed no objections to taking you back?"

"Actually, it's complicated. But yeah, he encouraged me to keep in touch; rebuild our friendship. Listen, the guy doesn't have a free minute. With his busy career, could I have really asked for more than this?"

"Megan, I'm confused by something," Katherine sarcastically evaded the question. "I thought you once told me this young man cherished you so that he'd walk through flames for you. If your assessment is correct, why wouldn't he simply pick up where things left off? Didn't you offer him the chance?"

Megan pounded the mattress in frustration. "Mother, it doesn't work that way. Have you forgotten that I'm still officially married, with a kid on the way? No matter how much Johnny may love me, don't you think he's entitled to at least mull over whether he wants to be involved with someone this close to motherhood?"

"But that's not the unconditional love you so eloquently described," Katherine calmly shot back. "You're supposed to be his match made in heaven, right? He even said in a press conference that he never got over you. I've got the news clippings to prove it. So here you show up at his door, offering him the chance to take back the best thing that's ever happened to him; the one who rescued him from his lowly, wandering existence, and he turns you down?"

"Mom, he didn't flat-out reject me. My showing up was a total surprise. And still he was very kind. He sat listening to my problems for hours. And he's fine with us meeting up again sometime soon. It's just… with so many issues swirling around, it's unrealistic to expect him to take me back with open arms."

"And just what kind of issues are we talking about? Didn't you tell him that I'd be entirely supportive? You must've told him I've had a change of heart."

"Well, as long as we're on that subject, I think it'd be fair to say that your presence doesn't exactly... put him at ease. He knew all along that your disapproval is what broke us apart. Who can blame him for having reservations?"

"So you're saying Johnny won't take you back because of me?"

"I didn't —"

"And here I am, allowing this parasite peasant to reclaim his cherished soulmate, only he rejects you because I'm still in the picture! How ungrateful! Or does he use me as his excuse to hide the real reason why he doesn't need you anymore?"

"Mother, what're you talking about?"

"Now that he's tasted a little success, he doesn't need our money any longer. I can read this drifter like a shoddy tabloid headline. And to think of all we did for him. You do know, don't you that it was my urging that helped elevate him from anonymity?"

Megan coughed in astonishment. "Mom, a little perspective. Johnny was always talented. Determined too. And he hasn't been sitting around all these months feeling sorry for himself. He isn't bitter. Probably just fears that you'll turn on him at any time. Honestly, can you blame him?"

Katherine stood from the bed. "Okay. I've heard enough. And I'm hardly encouraged. This so-called consummate boyfriend of yours is obviously unwilling to make the most of second chances. If he wants to blame me, perhaps he'd better think twice before voicing such opinions."

"But he didn't say any of it," Megan insisted, rolling to the empty side of the mattress. "He just needs time to work it all out. Johnny never claimed you were the reason he wouldn't take me back. I mean, would you accept a married, very pregnant ex-girlfriend if she came knocking on your door so many months later?"

Katherine abruptly turned and left the master suite. "That pathetic, unappreciative opportunist," she muttered, her stiletto heals clattering against the wooden floors as she headed for the living room to retrieve her overcoat.

Megan scurried to the front of the apartment. She encountered her irate mother once more, just as she was reaching the front door. "You didn't answer my question," she shouted, blocking her path to the exit. "I asked what you'd do if you were in Johnny's shoes. This your way of telling me you agree with his reluctance?"

"Megan, you're exhausted. I'm falling asleep. Neither of us is thinking clearly. Why don't we pick this up in the morning, like you suggested?"

"First I want a straight answer. And I'm not going back to bed till I get one from you."

Katherine let go of the doorknob. "Fair enough." She softened her tone. "If I were Johnny… what young man from his humble background wouldn't want to be with one of the most prized and eligible women in this city? If I were him, I'd be begging you to take me back."

Megan cringed. "Oh, c'mon! Now I know you aren't being objective. Put away your maternal rose-colored glasses. Maybe when we're both rested and thinking clearly, we can —"

"Don't bother," Katherine mumbled angrily, unlocking the front door. "Now get some sleep and let me be on my way. I've got to be in the office in just a few hours. At least you have the luxury of sleeping in."

With that pleasantry, Katherine Price nudged past Megan and stormed off into the cold New York night, never more determined.

24

By Perspective

When Risa Sheppard arrived for work around nine, she found Johnny in a deep slumber in his living room recliner. First she lowered the living room shades. Next, she shut the double French doors to keep the noise out. Andy and Jacqui arrived home at noon.

"Oh, hey guys," Risa spoke softly as the couple entered the room. "You need to keep it down. Johnny's passed out in the living room. Must be jetlagged."

Andy slid behind his desk. "That's odd. Why wouldn't he sleep in his bed?"

"Beats me. I found him that way when I got here earlier. Oh and by the way, Andy, I've got about twenty messages for you. They're right on top of that huge pile."

"Tell you what." Andy winked at Jacqui. "Why don't I catch up here, while you check on our favorite hit-maker?"

Jacqui poked her head inside the living room. She found Johnny sprawled out on the recliner. A throw blanket was hanging over the back of the sofa. Jacqui grabbed it and began to cover her slumbering friend. Suddenly, his bloodshot eyes popped open.

"Megan," he called out, lurching forward in a state of momentary confusion.

"Oh, hi, Johnny, it's Jacqui. Didn't mean to wake you. Funny place for a lie-down."

"Jacqui, you're back from the Falls. Andy too?" His voice was groggy.

"We literally just got in. Rumor had it I might find you here."

Johnny leaned back and began to work out the tightness in his neck after an awkward sleep. "Jacqui! Wow, some timing. You got a minute for me?"

Jacqui lifted one window shade. Johnny's tiredness and discouragement was visibly evident. She gave him a friendly hug. "What's the matter? Run down from the tour?"

"Oh, man!" Johnny sighed. "The tour, it's been mostly incredible. But you'll never believe the insanity of the past few days."

Johnny sat up and began to summarize the details of his personal dilemma. Calmly, Jacqui processed every word, nodding occasionally, but saying little. When Johnny concluded, Jacqui remained in quiet reflection. Soon, a wry smile emerged. "For someone with a top-selling album, and all those fans, you're one of the most unlucky blokes I've ever met."

"I wouldn't call it unlucky," Johnny countered with a grimace, "just terribly ironic. You know, when I was with Megan, she was everything to me. But her mother squashed the whole thing 'cause I was a nobody." He sighed. "Miserable as I was, I managed to convert the pain into music, and somehow became the success she predicted I'd never be. Now, when I finally feel like I've found someone new, this one gets scared off because I'm too successful. I'm just so confused."

"Johnny, can you imagine how many young musicians would ditch their most loyal girlfriends in exchange for a hit song? I mean, here you are at twenty-three with an unreal following, and all the critical praise anyone could ever want. If you'd just take a step back from your love-life - or lack thereof - you'll recognize that you may never have it better than this."

"Yeah, yeah, I know. It's been an amazing ride. Especially from where I started... all this respect, the fans, glowing reviews, it's just epic. But happiness ain't just about a hit record? You know, I never really had any stability before Megan. And now, without someone to really share all this..."

He paused, realizing how selfish he sounded. "Not that it's totally in my control, but if I could somehow make it all stop for a while, find a true companion —"

"But as you say, you just can't flick off fame with a switch. Certainly not at this level."

Johnny's eyes narrowed with concern. Jacqui took his hands in hers. "Hey, your music's not just yours anymore. Even if you never record another song, there'll always be people out there who'll claim it as part of the soundtrack of their lives." She pointed to a framed copy of his album cover hanging on the wall above them. "And as for this Lauren, did you tell her how you feel? Does she know you'd consider such drastic actions on her behalf?"

"I couldn't. I'd scare her away. We've only known each other a few months. And she's heard enough macho dishonesty to ever buy a line like that from me."

"How do you know for sure? If you're so mad for her, why not go over to her flat; confess your feelings?"

Johnny sat shaking his head. "I don't know if it's love, pure attraction, or just convenience. I do know it's not the same as being with Megan. Not yet anyway. Like I said, we spent a few intense weeks together. Now, the tour's over. Of course, I wouldn't mind the chance to find out, though it's looking kind of doubtful."

Jacqui sat gazing at the hardwood floor, until the tiny gaps between the slats appeared to become canyons. Carefully, she weighed the details. "Look, Johnny, if she honestly feels the same as you do, she'll come round. You know, she's being a fool if she gives you up over things that may happen in the future? Just who can predict what'll be in five years time?"

"I sure can't." Johnny stood up and stretched. "Just wish I knew the next move to make."

"Give her a week to mull it over. Maybe don't even ring her till right before the next concert. By then, maybe she'll have got her head straight. If not, tell her what you just told me. Let her know how far you're willing to accommodate her feelings. At least you'll have given it your best."

"And what do I do about Megan? I honestly want to reach out to her; be there in her time of need. And I feel terrible for losing it last night like I did. But I mean, first she shows up out of nowhere, catches me at a really weird moment. She's walks in majorly pregnant from this monster who she married, which freaks me out. Plus, she's so unstable and still very much under Katherine's manipulation. How was I supposed to handle it?"

"Sounds to me like you did everything right with her. But you can never say never, you know? You offered to keep open the lines of communication, and you've eased her conscience by accepting her apology. If somewhere down the road your paths happen to cross... hey, whatever. But I do believe from the way you speak of her that your feelings are more than compassionate."

Johnny washed up, then stepped into the office bedroom. He was instantly bombarded.

"Welcome back the conquering hero! Before you get comfortable, you do realize you're booked for Letterman next Thursday? Nice little sound-check for opening night at the Beacon, eh?" Andy reminded. "And now Lorne Michael's wants you for SNL too!"

"Hey, boss," Johnny deadpanned. "Nice to see you, too. Good to know we're still on a little roll of sorts."

"You kiddin' me?" Andy glared back. "You've just come off a tour that sold ninety-five percent of all tickets. And you rank among the top five best-selling artists of this calendar year. Am I missing something here?"

Johnny embraced Andy and patted him on the back. "No question we're doing a whole lot right. You especially. Just remind me to make time one of these days to sit back, sober up and let it all soak in. In the meantime, please do me a favor and call the band about the Letterman gig. I could really use a break from everything the next few days."

Sheila McLennan could tell by her partner's scowl that Katherine Price was up to something mischievous. Already she'd seen Katherine's secretary pull a file on supermarket tabloids. The Enquirer and the Sun were not the kind of mainstream media the agency targeted for their line of high-profile clients. Tabloids weren't even a desperate substitution for legitimate coverage. Now her curiosity was piqued.

"So what've you got up those Fendi sleeves of yours?" Sheila asked playfully. "A Giuliani smear campaign for November? Maybe another of your famous multiple exclusives? Hell knows the repercussions we avoid with you being the mayor's de facto mouthpiece."

"Right about now, I could give a rat's ass about the mayoral race, the fashion police or the next Manhattan high-rise. I've got a score to settle and I need it done discreetly. Presumably, I can count on you to get your little manicured hands dirty if necessary?"

Sheila smiled. "You know me well enough. But do tell: who is drawing your ire these days?"

"You recall my asking you about that pop star in the making, Johnny Elias?"

"You mean *your* Johnny? The kid who dated Megan back when she worked here?"

"Precisely," Katherine answered, opening a bulky file with Johnny's press clippings. "But don't you ever refer to him as mine. It seems this young man believes he has a bone to pick with me. I'd like to give him one to choke on."

"Oh, so now you want to strangle America's newest heartthrob and musical sensation?"

"Sheila, I'm serious," Katherine insisted. "Until now, his brush with celebrity has been an apparent joyride. Perhaps its time he gets a taste of media reality. Building up a hero, then tearing him down to size; that's their favorite pastime. Mine too."

Sheila shot Katherine a look of surprise. "So what's your strategy, Mrs. P?"

"For starters, I've got a couple of delicious possibilities. By the time we've planned the main course, his unassailable mystique will be scarcely recognizable." Katherine reached for a pile of nearby photos on her desk.

"Do you know any paparazzi? That and perhaps one of those computer retouch artists? A few misinterpreted photos should get us on track."

"Retouch? Why? What've you got to work with?"

Katherine took out the image of Megan, Johnny, Andy and Jacqui from Central Park. "I found this precious shot in Megan's old bedroom. You don't suppose we can get it to tell a different story?"

Sheila skimmed through her black address book. "With computers these days, anything's possible. I know a few graphic designers who might fit the bill."

"Excellent." Katherine flashed a sinister grin. "But remember, no matter how successful, it must be handled anonymously. Otherwise, the reputation of the sainted Johnny Elias isn't the only one on the line."

"Guys, we sound like a wasted bar band!" Ian shouted from behind his Ludwig drum kit. A fractured rehearsal take on *Shadows Of The Same Color* triggered his disgust. "We couldn't have gotten rusty after such a short lay-off. Let's get it together."

"Actually, Ian, the breakdown was my fault," Johnny volunteered, turning back to face him. "Sorry, I'm really distracted. Why don't we try that again from the top?"

"Well, better to hear you say it," Frank muttered, eliciting tense smiles all around. "This is only our biggest gig to date. One sour note on national TV can sink a career."

The first daytime rehearsal after a weeklong hiatus was proving strenuous. The band worked out over at *The Lion's Gate*; their unofficial practice stage. It was more than rust that had caused an uneven run-through.

It didn't help matters that Johnny and Lauren would barely make eye contact with each other. The awkward chill they generated could be felt by everyone in their presence. After Johnny departed, Frank took Lauren aside, pressing her for an explanation. "I know I asked you guys to cool it back on tour. But taking it to the opposite extreme ain't exactly working either."

Lauren wiped the sweat from her brow with a cocktail napkin. "Frank, it's gonna be okay. Johnny and I just need to sit down, clear the air. I'm thinking maybe after the five nights at the Beacon. We kinda left things precariously."

"Just don't let it go too long," Frank urged, tucking away his red Stratocaster. "Love 'em or not, that guy's our meal-ticket. If he ain't focused soon, we've all got resumes to polish."

Johnny returned to his apartment after the rehearsal. He darted through the foyer, past the living room and over to his home office. In the darkness, the red light from the answering machine flickered. Johnny flung his coat over a black leather couch. Sliding behind a cluttered antique desk, he hit play to retrieve his messages.

"Johnny, this is Fern from Highpeak. Just wanted you to know that your requested vinyl copies are going out overnight. Look for 'em tomorrow and enjoy." Beep.

Oh yeah, he thought nostalgically. You haven't really got an album out till you have a vinyl edition in your hands. Then the next message played.

"Andy, it's Jerry Goodman. Two phoners lined up for Johnny next week. A Thursday wakeup spot in Denver, and a 2PM Friday in Tulsa. Let me know if he's a go." Beep.

Hope that morning show isn't too early. I always sound scratchy after late rehearsals. And no more morning jumpstarts with those black beauty pills. Too scary; not worth it.

Johnny opened the top envelope from the mail pile. The machine continued on with one last message. "Hi Johnny. Larry Jacobs: program director and afternoon host on WNYR-FM here in New York. Hey, listen, next week's our big annual pledge-drive. We're doing it this time to benefit *World*

Hunger Year, the foundation Harry Chapin started back in the seventies. Anyway, I was hopin' you could maybe donate some signed memorabilia for the cause. Our listeners are really starting to dig your album. Please call me at home at 212…"

Interesting, Johnny thought. *That guy's a legend in this town. And what better cause than feeding the hungry? But all the same: is classic rock-radio finally ready to jump on the bandwagon?* With WNYR one of the last hold-overs, Johnny wondered if this call represented a turning point from their reluctance.

Yeah, I'll sign a few photos, he thought. He glanced over to his wall-calendar. *Only a handful of daytime rehearsals, and nothing else till Thursday.* Then another idea arose.

Although it was now half-past ten, Johnny recognized that one of his newfound celebrity privileges was the ability to contact people at any hour. No one ever seemed to mind receiving a late call from a rock star – especially an eager program director in need of fundraising assistance. Johnny grabbed the cordless phone from his desk. He dialed the number and spun his swivel chair toward the window, listening to a series of rings.

"Larry Jacobs," a familiar voice answered on the other end.

"Larry, Johnny Elias returning your call. Hope I haven't disturbed anyone at this hour?"

For a brief moment the line went silent. Then Larry chuckled. "No, no not at all. I'm just thankful you aren't my ex, crying for an alimony upgrade. Calling at this hour is her MO. Anyway, I live alone down in the West Village. And yeah, kind of a night owl."

"All right then. So what's this about a pledge drive?"

"Yeah, thanks for getting back to me so quickly. I know its short notice, but we really could use a signed item if you're comfortable with that sorta thing. We're usually set weeks in advance, but this year we only have an autographed BB King guitar and some U2 concert posters. Think you could dig up something worthwhile, sign it and send it over to the station?"

"Hey, Larry, you say you're a Village night creature?"

Again quiet for a moment, Larry then answered, "Why? What've you got in mind?"

"You know Café Figaro, corner of Bleecker and MacDougal?"

"Ahh, Figaro's one of Dylan's old haunts from the early sixties. You wanna go there now?"

Johnny laughed. "I heard Dylan once hung out there too. But these days they make the best hot cocoa in the city. What do you say we meet there in half an hour?"

"You for real?" Larry asked, wondering why this burgeoning pop star – one of the hottest names to evolve on the local music scene – was so eager at this late hour, on a weeknight, no less.

"Why not?" Johnny countered. "What've you got to lose?"

"Well, aside from a little extra sleep, nothing I guess. If it's not too busy we can meet next to the old jukebox."

"Great," Johnny answered, throwing on his coat. "I'll be there. See you in a few."

Johnny arrived to find the café nearly empty, except for a side table occupied by three NYU students. He easily spotted the colorful neon jukebox. The classic Wurlitzer was loaded with 80s pop records: Simple Minds. Crowded House. The Fixx. While he studied the song selections, a waiter approached with menus in hand. Johnny waved him off. "Two hot cocoas," he requested. "And some of that famous whipped cream in each."

The waiter headed back to the counter. The front door swung open. In walked a man sporting a dark trench coat, black jeans and a baseball cap with a Rolling Stones tongue logo, covering long messy hair. He appeared nothing like his youthful visage splashed on city billboards. "Johnny?" he questioned, unbuttoning his coat.

"You're late," Johnny joked, as the radio icon sat to join him. "But after years of hearing you on the air, I feel privileged all the same."

"I tried getting here fast as I could. You live around here too?"

"I'm up on the West Side. But at this hour, might as well be two doors down." Johnny watched Larry drape his coat over a chair. "So, I guess you're wondering why I asked you here?"

"That'd be a good start. I only called about the fundraiser. Not that we'd –"

"Well, I'll certainly donate something for the good cause," Johnny interjected. "But maybe we could start out by talking about radio. You guys are called the city's classic rock station."

"And we're damn proud of it." Larry flashed a wide grin. The waiter placed two foaming mugs on the table. "Oh, thanks, man. This is what I get whenever I come here."

"No problem." Johnny nodded. "The thing is, I'm seeking clarification about the way you guys treat new artists. I'm not one to make demands, but when the station I grew up listening to is resistant to playing my music, well… it's slightly disappointing."

Larry took a first sip of his cocoa, then set down his mug. "Johnny Elias, you're truly a gifted artist. That's clear from your popularity alone. And you've written some thought-provoking tunes. We play 'em on occasion – as I'm sure you know."

"On rare occasion!" Johnny shot back. "You guys always air current releases from Jackson Browne, Peter Gabriel, Warren Zevon. There a rule that says you can't play someone new in regular rotation?"

"Johnny, we played your title track for about two weeks strong, when it came out as a single. And we always spin your tunes during the all-request lunch hour."

"Exactly my point!" Johnny slapped his thigh emphatically. "That your listeners request my music only underscores that they wanna hear it on your station."

Larry stared across the table. He appeared ready to reply, but instead compressed his lips, allowing Johnny to vent.

"NYR plays folky mellow stuff too, like CSN, Paul Simon, even James Taylor. Not rockers in the traditional sense, but you place 'em all under the

same banner. I realize I'm clearly nowhere in their class... not yet, but..."
His voice trailed off.

Larry tore open two sugar packets and added it to his still steaming
cocoa. "I forgot how bittersweet they make it here." He smiled awkwardly
from behind the tall mug. "You raise a few good points; hard to argue with
any of 'em. But, I mean, you're a popstar riding high on the big revenue Top-
40. Why would you want to be lumped in with the old guard?"

"Larry, pop-stardom is transitory. Here today, forgotten tomorrow.
Classic rock is immortality... staying power. And you guys in New York set
the trend for everyone else."

"Point taken," Larry nodded. But a new artist like you, regardless of
how promising, isn't the perfect fit for a playlist loaded with classics. You do
understand this?"

"And what if the young upstart were agreeable to some kind of mutual
affiliation? What if he were to arrange for the rock station to get first dibs on
future releases; even make himself available for gigs like your fundraiser?
Might his airplay increase, meeting listener demand?"

Larry stared across the table, now certain as to why he'd been invited.
While he was not the only decision-maker at WNYR when it came to for-
mulating the set list, as the signature voice and program director he held
his share of influence. And this idea of reeling in this big fish for the station's promotional activities... how many radio execs wouldn't leap to strategically align themselves with the "can't miss" singer-songwriter of the
moment? "So what'd you have in mind, Mr. Elias? I'm listening."

Johnny wiped the foam from his upper lip and dropped his napkin.
"You say you're in a rut for auction items. I'm prepared to join you in-studio
on the radiothon. I can bring my band; play a few songs. I'll even offer a
prize package if you think it'll raise a few bucks. Maybe a handful of your
listeners can watch us rehearse for our upcoming gigs, not to mention a
stack of exclusive tickets to our Beacon shows. We can start there - if the
station has any interest?"

Larry raised his mug and downed the last of its contents. "Cheers," he declared, tipping it in Johnny's direction. "I admire your moxy for voicing your feelings on the state of classic rock radio. I've no doubt that as long as you keep making great music, we'll be playing it here-and-there… providing it isn't too sappy."

Both men laughed. Then Larry finished his thought. "Johnny, you seem really down to earth for someone on your first bite into stardom. That's cool. I'm also tickled that you happen to be a long-time listener. Of course, I can't promise anything as far as consistent airplay goes. But I'm sure any participation in our charity event will prove beneficial to you and to the cause."

Larry saw the disappointment on Johnny's face. Some words of encouragement were in order. "Look, John. You simply can't become the next Paul Simon overnight. No one can. But you're on one hell of a spurt right now. And I'm sure our station would love to work with you. Showing up next week'll be a great start. From there, we'll figure something out."

Johnny polished off the remainder of his cocoa. A modest grin was concealed beneath a foamy mustache on his upper lip. "Just name the time and place, Larry."

At that moment, one of the students dropped fifty cents into the Jukebox. The song selection was a semi-familiar hit of yesteryear, *I Ran* by the eighties new-wavers A Flock of Seagulls. Larry glanced across to the jukebox, then back to Johnny. "I think those guys played our holiday concert back in '82; haven't been heard from since. You sure you still wanna do this?"

Johnny slid his arms into his jacket sleeves. "Remember, man, it was you who called me. Oh, and I look forward to hearing promos for my appearance, beginning tomorrow on WNYR. If I can't get you to play my songs regularly, at least you can mention my name from time to time."

Johnny and the band gave a stirring performance at the *Ed Sullivan Theater* for the afternoon taping of the *Late Show with David Letterman*. They stepped onstage to a wild hometown welcome. The reinvigorated group played *Poet of the Wrong Generation* and the album's closing track, an environmental protest, *If I Close My Eyes and Half Pretend*. Johnny's voice soared to the upper reaches of his register, an octave higher than on the studio recordings. Lauren had to sing her harmony in falsetto to keep up with him. The crowd appeared mesmerized by the added gusto.

During his four-minute interview, Johnny deferred most of the credit to his bandmates, past and present. From his introduction, until the obligatory handshake at the segment's end, sections of spectators held up supportive banners and shouted his name. Even the host made light of the fact that this was not your typical guest appearance.

This has been one heck of a homecoming for a performer who's certainly captured the hearts and minds of the people in this city. Now imagine if they actually liked his music?

Momentum from the nationally televised performance easily spilled over to the *Beacon Theater*. Following Larry Jacobs's introduction each night, the group played lively sets of just over two hours, completely energized by thunderous ovations and raucous intensity. There were no pyrotechnics, no lasers, flash bombs, choreography, or intricate lighting – just a dynamic quintet of capable musicians, fronted by a charismatic high tenor, whose music was the prevailing message.

The New York audiences were even more eclectic than those around the country. They appeared to range from teenaged girls to fifty-year-old men. Johnny's folk-rock sound had clearly struck a chord with the baby boomers, who appreciated his throwback style and textured harmonies. For the younger fans, Johnny Elias was a hip, handsome new artist with something to say, even if much of his message went straight past them.

Johnny's songs of conscience, misfortune and topicality continued to raise his status to that of a working-class musical renegade. And hearing him wax poetic on such topics as racial unity, alienation, and a yearning for the musical artistry of yesteryear, his growing audience rapidly embraced him on a national scale.

By the time his debut concert tour was wrapping up, the mainstream media had caught on in full-force. Ironically, they touted him as something of a new musical spokesperson for his generation. From *Newsweek* to *TV Guide*, the most widely circulated publications were plastering his face on covers. An unlikely superstar was created almost overnight.

Johnny called an informal group meeting in the dressing room just before the final show. To each of the guys he presented a bonus check and a gold Rolex watch, engraved with their names and the words *Poet of the Wrong Generation Tour 1992-93*. Lauren received a customized ladies diamond Rolex, along with a box of long-stemmed red roses. This thoughtful gesture garnered teasing applause from the others.

Lauren tearfully threw her arms around Johnny. The tension was broken. Everyone playfully cheered them on. Lauren leaned in and whispered, "Can we talk outside for a minute?"

In a suite designated for the post-concert buffet, Johnny and Lauren sat on opposite sides of a lime-green leather couch. Each nervously waited for the other to start. "Why don't you go first this time?" Lauren suggested, as she sank into the sofa.

"All right," he smiled, inching closer to her. "There's something I've been wanting to tell you since flying back from the coast. With tonight being the last show, I didn't know when I'd get another chance."

Johnny took note of how Lauren leaned toward him with anticipation. Affectionately, he took her left hand in his. "You know, I've been incredibly blessed with all this lunacy: Cheering crowds, radio play, chart watching. No one would ever believe this. Especially me. It's just, even mind-blowing adulation can feel pretty hollow when there's no one to really share it with."

"But Johnny, you do understand it's only a matter of time."

"You'd think so, Lauren. But in my shoes, you just never know who's out to swindle you for your fame. For as long as I can remember, all I've ever really wanted was a little steadiness. That, and a place to belong – whatever that means."

"I know where you're coming from," Lauren acknowledged. "Really, I do."

"But in meeting you, I never felt the need to put on a show for your affections. Don't know what happened to us that night in San Francisco. Maybe playing you that song carried the wrong message. Or was it the words I chose –"

"It was none of that." Lauren squeezed Johnny's hand tighter. "Your song is lovely. And you should record it someday... You know, you have an amazing gift to articulate feelings. Just look out into the crowd every night and really gaze at the faces. Some have tears in their eyes. Others are mouthing every word. You capture their imagination."

"Yeah, totally amazing from up there. But what does it really mean? Call me crazy for saying this, but I'm willing to ditch the superficial devotion, or at least a chunk of it, if it means finding the right kind of harmony. Sure, there are no guarantees. But I also believe chances are meant to be taken. That's what I wanted to tell you that night. I only held back 'coz I figured you'd never believe me."

"I do believe you, Johnny. And I don't for a minute doubt your ability to stay faithful. But you do realize that I can't allow my selfishness to interfere with your destiny."

Johnny released Lauren's hand. "Destiny? I don't understand."

Lauren slid closer and again took Johnny's hand in hers. "You, Johnny Elias, are on course for something larger than life. Of all people, you should certainly recognize the unprecedented history you're carving for a modern day artist. There's no way I could live with myself, knowing I held you back from touching the sky... or soaring above the clouds."

Johnny pulled back abruptly. "So what're you implying? Am I destined to meander for decades though the world of celebrity writing sad songs for the masses?"

"Johnny," Lauren sighed. "I'm certain that there's someone who'll see through it all. But for now, for me, I'm afraid I'm just gonna get in the way of your unlimited potential. Women like me will come and go. But they should never obstruct talent like yours when something legendary is within your reach."

That night's final concert was decidedly emotional – heightened not only by it being the tour's last, but also the bittersweet sentiment felt by two particular band members. Johnny fed off the hometown frenzy to render one of his most intense performances to date.

From opening night in Cincinnati, to the last New York concert, the five-member band had conquered fifty-two audiences in forty-four cities. Along the way, they became a polished display of musical unity. And although Johnny Elias was clearly the name on every marquee, none of the supporting cast ever felt anything short of indispensable – at least onstage.

Only Johnny reemerged for the last encore to a prolonged standing ovation. It was Lauren's spontaneous idea to have the others stay back by the dressing room door. "Hey, guys," she held out her arms wide. "This is *his* moment. His fans. His music. Let's let him have this… alone."

Nervously, Johnny made his way to the piano at the center of the stage, perspiration pouring down his cheeks. The lights dimmed. The standing crowd quieted. A set of jittery fingers touched the ivory keys for the first time in a public setting. A heartfelt rendition of *Poet of the Wrong Generation* followed. It was hardly a solo effort.

Much of the sold-out audience harmonized to the wordless chorus, singing louder with each repetition. Johnny took a slow final bow at the song's conclusion. The decibel level was mind-numbing; the stage was pulsating. The tears were genuine. It was a poignant high point to end the tour – a journey in which Johnny Elias had evolved from a promising newcomer to a rising luminary. An improbable overnight sensation.

25

SObERiNq PROSpERiTY

The note read: *Welcome to the top, Johnny Elias. Enjoy the view. But remember, you've now got one helluva reputation to live up to.* – Ron Neswick

It was waiting backstage after the final concert where Johnny first received the extraordinary news. Aided by his recent media surge and his weeklong stand of sold-out concerts, *Poet of the Wrong Generation* had become the best-selling collection of songs in America some six months after its release. But with chart-topping success breeding lofty expectations, Johnny was in no frame of mind to enjoy the achievement.

Intense pressure mounted to begin work on a follow-up album. A *Goldmine Magazine* feature covering Johnny's milestone was accompanied by a sidebar about debut wonders who were never heard from again. Stacks of fan mail were laden with questions about when his next CD would be coming out. Even Ron Neswick's congratulatory note was tinged with motivation.

Johnny took some time off following the New York concert run. He enjoyed easing off of the accelerator: sleeping in late, ordering Chinese, and catching up on recent movies on cable. But the unstructured routine quickly grew tired. Within three days, he was ready to get back to work.

In the second week of January, Johnny phoned René Fontenot to arrange studio time in Manhattan. He also intensified his writing efforts, hoping to stockpile enough usable material. Johnny could count as many as ten songs meriting a tryout. Realistically, he considered only half to be good enough.

"Elias, you'll be happy to know that we've secured a West Side studio for your convenience," René told him. "Regrettably, Joe Rivera has a prior commitment. But not to worry. Ron's recruited a big-time veteran. You'll be really pleased with Dan Krueger."

Unlike his first recordings, which had breezed by without incident, the first four days of the new sessions appeared to be a harbinger of negativity. The opening track, *Contemplations*, was intended to be a mid-tempo pop song, yet somehow it evolved as a power ballad, later bursting into borderline grunge. Johnny sparred with Dan Krueger over vocal levels, single-tracked harmonies, and excessive percussion. But it was the constant retakes that ignited his temper.

The vocals on a psychedelic rocker, *Curious Delusion*, were correctly deemed mediocre by the new producer. Instead of capturing the track in a straightforward manner, Dan insisted it be recorded purely as an instrumental. Johnny detested the result.

"I don't care if you tweak the arrangement, but don't mess with the song's integrity! I take that personally!" he shouted.

Further complicating matters was the lack of availability of Johnny's trusted band. Only Frank and Ian – who never refused a paying gig – were available part-time. This left Johnny to adjust to a new bassist, backup singers, and assorted studio musicians with whom he'd never played. The atmosphere was toxic. Johnny enlisted the help of Howard Greffen to revitalize the mood.

"Hey, looking good!" Johnny shouted, applauding his mentor's studio arrival. "Great to see you taking care of yourself."

"Been trying, man." The songwriter grinned, showing off his healthier physique. "Since you hit the road, I've turned over a new leaf, so to speak. Even my doctor seems full of compliments – my fashion sense notwithstanding."

"Well, we didn't expect miracles," Frank said with a straight face before his laughter got the better of him.

The song, *Tomorrow's Door*, was the very first Johnny attempted that was not one of his originals. As a precondition, he promised Howard to withhold the mystery behind the highly personal lyrics. With the composer at the piano, Johnny delivered a heartstring-tugging vocal. Even the combative Dan Krueger was pleased by the results achieved over two separate sessions.

"Good job, guys. Real solid. Let's try and carry these vibes over to tomorrow for a change."

That evening as they broke for dinner, Johnny headed home for a briefing with Andy. The sound of familiar laughter greeted his arrival. But as he entered the back office, Andy and Jacqui both seemed deadly serious. "What? Did I miss a good joke?"

Jacqui held up the latest edition of the *National Stargazer*. Her stern face melted into a giggle. "Johnny, did you know that you and Andy are lovers?"

"Lemme see that." Johnny snatched the copy from her hands. "What the hell?" To his dismay, the front-page carried a photograph of himself with his arm draped around Andy. It was adorned with the headline *The Secret Lifestyle of Johnny Elias*. Inside, a two-page "exposé" used several unnamed sources to support the allegation. There was even a selection of recent photos taken of Johnny around town, interacting with a variety of men, including his bandmates.

"I'll sue their asses!" Johnny shouted at Andy. "Where'd you get this?"

"Jacqui found it at the check-out counter in the bodega. And did you notice the doctored photo? I think it's Central Park. That picture Megan gave you, only with the girls cut out. You don't suppose she supplied it?"

"No chance! Meg hardly needs the money. And she'd never hurt me again." Johnny grimaced, his focus to shifting to retribution. "So, Andy, can we sue them? It's obviously false."

"Unfortunately, we can't do much. The lawyers already have it on their desks. Problem is, the article only makes strong overtures. Even if we did have a case, Jerry Goodman says the idea of a lawsuit might make you look overanxious. That'll cause some people to actually believe it."

"So how do we make it go away?" Johnny threw his hands up in the air. "Do I hit the airwaves to deny it? Do I start dating every starlet in the city? I mean, look at Elton John. Freddie Mercury. Those guys set up sham marriages just to keep people off-track from their hidden lifestyles. I don't even have one. But once this hits the mainstream..."

"Well, I had an idea," Jacqui chimed in. "I suggested to Andy that we get hitched tomorrow, so it'll be obvious that at least half the story is rubbish."

Andy folded his arms. "Only problem, of course, is what my folks'll think if we elope."

"Guys, I'm really touched. But I don't think it'll quell the rumors. We oughta speak to our PR people, get a plan going. Meanwhile, let's at least put some pressure on that tabloid; make 'em tell us where they got that photo. We must be paying those lawyers for something!"

Within thirty-six hours, Jerry Goodman's office had issued a statement expressing Johnny's regret over the false rumor from dodgy sources. It also threatened a lawsuit, which never materialized. Then came the "be-seen" campaign: A series of high-profile dates around Manhattan for the sake of fending off the slanderous gossip. A fashion show with supermodel Christy Turlington. A Broadway red-carpet stroll with actress Winona Ryder. Johnny reluctantly went along. The tabloids feasted on the photos.

Throughout February, Johnny showed up uninspired at the studio for four or five-hour intervals, halfheartedly fighting through mostly mediocre material, lackluster results and hostilities with a volatile producer. Just when the sessions appeared to have hit rock bottom, a visit one afternoon by René Fontenot only added to the tumult.

"Elias, what the hell's happened to you? One day you're the reincarnation of James Taylor. The next, you're a worse than a poor imitation."

"Reincarnation?" Johnny squinted at him. "James Taylor's very much alive, last I heard."

"Ah, but every one of your session tapes is dead on arrival; not one lead single in the batch. Maybe if you took some time off for —"

"And maybe if you guys would get me a cooperative producer, these sessions wouldn't be so morose!" Johnny shot back. "Everyone loathes Dan. And if I have to sit through one more wasteful retake…. Tell me why an established artist needs to put up with this crap?"

"You need to deal with it, Mr. Elias, because you're under contract and we're paying you handsomely." René flashed a pseudo-smile. "Given your attitude, I'm starting to wonder if arrogance is blocking your creativity." He exhaled through his teeth.

Johnny sighed and jammed his hands in his pockets. "Rene, I'm giving it everything I got. Honest. It's just…great material needs time and inspiration. Like the Poet album."

Rene ran a hand across his long mustache. "I hear what you're saying. But I can't impress upon you how crucial this sophomore effort is. One hit record puts you on the map. Two in a row makes you a star… or simply a flash in the pan if it turns out awful. I'll talk to Ron about the problems. Meanwhile, you come up with something we can all get excited about!"

Amid the studio chaos, Johnny's dismal outlook took a sudden turn toward the bizarre. Charles Dudley, a forty-seven year-old, unemployed computer programmer from Edison, New Jersey, brought a copyright infringement complaint into a New York courtroom. He claimed that Johnny had plagiarized the tune and some lyrics for his album-track, *One Frame At A Time*. Even before preliminary evidence was presented, some New York papers carried the headlines: *Johnny Copycat?, Johnny Be Bad,* and: *Elias In Song Theft Probe.*

This latest firestorm seemed to have little bearing on Johnny's airplay or record sales. It did, however, create a stain of controversy on his previously unblemished persona. It also further agitated the Highpeak executives, who were notably absent from the court hearing.

Given the option of skipping the proceedings, Johnny instead used the occasion to try and reverse the damage. He showed up in a flattering Italian suit, smiling confidently for the cameras. "Hey guys. No story here. Just someone trying to cash in on my name." He even brought along a keyboard and gave the courtroom a solo performance of the song in question. More than skeptical headlines, he hoped what people would best remember were the front-page images of a stylish musician at the height of his talents.

The case was thrown out in under two hours. But in some ways, the media circus had seemed a bit too well-organized, particularly in view of the feeble accusations. Even victorious, Johnny left the downtown court-room wondering why his case was tried more in the tabloids than in front of a real judge and jury.

This frustrating ordeal, coupled with his generally overcast perception of the moment inspired a new purpose to Johnny's songwriting. One par-ticularly biting song, *Depraved Indifference* was a radical departure from anything he'd previously composed.

> *Who can you trust in a world so uncertain?*
> *Who's out on stage, and who's behind the curtain?*
> *Friends when they need you and when it's convenient*
> *Where are they now in the times when you're hurtin?*

Early 1993 saw New York City in a state of unease. The economy was faltering. Tourism was down. The job market was at a depressing low. In 1993 alone, there would be 2,085 murders in the five boroughs, establish-ing a dubious record. One didn't need to look far to find people mumbling to themselves in a state of discontent. But if society's declining values, political incompetence and a dissolving ozone layer were weighing on the minds of locals, it was all instantly placed on the backburner in one hor-rifying moment.

It was Friday, February 26th. Johnny was in the studio, taking part in a late morning session. Dan Krueger was out battling the flu. Cliff Zacario – a two-time Grammy-nominated studio virtuoso from Los Angeles – sat in Dan's place at the console.

The timing was excellent, since Johnny didn't trust Dan to oversee his most treasured material. Under Cliff, he felt motivated to break out one of his more inspired tunes, *A View from the Top of the Word*: the song Lauren Minton had made him promise to someday record. And with Cliff, he believed an appropriate arrangement could be provided.

From 10am until noon, Johnny sat at the piano in studio C, belting out his upbeat ballad with a passion that had been lacking before. Frank's wailing guitar and Ian's steady percussion set the tone for two cohesive run-throughs. Then the red light went on. Johnny held nothing back. The first recorded take came off flawlessly, save for one minor hesitation in the last chorus.

While Johnny overdubbed his vocals in a soundproof booth, the rest of the musicians broke for lunch. It was approximately half-past twelve when Frank Traber suddenly appeared, pounding on the glass. Johnny was wearing headphones and couldn't hear anything, but the expression on Frank's face made him stop at once. "Hey, what's going on?"

Frank could only grab his arm and propel him into the studio lounge. The other musicians were all there, staring transfixed at the television.

A bomb had exploded beneath one of the soaring World Trade Center towers.

Soot-covered faces held expressions of terror and exhaustion during a mass evacuation. People had been stuck in smoke-filled elevators, or rushed down dozens of flights of stairs to safety. With the sound of emergency vehicles blaring in the background, scores of workers poured out onto the downtown streets and into a snow flurry.

If the surreal scene itself were not enough, the word "terrorism" began cropping up in the reporters' voiceovers. Johnny felt his stomach tighten in fear.

Was there another bomb? How much damage had the blast caused? Was anyone killed?

Through all the unanswered questions came one grim certainty: New

York City had become a target. Even in the broad daylight of an ordinary winter afternoon, it was no longer safe from a cowardly act of terror.

Johnny spent the afternoon glued to the TV in the lounge. At home that evening, he felt compelled to turn it on again so he could continue to watch with Andy and Jacqui. They sat in silence, watching the replay of the evacuation, over and over again. Johnny couldn't tear himself away until well past midnight. "Those bastards!" he kept repeating. "Can't believe they did it here!"

Unable to sleep, he wandered over to his bedroom window, looking out at the vacant serenity of Central Park. A drift of fallen snow blew past the empty benches. A plastic bag rustled in the branches of a bare oak tree. Johnny appreciated the stark contrast to the troubling news footage.

And then he spotted her.

Just in front of the low stone wall at 93rd Street lay a shivering homeless woman in a crumpled cardboard box. Occasionally, a taxi or limousine pulled up to the nearby curb; their passengers stepped out and callously walked on by.

Man, am I blessed. It was the only possible reaction, and it spurred Johnny to action. In the kitchen, he reheated his untouched dinner in a plastic, microwavable container. He threw on a heavy coat and took the food downstairs and across the street. "Care to come inside?" he asked the woman as he handed her a hot meal and one of his hooded sweatshirts.

"Nah, this ain't too bad tonight. Once you get used to it, you don't feel a thing."

"I kinda know what you mean," Johnny answered, reaching for the cash in his pocket.

Back upstairs, his adrenaline still running from his quick excursion, Johnny pulled a notebook from the top drawer of his desk. A cold rain had begun to fall, pattering a rhythm on his bedroom window. In freeform, Johnny jotted down his thoughts about the troubled world outside.

Terrorists in New York City
Unemployment on the rise
Pollution in the air we're breathing

and a hole right through our skies
There's a deficit growing – lots of hot air blowing
Can our government get it right?
And there's a hard rain crashing against my window
It's keeping me up in the night

Lonely people with no direction
Homeless people begging everyday
Tainted souls seeking out perfection
Those who prosper turn the other way
There's a battle we're losing – Just what side are we choosing?
Will we somehow win this fight?
And there's a hard rain crashing against my window
It's keeping me up in the night

(Chorus)
Our future is fading – Stop observing, start participating
For our own protection – Let's get moving in the right direction
This is a call to action – A call to get it right
This is a call to action – See the world in a different light

Television as education
Parent figures of the modern day
Program quality disintegration
A generation full of mind decay
Culture lost with tradition – Are we only left wishin'
it'll work itself out right?
Well there's a hard rain crashing against my window
It's keeping me up in the night

Expect no salvation – Can't rely on empty expectations
Our problems – Deplore them

They won't go away if we ignore them
This is a call to action – A call to get it right
This is a call to action – See the world in a different light

No determination, loss of values
People living in hypocrisy
Doing anything to make a dollar
It's become a moral bankruptcy
Call it modernization or deterioration
Yet we carry on in spite
And there's a hard rain crashing against my window
It's keeping me up in the night
(Chorus- End)

Within days Johnny was back in the studio, recording this powerful up-tempo march, with Frank's searing guitar intro and Ian's pounding back-beat. Topped off by a gritty lead vocal, *A Call To Action* was just the kind of song rock stations were clamoring for.

"Now that's what I call memorable!" René Fontenot exclaimed. "It's timely. It speaks the language of the people, and it's empowering without being too preachy. I think we have our lead single for the next disc!"

Was it loneliness or curiosity that got the better of him? Either way, Johnny saw no harm in calling Megan before his trip out to California. Surely he had missed her voice, her warmth and the comfort it provided him for so long. When Megan answered her cordless phone, Johnny hardly recognized the relaxed tone on the other end.

"I was beginning to think I'd never hear from you again," she said. "How've you been?"

"I'm okay. More importantly, you must be what – a few weeks before the due date?"

"I'm about seven months; due in mid-April. Feeling great, though you wouldn't believe how big I've gotten." Megan paused. There was a splash of water in the background. "Speaking of getting big, I saw you on Letterman a little while ago. Wanted to call and say congrats, but I figured you were likely bombarded."

"Yeah, it's been busy; working hard. Though it's probably not as much fun living it as it must look on TV. Hey, are you washing dishes?"

"Actually, I'm taking a bath. Anyway, weren't you one to always worship the glamour of rock and roll mythology? I figured all this excitement would launch you into orbit."

Johnny coughed. "Yeah, I shouldn't complain. But you know, being a fan, I always pictured my heroes living the life. Never thought about what it really was like." He hesitated. "I mean, sure, the pay is great. The chance to have your music heard: *unbelievable*. But everyone wants a piece of you, you know? No time for a real life. Not a normal one, anyway. And I feel sometimes like I've compromised who I really am just to live up to the hype."

"But you were always so in awe of anyone who ever stood on a stage! I remember that night with you and Andy at Radio City, waiting for Dylan to come out. You totally lost it when he walked onstage with his guitar."

Johnny nodded, forgetting that she couldn't see him. "Yeah, but that's just my point, Meg. For a performer, nothing beats that rush when the lights go down and the crowd goes wild. But the fact is, it's not all stepping onstage, you know? I go home at night, just like everybody else. And most of it isn't magic."

There was the sound of sloshing on the other end; Johnny imagined Megan getting out of her tub. She cleared her throat. "So – don't tell me you're already tired of success! I know you too well for that. You're not dispassionate about anything. No matter how much life changes us, good or bad, some things...." There was another long pause, punctuated by some short breaths. "Hey, I'm back. Listen, I don't suppose you want to take me up on breakfast one morning? These days I'm at my best after eight to ten hours of sleep."

Johnny laughed. "I've never had the pleasure of watching a pregnant woman devour breakfast for two. We'll have to do it when I'm back from L.A. My record label's sending me out there tomorrow to wrap up my album with a producer I've been petitioning to stick with. Not sure exactly when it'll be finished, but let's do it right when I get back."

At Highpeak headquarters, Ron Neswick contemplated the expected bad news. A comprehensive sales report for the past six months merely confirmed that the numbers were, in fact, dwindling. Aside from Johnny Elias and two heavy-metal bands, figures for the label were down by twelve percent from just a year earlier. Ron was already feeling the pressure from his CFO. He was beginning to get the sense that even his job could be on the line if things failed to turn around quickly.

At a mandatory staff meeting, Ron gathered the hierarchy to announce several innovative ventures.

"On the recruiting front, we're going to organize a citywide competition to find the top amateur band. I'm talking events in all five boroughs. Major publicity support. Heidi, that means you." Ron tapped her on the shoulder with a wrapped cigar. "Complementing the talent search, I want self-congratulatory ads running in all the trades. Let's encourage unsigned artists to follow in the footsteps of our current stars. Jessica, that's your territory." Ron pointed a cigar in the direction of his assistant VP of marketing, then lit it.

They waited for the first inhale. "Lastly, new releases from our top-selling artists are a must next quarter. I hear Johnny Elias is almost done with his second disc. Let's get a jumpstart with the first single, a video, an album cover."

"Just one question." It was René. "Are you at all concerned about overexposure? I mean, the Poet record is still on the charts. Do we really want Elias competing with himself?"

"Overexposure's perfectly overrated." Ron mashed the burning end of his cigar in an ashtray. "I see no reason why a second release can't come approximately a year after the first one. Early July seems about right. And as for competition, let's just say that our own long-term future might just be a little more important than any single artist, if you catch my drift."

Andy Raymer stared at the hand-delivered package. The return address read: *By The Hand – The Blind Children's Center.* On an average day, Andy opened a dozen similar personal appearance requests. He usually had Risa send out a form letter with Johnny's signed 8 x 10. If it appeared more important, he'd draft a page in Johnny's name and have the boss sign it on a rare day off.

Perhaps it was the slick, professional appearance of this envelope that caught Andy's attention. Inside, a personalized letter requested Johnny's attendance at a Manhattan fundraiser on Tuesday, June 22nd. However, unlike the stuffy black-tie dinners that usually sought celebrities to hobnob with wealthy guests, this one seemed to be truly an event for the kids.

The appeal was for Johnny to perform five songs at the grand opening of an upscale midtown auditorium. Six hundred sight-impaired children and their parents would attend for free. Monies would be raised through ticket sales to paying guests, who would fill the remainder of the 2,500-seats. The event had already secured the participation of two stand-up comedians and a renowned classical violinist. Johnny was being sought as the headliner.

Andy checked the master calendar, then called Johnny in Hollywood. "So what do you think about this one? Personally, I love the idea, especially after all that copyright courtroom crap. You can never have enough good press."

"Sounds good if you say so," Johnny agreed. "Besides, you know I'm partial to kids who can stand to catch a break. Just do your homework on that organization and make certain everything's legit, okay?"

The sessions under Cliff Zacario were sounding notably better than the ones recorded with Dan Krueger in New York. Johnny was delighted.

Beyond the studio, Johnny and his Brooklyn bandmates relished the warm California weather at a house they had rented together just outside Beverly Hills. The guys enjoyed exploring the city at night, occasionally taking in red-carpet Hollywood premieres.

Despite stardom's privileges, Johnny never stopped feeling awkward when fans recognized him on the street. He often surprised people by pausing to sign an autograph, pose for pictures, or discuss the meaning behind songs on his landmark album.

One night, between courses at The Ivy – a trendy LA eatery on Robertson Boulevard – the tables were turned. "Hey, Ian, you notice the tall guy in the glasses, two tables to the left?"

"You mean the dude behind the menu?" Ian guessed, turning to get a better glimpse.

"Yeah, I could swear that's Ray Manzarek."

"Manzarek… keyboard player from the Doors, right? Guess it could be." He began humming a few bars of *Love Her Madly*.

"Yeah, I'm sure it's him. Hey, Ian, don't keep staring like that! Probably out to dinner with his wife or something. Privacy, you know?"

Johnny hardly touched his Cajun prime rib. He tried to remind himself that he treasured his own privacy and should afford the same courtesy to those he admired. Finally he gave in. When he got to the other musician's table, he was surprised to find that Manzarek had heard of him, as well.

"Hey, I just wanted you to know I really dig your album."

"Thanks… thank you!" Johnny stammered, his eyes wide as cymbals.

"So, you working on a follow-up to Poet?" Manzarek asked.

Johnny felt his legs wobble as though he were standing on the floor of a carnival bounce house. He leaned against a chair for support. "Um, yeah, my band and I, we're out here to wrap up the last few tracks. It's sorta getting there… I think."

"Well, good luck with it, man." Manzarek extended a hand. "And bear in mind: the key to sustaining it is to never stop expanding the horizon of your creativity. Just don't ever lose sight of what made it work for you the first time around and you'll be okay."

Johnny stood gaping in amazement. Even in having achieved a number one album, and played to tens of thousands, he found the recognition from a music legend the ultimate confirmation of his success.

"How cool was that?" Ian patted Johnny on the back as dessert was delivered. "You really know your rock icons. And apparently this one knows you, too."

Johnny blushed and turned away. "You know, till now, I've never allowed myself to believe in all this; that I've really made it big." Then, chuckling, he added, "You don't suppose Frank'll believe us when we tell him who we met here tonight?"

26

WHAT MIGHT HAVE BEEN

For Megan Price, the finalization of her divorce delivered a sobering reality. Although she had to face Gerald Ridgewell one last time in a Manhattan courtroom, she managed to maintain composure throughout the appearance. Megan took some satisfaction in hearing the judge admonish her former partner for his sickening behavior. She stared straight ahead, refusing to make eye contact with the father of her unborn child.

Outside the family courthouse, Gerry tried catching up, possibly to offer some form of apology. But escorted by her mother and a trio of attorneys, Megan was whisked away into a waiting town-car before he could come within an earshot.

The morning after, she awoke feeling renewed. Megan showered quickly, then threw on an oversized blouse to match an early-spring sweater and a loose-fitting skirt. A yellow cab delivered her over to Columbus Avenue for a nursery-shopping excursion. She picked up some receiving blankets and a musical mobile to hang over the soon-to-be delivered crib. The prospect of motherhood felt suddenly exciting.

As she approached a long line near the checkout counter, Megan abruptly felt overcome with fatigue. Though it was not uncommon for her to experience tiredness, this particular sensation was especially draining.

Sweat began pouring down her cheeks. She could feel her legs weaken and feared they'd buckle under the weight of her pregnant belly. A terrible cramping in her abdomen soon followed. Megan winced in pain.

"You all right?" asked a gray-haired grandma standing just before her in line. "You're looking rather pale."

"It'll pass." Megan cringed as another cramp hit her, holding her balance against the rolling cart. "I've had this before – just not as bad." As the words left her lips, Megan felt a rumbling in her lower half. This was followed by an explosion of pressure, leaving her legs drenched with fluid trickling down to the floor. Mortified, she looked around, hoping no one else had noticed. But all eyes were now fixed upon her.

"Call an ambulance!" shouted a man standing one cart behind her. "I think this woman's water just broke."

Megan was rushed by paramedics to a birthing room at Lenox Hill hospital. Two hours later, she prematurely delivered a healthy five-and-a-half-pound baby boy.

As she sat alone with her newborn, Megan filled out the birth certificate. Leaving out the father's name was the easy part. She deliberated a while before writing in the name of her son.

Katherine Price arrived later that evening. She was ecstatic to cradle her first grandchild in her arms. "My precious little one," she cooed. "You're so lucky to be born into our loving family." When the infant began screeching, she handed him back to Megan and switched on her adult voice. "So what've you named this sweet boy? He looks a lot like Daddy's grainy baby pictures."

Megan smiled proudly. "Yeah, he's got a bit of that in him. Daddy's hair. Grammy's face. Best of all, he's got Grandpa's blue eyes. I decided to name him Alex after Grandpa Alexander. He'd be so proud."

Katherine inhaled deeply, then let out a deliberate sigh. "That's all very nice, Megan, but don't you think it would've been more appropriate to name your firstborn after the man who named you."

"Mother!" Megan's face turned dark red. "I just had a baby. Lemme rest peacefully, okay?"

Katherine backed off. Her voice softened. "I didn't mean to question your judgment, honey. I know how much your grandfather meant to you. I was only hoping you wouldn't still be angry with Daddy after all these years. He did love you very much, even if he sometimes had a funny way of showing it."

She turned away and looked again at her grandson. "I must admit, I wasn't really expecting this early delivery. But with a few calls, I'll have the apartment set up for when you go home."

Megan frowned. "Actually, all things equal, I'd rather deal with it when I get home. I don't want anyone in my apartment while I'm away."

Johnny learned of Megan's good news while still recording in LA. Unable to extend congratulations in person, he instructed Andy to send a gift basket for both mother and child. "Spare no expense. And please make sure she knows it came from me."

"No problem," Andy assured him, talking from behind a pile of mounting papers on his desk. "I'll have Jacqui pick something out and send it on over."

As he spun around in his chair, Andy inadvertently knocked over a stack of publicity photos. "What was that?" Johnny asked, hearing the thud.

"Listen, John. We need to get ourselves a real office. And I'm not talking about a one-room makeshift place like we've got up here. We're already out of filing space. I've got Risa working at your kitchen table. And Jacqui's turned your dining room into her art studio."

"Yeah, I had a feeling this was coming. Have you got something else in mind?"

"I've started to get pricing. There's this space on Madison in the sixties."

"The upper East Side," Johnny sighed. "Can we afford it?"

Andy chuckled. "You kidding? With the royalties you're raking in, there's no reason we can't afford the Waldorf penthouse. In fact, when you get back here, might be a good idea to talk with a financial planner. For tax purposes, there must be a better way to hold on to it."

Johnny had mixed feelings when he heard the completed thirteen-song collection in mid-April. Even with the solid work turned in under Cliff Zacario's supervision, he was convinced that this was not nearly the equal of his first effort. There were a few notable highpoints, and a wider array of sounds. Still, if only he could buy another month for additional writing and recording... He placed a call to Ron Neswick.

"Ron, I feel like I've been working from behind from the get-go. First you guys set that crazy songwriting timetable. Talk about added pressure! Then you stick me with a producer who'd rather make his point than a hit record. And now that I've finally gotten into a groove, I have to come home; call it a day? Ron, this is my reputation. I'd hate to see it pissed away over a matter of weeks."

"You make some fair points, Mr. Elias," Ron acknowledged. "But will another month really turn this into a masterpiece? You need to think about this; grow up a little. We've already caved in to your demand to switch producers. And we sent you to record out west to accommodate this request. We don't have the luxury of time or budget to keep tweaking it to perfection. If I continue letting you have your way, this record'll never come out."

Johnny called an informal gathering of his inner circle the very night he came home: Andy and Jacqui; Frank and Ian; Larry Jacobs – for his commercial perspective – plus Howard, who Johnny hadn't seen since the early recording sessions in New York. Johnny played the tracks in sequential order. Then he went around the room seeking reassurance.

"Absolutely stupendous!" Jacqui shouted, applauding from the couch. "Slick, introspective pop. Nice stuff."

"It's got some tracks to take on the road." Ian was holding a bottle of imported beer between two fingers. "Add it to the songs from the first disc, and it should make for a helluva set."

Frank shrugged his shoulders. "It isn't *Poet*, but I wouldn't mind hearing it again. Hard to make a definitive comment on something you've only heard once. Even if I did play on it."

"Johnny, this is solid," Andy proclaimed from the piano bench. "Tough to top the original, but the fans and critics are already on your side."

Larry Jacobs clapped his hands. "From a radio standpoint, this rocks! These tunes have a harder edge than the debut, without losing any cleverness. Unequivocally works for my format!"

Johnny popped the disc from its tray and turned to his musical mentor. "And what about you, Howard? You've been awfully quiet since I hit play. I'd love your honest opinion."

"And my honest opinion you shall have," Howard answered cheerfully from the recliner. "As a whole, I'd say it rates a notch below the Poet record, just 'coz I get the sense that not every song plays from the heart. I can tell when you've been writing to meet a deadline. Overall, it's good. Though I agree that if you weren't feeling rushed; yeah it could've been stronger."

Johnny nodded in agreement, even as the truth had stung. "Right, well I was kinda thinking along the same lines. Guess I just needed to hear it from someone else."

"Hey, kid, don't get me wrong. You have a lot to be proud of with this record." Howard softened his tone at the sight of Johnny's disappointment. "Someone like me would kill to put out something half this caliber. I've little doubt your lofty stature will stay intact."

"I sure hope so," Johnny answered through a shrug of insecurity. "I've worked too hard to see it all unravel over petty deadlines and overanxious executives. I really hope you're right."

Wishing to escape the doldrums of his perceived mediocrity, Johnny dropped by Megan's apartment the following afternoon. He was pleased to find the new mother in good spirits, albeit weary from a lack of sleep. "So – how've you been coping?" he asked, arriving at her door. "Can't imagine caring for a baby by myself."

"Actually, I haven't been altogether alone. There's a nurse who shows up each afternoon for a few hours. Plus, you probably figured that you-know-who would be getting in her grandmotherly fix." Megan grimaced. "Don't just stand there, come on in. I'm not enchanted by her constant presence. But as a single mom, I'll take all the help I can get."

"Ah, your mother," Johnny sighed, hanging his jacket in the front closet. "I thought you told me that you'd grown apart since you moved here?"

"Honestly, John, she's mostly a nuisance, you know? Filled my place with baby stuff while I was in the hospital, even after I told her not to. And she shows up unannounced so often, I've almost come to expect it."

Johnny sat down on the living room sofa. "You don't have to let her in if you're too tired, you know. Your home. Your rules."

"Yeah, you try restricting a new grandmother from seeing her first grandson!" Megan laughed. She didn't want to tell him about Katherine owning the apartment, so she made light of it and changed the subject. "Oh, I think I hear Alex waking. Can't wait to have you meet him. Don't go anywhere."

Megan returned to the living room minutes later; her month-old son, wrapped in a blue receiving blanket. "Here's my little angel," she announced, rocking the newborn in her arms. Then she asked the baby, her tone playful, "Alex, would you like to meet Uncle Johnny? He's very special to your mommy. Can you say hello?" She turned back to Johnny and smiled. "So, what do ya think?"

"Looks a bit like you," Johnny pronounced upon seeing the boy's miniature face. "Does he talk at all? How's his singing voice?"

"Well, if his screaming's any indication, he certainly has a bright future in some new-age punk group," Megan joked. She inched her way closer to

Johnny, who was now standing. "Wanna hold him? He's not heavy, even with all those pounds I packed on."

Johnny took a step back. "Me, hold him? I've never held a baby before; wouldn't wanna hurt him."

"Nothing to be afraid of," Megan assured him. She stood up and gently placed the boy against Johnny's chest. "Just use two hands and don't squeeze too hard. He may squirm a bit, but I promise he isn't going anywhere."

Johnny wrapped both arms around the boy. Megan slowly let go. Gradually he was holding the baby on his own, and his trepidation subsided. Those miniature fingers. The baby-smooth skin. Johnny peered into the boy's tiny blue eyes. Suddenly, he was transported to another place and time: a looking glass to a world of what-might-have-been.

What if he had taken Megan's calls, or answered her letters in the weeks that followed her betrayal? Conceivably, he might now be standing here, not as a visitor, but cradling his own flesh and blood.

Of course, if this scenario had played out, his path to becoming a musical hero would never have materialized. Yet the thought of a quiet domestic life - the stability he had forever craved but never tasted - suddenly seemed more appealing. Especially when compared with the pressures of living up to everyone's high expectations.

His thoughts were interrupted by a ringing telephone. Megan went to take the call. From the exasperation in her voice, he knew who was on the line.

"Yes, Alex is fine... don't need anything right now... I have enough diapers... Not really up to company... No, I haven't heard from Zach; don't need him coming by later. Please just let me go. I have a delivery waiting... Okay, bye."

Just as Megan was hanging up in the other room, young Alex unleashed the unmistakable cry of a newborn. Instinctively, Johnny tried to calm the infant, singing *Frère Jacques*: the first lullaby that popped into his mind. The baby carried on for what seemed like hours; no pacifier in sight. *Well, this kid's no fan of mine.* It was an awkward reminder that his long-shot daydream of a future with this child's mother was very unlikely. Not only wasn't this his screaming infant, but as long as Katherine Price remained in the picture, uneasiness would always be lurking.

"Don't feel bad, John." Megan rushed back into the room and took the baby from him. "He's just craving something you can't give him." She turned away and undid the top two buttons of her maternity blouse. "Please don't take it personally. He's just hungry."

"Well, maybe I should be going then. Lemme give you guys some privacy."

"Hey, wait," Megan urged, catching up to Johnny near the coat closet. "I'd offer you to hang around, but I know you must have someplace to be."

"Actually, yeah, I'm meeting my tour promoter in an hour. Rehearsals after that." Johnny slipped on his coat and stepped out into the hall with Megan following closely behind.

"Well, Alex and I really enjoyed your stopping by," Megan said as the elevator arrived. "And next time, maybe we can spend more quality time together, just you and me?"

"Yeah, we should. I'd like that." Johnny nodded, though his words seemed unconvincing.

Johnny planned to sleep in the next morning. A readjustment to the Eastern time zone would have been useful. But it was just 7:25 when the ringing of his private line awaked him.

"Elias, it's René. I wanted to give you a heads-up before you heard directly from the boss. Boy is he ever pissed this morning."

"What about?" Johnny asked, his voice scratchy. "I thought we were on the same page with the album?"

"Album? This is about what's in today's papers. You have access to the Post? It's right there on Page Six."

"What? More gossip?" Johnny was still waking up. "Haven't seen anything except the flip side of my eyelids."

"Not a rumor, Johnny. A photo! There's a shot of you at some bar. You're holding this long needle. The accompanying caption insinuates you've been shooting up... in public! I don't want to pass any judgments, but —"

"Don't, then," Johnny interjected forcefully. "That's not my scene. You sure it isn't doctored? Wouldn't be the first time a tabloid did that to me."

"Johnny, why don't you grab a copy, then call me back? Very concerned to say the least."

Johnny stepped into a pair of jeans and raced out, barefoot, into the hallway. On the ground floor, the tousled star was bombarded by a gathering of TV cameras and microphones. He stumbled past them and crossed the street to a newsstand on the corner of 96th, where he bought the paper with the change in his pocket. He then gingerly crossed back over, where again the media cluster began to swarm.

"Johnny, is it true you've used heroin for inspiration?" asked one man with a tape recorder in his outstretched hand. "What can you tell us about the picture in today's paper?" asked a well-dressed woman from the all-news radio, pointing a microphone near Johnny's mouth.

"I've never messed with drugs... nothing heavy anyway. And I've yet to see the photo in question." Johnny maneuvered through the crowd toward the building entrance. "Just wanted to see what all the fuss is about."

With flashbulbs popping around him, it occurred to Johnny that he'd not yet put himself together for the day. *Not a terribly flattering image,* he thought ruefully. He shielded his stubbly face with the newspaper and kept walking until his bare feet found the cold marble floor of his lobby.

The disturbing image on Page-Six stared back at him in black and white. Once upstairs, he located the cordless phone in his kitchen and quickly dialed the Highpeak office. "René, that's no drug needle. I was photographed months ago holding Howard Greffen's insulin. He's diabetic. I was probably looking after him; reminding him to take it."

"But the look on your face: way too recreational," René countered. "Have you any idea what our label has riding on your next record? Already you've been accused of stealing from some starving artist. Sexual orientation rumors. Now this needle thing pops up and goodbye credibility."

Johnny's temper began to twitch. "Damn it, René. Don't you listen to a word I'm saying? That syringe is insulin. And it's not like I'm sticking it in my arm."

Another voice cut in. "Johnny, even if the Post runs a front-page retraction, you've just made things notably worse. You looked like hell on the telly just now; shielding your face like that. Gives the impression that you have something to hide," shouted Ron Neswick over René's speakerphone. "Tomorrow, this is only going to spin further out of control. Don't you own a pair of shoes with the money we pay you?"

"Ron, can't a man pick up the morning paper without being stalked? How the hell could I have known? I'll go throw on a suit; comb my hair. I'm sure I can rationally explain everything if they're still salivating for me down there. And if not, I'll call my own press conference; announce my lawsuit for defamation of character."

"You'll do nothing of the sort," Ron snarled. "You'll find a quiet way out of your building and head straight here. Then we'll sit down and figure out how to undo this mess. Last thing I need is to have you say something else we might all regret."

Johnny arrived with Andy at Highpeak headquarters. They were ushered straight into the conference room. "Have a seat, gentlemen," Ron grumbled. He watched the two men pull out the two remaining empty chairs around the oval table. "So much for our media darling, Mr. Elias!"

"But I swear this is all someone's idea of a sick joke! Let's get Howard Greffen on the phone. He'll verify it for you."

"None of that matters now." Ron shook his head. "How do you expect us to try and set the record straight when everything looks so firmly crooked? I'm not even sure what to believe myself."

"And where there's smoke, there's usually fire," Heidi Ellison cut in, putting down a coffee mug. "You can only deny so much before people tune you out."

"Oh, please!" Andy scowled back at her. "As if anyone believes this crap."

René stood up and walked over to the other side of the table. "Do us a favor, Johnny. Roll up your sleeves, if you don't mind."

"What the hell's this about?" Andy protested, his voice irate.

"Mr. Raymer, are you familiar with the Blake and Riley Gibson tragedy? A rather dark day in our company's history." René was now standing directly behind Johnny.

"The Gibson Twins?" Andy rolled his eyes. "Yeah, everyone's heard of their inauspicious demise. But what's that got to do with Johnny?"

"We want to see his veins," Neswick demanded from across the room. "We're not too keen on our star attractions linked to hazardous recreational activities… if you know what I mean."

"Oh, so that's what this is about." Johnny stood up. "It's fine, Andy. I've got nothing to hide." Without hesitation he unbuttoned his long sleeve shirt and dropped it on the conference table; his bare arms and chest on display for all to see."

"Doesn't look like he's got any needle marks here," René commented after a close inspection. Then to Ron he asked, "Should I ask him to remove his pants as well?"

Andy jumped out of his seat and quickly intervened. "Are you people kidding me? Sheer insanity! This guy's purer than pearl. Johnny, you've shown them plenty."

"That's fine for now, Mr. Elias. Put your shirt back on," Neswick shouted above the commotion. "Though I must say, your erratic behavior of late has us all scratching our heads. Then these rumors crop up and—"

"And even if he's not shooting up, he could be snorting the stuff, or doing something else," Heidi interrupted. "I think we should have him tested. Blood and urine to be sure."

"Are you for real?" Andy was again livid, throwing his hands up in Heidi's direction. "On what legal grounds? Oh, wait. Maybe he should just run over to you now, drop trough and piss in your coffee cup! Bet you'd be drooling?"

Heidi's flashed her middle finger at Andy. Andy took two strides in Heidi's direction. A stunned Jessica Frazier raced quickly to get between them.

"Enough, already! Enough from all of you!" Neswick shouted. He pounded the table in fury. "In all my years in this business… absolutely asinine!"

A hush fell over the room. Johnny stood shaking as though the floor were rumbling beneath him. Up to that moment, he had never perceived his career as fragile. Even while becoming an overnight media darling he'd always been protective of his image, of his privacy. If anything, he'd taken too little time to enjoy this improbable ride. Recreation was virtually nonexistent.

Yet here was all this vicious innuendo about a darker side that didn't exist. Just where was it coming from? When would it dissipate? And to think of the damage it had already caused…

Johnny tapped his knuckles against the tabletop. He looked around the room studying the executives' faces, blood rushing through his veins. "Okay. Here's the part I don't get. Instead of buying into this BS, why aren't you guys rallying to my defense? Hasn't my music brought millions to this company? I thought you'd all protect me, not point accusing fingers. I mean, does anyone in this room actually believe I'm a junkie? Yeah, so I've popped a few pills on tour. Who hasn't? But have I ever shown poor judgment; blown off a gig? A session? A commitment? You've all seen my work ethic. Where does all this mistrust come from?"

"It's not that we don't appreciate your importance," René responded. The others nodded. "But let's not lose sight of who made you a star! We are your employer. And we've never been more conscious about the perception of our artists. We simply can't afford to sit idly by and ignore another tragedy in-the-making."

"And you claim none of these stories are the result of anything you've done," Heidi tacked on. "But when they keep surfacing, how're we supposed to keep defending you?"

There was an awkward moment of silence. Then Ron Neswick rose from his chair, walked across the room and put his arm around Johnny in a fatherly manner. "Listen here, young man. This all may seem hostile, but it's coming from a good place. I just need you to look me in the eye and tell me honestly if you have a drug problem; if you need us to get you some help. Rehab isn't a punishment. But if you're sick, it can save your life."

Johnny looked up and locked eyes with his boss. His indignation was still visibly apparent. "No, Ron, I'm totally clean. Honestly, no addictions. The only problem I seem to have is with whoever's going round spreading these rumors that I do. That and the fact that your people are so damn gullible. I just don't understand."

Ron stood quietly, staring into Johnny's unblinking eyes. Slowly, he exhaled. "Well, okay then. I'll just have to take you at your word. And I, for one, believe that yes, it is our responsibility to protect our assets when they've fallen victim to disreputable idiocy." He removed his arm from around Johnny's bare shoulders and pointed across the table. "Heidi: go draft a release admonishing the so-called journalism exhibited today by the *Post*. And get a quote in there from a medical expert to prove the diabetic angle. When that's done, I want you to investigate the origin of these rumors. If it's a rival label, shouldn't be too hard to pin down."

"On it, boss." Heidi nodded, jotting down some notes on a memo pad.

"Make sure I'm also kept in the loop," Andy grumbled as he stepped toward the door. "Any release crosses my desk before it goes out."

Ron waited for Johnny to finish buttoning his shirt before walking him out to 57th Street. When he returned to the conference table, his curious strategy came into question.

"What was that all about?" René protested. "I thought this was an intervention. Did Elias say anything to change your mind?"

"Well, there's the small matter that Johnny Elias just happens to be our current bestselling mainstream artist. Let's not forget that he still has a top-20 album. Not to mention a brand new one with a can't-miss single on tap."

"Oh, so now we're willing to overlook his character flaws because he's bankable and convincing? Ron, even if he's telling the truth, I'm tiring of the excuses and his who-me attitude. You can't help but wonder what kind of enemies he's got out there. That guy is definitely hiding something. He needs some real help."

Ron leaned forward against the top of his big chair. "René, my friend, have you ever considered that a little controversy might just be what we need to drum up some much-needed business around here. Fact is: our boy hasn't exactly been arrested, institutionalized, or caught in a compromising position. No track marks. No red flags. I may despise this ugliness as much as you do, but I'm not about to let an opportunity slip by. Especially with jobs on the line."

René's face reddened in fury. Ron took a moment to light up a cigar, then stepped in René's direction. "Might I also remind you of the financial commitment we have for his next three albums. Unless Mr. Elias violates his terms, or seriously tarnishes our reputation, we're not letting him walk."

"But I thought we were trying to rebuild a once mighty label with an influx of new talent. Johnny Elias may swear his innocence. But if he's really this magnet for scandal… we can hardly afford another high profile catastrophe."

Ron blew a trail of cigar smoke through his nostrils. His patience was wearing thin. "René, show me hard evidence that our golden boy's an addict. Something more than unsubstantiated hearsay. You wanna put the fear of God in him? You've fired a warning shot, and that's fine for now. In the meantime, we've got a record to release. And I want it on the shelves before the summer. Remember: our bottom line supercedes any tabloid fodder."

27

Greasing Tall Skids

A *Call To Action* received furious airplay on both top-40 and rock stations from its first day of release. Switchboards in every control room lit up with requests, prompting program directors to insert it into heavy rotation. Whether it was sheer quality, its social conscious, or timely lyrics, the song was instantly adopted as an unofficial anthem for nearly every dissatisfied young adult in America. And the stores barely kept up with demand.

Just before the new single's release, Johnny found himself front-page news again for all the wrong reasons.

Although media outlets ran Johnny's denial of the narcotics story, it was his ill-advised barefoot jaunt that grabbed screaming headlines on a slow news day. Not even quotes from two prominent doctors to explain the diabetic needle could offset the unbecoming black-and-white images – visual evidence of his supposed erratic behavior.

For six days, Johnny found reporters camped in shifts outside his building. Just to safely run local errands, he'd dress in disguise and exit from a side-door with an entourage. It was only after he came out for an informal press conference that the bloodthirsty hoards were finally satiated. Yet even his candid remarks about recent rumors were twisted in some publications to make him appear combative.

Johnny was so preoccupied with his invasion of privacy that he didn't immediately realize the rush-distribution of his new single. He had never been shown the packaging, or been told of a release date, so he was entirely startled when hearing it in the back of an uptown taxi.

"Andy, how the hell did this happen? Aren't they supposed to get our okay on things like this?"

"Technically, it is a contractual violation," Andy admitted. "But in light of recent tensions and all the larger issues, do you really want to challenge it? At least they've managed to score some serious airplay."

Both critics and the record-buying public were unfazed by personal gossip dogging Johnny since the recent outbreak of indignity. One trade magazine described the song as "*a rock anthem for the early 90s.*" Another described it as "*Dylanesque in nature, with a clever social message.*"

Just the thought of having one of his songs compared with those by the iconic Bob Dylan was enough to raise Johnny from his temporary malaise. But as he digested the visual interpretation of *A Call To Action* in a music video – a montage of High School cheerleaders shouting through megaphones – he was left with no choice but to protest his record label's unauthorized actions.

Meanwhile, the execs at Highpeak – who figured Johnny was in no position to criticize a chart debut at number four – simply pushed on to the ringing of cash resisters. A few broken rules were well worth any legal risk at this time of need. Highpeak acted unilaterally in planning a rush-release of the new thirteen-song collection. It wasn't until Andy caught wind of these covert intentions through a misdirected internal memo that he asked his lawyers to intervene.

Ron Neswick, it seemed, anticipated orchestrating everything, including the very naming of the album. A preliminary cover was designed with the title *Second Time Around*. But after meeting fierce resistance from the stunned Elias camp, Highpeak eventually relented.

René Fontenot's alternate choice to make it a self-titled release infuriated Johnny, who instead came up with the name, *A New Beginning*. This of course, was in reference to a lyric on the album's closing song, written by Howard Greffen. If the title, or Jacqui's rushed cover design – a multi-colored sunrise - lacked the imagery of *Poet of the Wrong Generation*, it was a vast improvement over some generic designation chosen with artistic indifference.

Nearly overlooked through all the bickering was the fact that *A Call To Action* had amazingly hit number one on the US singles chart in just its second week of release. Johnny had no time to celebrate his achievement. An extensive satellite radio tour and the taping of a *VH-1* special assured him of preoccupation.

In the eye of the storm, Andy received a congratulatory call in his new East Side office. It came from a Sheila Sterling, coordinator of the upcoming benefit for the sight-impaired children.

"Mr. Raymer, we're delighted to learn that Johnny Elias has the new number one hit. I suppose we're getting even more than we bargained for."

Andy scratched his head. "I appreciate the kind words, though I'm not sure I follow you on the second comment. Is there something I've overlooked beyond Johnny's commitment to play your event?"

"Not at all." The woman stifled a laugh. "No other requests. What I meant was, now that he's topping the charts, I imagine his appearance'll only bring greater coverage to our cause. Not to mention how excited the children'll be if he plays his latest hit."

"Well, I can't speak for Johnny, but I'm fairly certain he'll be playing *A Call To Action*. He's truly excited about participating on the twenty-second."

"*That* was actually my other reason for calling." The woman's voice grew serious. "I pray this won't mess anyone up, but unfortunately we had an unforeseen schedule alteration. Instead of the original Tuesday date, we were forced to push it off to Wednesday the twenty-third. All other details – the start time, the venue, all that – remain the same. Please tell me that Johnny can still make it for the children one night later?"

Andy fumbled through the date book, then double-checked the master calendar on the wall. "Shelia, looks like the twenty-third's clear, although I still need to check it with the boss. Can I call back tomorrow to verify?"

"Not to pressure you Mr. Raymer, but might it be possible you'll be speaking with him today? Everyone here is terribly anxious. If I'm not being too much of a pest, I'll call again later to confirm."

"Mr. Elias, you were just getting your feet wet when I booked your first tour. Feels like yesterday. Today, you've officially graduated from theaters to arenas. Instead of a diploma, I'd like to present this outline: Eighty prospective dates for your consideration."

Sandwiched between a nationally syndicated radio interview and a *People* Magazine sit-down, Johnny met briefly over lunch with concert promoter, Herb Cantor. Herb did most of the talking… and the eating.

"So what do you say, young man? You addicted to the touring life yet?" He reached out for a ketchup bottle.

Johnny glanced at the itinerary, then dislodged a lemon seed from the straw in his Diet 7-Up. "Mr. Cantor, your terrific enthusiasm aside, I'm not sure I'm ready for this. Not used to this pace."

"Not ready? Don't tell me you're not prepared to make the leap to the next echelon. If you thought the last tour was big…" He sank his teeth into a large hamburger; juices spurted everywhere.

Johnny shrugged, then handed Herb a napkin. "Listen, I understand it's inevitable. But if opening night could be pushed off by even a month or two, I'd consider it a moral victory. These days I'm just running on fumes."

At his empty apartment that night, Johnny found piles of autograph requests, phone messages, and an endless stack of paperwork to review. He signed the first bundle of fan reply letters, then decided he needed a break.

He traded in his business attire for a white denim shirt and blue jeans. Johnny was lonely, tired, and still stung by the recent wave of disharmony.

He pulled out his black phonebook and began to flip alphabetically through the pages. Under the letter M, he spotted Lauren Minton: a voice he hadn't heard from since his last concert, six months earlier. *Gotta wonder what she's up to?* He hesitantly picked up the receiver and dialed. But before his imagination could wander, the piercing tones that her number was no longer in service came through loud and clear.

Johnny next attempted reaching Andy over at Jacqui's place. He disconnected at the pick-up of Jacqui's answering machine. Next, he tried Larry Jacobs at his downtown apartment, knowing it was never too late to call. Even his attempt to reach Howard Greffen was in vain, when his marbly pre-recorded voice declared that he wasn't at home. Johnny shook his head in disbelief. *For someone in such demand, how'd I become so isolated?*

He aimlessly paced the living room for more than half an hour. At one point, he casually ran his fingers across his scalp. A loose clump of hair caught on his knuckles, and easily came free. He stared down at it in disgust. *Damn the pressure. If it don't kill me, it's gonna sink my career. Ain't too many balding pop stars burning up the charts.*

Johnny lifted the handset again at eleven-thirty. Was it too late to phone Megan? Surely a call at this hour would disturb her sleeping newborn. Instead, he settled into a red beanbag chair in the den. He flipped through the sixty or so channels on city cable. Nothing of interest. In the kitchen, he switched on the radio and made himself a grilled cheese sandwich. He found little comfort in hearing his own voice sing *A Call To Action*. Promptly, he turned it off. Even at his treasured baby grand, Johnny remained uninspired. His eyes glazed over; his mind elsewhere. He could hardly string together more than a few notes before conceding defeat.

Johnny stepped toward his bedroom, kicking off his black loafers in the process. "Another day's useless energies spent," he muttered. His king-sized bed felt more empty than usual. For close to an hour he lay awake, tussling with his quilt.

Then the phone rang.

"Hi. If I'm getting you at a bad time just tell me."

"Megan," Johnny sighed. "No… it's not too late. Couldn't really fall asleep tonight."

"Everything all right?" she asked, sounding concerned. "I really wanted to congratulate you on the number one song, but I only just got Alex down. Been trying since around ten."

"Putting things in perspective as always," Johnny said softly, seeing the irony.

"What do ya mean? Hey, you feeling all right? Wanna talk about it?"

"Okay, yeah, I suppose we could."

There was a pause, then Megan spoke. "Hey, I know it's late, but you're welcome to swing by my place. It's not like I had any other plans at this hour!"

Johnny was startled by the timeliness of her call. He paused to reflect if this was all somehow meant to be. *How could she have known?*

He found himself going over to Megan's place as though it were the most natural thing in the world. Megan was waiting in her doorway. His eyes lit up at the site of her. "Wow! You're looking great," he said, noticing her more slender figure beneath a lilac silk robe and a pair of black sweatpants. "What's it been, two months since you had the baby?"

"It'll be nine weeks tomorrow." Megan gestured proudly at herself. "Thanks for noticing. Been working out to get my figure back. Now, come here." She took his hand and led him to the sofa. Her blonde hair smelled sweet like fresh pineapple. There was a bucket of ice and two crystal goblets on the marble-topped coffee table. "Can I get you anything to drink?"

"Sure, that would be great." His eyes wandered around the room.

Megan briefly departed. Johnny stared at the glasses on the table. He wondered if they were being used for the first time, considering how brightly they reflected the amber candlelight from a nearby flickering votive. Relaxing music emanated from a pair of speakers atop the fireplace mantle. The song was one from his youth – *Time*, by the Alan Parsons Project. Softly, he picked up the chorus in the middle. *Time, flowing like a river. Who knows when we shall meet again, if ever?*

"You say something?" Megan returned to the room with a pitcher of cold lemonade.

"No… just singing with the radio for a change." He was slightly embarrassed. "You know I can't resist."

"Good to see you still haven't changed! Yeah, I hum along with my favorites too. Even memorized some of your songs, hearing 'em so often. You know, sometimes it's hard to believe I actually know the man behind the voice." She poured the lemonade and handed him a glass. "So tell me what's going on, John. You sounded really down on the phone."

"Yeah, pretty remarkable that through all these years you're the one person who truly understands me."

Johnny opened up about the damaging gossip and the never-ending demands. Megan sat quietly, hands folded, her eyes loving. Johnny told her everything, breaking off occasionally to pour another glass. "And I'm feeling lonely," he concluded. "Guess I have ever since I wrote *We've Already Said Goodbye.*"

"You ever consider what might've happened if you never had to write that one?" Megan found she had tears in her eyes.

"That's a question I've asked myself at least once every day since I wrote it." His voice cracked. "That song… it was the most painful thing I ever put to paper. And while it's brought me unbelievable success, it's delivered about as much happiness as the incident that inspired it."

Megan softly sighed. "Sorry you feel that way." She inched closer to him on the sofa. "Thing is, while the past is unchangeable, we can always make up for lost time. Life may've gotten far too complicated for us, yet every night I fall asleep to the sound of your lovely music box and… Hey, I can dream, can't I?"

Megan rested her head on Johnny's shoulder. Johnny sat in complete silence, conflicted by passion and fear. Was it desperation or destiny that led him to her door at this late hour? No matter, he decided to let his instinct take over and decide. One hand began to stroke her arm; the other cradling her back.

Megan took comfort in the tenderness. With nothing left to say, and afraid to make another move, she instead lay peacefully against him, waiting for his initiation.

Johnny's heart was thundering. Closing his eyes, he felt strangely reassured by the sound of Megan's familiar breathing against his neck. Somehow, it all felt surprisingly comfortable, despite how long it had been since he had been close to her.

Soft music continued to spill out from the speakers above. As *Drive* by The Cars faded out, the piano intro to Bob Seger's *We've Got Tonite* suddenly began – another song that had once already altered Johnny's fortunes. His eyes popped wide open. He removed his arm from around her, then stood from the couch. His hands were trembling. Johnny reached out to Megan, pulling her up to join him. He gazed deeply into her loving blue eyes, then whispered, "I can't recall the last time we danced together."

"August 15th, 1991." She flashed a telling smile and quoted: "You remember. It was late in the evening and all that music was seeping through."

Johnny smiled in recognition, then pulled Megan close, his desire growing within him. Slowly, they began to move in unison to the melody filling the room. The adoration in her gaze told him everything he needed to know.

Megan leaned in with eyes firmly closed and brought her open lips to his. Her body pressed snugly against him. She clutched his shirt, feeling his warmth, wishing to never let go. In return, Johnny tenderly kissed her, caressed her soft blonde hair, untied the belt of her robe. Soon, he was running his fingers over unfamiliar, fading lines of stretched skin across her belly. This alluring vulnerability only further excited him. For one breathtaking moment, two tortured, wandering souls had rediscovered a common spiritual bond.

But before their passion could carry any further: a sudden piercing cry from down the hall. "Alex," was all Megan could say as she gently pulled away and began trotting in the direction of her boy's bedroom.

When she returned to the living room minutes later, she found Johnny sitting on the sofa, head in his hands. "So sorry for that. He's still got a fever.

Do us a favor. There's a 24-hour Duane Reade just around the corner. Can I ask you to please run over and pick up some Tylenol for infants? The one with a dropper."

By the time Johnny returned with the medicine, all sparks from their magical exchange had dissipated. It was 4:45am. Alex was still screeching. Johnny yawned, stretching his arms above his head. "Well, you know how helpless I am around babies. If you've got things under control…" His tired voice tailed off. He dangled a key-chain in his left hand.

"You don't have to leave, you know," Megan said quickly. "I'll probably have him back asleep soon. Meantime, you're welcome to crash in any of the bedrooms if you like. I've got one big empty place here."

"Meg, you're so sweet." Johnny shook his head. "Wish I could, but I'm actually booked on *Good Day New York* tomorrow morning… which now is actually today. Gotta be there in an hour for hair and makeup, or so they tell me."

Megan held Alex against her chest. She stood to walk Johnny out in a scene becoming all-too-familiar. "I'm not even gonna ask this time when I'll see you next," she said, smiling. "With your crazy calendar… hey, how about this weekend? Hopefully Alex'll be better by then."

Johnny smiled and brushed Megan's cheek. "Yeah, it's been far too long. All that precious time lost." He leaned forward and kissed her forehead. "Listen, the next few days are hell for me: endless promo for the new album, and a major charity gig. My life's just not my own. But Meg, I'll call you the minute I'm free. I promise. Maybe we'll even run off together somewhere for a while; do some serious catching up." He leaned closer. "You won't be waiting very long." The elevator arrived. He delicately embraced both Megan and Alex. "Oh, and thanks for being here for me tonight."

"I've always been here for you," Megan said. "Always will."

Early reviews for Johnny's soon-to-be released album were more flattering than anticipated. *The Newark Star Ledger* gave a solid three out of four stars review, mostly focusing on the strength of his single. Long Island's *Newsday* called A New Beginning *"solidly spectacular,"* although they did note the oddity of an artist releasing two albums in the same year.

On the airwaves, top-forty stations continued to play *A Call To Action* in saturation. Rock radio picked the edgier cuts to generate early hype. Light-music stations altogether ignored the single, instead opting for the album's two ballads: *Tomorrow's Door* and *A View From The Top Of The World.* Steady advance exposure, indeed.

Over at Highpeak headquarters, Ron Neswick and his staff were fired-up by all the goings-on. Not only was Johnny Elias still holding down the # 1 single, but the label's recent talent search had successfully yielded three new promising acts.

Ron was encouraged by Johnny's participation in the upcoming charity concert. He privately arranged to purchase the last remaining high-priced tickets. Unbeknownst to Johnny, he then offered them as a perk to the newly signed contest winners. Ron owned no desire to burden his busy star with further details. But he saw little harm in popping in unannounced for formal introductions once the concert had ended.

Since returning from Los Angeles, Johnny's time at home had been mostly spent rehearsing in solitude. Andy was no longer a fixture in the apartment. These days he was crashing every night at Jacqui's East Side rental, close to the new office. But popping up to fetch a fresh suit and some misplaced papers, Andy noted the change in Johnny's playing.

"Whoa! Fairly obvious you won't be needing another piano player in the band anymore!" he said, applauding, after catching the tail end of a solo rendition of *Tomorrow's Door.* "How long ago was it that you played on a mini-keyboard, using only two fingers?"

"Oh, hi there, stranger." Johnny rotated on the piano bench in the living room. "Yeah, I guess the extra day bought me some time to polish my act. But I'm really nervous, man, going up there without a safety net. Other than one encore at the Beacon, I've never really played solo before. Every mistake'll surely be magnified."

Andy chuckled. "John, no disrespect, but Wednesday's show is in front of a room full of blind children. They'll hear you just fine, but they won't notice a grimace if you go out of tune. And remember, you're doing this out of the goodness of your heart. Making a few kids happy is all that counts."

"Actually, it's not the kids I'm concerned about. They'll have a blast." Johnny wiped his brow with his sleeve. "It's those senseless tabloids. *Somebody* out there has it in for me. I've got a strange premonition that if I'm not perfect, those hawks will be circling to pick me apart."

Andy tucked two sport jackets into a garment bag. "Hey, don't lose sleep over what you can't control. Long as you bring your A-game, you've got nothing to worry about."

28

Brilliant Demise

Tuesday June 22nd, 1993, began as a regular day for Johnny Elias. Or at least as normal a day could start off for a burgeoning pop star with a new album set for release.

Johnny received a 7:30 wake-up call from Heidi Ellison. He showered, shaved, then dressed casually in a black sports jacket and stylish blue jeans. After a brief radio phone interview, he headed downstairs past a small media contingent and into a waiting black sedan.

The car arrived thirty minutes early for the signing. Johnny was escorted through a growing crowd outside the flagship Tower Records store. Once inside, he got the urge to greet the salespeople on the retail floor during morning set-up. Upbeat and relaxed, he scribbled autographs and sang requested snippets as the room took shape for a large gathering.

At exactly ten o'clock, the front doors opened. Over 800 people noisily queued up between stanchion and rope, waiting to meet their hero. Excited fans approached a raised counter to buy the new CD and move along to a desk where Johnny exchanged pleasantries and signed the cover.

The event had been scheduled to last two hours. By eleven-thirty, the volume of autograph seekers had swelled to over two thousand. Heidi barked out orders to cut off the line, but Johnny turned to the store manager. "Hey, we've got no place to go till two. Let's keep it going till my right hand falls off!"

Immediately after the signing, Heidi ushered Johnny into another car, this one en route to a midday radio program. The vapors from Heidi's perfume made Johnny's eyes water, which was fortunately not visible on radio. *Man, she's overwhelming.* From there, it was off to an interview segment for *CNN*, and another for Canadian television. It was 4:35pm when the car dropped him off at the apartment. "Wow! For three spots, we made great time. We'll talk later!" Heidi shouted. "Unless you feel like inviting me up?" Johnny closed the passenger door, drew a breath of fresh air, and headed inside.

On his key table in the foyer, Johnny found a fresh stack of album reviews awaiting him. Halfheartedly, he opened the envelope and glanced at the first several from the top. Feedback ranged from *"Another Landmark Effort"* to *"Maddeningly Inconsistent." Looks like some are a little too kind, while others are selling it short,* he thought, shrugging. But with a massive hit single and a whirlwind of publicity, Johnny remained confident that his album would sell big.

Tired from all the earlier commotion, he stepped sluggishly out of his stiff shoes and flung himself on the living room sofa.

Johnny awoke an hour later feeling refreshed. A to-do list for the benefit concert sat atop his piano. Johnny narrowed his seven song favorites down to five and tinkered with the arrangements until he was satisfied. When he clicked on the TV for background noise, he caught the end of the six-o'clock news telecast.

"On the West Side this morning, hometown hero Johnny Elias celebrated his brand new CD with a signing for thousands of his most loyal fans. Lines stretched across two and a half blocks on Broadway."

Within moments, a barrage of calls began ringing on his private line. First to get through was Carolyn Green, Johnny's onetime foster mom. "Oh,

Johnny, just saw the report. What a wild scene you caused today! I couldn't be prouder!"

Next was Risa Sheppard. "Johnny, that footage from today's event actually appeared on channels four and seven. As usual, I'll have the clipping service order up copies for the archives."

Johnny let the answering machine get the next several calls. A microwavable pizza was nearly ready. He figured all messages could be returned at his convenience. But with a steady stream of rings drowning out his television, curiosity would eventually prevail.

"Johnny, it's Megan. Can you hear me?"

"Megan," he answered, attempting to lower the TV with a remote. "You gotta speak up a little. Bad connection."

"Johnny, I need help," she pleaded on a static-filled line. "I'm really in trouble; didn't know who else to call."

"Megan, where are you? What's the matter? I can hardly make out a word you're saying."

"It's Gerry!" she whispered. "He's got Alex. I'm at his apartment trying to get him back."

"Call the police, Megan! Or tell me where you are." He pounded a fist on the countertop. "I'll have the place surrounded in a minute. This asshole should be arrested!"

"Please, don't," she urged. The connection crackled. "If the cops show up, he might hurt us. I'll explain it all when you get here, but please come, Johnny. You gotta hurry!"

"Where are you?" he asked, pulling a pen from his pocket.

"A six-story building; corner of Amsterdam and 176th. There's a bodega next door with a yellow awning. I'm in the last apartment on the right. Third floor."

"What's the address?" Johnny competed with white noise in the background. Getting no answer, he repeated the question and Megan's name intermittently. But after more static and indiscernible clamor, the connection cut out.

Johnny's initial instinct was to dial 9-1-1. But the thought of Megan in danger had his mind racing toward irrationality. Instead, he quickly jotted down the location he believed to have heard, so as not to forget it along the way.

"I wonder what's keeping Johnny Elias," Katherine Price said. She was in the dressing area of the Alexander Hamilton Auditorium. "Wasn't he slated to be here by seven for a meet-and-greet? I guess traffic at this hour must be murder."

"There must be a reasonable explanation," noted Christopher Gruen, director of *By The Hand*. He adjusted his tuxedo jacket. "My people say he's excited about this. He'll show. Anyone try reaching him at home?"

"At least a half-dozen times," Sheila McLennan said. She sounded exasperated. "I keep getting his answering machine; must be on his way."

"How 'bout his manager? Anyone try calling his office?"

"I tried Andy Raymer too." Sheila shook her head. "It's now past seven; must've all gone home for the night. Or maybe they're on their way. People from his record label are out in the lobby. Maybe they all arrived together."

At that moment the classical violinist, Joseph Muravyov strolled in, sporting a white tuxedo with long tails. In his hands was a protective case for his precious instrument. "If Mr. Elias is delayed in arriving… well, I've prepared up to forty minutes of music. That should keep everyone happy for a while."

The crowd filed into the posh auditorium. It was visibly apparent that they hadn't come to see stand-up comics, or to hear classical music. Beyond the first thirty rows – which were reserved for sight-impaired children – fans gradually filled the remaining seats, having spent up to three hundred dollars for the privilege. Many sported Johnny Elias concert t-shirts.

By seven-thirty, three-quarters of the room was occupied. Dozens more mingled in the lobby, or lined up for refreshments. Onstage, in clear view stood a central podium, draped with the logo for the *By The Hand* organiza-tion. To either side stood separate microphone stands. And to the far right: a shiny black grand piano with a matching bench.

In the crammed orchestra pit, two-dozen photographers jockeyed for prime position. And behind the back row of audience, a twelve-foot wide platform progressively became occupied with local TV crews. Numerous Price & McLennan staffers kept the media exceptionally well organized in a tight setting.

Soon, the children were escorted to their assigned seats. A buzz of excitement overtook the room. Backstage, Christopher Gruen and his staff were doing their best to stay calm as showtime neared. "Who spoke to Mr. Elias most recently? Anyone confirm his arrival time? I hope this isn't some kind of a prima-donna rock-star thing, where he just shows up whenever he chooses."

"I faxed Andy Raymer tonight's schedule just yesterday," Sheila assured him confidently. "He personally verified they'd be here. I've no reason to believe differently."

Christopher Gruen scratched his head nervously. "You don't suppose he somehow forgot about us? Maybe we should send someone up to his place."

Before Sheila could object, Christopher turned to one of his well-dressed assistants. "Stacy, I hate to do this to you, but can you please get the home information for Johnny Elias from Ms. McLennan? Then drop by his apartment; see what's keeping him."

"That should be it," Johnny yelled from the back seat, pointing to the far corner of Amsterdam and 176th. The cab came to a screeching halt. He reached inside his wallet and handed the driver a folded fifty-dollar bill. "Thanks, and keep the change," he muttered, stepping out onto the curb.

As he looked around, it was clear to Johnny that the neighborhood he'd just entered was as run-down as he earlier visualized. *What on earth would Doctor Gerald Ridgewell be doing up in the Heights?* The thought was lost as he spotted the yellow bodega awning. The front entrance was where he expected it. There were no doormen in this part of town. Johnny walked inside.

There was the smell of stale cigarette smoke, and streak marks along the light blue walls. The elevator was – according to a hand-written note taped to its door – out of order.

Johnny pounded up the stairs. At the top of the second flight he yanked open another door leading to the third floor. He turned right and knocked on the door at the end of the hallway. The unmistakable odor of marijuana inundated his nostrils. "It's open!" a Spanish-accented male voice called from inside.

Johnny thought twice before turning the knob.

"Megan," he called out. "You in here?"

Stacy Mills' high heels clacked urgently as she hurried to the backstage entrance. Katherine Price opened the door, worry on her face. "Any luck?"

"This honestly makes no sense," the receptionist reported, trying to catch her breath. "His doorman said Johnny rushed out to a cab around six-thirty. Should've been here by now."

Katherine concealed a contented smirk. She whisked an invisible piece of lint off her navy Prada jacket, before heading back up to the stage level.

Onstage, violinist Joseph Muravyov was completing his impressive set with a performance of the main theme from Copeland's *Appalachian Spring*. Much of the audience stood to applaud, believing this would be the evening's final instrumental. But as the virtuoso turned to the side, he noticed Christopher Gruen motioning to keep going. Given the crowd's casual makeup, he figured they'd appreciate something more contemporary. Muravyov waited for the clapping to cease. Next he began a medley of pop songs to feature the violin, beginning with, *Eleanor Rigby*.

The attendees settled back in their seats. Mr. Gruen met behind the curtain with his event organizers. "So what's the latest on our truant pop star? Tell me someone has good news."

"I'm afraid I didn't learn much," Stacy Mills said, apologetic. "Either he had somewhere else to go first, or he's totally blown us off."

Sheila McLennan grimaced. "Entirely appalling! If he doesn't call in with a believable excuse, I say we announce that Johnny Elias simply couldn't be bothered to show up for these special children, for his fans, despite his commitment to be here."

"Now, hold on a second," Katherine cautioned. "We don't need a riot on our hands with all those defenseless kids in the crowd. Let's say nothing until the last comedian has left the stage. Then leave it to me to address the media. Privately."

"I think she's right." Gruen mopped his neck with a handkerchief. "We don't need to supply any more ammunition."

At that moment, Ron Neswick popped in, a troubled look on his round face. "Anyone hear from Johnny Elias?" He didn't have to ask a second time. His expression clouding, he stomped off to the bank of payphones in the lobby.

On the other side of the curtain, a comedian called Gus Fandango got only modest laughter with a routine better suited for a small club than a large theater. He'd also forgotten that children occupied the first several rows. Many parents cringed at his raunchy humor.

Christopher Gruen emerged from behind the curtain just after 9:45. With no sign of his headliner, and the spectators growing impatient, he delivered a stall-tactic speech about the merits of his organization. By the time he'd covered the list of primary services, some of the audience began chanting Johnny's name. Soon the majority caught on.

The director appeared flushed and uneasy. He tried to sway the crowd by introducing a few of the children's special instructors to the sound of polite clapping. When the "Johnny!" chant resumed, he staggered backstage to huddle with his organizers. In desperation, they decided to ask Joseph

Muravyov to take a final turn onstage, hoping to give the paying crowd their money's worth.

Unfortunately for Muravyov, only rock and roll would suffice for the fired-up spectators. The fans grew restless. Many filled the aisles during his rendition of Mozart's fourth movement of Symphony Number 40. The twenty rows of children were carefully evacuated until the entire front section sat empty. Even the ordinarily unflappable Muravyov became momentarily distracted by the mass exodus, actually striking a few sour notes. The audience hardly noticed. Those who remained sat wondering aloud if their hometown hero had failed them.

When the lights came up, a visibly frustrated Muravyov exited stage left to a smattering of boos. Handfuls of peanuts and popcorn showered the stage. Backstage, Christopher Gruen unbuttoned his tuxedo jacket, removed his bowtie and turned to Katherine Price. "Think you could break the bad news tactfully?"

Katherine hesitated before heading out to the podium. "Ladies and gentlemen. On behalf of *By The Hand* and all our wonderful performers, I'd like to thank you all for coming out to support our special children."

The escalating chant of *"refund!"* rained down from the rafters. Katherine raised her voice a notch. "Unfortunately, our main performer is not here with us for reasons we don't yet know. To all who were hoping to see Johnny Elias, we apologize for his unforeseen absence and thank you all for your incredible support. Please exit peacefully and have a good night."

The chorus of boos grew louder. Much of the remaining crowd arose from their seats and stomped disapprovingly to the exits. Others refused to leave. Two sections of disgruntled fans began hurling their programs toward the empty stage. Some in the balcony showered the lower level with jellybeans and cups of soda. One man ignited his seat cushion with the cigarette lighter he'd brought for an encore. The smoke set off the theater's fire sprinkler system.

Out in the lobby, a throng of furious fans smashed a glass showcase containing assorted souvenirs. Mass looting ensued. A trio of teens grabbed a fire extinguisher and shattered two plate-glass windows at the front of the theater. A wailing alarm sounded. Within minutes, an NYPD riot team was summoned to apprehend the hooligans. Popping flashbulbs captured the chaos.

By the time the theater cleared out and lights were restored, this plush room, reserved for elegant performances, sat in disarray. Piles of papers and broken glass were strewn across the drenched designer carpet. In the entranceway, twelve vandals were handcuffed, and nine innocent bystanders were treated for cuts and bruises.

Katherine Price refreshed her lipstick in the rear of the ransacked auditorium. Surrounded by TV cameras and microphones, she was entirely in her element, aside from the smirk she tried to suppress. "The good people at *By The Hand* have no answers as to why Johnny Elias was absent tonight. I do know that this paying audience was terribly disappointed, not to mention all those sweet children. It's tragic, really, given his famous humble upbringing. I only hope he has a worthy excuse. From the kids to his loyal fans, he's let down an awful lot of people."

The last of the crowd to exit that night was a soggy Ron Neswick. Ron – having been doused by a flying soft drink – found a despondent Christopher Gruen backstage, making yet another failed attempt to reach Johnny's apartment by phone.

"Mr. Gruen, I wish to extend my apologies. There must be a reason for his no-show tonight. Just wish I knew what it was."

"Mr. Neswick, I realize this isn't your fault. But I do hope there's some fallout from this travesty. Johnny Elias may very well be a gifted talent. I just don't understand how he expected to get away with this."

"I assure you there'll be repercussions," Ron promised emphatically. "Unless he's encountered some emergency, I intend to address this harshly."

Johnny stepped inside a brighter room at the end of a dark corridor and did a double-take. Cigarette butts and beer cans lay scattered across the

uncarpeted floor. The stench grew worse with every step. This was unques-
tionably the biggest dump he'd ever seen.

Johnny called out for Megan again. Instead, he encountered a short,
well-built Latino man dressed in a black leather jacket, a white t-shirt and
torn black jeans. Four gold rings on his right hand matched a solid gold
necklace hanging over the v-neck cutout of his ragged tee.

"Hey, you here for a pick-up?"

"You're obviously not Gerald," Johnny guessed aloud. "I'm looking for
someone; a woman with a small child."

The host folded his formidable arms. "Don't know 'bout no bitches or
babies. This is Octavio's place for business. Ain't no hangout."

"Somehow I believe you," Johnny muttered beneath his breath. He
scanned the room for more openings. "Can I at least have a look around?"

"Not much to see, but if you insist. Long as you ain't here to waste
Octavio's time."

The man led Johnny through a rusted doorframe. A naked overhead
bulb revealed a grimy bathroom to the right, complete with a cracked toilet
and rusted sink. A nearby bedroom proved equally tattered. Two worn-
out mattresses complemented a set of dented filing cabinets. Inside a small
closet, Johnny found only empty wire hangers.

Under the watchful eye of his host, Johnny dejectedly stepped back into
the main room. "Guess I should be going," he announced, heading to the
front door.

"Hey, man, wait a second. What I can interest you in before you go?"

Johnny turned back and stared awkwardly. "Sorry to bother you. I only
came here to find someone in trouble."

"But you haven't even seen my merchandise. You've come all this way.
Mize well check out my goods." Octavio placed a briefcase atop a small card
table. "Sure you don't wanna sample the good stuff?"

Great, a coke dealer! No time to waste here. Gotta find Megan. Johnny
hastily tried to flee via the front hallway. He pushed opened the first door

and found himself back in the dark corridor leading toward the entrance. But as he reached the outer door, he was unable to budge it.

"Señor," Octavio said, catching up to him. "You didn't expect me to leave it unlocked with my valuables inside?" He turned the latch to the top lock. Then he attempted to slip something in Johnny's pocket. In the darkness of the narrow space, a plastic bag fell to the floor at his feet.

Johnny stepped out into the third-floor hallway. Inadvertently he kicked forward the ten-gram bag. As he did so, a blinding crossfire of flashbulbs was followed by the sound of cameras resetting for the next shot. Johnny's eyes were still adjusting to the light. He could barely make out two crouching photographers to either side of the doorway.

"What the hell?" he yelled to the squatting man on his left.

"Just doing my job," the man replied, firmly pressing down on the button.

"Who sent you here?" Johnny turned wildly to the kneeling photojournalist on his right.

"My editor, of course." The second man calmly snapped away.

Johnny grew sharply agitated by their not-so-coincidental presence. To his right, he caught a glimpse of a long tan overcoat sprinting toward the exit sign at the end of the hall.

"Get back here!" he yelled, picking up speed in pursuit. The loud clang of flesh and bone against metal echoed through the hallway. Up ahead, the photographer was struggling to open the far stairwell door. Johnny managed to close the gap. He used his size to seize the smaller man by the wrists and wrestle him to the floor. "Gimme the film, jackass!" Angrily, he extracted the camera from a pair of sweaty hands.

"Hey, let go, ya bastard," the man hollered.

Johnny tried forcing open the film compartment to expose the contents. And then suddenly, he was upended. The photographer had kicked out Johnny's legs from under him and pounced on his photographic subject. Through the exchange of punches, Johnny forgot about the second paparazzi… until the alarming assault of flashbulbs that came from down the hall.

With a jolting rush of fear-induced energy, Johnny unleashed a right uppercut to his opponent's jaw. The force of the blow left the man crumpled in a tan polyester heap. Johnny grabbed the camera, spun in the opposite direction and ran, perspiration and blood raining down his forehead. Incrementally, he closed in on the other photographer as they charged down two flights of stairs. They reached the ground floor and burst out of the stairwell seconds apart.

The second man panted heavily through the lobby. As he ran, he secured his Pentax, dangling loosely over his shoulder. Only steps from the exit, a glass door swung open, followed by an incoming resident with a bundle of grocery bags. The elusive photographer jumped three short steps to the sidewalk, sprinted to the curb, and dove headfirst into the backseat of a waiting silver Toyota. It sped away with the passenger door ajar.

Johnny could only watch helplessly as the getaway car ran three consecutive red lights. He was left with one photographer's camera, two black eyes, and the taste of warm blood trickling from his nose and forehead.

When he spun back toward the building no one was there.

Johnny sprinted two more blocks and ducked into a downtown subway station. He paused on the platform to catch his breath and rein in his emotions. *Where to turn next?*

Instead of heading home, Johnny switched to a cross-town train. He made it over to the East Side and ran straight for the office building where Andy had recently set up shop. The lobby was eerily quiet. Johnny scrawled his name hurriedly in the after-hours reception book before riding up to the ninth floor. It took several keys and multiple attempts, but he managed to locate one that turned the deadbolt. Overhead fluorescents flickered in the darkness. Johnny went straight for the phone on the front reception desk and dialed Megan's home number.

"Hello," he heard her repeat several times, as he held his breath. "Who's calling?"

Startled by her calm intonation, Johnny remained speechless. At first, all he could hear was the thumping of his own heart. Then came the babble of baby Alex in the background.

They're safe, he thought. Neither Megan nor her son was being held against their will. His search to find them was over. *But how could she do this to me? Again?* Familiar tears streamed down his swollen cheeks. Johnny leaned against the wall and slammed down the phone. *How viciously calculating*, he surmised. *How could I have been so stupid?*

29

Suburban Escapism

"**W**here do ya want this piano?" one of four burly moving men asked impatiently. "Can't lug this thing forever."

"Bury it in the basement," Johnny said, rolling his eyes. "Doubt I'll be needing much access to it."

It was a muggy September afternoon in Stamford, Connecticut. Johnny Elias stood outside his new home, waiting for the second moving truck to arrive. He reached down to the manicured lawn and plucked a dandelion between his right thumb and index finger, then watched contentedly as the delicate fuzz blew off in a summer breeze.

It had been three months since the disastrous turn of events back in the city. Johnny began to pace on the lowest of six concrete steps below the main entrance when he spotted the brown van. He waved until he caught the driver's attention.

Outfitted in a red baseball cap, a bulky t-shirt, and a pair of cheap sunglasses, the one-time musical troubadour bore little resemblance to the matinee idol who had previously filled theaters and adorned magazine covers.

After the movers unloaded the cargo, Johnny stood alone amid a pile of boxes in the living room. Silverware. Clothing. Appliances. Files. One by one, he unpacked his possessions until the stack dwindled to a precious few. A collection of framed mementos from his once-prominent career was piled in one area. But with the wounds of resentment still raw and oozing, he resealed the cartons and carried them down to the cold, cavernous basement. *Out of sight, out of mind.*

The night of his missed appearance for the charity benefit had slowly morphed into the morning of his discontent. Johnny returned home at 5am. He got hold of the early editions of all New York papers, fully expecting to find his fisticuffs on the front pages. Instead, he was taken aback by an alarming story, claiming that he had missed a scheduled performance for a room full of helpless children, sparking a riot no less.

"They've got it all wrong!" he shouted, shattering the early-morning silence of his empty apartment. "That show's tonight. Won't miss it for the world!" Then he read on. Headlines such as *Johnny No-Show*, and *Blind Benefit Snub*, made it clear something had gone terribly wrong.

Johnny ran to his home-office for a check of the answering machine. Twenty-six new messages flashed, most of them from Christopher Gruen and his staff, desperation in their voices. *How could this be? Andy told me the gig was rescheduled.*

Near the end of the prerecorded barrage came an unmistakable raspy voice of authority. "Johnny, you'd better be dying or kidnapped to explain this classless act tonight. Phone me at home as soon as you get this message. I'll be waiting."

Neswick was there too? he wondered fretfully. *This keeps getting worse by the minute.*

At the end of the tape came the final message – Andy Raymer calling from Jacqui's apartment, clearly shaken. "Johnny, we just got back from a show and… I think all hell's broken loose. You've probably seen the news by now. I swear, they told me that concert was changed to tomorrow night. It's a total set-up. If it helps any, I think I at least know who the culprit is. Call me the minute you get in."

Frantically, he dialed Jacqui's number. Andy answered after just one ring.

"Johnny, I'm so sorry, man. Don't know how we're gonna fix this, but leave it to me. I got you into this, and I'll put it all on my shoulders if that's what it takes to protect your rep."

"Well, I didn't get the license plate of the truck that hit me. I'm also pretty sure this isn't your doing. Before you start taking the blame, get yourself over here and let's sort out the details. Oh, and I'll tell you how I spent *my* evening. If you haven't read about it yet, that is."

Within a half hour, Andy was standing in Johnny's doorway, tired, glum and with a later edition of the *Post*. "You know the old proverb about being careful on what you wish for?" He held up the front page. *Johnny's Drug Den Dispute* screamed in bold-type, with a photo of the young pop star brawling on the floor with a bloodied *Daily News* photographer. From the accompanying *Star Slugs it out at Drug Den* caption, it was now obvious that the situation had grown imminently worse. "Man, you look terrible. What's with your face?"

"It's sore." Johnny touched his swollen, aching cheek. "But never mind that. What does the paper say?"

Andy turned the front-page back, then read the opening paragraph:

He should have been entertaining a room full of sight-impaired children. Instead, rocker Johnny Elias brawled last night at a notorious uptown crack-house.

Johnny, this is bad," Andy understated. "I know I screwed up on the performance date, but how'd you end up there?"

"You're not gonna believe this," Johnny sighed, "but it was Megan."

"Megan! What gives? I thought you guys were getting back together!"

"That's exactly what I don't get either." Johnny could feel the adrenaline coursing through him. He had to do something, had to... he didn't know what he had to do. "Just last week we were – I guess you'd say... well,

I thought I could trust her." He shook his head. "I was wrong. Come, sit down, I'll tell you everything."

As he listened, Andy made mental notes. He was trying to fit together the jagged pieces of this sordid puzzle. A folded envelope protruded from Andy's jacket pocket. It had earlier contained a complimentary pair of tickets for *Phantom Of The Opera*. He hadn't questioned their provenance; he and Jacqui had enjoyed the show. Now he removed a letter-sized packet from the outer envelope. Printed in the upper left-hand corner was the Price & McLennan masthead.

"That wicked bitch," he blurted. "This has Katherine Price's fingerprints all over it. From the media turnout, to the photographers who followed you, it's all gotta be her. Even had her own daughter in on it!"

Johnny was feeling nauseous. "Can't believe I allowed her to get close again. I never honestly thought she and her mother saw eye-to-eye, let alone worked together!" He involuntarily flashed back to that awful night at the Price's apartment, with Megan and Katherine sneaking another man down the back stairs. "It's like they take pleasure in playing some twisted game to torture me. Why don't they just leave me the hell alone?"

Andy desperately wanted to help. But perhaps more importantly, he needed to devise a plan to stop the media avalanche before Johnny was snowed under.

In the far corner of the living room, Andy extended his arms and pulled his friend up to his feet. "Hey, so sorry, man. I'll find a way to fix this. We'll get the papers to report this right."

"Never mind the tabloids. How am I gonna explain this to Neswick? He apparently showed up to see me last night with an entourage. Claims to be waiting for my call. Not a very happy camper, I'd say."

"I'll deal with Neswick," Andy said. "I'll pop by his office first thing this morning; lay it all out on the table. What's the worst that can happen? He can't exactly fire you over this misunderstanding. You're his bestselling artist, not some backroom secretary. I'll take the heat; let him know where the real blame rests."

"Andy, I'll handle Neswick. This isn't your fault. But what about the charity? How do I make it up to them? And what about my so-called brawl? Hell, I've still got some guy's camera. How do I explain all this? Not to mention the crack-house photos? I'll bet by morning rush, half of New York'll have me pegged as a hopeless addict."

"That's what we've got Jerry Goodman for." Andy rubbed his brow. "We'll catch him before he leaves for work; have a plan of action by lunchtime. I'm certain that once people sort through the hogwash, they'll be able to draw a more realistic conclusion."

Unfortunately, Andy's portrait of optimism only lasted into the next hour. By then, the two men were on the phone with their PR guru, discussing a media solution to this growing crisis.

"I know you aren't gonna like this, but I believe the best remedy is to get Johnny into rehab. Even if it's one of those exotic country clubs, we need to get him out of the spotlight; get fans to sympathize with his problem."

"No chance in hell," Johnny said, leaning closer to the speakerphone. "That's also what Neswick wanted me to do. Why should I create the impression that I have a drug problem? That'll only make things worse."

"But you do have an image problem. And we need to change public perception," Goodman replied. "A year from now, no one will remember this, providing you avoid future incidents and keep on writing great songs. Johnny, everyone in music, from Aerosmith to Zeppelin, has had their addictions at one time or another. Right now, what you need is an escape hatch. Rehab may be the best thing. You get to relax poolside somewhere for a month, then come back to your fans with the respect of a conquering hero."

"There's got to be a better way," Johnny said. He could feel a headache building from stress and lack of sleep. He rubbed a hand tiredly over his bruised face. "If I admit to drug abuse, I'm playing right into the hands of whoever's out there trying to wreck me. Plus Highpeak will assume I lied to their faces. What I need is to prove my innocence!"

"What if Johnny agrees to pay for the theater damages and makes a sizable donation to *By The Hand* as a public apology?" Andy proposed. "He'll even play another free show to make up for the miscommunication. I'll bet we can arrange it within a week."

"At this point, I think its best for him to lay low until this blizzard of negativity passes. The apology's fine; a donation is nice, but it won't be front-page news like scandal. Kindness unfortunately doesn't sell papers."

"So just what're you saying?" Johnny demanded. "Bottom line?"

"My advice to you is to issue the apology, then duck out of site. Making counter-accusations about being set up by old adversaries won't sit very well with the public. The less you say, the better off you'll be in the long run."

Within an hour, Johnny's press release hit the wires. He promised to repay the charity organization, the theater and all those who purchased tickets. It came off as well-intended. But almost as the statement was circulated, Highpeak Records made even a bigger splash.

Fed up with Johnny's continuous negative headlines, and capped off by the drug-den donnybrook, the label announced that it was dropping him, effective immediately. And in a highly unprecedented move, they were recalling his new album from all stores, just two days after its commercial release. Invoking a morality clause in his contract, Highpeak issued a terse statement declaring they'd severed all ties to "the troubled Johnny Elias."

"Can they just go ahead and do that?" Johnny gasped. "We have a deal for three albums! Don't they need to buy me out before they can cut me loose?"

"I'll have the lawyers check into it, but I don't think they can," Andy guessed, pulling a copy of the agreement from the files. "Unless you're convicted of a felony, I don't think they can pull the plug. And last I checked, wrestling with a paparazzi shouldn't get you jail time. Highpeak will probably have to reinstate you."

"And what about my album? Can they just yank it off the shelves because of some bad press? I thought I *owned* the music!"

"The deal is: they own the *rights* to these recordings, even though you own the actual music and lyrics. If it came down to it, I'm sure we could buy 'em back; have it released by another label in no time. But – the bad news is, I think a product recall is within their jurisdiction."

Andy was right. Within the course of one week, nearly five hundred thousand CDs and cassettes of *A New Beginning* had been shipped back to the factory for destruction. Though stores across the country were reluctant to part with their bestselling album of the moment, most complied and were refunded for their troubles. However, with radio still playing a variety of the tracks in regular rotation, some chains managed to hold onto a few copies. Eager customers snapped them up at a premium, creating an instant collectible. Bootlegged copies soon followed.

Between first-day sales and the discs that never came back, *A New Beginning* had sold enough units to make the number two position on the *Billboard* charts in the first week of release. Yet because of the recall status, these figures were never publicly disclosed.

Johnny dove headfirst into deep despair. For two weeks he hardly spoke a word, feeling bewildered as the lawyers hammered out the final settlement. He was unable to eat, sleep, or even to get out for air. His eyes became bloodshot, his complexion pale. Catching sight of himself in a mirror, he was shocked at his emaciation, his air of depression. *I look more like a war zone refugee than a pop star,* he found himself thinking.

Howard arrived to give moral support. "Chin up, kid. It's not as bad as you think. Highpeak was just a stepping-stone to bigger things. Don't let the bad guys win."

"Howard, I'm not sure it's even worth the fight." Johnny said listlessly. He was slowly taking apart a cardboard coffee cup. "I feel like I've let everyone down. And I have no clue where to go from here; how to make things right."

Howard went over to the younger man and put his hands on Johnny's shoulders. "Well, for starters, you've got your whole career ahead of you. Add to that the many great songs cultivating in that fertile imagination of yours. Andy tells me he has four offers for your next album."

Johnny slouched deeper into the vinyl fabric of his beanbag chair, his head tilted to the floor. "Howard, I love you, man. But you know what the pisser is?" He looked up. "Music was a gift to me. It brought us together; made me famous… and yeah, a whole lotta money. But at times, I just hate what it's turned me into; screwed up my priorities. And now, I've let you down as well."

"Let me down?" Howard raised his eyebrows. "And just how do you suppose you've done that? Listen, I could care less about Ron Neswick. Look at the way he failed to support you! He's probably gonna lose his job if Highpeak can't replace your sales figures. And he was never the most beloved individual in my phonebook to begin with."

"But what about your song? *Tomorrow's Door* was supposed to be a huge radio hit."

"Johnny, you've had plenty of hits. And you'll have plenty more. Stop acting like someone died. You're starting to scare me, man."

"This isn't just about me. Howard, I wanted to show the world how good you are! And maybe have your kid hear his song; reach out to you! Now I've failed everyone. You, my fans, and myself."

"You haven't failed me," Howard insisted. "Hey, some things just aren't meant to be. You did your best. And your recording of my song melts my heart. But remember, this isn't the end. You'll again have opportunities to re-record it down the road. Nothing is over."

Johnny reached forward and snatched a copy of his latest disc off the floor. "I spent ten months writing, recording and producing this album! Battled tooth and nail to prove I wasn't a one-hit wonder! And yet it all gets deleted like it never existed. Wasn't it Oscar Wilde who said the only thing in the artist's world worse than being talked about is not being talked about?"

"Oscar Wilde also said that all art is useless," Howard chuckled. "A bit of a cynic, wasn't he? Listen, if there's anyone who can relate to having their music ignored, I think you're facing him." Howard put his arm around Johnny. "You've gotta realize that when you get to be my age, you'll find there are far more failures than success. Human nature, you know. But the key to happiness: make sure we savor our victories beyond the bitterness of all combined defeats. Put it in perspective, will you? You've been lucky enough to have a best-selling album and multiple hit songs. And you're only still a kid. I've been at it much longer than you, and I've never even had one bite of the cake, let alone a smidgen of frosting on the tip of my tongue."

Lying in bed in Connecticut, Johnny felt numb. It was good not to have reporters hanging around his door anymore. And he was happy about waking up without fears that his name would resurface in another scandal-ridden headline or the gossip columns. In fact, the relative calm suited him just fine.

What troubled him most on this overcast morning wasn't his future, his finances, or his ongoing battle with Highpeak. Instead, it was that last, desperate phone call he had received from Megan Price on the night of the benefit concert. *Why would she work so calculatingly, when she seemed sincerely affectionate?* Johnny replayed the frantic call in his mind. He vividly remembered the static on the line, the background noises and the constant disruptions. In this moment of clarity, he reexamined if perhaps he'd jumped to mistaken conclusions.

Only now it was obviously too late.

In the days of his self-imposed seclusion, Johnny's professional meltdown had taken a backseat to his personal disillusionment – namely, Megan's unfathomable second betrayal. He didn't want to hear from anyone back then. Screening his calls, he was flabbergasted when twice after the scandal broke he heard Megan's voice leave concerned messages on consecutive days.

On the first call, she seemed curiously unaware of the severity of his troubles. "I'm sure there's a logical explanation for the other night," she told his machine. At the time, it seemed galling. Johnny believed she was only mocking him, further twisting the knife in his side.

The second message seemed of greater urgency. "Johnny, please, I know you're hurting. Just call me back. I'm here for you at any hour." Johnny dismissed it as another punch to the gut. He could only see things through the eyes of a wounded skeptic. There was no chance he'd be calling her for elucidation.

The only decision Johnny felt obliged to justify during that dark period was not going forward with a new recording contract at a different label. Even at Andy's insistence, Johnny refused to be swayed.

"You've still got a top-five single and a major fan-base. Consider the buyout like Roger Maris being granted free agency in the middle of his sixty-one-homerun season! You may never have this kind of leverage again. And the radio stations, some are still playing the songs, even with the album recall. It's time you wash the bad taste from your mouth; start fresh somewhere."

"Spoken like a true businessman." Johnny rolled his eyes. "Don't you get it? This isn't about money, fame or bargaining power. I'm twenty-three, and I'm completely fried! From the day I began recording *Poet*, seems like I haven't had an hour's peace. It's been rehearsals, touring, writing, recording, negotiations, papers to sign, some ill advised pill popping - an endless cycle of exhaustion. When do I get to start enjoying the benefits of stardom? Being recognized when I go out to dinner doesn't cut it, you know."

"Sounds to me like you need a vacation," Andy said, unperturbed. "Get yourself down to the Caribbean for a bit; enjoy the sunshine. Or hop on a cruise and let 'em pamper you. Spend a few bucks, recharge your batteries, and come back feeling yourself. Some time away will do you wonders. And, quite frankly, you deserve it."

Johnny shook his head. "Andy, you think I can just disappear for a while, come back, and everything'll be cool: like slapping a Band-Aid on a gusher to stop the bleeding? What I'm trying to tell you is: I need a new deal right now like I need a clone of Katherine Price."

Andy nodded, thus reminded. "I'm already on the case with that witch.

She'll be crawling on her knees, on national TV, by the time I'm done with her." He pulled a three-ring binder from his briefcase. "There's enough dirt in here to fill the Staten Island dump twice! No sweat, man. Soon you'll be able to start enjoying your career without looking over your shoulder."

"Don't kid yourself." Johnny folded his arms. "This isn't only about her. Not really. I'm just not interested in playing pop star for now. You know, when we were in school, I thought music stardom was the pinnacle of – of everything. Man, we spent *days* studying album covers, memorizing lyrics. You remember. We used to sit in those packed arenas, screaming our lungs out. And it all looked incredible from up there, like once you had all that, you were set for life."

"I hear what you're saying, Johnny. I'm just not sure I fully understand – do you need more help? You've got enough income to surround yourself with a whole team. Just tell me what it'll take to make it work."

Johnny stood with his arms folded, seeking the right words to explain that he'd reached the end of his rope. He wished to be convincing, yet in a way that would not be an assault on his best friend's personal sacrifice.

"Andy, please don't take this the wrong way. I know how attached you are to my success. And I couldn't ask for a more trusted friend if I lived five lifetimes. No shortcomings on your part. I just don't know if I can do it anymore."

"Can't do what?" Andy leaned forward.

Johnny sighed impatiently, got up from his chair, and started pacing, his negative energy sizzling around him. "I haven't got any music left in me! I hate the thought of going back on tour without a chance to blink. I'm drained from building an identity, only to have someone else tear it down. I'm worn out from the bickering with producers, bandmates, self-serving execs." He paused, looking at Andy. "You know, most of all, I just want a normal life; away from all the cameras; the expectations; people with ulterior motives." He took a deep breath. "Is stability too much to ask for; a normal relationship with someone who isn't chasing you for fame or money? I want someone to fall for me, not 'coz I'm *Johnny Rock Star*, but because I'm Johnny Elias: a guy from Brooklyn who just happened to write a few decent songs."

Andy sat still, silently assimilating Johnny's words. He hadn't put himself in his friend's place, hadn't realized how hard things had been. At the same time, Johnny was clearly showing signs of depression, and *depression doesn't last forever. He needs a break, then he'll refocus. A break – and maybe a trusting relationship so he can start enjoying his success.* Just as Jacqui had been his pillar of support throughout the craziness, he was certain that Johnny could rediscover the upside of stardom if he had someone meaningful by his side. *No way I'm giving up on everything we've built together.* He tried instead to compromise. "Tell you what. Why don't we get you away from all the lunacy? I'll find you a place where you can just blend in, without the fanfare or molestation."

Johnny perked up at the suggestion. Andy smiled.

"I don't suppose you need to be living ten blocks up from Megan Price. Or, for that matter, across the park from her wretched mother. This place has never really been home to you. Let's get you out to the suburbs; commuting distance to the city, but far enough away that no one'll hound you. Once you're out of the limelight, I just know it'll all come back to you."

Not wishing to burst Andy's bubble, Johnny nodded. "Maybe you're onto something. If we're gonna do this, let's not make it too close a commute. In fact, once I'm gone, I wouldn't mind if I never stepped foot in this godforsaken town again."

Johnny opted for an unassuming relocation. Rather than the kind of showplace someone of his status might covet, he sought to cultivate a sense of normalcy in his anything-but-normal life.

Andy found him an unpretentious three-bedroom Victorian up in Stamford, Connecticut. The grounds were in desperate need of a landscaping overhaul. The inside was cozy, though it was going to require a good deal of modernizing. Johnny was unfazed. Impulsively, he offered the full asking price. A deal was struck on the spot.

On his final afternoon in the apartment, Johnny found himself once again engulfed in thoughts of the enigma that was Megan. It was triggered by the box containing her old apology letters. Johnny rediscovered them in the center of a cluttered pile. He took a minute to read one opening paragraph. The words on paper were so loving and thoughtful... just like they had been the night over at her apartment. And yet she had turned on him; deflating both his soaring career and his desire to recapture the happiness they once shared.

Fortunately, he was not alone.

"What's the matter?" Jacqui asked, sounding sympathetic. "You look reflective."

"Tell me what's wrong with this picture. I can't seem to make any sense of it, no matter what angle I view it from."

"The photo from Central Park?" she asked, picking up the framed image of the four friends at Paul Simon's concert.

"Actually, I'm talking about everything. I mean, I've never known Megan to be disingenuous, aside from one unfortunate night. But the way she screwed me over this time – it's almost as if I never really knew her at all."

Jacqui sighed. "Maybe it'd be best if you could find a way to stop fussing over that woman. Dwelling in the past isn't going to make you feel better, you know?"

"Wish it were that easy." Johnny closed the lid. "But I just can't help myself; so many questions." He shrugged. "Sometimes I wanna ask her, go see her, do something. But then I'll probably walk into a hidden camera crew; end up on the news again. Maybe that's what she wants."

"You could write her a letter," Jacqui tapped the box top. "Megan once wrote you fairly often. Maybe that's the best way to approach it now."

"A letter?" Johnny squinted.

"Hey, it doesn't have to be a masterpiece. But sure, go get all your anger off your chest. Tell her how much she hurt you. Maybe this can be your closure.

Johnny decided to follow Jacqui's advice. It took him eight pages in almost as many hours. He shared his pain, his anger, his inability to understand her cruelty, his inability to forgive her. Johnny saved his harshest criticism for Katherine, accusing Megan of allowing her mother to corrupt her. *If there's any justice in the world, it'll all catch up to both of you some day*, he wrote. *You deserve each other.*

Megan Price shoved past the office receptionist, heading straight for the Price & McLennan conference room.

"Ms. Price, you can't go in there now! She's with a client!"

"Like I care," Megan muttered. She slammed the door open. "Mother!" she screamed. "You selfish megalomaniac! You've ruined my life for the last time!"

There was a moment of shocked silence in the room. Then the receptionist said, from the doorway, "I tried to stop her. I'm sorry, Mrs. Price, she wouldn't listen to me."

"It's all right," Katherine said smoothly. "This is my daughter. She can see me any time." The door closed and Katherine turned to Megan. "Sweetheart, if you give me a few minutes to finish up here, I promise you my full attention."

"No more promises! No more plans and schemes!" Megan seemed unaware that they were not alone in the room. "This is it! I don't even owe you the courtesy of being here. We are so through!"

Katherine never lost her poise. Arching her eyebrows, she smiled at her clients as if to indicate that she had seen many such tantrums before. "Let's take a break here. Can you give me the room for a moment, please?"

Megan was still seething as people filed past her to the door. Katherine hadn't even bothered to stand up. "All right, so now tell me what's so important you have to interrupt the most important meeting of my day. That was the mayor's campaign team!"

"The most important meeting of your *day*?" Megan gasped. "How 'bout you wrecking my entire *life*! Don't worry, Mother: I'll make it short and sweet so you can get back to your *meeting*. From this day forward, you're banned from my home, forbidden from seeing my son, and no longer welcome in any aspect of my pathetic life. I've changed my locks; gotten an unlisted number. If you make it necessary, I'll get a restraining order. We're done!"

Katherine tried to speak, but for once couldn't find the right words. She was stunned by Megan's sudden eruption… and her surprising determination. She reached out toward her daughter. "Megan, let's talk about –"

"No!" Megan jumped back from her mother's hand as if it were a weapon. "I've never been more ashamed of being your daughter."

It wasn't until she was at the elevator that Katherine managed to catch up to her. "Sweetheart. I don't understand. I'd never hurt you knowingly. What could possibly have brought this on?"

"You've heard all I have to say." Megan, repeatedly hit the down button. "It's probably far too late for me to ever be happy. But at least I know you'll never interfere in Alex's life. You'll never do to him what you did to me. Consider yourself disowned."

"Why are you being so harsh?" Katherine asked with increased concern. "I'm sure there's a logical explanation."

"Save your excuses for the media and your precious clients. You never cared about my happiness. It was always about appearances and your public persona. But this time, you've obliterated the boundaries of common decency. Now there's really nothing more to talk about."

The elevator door opened and she stepped inside. Turning, she refused to meet her mother's eyes; the doors shut between them. She truly believed that for the first time in her adult life, things might finally be different. It was a bold but necessary step. Long overdue.

30

Fallout Shelter

Winds of change blew through New York City in the autumn of 1993.

On November 2nd, Brooklyn-born Rudolph Giuliani defeated David Dinkins by nearly 45,000 votes to become the City's 107th mayor. A bold effort was made to reduce crime, resurrect the city's faltering economy, and refurbish public perception. Graffiti-covered subways and long unemployment lines were gradually replaced with safer, cleaner streets and increased tourism. It became hastily clear that New York had a new sheriff in town.

For Katherine Price, the disappointment of David Dinkins' defeat was far easier to accept than the sting of her daughter's imposed banishment.

Katherine knew full well why Megan had drawn a line. She was almost proud of her daughter for taking a stand, after years of coping with her own overbearing tendencies. Yet being unable to communicate with Megan, or see her grandson grow up became increasingly intolerable.

Megan's tirade that afternoon in the conference room had sent Katherine spiraling into a professional black hole as well. Shortly after the mayor's defeat, Price & McLennan not only lost their most prominent ally, but they also witnessed a mass defection of many key accounts. Word got around that this once top-ten agency had lost serious credibility with the media. Past indiscretions and shady practices had gotten them blacklisted in some circles.

By June of '94, the agency had lost forty percent of their clients, forcing Katherine and Sheila to eliminate a number of staff positions. Further complicating matters was Katherine's insistence on indoctrinating her son Zach for his eventual inheritance of the business. Zach Price was only a college sophomore by the time Katherine deemed him ready to come onboard.

Inexperienced, undereducated and overmatched, Zach seemed to create more fires than press clippings, to the dismay of the remaining staffers. It wasn't long thereafter that Sheila McLennan too defected, taking not only her name but also a handful of clients to her own mid-sized agency… sparking an acrimonious rivalry.

For Megan, the next few years brought peace, if not happiness. She took satisfaction in the freedom of raising her son without the constant interference to which she'd grown so accustomed.

Megan shut her mother out in every aspect of her existence. No birthday celebrations. No holiday dinners. Her only concession was the occasional photo she would share with Zach on his random visits.

Oh her 25th birthday, Megan inherited a sizable trust fund left to her and Zach by their grandparents. She used some of the money to purchase a second residence – a condominium in Floral Park, Long Island – as a place for her and Alex to escape to when deemed necessary.

By the time Alex turned four and started nursery school, Megan grew bored of being a stay-at-home mom. She took a volunteer job working part-time with battered women. Other people's problems were surely easier to solve than her own.

Megan could never get over Johnny Elias. She spent much of her free time trying unsuccessfully to track him down. His angry letter did not carry the emotional impact of *We've Already Said Goodbye*. But it did leave her distraught and inherently sad.

She tried dating again, and there were a few men who made an impression. But like the wife of a missing soldier, she always kept hope, against all odds, that Johnny would someday resurface to sweep her off her feet. If it was an empty dream, at least it enabled her to carry on.

Occasionally, Megan would hear one of Johnny's songs on the radio. With the vivid memory of their special dance in her living room on that early June morning, she'd often raise the volume and close her eyes.

The loss of Johnny Elias and the expense of an unprecedented album recall proved too great a setback for Highpeak Records to overcome. Within four months of cutting loose their most commercially successful artist, René Fontenot was shown the door, ending a solid twenty-year run with the company. Though he would eventually team up with Herb Cantor in the concert business, he never quite managed to get over his own second-guessing in the handling of Johnny's situation.

Ron Neswick was next to take the fall. With declining sales figures and the inability to breathe new life into the label, he was first stripped of his title and later his job, all within ten months. Facing the *what-have-you-done-for-me-lately* attitude, Ron found it increasingly difficult to latch on elsewhere at the age of sixty-two.

Andy Raymer never quite gave up hope. But as requests dissipated, so did Andy's optimism for a return to past glory by the poet of a forgetful generation. Soon after Johnny ducked out of sight, Andy found himself in need of full-time work. The East Side office was initially retained to oversee Johnny's gradually waning fan club. Eventually, Andy revisited the idea of creating a music management company. Previously established connections made through Jacqui's album cover designs proved invaluable. Raymer Music Management was off and running.

In the summer of 1994, Andy and Jacqui ended their long engagement by tying the knot in a small, festive ceremony in England. The memorable day was capped off by a special impromptu performance at the piano by the reclusive best man; the most famous guest at the gathering.

The Raymers became first-time parents two years later, when Jacqui gave birth to a red-haired baby girl. They named her Julia. The role of parenthood became a great source of joy to the energetic Andy, though no longer was he able to live at the office as he had in the early days. Jacqui, meanwhile, continued her freelance designs from the couple's new two-bedroom co-op on Manhattan's East Side. Together, they remained a portrait of teamwork.

It took a while for Johnny, but he eventually came around to getting out and doing "normal" everyday activities. Household errands had to be run, even if on occasion he received a second look from a neighborhood grocery clerk, or a knowing wink from a sales attendant.

Johnny occupied himself with the things he always wanted to do but never had time for. Initially, it was learning to drive. Living out in suburbia, he hated the idea of waiting for taxis in a town lacking public transportation. Instead, he purchased a used pick-up truck, and took on home improvement projects such as landscaping and painting. The former star even briefly tried his hand at gourmet cooking. Successful, or not, he was at least wholeheartedly pleased with his attempts. And with no one to criticize or rush his work, there seemed to be little downside.

Johnny next sought to use his considerable time and resources to become a difference maker. He was forever troubled by the memory of that shivering woman camped across from his former building in sub-freezing temperatures. Anonymously, he put up more than a million dollars to establish *The Coat Coalition*. Johnny placed Carolyn Green - his foster mom from his high school days - at the helm. Within six months, they had purchased a fleet of trucks to travel the tri-state area and collect used winter jackets. Volunteers would then distribute the coats to homeless shelters and those in need on city streets. Johnny kept his name off all organizational literature. He sought no fanfare or publicity through this worthy cause. In an otherwise murky era, this would prove his most gratifying venture.

A year later, Johnny finally grew reflective about music for the first time since leaving it behind. An ad in the local paper for guitar lessons triggered fond college memories of blowing "big money" to sit in a booth and hear his instructor play his requested favorites. This time around, he purchased a Gibson Hummingbird acoustic and enrolled in a one-hour, twice-a-week lesson at the local music shop. Johnny managed to go totally unrecognized by his fifty-year-old instructor. Through diligent practice, he was soon on his way to proficiency.

Bitter memories were Johnny's excuse for allowing old friendships to lapse. He heard that Ian and Frank – still without full-time employment – had formed a new band back in Brooklyn, and were again out on the club scene. Andy had sent him a tape of one of their gigs. He was amused to learn that Ian was trying out his vocal talents from behind the drum kit.

Art Tillman was rumored to have gotten married right after the Poet tour. Though no one heard from him directly, Ian later learned that the bass player had latched on with a major summer touring attraction.

Howard Greffen completed his degree and was now teaching in Brooklyn Post's music department. He and Johnny would speak periodically. But Johnny's New York boycott and Howard's full-time work commitment kept them from meeting in person. Howard, in fact, rarely had a need to leave Brooklyn. Between his day job and his music tutoring three nights a week, he was constantly surrounded by the things that he loved.

As for the women of Johnny's past: Lauren Minton remained a mystery; Megan Price an enigma.

There were instances when Johnny considered phoning Frank, back in Brooklyn, to see if he and Lauren were still in touch. Yet despite his curiosity, a part of him preferred not to know, given the friction his interest in Lauren had generated between them.

The accusatory letter Johnny sent Megan prior to leaving Manhattan was supposed to have created some closure for him. But biding his time in the obscurity of suburbia, there were still far too many hours spent wondering if he hadn't made a mistake. On New Year's Eve, 1996, Johnny found himself alone, with no plans and not much desire to revel in the changing of the calendar. The clock would strike midnight whether or not he was awake for it.

He went to bed at ten. But unable to sleep – and instead of switching on Dick Clark and the insanity of Times Square – he decided to finally read all of Megan's old apology letters, start to finish. The logs in his fireplace crackled a few feet away. He couldn't avoid feeling similarly charred by the contrast of Megan's words to her actions.

Johnny wrote his heart. All of his songs embodied his true feelings. He couldn't understand how someone could write so lovingly yet behave with such contempt. Out of curiosity, out of need he reached for the phone and dialed her number from memory. Eight times the phone rang without answer. He tried again an hour later with the same result. *Maybe she's changed her number. Maybe it's for the best,* he thought. *Well at least* that *ghost isn't gonna haunt my new year.*

Howard Greffen sat behind the same rickety piano stool he had known since childhood. Ordinarily, on a school night, Howard might have sat proudly opposite a youthful face, teaching the language of his soul. But on this invigoratingly cold February evening of 1997, Howard was enjoying the companionship of a younger woman who had caught his eye at school.

"Nice signing, babe. Your Jennifer Warnes is far better than my Joe Cocker."

"No way! Your imitation was hilarious. Plus you had double-duty playing the piano."

Marlene Harris was not a student at Brooklyn Post. She had joined the music faculty just one semester after Howard had begun. At forty-two, she was nearly eight years his junior, though she could easily have passed for thirty-five.

Howard hardly seemed a candidate for the attention of the bubbly music theory professor. For months, the pair barely exchanged a word in the teachers lounge, or while passing in the hallway. Then one quiet afternoon Marlene overheard the sound of her favorite nostalgic tune, *It Might Be You,* the theme from the Dustin Hoffman film *Tootsie.* Curiosity sent her exploring to find from where it was coming.

Several weeks later, Howard and Marlene had become inseparable. In the partially dusted back parlor, the pair took turns sharing lines in an impromptu duet, *Up Where We Belong.* Whatever this rendition lacked in vocal range was made up for in pure sincerity.

"That was entirely brilliant," Marlene said, chuckling. She came over and kissed his lined forehead. "We make a great little team!"

"I tend to agree." Howard bashfully turned away. "Now if only I could come up with another dozen of these, I can sidestep the matter of showing you around the rest of my house."

"Oh, Howard!" She smiled at him. "For someone like me, living in a Kings Highway studio, this place is an absolute palace. A dusty, cluttered palace, but a palace all the same."

"I suppose that's one way of looking at it," he answered, tugging on his salt and pepper goatee. "Though as you can probably tell, it's awfully big for one lonely musician to care for by himself. And admittedly, I'm a packrat; just can't throw anything away."

There was a knock at the front door. "Were you expecting someone?" Marlene asked, sitting down on the sofa.

"You kidding me?" Howard rose to his feet. "You're the first real guest I've had over in ages. Excuse me a minute. Be right back."

The door swung open and Howard found himself looking at a young man in his twenties. He looked terrified. He had thick glasses, a brown goatee, and he was holding... an infant.

No wonder he looks scared, Howard thought. Then he looked into the young man's eyes. "Can I help you?"

31

COMING TO TERMS

"**A**s I read your name alphabetically, please come forward and get your paper. Stephanie Baker… Laura Davidson… Scott DiVito." The voice droned on. "John Elias."

Johnny stepped out from behind a desk on the left side of the classroom. He approached the professor's lectern and reached out for the fifteen-page report on Rossini's *The Barber of Seville*. A lengthy set of barely legible handwritten comments appeared in red ink on the last page, followed by a letter grade encircled at the bottom. *A C-plus!* he thought angrily. *Can't believe this wasn't an A.*

Johnny read the teacher's analysis at his desk. He then waited until the classroom emptied before walking to the front once again. "Pardon me, Mr. Werthimier. Can I have a word?"

"If it's about your grade, Mr. Elias, I think I've already shared my thoughts quite generously in writing."

"Yeah, I've read them. And I appreciate your feedback," Johnny took a deep breath. "It's just… I spent hours listening to this opera; cited countless references. I don't know how many A's or B's you've handed out, but —"

"Mr. Elias," the teacher interrupted. "I am well aware of your waltz with fame outside this classroom. Your popularity may be indisputable, albeit debatable, but it carries no weight with me. The report was fair and it received a grade based solely on merit. Other professors may allow you a forum to challenge their grading system. I assure you it won't happen in this room."

As he walked away, Johnny's scowl gave way to a grin of satisfaction. Sure, he would have preferred a grade adjustment. Yet being viewed as something other than privileged felt oddly gratifying. Suddenly, he was just one of thirty undergrad students, working for three hard-earned credits in Advanced Elements of Musicianship.

Johnny had signed up for his final fourteen credits at Stamford State College, convinced that his considerable empty time would be better served doing something productive. For the spring semester of 1998, he found his renewed undergraduate experience both humbling and revitalizing. It had been five long years since his self-imposed hibernation began. At twenty-seven, he was considerably older than those with whom he now shared a classroom.

Johnny grew a short beard and donned a pair of metal-rimmed glasses, changing a once-familiar face. He also trimmed his trademark long brown hair in an effort to blend in with the student body. Still, as word-of-mouth spread that a celebrity might be on campus, there was no shortage of unwanted attention.

At first he considered the occasional autograph request a nuisance. Sometimes, he'd even shrug off his true identity. Gradually, he mellowed to the point of feeling an uneasy sense of flattery. He was genuinely surprised at how many students felt impacted by his music. Between classes he posed for photos and signed every paper waved in front of him.

Johnny also drew his share of attention from the campus co-eds. Often, there'd be one or two waiting for him inside the cafeteria, or even outside the men's room. But trying desperately to avoid being superficially admired for past accomplishments, he'd rarely reciprocate their attention. And even when he did in his moments of weakness, Johnny remained emotionally uninvested.

It happened one rainy evening in the student parking lot. Johnny sensed he was being followed by a guy with a guitar case slung over his shoulder. Instinctively, he picked up the pace through the puddles, figuring he could avoid the inevitable encounter. But just as he placed his keys in the driver's side door, the voice caught his attention.

"Mr. Elias, please wait up! Just a quick question."

Johnny lifted the door handle to his second-hand Dodge pick-up. He paused briefly and smiled.

"Oh, I really appreciate this!" the wide-eyed student said. "I doubt you've noticed me, but we take the same class. And everyone's wondering what someone of your caliber was doing here with us? Not that we mind having you around, but..." His voice trailed off uncertainly.

Johnny leaned against his truck, ignoring the rain. "So you're in my class, eh? Well, if you must know: I never graduated. Guess you could say I got a bit sidetracked." Johnny turned and set down his bag on the front seat. "So what'd you say your name was?"

"Gary. Gary Gaines. I'm three seats behind you in Advanced Elements."

"Well, nice to meet you, Gary." Johnny extended a wet hand. "I don't suppose you chased me all this way just to introduce yourself. Was there something else?"

A burst of thunder rumbled through the parking lot. Gary wiped the raindrops from his forehead. "Actually, I'm in a band with a few guys here at school. We're called BQE. Got this monster gig in a couple of weeks. I figure it's a long shot, but I was hoping you were free to come hear us practice one night... if you have the time."

"BQE? That's not the Brooklyn-Queens-Expressway, is it?"

"Well, sort of," Gary shrugged. "Our front man's a guy called Brian Quigley. He's the BQ part. Named his first band the Brian Quigley Experience; they were pretty good. But people had a hard time taking 'em seriously. So when my friend Matt and I joined last year, we shortened it to BQE. We're both from Canarsie."

"Really," Johnny said, smiling. "And what do you guys play?"

"Oh, I'd say we're a cross between Cheap Trick and Foreigner. A rockin' quartet with a polished pop sound. Mostly originals, but we'll slip in some covers here-and-there."

"Originals, nice. Well, playing 'em for others is the only real way to prove your songs are any good."

"So you'll come by; hear us play?"

Johnny got in and fastened his seatbelt. A flash of lightning lit up the sky. "If I can free up some time, yeah, I'll consider it. Hey, it's pouring man. Hop in. Where you headed?"

Two nights later, Johnny strolled into a largely empty reception hall in nearby Darien, Connecticut. A janitor was operating an industrial carpet cleaner. The deafening noise forced him to cover his ears until the sound of machinery was replaced by something more melodic.

The backbeat of a steady drummer was followed by a gruff lead vocalist and three searing guitars. Johnny looked around the partially lit ballroom. He observed a cheering section, comprised of four attractive young women in BQE t-shirts, and one man running with an extension chord and guitar picks. *Girlfriends and a roadie*, he surmised with an odd jolt of nostalgia.

Johnny swayed gently to the rhythm as the band completed an animated run-through of four songs. A long gray raincoat and black chinos rendered him inconspicuous.

The short set soon ended. Gary Gaines placed his bass guitar down behind the raised platform and looking around, spotted Johnny. With a whoop of delight he scrambled off the stage. "Hey! You're really here!" he cried drawing attention from the others. "I totally appreciate this! Really, we all do, Mr. Elias."

"Uh, actually, call me Johnny. I'm not that much older than you guys."

"Thanks, Johnny," Gary said, grinning widely. "Man, this is so cool! If it'd be all right, I'd love to introduce you to Brian and the band. None of 'em believed you were gonna show." He raised his voice. "Guys, look who's here! C'mon over!"

Johnny shook calloused musician hands all around. "So what's this I hear about a show that you're all so nervous about?"

"Oh, it's the annual battle of the bands," Brian Quigley explained. "Every April, New Haven's rock station, they hold a kick-ass competition – like fifty local groups. The top five get prize money. And the overall winner gets airplay for an original song."

Gary enthusiastically cut in. "Some get recording contracts, or get to open for a big summer gig. Hell knows, we'd sell our baby sisters for that kind of exposure."

"Sounds like fun," Johnny said, nodding. "I take it you guys plan to win it this year and go on to be rich and famous?"

Brian snatched a rubber comb from his pocket to tidy his slick, jet-black hair. "You make that sound like a bad thing, the way you say it," he said, grimacing. "I'm sure you get this a lot, but the songwriting on your *Poet* album… absolutely righteous."

Johnny blushed and looked away. "Sorry if I sound bitter. It's just, not everyone finds utopia with a hit record. Still, I'm not here to discourage. Oh, and thanks for the compliment." He removed his hands from his pockets. "Anyway, I wouldn't mind catching more of your repertoire before passing judgment, for what mine's worth."

"Well, how about so far?" Matt, the drummer chimed in, toweling off his forehead. "Any pointers?"

Johnny rubbed his chin. "Overall, I like the energy and tempo. But I think you need to lose the theatrics. Don't know who you're trying to impress with the grunting and grimacing but it doesn't suit your style. Oh, and Gary: go easy on the baseline in the chorus of that last song. Too much reverb."

Without further coaxing, Johnny quickly became a familiar fixture at BQE's rehearsals. Alternating roles between cheerleader and chief critic, he was impressed with how each successive run-through offered a higher level of cohesion. It was a fond reminder of the early days on the road with Howard, Frank and Ian, when they were first learning to please a crowd. *Almost forgot how much fun this can be when you're not a phenomenon.*

Time seemed to fly by as the competition neared. Years of living in virtual slow motion gave way to counting down the days.

On Sunday, March 22, 1998, Johnny strolled inconspicuously into a sweaty hotel ballroom, one of over twelve hundred spectators. General admission for all non-participants was $17.50. In a plastic folding chair on the aisle, he flipped through the eight-page program, cluttered with local advertisements. Tinted glasses and a black baseball cap enabled him to sit incognito.

Minutes later, a local DJ from the sponsoring radio station took the center-stage microphone. A bit of hype and pandering was followed by an explanation of the rules.

Folks: we have thirty-six bands here tonight! Each plays one original in the preliminary round. Your cheers'll decide who moves on. In round two, five groups'll be brought back to do a cover. Your ovations will narrow it down to two finalists. And the end… you the audience will be picking the grand prize winner! Good luck to all contestants and let's make some noise!

As is often the case with amateur competitions, many participants were less than first-rate. They ranged from the grungy boy band *Well-Fed Waifs* to the visually striking but vocally challenged women's trio, *Strategic Bikini.* BQE was the sixteenth to play. By the time they took the stage, much of the early, anticipatory buzz had left the stifling room. "Plug and play," a stagehand shouted, and so they did. BQE performed a fiery take on their best original song, a moody, keyboard-heavy rocker called *Winter Comes.* Brian Quigley's vocals were pitch-perfect. Strong applause followed. Their likelihood of advancing seemed a mere formality.

Johnny watched patiently as each amateur band gave way to the next. Upon completion of round one, the stage-host called out the names of seven bands for which the noise meter had registered highest. This exercise elicited intensified cheers from different sections of the room. After conferring with off-stage judges, he announced five semi-finalists.

BQE was the fourth name called. Johnny exhaled.

A re-explanation of the rules preceded the second round. The five advancing groups soon re-energized the audience. One band, *Rainbow's Gold*, comprised of three young men in gold lame' suits, did an excellent take on the Police hit, *King Of Pain*. Their performance drew a standing ovation. *These guys'll be tough to beat*, Johnny guessed from his vantage point.

An all-girl band, *Summer Solstice* next performed a beautiful rendition of the Crosby Stills & Nash nugget, *Suite Judy Blue Eyes*. Their three-part harmonies were so good that even Johnny felt compelled to stand and applaud, despite his vested rooting interests.

The third semi-finalist proved a pretender. A group of three men and two women called, *Just Us* attempted a radically altered version of Stevie Wonder's *Living for the City*. If inconsistent timing on the backing vocals wasn't bad enough, an aborted stage-dive by the lead singer doomed this effort, sparking obvious groans from the revved-up observers.

BQE required several minutes to fix an amplifier problem before getting their second opportunity. Having heard their faithful cover versions of Foreigner's *Cold As Ice* and *Jukebox Heroes*, Johnny fully expected one of those. But when the band finally took their positions and Brian Quigley stepped up to the microphone, all bets were off.

"We'd like to dedicate this song to someone in this room who's inspired us all. This one's about injustice and hope for a better future." A smattering of courteous applause followed. Johnny squirmed in his chair. Then came something entirely unexpected: *Shadows of the Same Color*.

From the opening notes, it was clear that the audience recognized the tune. Some rose from their seats, singing aloud with the early verses. One man held up a flickering lighter. Others soon followed. As the repetitious chorus began, the echo in the steamy room grew louder, until it seemed as though close to a third were on their feet, rekindling a triumphant glimmer of 1992.

Johnny looked in all directions, paranoid that the song selection might blow his cover. He scurried to the far corner of the room and bit down on his lower lip in a valiant effort to keep his emotions in check. But here were several hundred voices spontaneously recalling the poignant lyrics to his anthem of unity. The composer grew progressively choked up. *Is this for real?* Hundreds of music fans retained the memory, singing from the heart in stunning togetherness. Even when the song ended, much of the standing crowd continued their vast sing-along, prompting Brian and the band to improvise a repetition of the last verse and chorus. A roof-raising ovation followed.

Johnny was clearly taken aback. This uplifting episode once again underscored his staying-power, his musical relevance. Regardless of which band would be declared victorious, there remained little doubt as to who the biggest winner in the room would be on this night.

Backstage, Johnny expected to find a disappointed runner-up. BQE's eventual defeat to *Rainbows Gold* in a hotly debated finale had nearly spilt the room in two. But when he entered the makeshift dressing room, all anyone could talk about was that one thrilling moment.

"Bloody hell, that was awesome!" Gary was grinning, his shirt soaked in sweat. "That reaction to *Shadows*... unbelievable! Hardly matters that we shoulda finished first."

"Guys, what can I say? I really think it was the performance and not the song that took you to the finals. But, what the hell? Didn't even know you had one of mine in your bag of tricks!"

"Actually, we've got arrangements on four of your tunes," Brain admitted, turning to pack away his Les Paul electric. "Just never played any of 'em since you started coming round. Didn't wanna turn you off if we butchered it."

"Well, boys... you blew me away tonight. Hearing you up there, it took me back to a time when making music was meaningful. That's no small feat."

32

THE PLACE I USED TO GO

A tranquil mid-December evening in Stamford, Connecticut was suddenly interrupted by a knock at the front door. In past years, Johnny generally ignored unannounced visitors, dismissing them as crazed fans from an era gone by. But on this night, curiosity won out.

Six months had passed since Johnny's belated college graduation. It was nearly as long since he'd been in regular contact with those closest to him. Wondering if perhaps this surprise visitor was Andy Raymer, here to check on him, he skipped down the creaky steps with a sense of anticipation.

"Johnny! I know you're in there! Please don't let me freeze out here!"

The voice was familiar. Through the peephole, Johnny recognized the New York radio icon. It took him a minute to disable the alarm system and undo both the upper and lower locks.

"My, my, it's been a while." Larry Jacobs extended a hand for a courteous shake. "Hope I'm not disturbing you at this late hour."

Johnny gave out a hearty laugh. He took the outstretched hand of his one-time rock radio advocate and pulled Larry up into the entranceway. "I suppose you didn't come all this way to stand out in the cold. But how'd you find me?"

Larry stepped into the modest living room at the top of the stairs. "Can't an old friend pop by impromptu once every decade or so? I must say, this place is hardly what one would expect from a pop star. Very… domesticated. Laid-back, you know?"

"You mean a former recording artist," Johnny corrected. "I don't dwell in the past; don't live there, either. I hardly need memorabilia or keepsakes to know who I am." His tone softened. "So can I get you a drink? You hungry? I've become pretty handy in the kitchen."

Larry waved away the offers. "Johnny, I could really use a favor. I know you prefer meeting in person to phone chatter. Just need to talk for a minute."

"Sure, man. Have a seat." Johnny sat on his couch and looked at Larry expectantly. The other man started to sit down, then changed his mind.

"Nah, never mind. Maybe its best that I be going. Good to see you looking well, and apparently doing well after lost time."

Johnny wondered how he could put him at ease. *Difficult to do when I don't know why he's here.* "So I hear you still play a few of the old songs on WNYR from time to time."

"Well, that's part of what I wanted to tell you." Larry jumped on the topic and this time really did settle on a nearby chair. "Might've started as nostalgia. You know the drill: sneak one on during my afternoon shift. Next thing I know, we're getting calls, faxes, and now email requests for a bunch of your old tracks. Honestly, I think there's still a lot of people out there who never stopped digging your music. Even the ballads."

Johnny smiled. "Good to know people still like a decent song or a fond memory. But really, that's all those are to me. It's like listening to someone else. I laugh whenever I catch you playing 'em. Mostly, I'm just numb to it."

"So you have tuned in to my show, you bugger! I was always certain that somewhere, you'd have a radio on when I played one. Never imagined you'd be the type to sing along with Puccini in the shower."

"Hey, don't flatter yourself," Johnny warned, grinning. "It's not like I do it often; just a minute in the car, or working round the house. NYR is one of the last listenable stations. These days, most of 'em play nothing but fad groups, boy bands and Madonna wannabes."

Larry laughed. "I'm surprised you even get reception up here. But yeah, I agree that FM's taken a nasty turn toward manufactured, no-talent, under-aged beauty queens who can't sing a note. Hard to argue with your theory."

"So tell me, Larry: you have another fundraiser coming up and you need me to sign a few items for a good cause?" Johnny laughed. "Hell, I'm sure you could raise at least ten bucks for one of my original lyric sheets. I hear memorabilia from disgraced former pop stars is hot these days."

Larry leaned forward. "Johnny, I've gotta tell you, most people never believed those old rumors. Others never cared – or don't remember any-thing except your music. You do know how many rock legends did drugs; fathered kids out of wedlock; got arrested? Even Paul McCartney once got busted with pot in his suitcase at a Japanese airport; went to jail for ten days. And *he's* been *knighted* by the bloody Queen of England!"

"And your point is?"

"My point, Johnny, is that you're sorta like the JD Salinger of rock and roll. You had one massive popularity spurt, then disappeared. Only, unlike Salinger, you still have a professional lifetime in front of you. Oh, and people don't read your music as a prelude to shooting celebrities. At least not yet!"

Johnny grinned in spite of himself. Larry leaned back comfortably. "Johnny, I'm in a bit of a rut. I could really use your help."

"What's your trouble?"

"For starters, WNYR is in serious jeopardy. My station's losing steam, both in ad revenue and listenership. Ratings have dipped twenty-percent the past eight months. It's starting to look like more than just a bad cycle. Management's been toying with a format change, letting us all go. But due strictly to my longevity, I've managed to buy another two months to get things righted."

"Man, I'm sorry Larry. That really sucks. But you know people do get older. And even the most successful stations need occasional tinkering." Johnny slowly leaned forward. "So where do I fit into this deal? I don't sup-pose you want me to come back to the city and spin some of my favorites to boost ratings? Might be fun, but that's hardly an option."

"Funny you mention that. Remember Dee Snider from Twisted Sister? He's now a popular morning man up here in Connecticut? And Greg Khin, another eighties front man, he's a morning icon in the Bay area. But no, I had nothing like that in mind."

"So what is it?"

"Actually, it's our annual holiday concert – the one I've organized all these years. It's about to fall apart. Could mean the death of the station as we know it."

"A concert?" Johnny straightened his posture. "You gotta be kidding me?"

"Johnny, I'm under huge pressure. I had everything in place. We always book two major acts at a theater like the *Beacon* or *Radio City*. I managed to snag the Pretenders as the headliner. Then I lost my opening act. Van Morrison was supposed to go on first. We actually sold out the Paramount theater at Madison Square Garden. Apparently, Mr. Van had some unforeseen emergency; now he's out. It's all last minute and I can't get a replacement."

"So why not have the Pretenders play a full show? I'm sure no one'll mind."

"Their management won't hear of it. It's just a promo gig for them – one hour - not a full-blown set. Now there are rumblings that they might pull out altogether. Guess who's going to pay the piper if this falls through?"

"So you want me to bail you out; play a partial gig?" Johnny stood up and moved toward the kitchen. He grimaced. "First of all, I haven't stepped on a stage in years. Second, I've got no band to play with. Lost touch with the guys from '92. And third, I'll almost certainly get booed off the stage once they recognize me. To the public, I'm still the overindulged orphan who blew off a room full of blind kids to visit a crack house, or whatever the papers called it. You can't possibly expect me to say yes?"

"Listen. A band is no problem. I'll get someone to back you for six or eight of your tunes. You can even cover a couple of standards, whatever you want. As for stage rust, you couldn't possibly have lost your voice at what, thirty years old? A handful of rehearsals and you'll be fine. But more than anything, I swear: once the crowd sees you, they'll be on your side. People still love your music. And I really wouldn't be asking if my ass wasn't on the line."

Johnny filled a martini glass with orange juice. "Cheers," he said, downing the contents in one gulp. "Guess I should have had something stronger, huh?"

Back in the living room, Johnny sank into his chair and sat quietly for several minutes. In his heart, he genuinely felt for his friend's predicament. And what if Larry was right? What if there was another of those elusive ovations to be had? And what if he had a good time in the process?

What Larry didn't know was how close to Johnny's heart his words were cutting. For quietly, unobtrusively, Johnny had begun writing again.

It had been about five months since he dusted off some old songbooks to complete a few unfinished stanzas. Coupled with his new skills on guitar since taking up lessons in earnest, the musical floodgates – stagnant for years – suddenly burst wide open. The result was more than two-dozen songs. Songs that had not yet been heard by anybody. They were different... more introspective than his earlier work. And even if no one else were to hear them, their existence served as a source of secret pride.

As for Larry's predicament, Johnny was not unsympathetic. Larry had helped him in the past: it was his turn to give something back.

But the reality was: he didn't believe he was ready. Stage rust was a certainty. It had been nearly six years since he had last stood before an audience. And with a hidden wealth of new music to perhaps share with the world, there was far more at stake than just his former reputation.

"Larry, this may sound crazy, but I'll really give it some serious thought. You're a true friend."

"Johnny, wow... I'm touched you'd consider doing this for me; with what you've been through and all." He cleared his throat. "Unfortunately, I don't have the luxury of a lengthy decision process. Hate to push my luck, but I'm gonna need your answer before I leave tonight." He paused. "The show is on Thursday."

"*This* Thursday? Man, there's no time to prepare, band or not." He shook his head. "It's not enough time."

"Wait, Johnny. I can have you working with a band tomorrow. Everyone knows all the old tunes. You'll have three days to rehearse; not impossible." Seeing Johnny's face, Larry swallowed hard and continued. "You do realize if this show unravels, we have to refund nine thousand tickets. We're already fighting a losing battle. Could be the final blow. Johnny, these guys've been my family for twenty-six years! I'm begging you!"

There was another uncomfortable silence. Larry mopped sweat from his forehead as unobtrusively as possible. Johnny was lying back in his chair, his eyes closed, as if meditating. "Listen, I have an idea. But I'll need your full cooperation."

"Anything!" Larry exclaimed. "Is it money? Transportation? Accommodations? Tell me what you need."

Johnny opened his eyes, straightened the chair, and shook his head. "It's nothing like that. What I need to know is: if I open the show, can my appearance be kept an air-tight secret till I take the stage?"

"Uh, I suppose it could. Although I'll need to inform the station honchos and the Pretenders' people that I have an opening act. We certainly don't need to announce anything to the public, if that's what you're implying."

"Yeah, that's it." He took a deep breath. "Larry, if I do this, I won't be needing a band. Don't even want my name introduced when I go out there. Think you can honor that?"

Larry clenched his left fist and shot it skyward in partial celebration. "Consider it done. You can't possibly imagine what this means to me. And you have my word: if there's any way I can ever repay this... oh man! You may have saved my career tonight."

Johnny stood up, as if with something important to do. He headed in the direction of the door leading down to his basement. Then he looked Larry in the eyes. "Maybe at some point down the road... well, you never know. But for now, if so much as a single word gets out about this, I won't ever let you live it down. Now not to be rude, but it's probably best that you get outta here before I have time to change my mind."

It was half-past six when Jacqui Raymer grabbed the ringing telephone from her nightstand. She answered in a groggy, early-morning voice.

"Jacqui, it's Johnny. Hope I didn't wake you."

"No, I was up," she lied. "You okay?"

"Well, I'm feeling fine, thanks; no bad news, or anything. It's just, I need to catch Andy before he leaves for the office."

She looked at the other side of the bed. "Johnny, he's in the shower. Can he phone you right back?"

"If you can get hold of him now, I'd really appreciate it."

Johnny waited for the next reply. In the background, he heard the sound of running water and muffled voices. Then swiftly, the water ceased and the voice of his most trusted friend was on the line. "What is it, Johnny? You okay?"

"Andy, something's come up. I could really do with your wisdom up here today before I make a stupid decision."

"Nothing like short notice, John. I've got an early staff meeting today; clients coming in at nine and eleven. A lunch powwow with a promoter at noon. And tonight Jacqui and I have dinner plans at *Tavern on the Green*. Let's just say it's a full docket."

"Hey, I know you're busy. But this isn't some request to just hang out. This is business."

"Look, if it's about the proposed website we talked about... What do you say to Thursday? Much easier day to move things around."

"Well, if you have no time till then, you may as well just come by to hear me sing in front of nine thousand people at the Paramount theater."

"What the hell? How'd this —" Andy could barely get the words out of his mouth when Johnny began to explain.

"It's something I've been weighing for quite some time. And last night an unexpected opportunity presented itself."

"What kind of opportunity?"

"I'm kinda committed to open the WNYR holiday concert. Of course I've got no band, no rehearsals and, frankly, no sleep since I said yes. Please come talk me out of it, before I do something regrettable."

Andy took a long, deep breath, pondering how he could rearrange his busy calendar. Suddenly, nothing else he had to do that day seemed terribly important.

"Johnny, hang in there. I'll call you in an hour. Just don't sign anything till you hear from me."

It was five past eight that morning when Andy knocked on Johnny's front door. Johnny rushed down the stairs and turned the knob.

"I got here quick as possible. Even outraced the cops up I-95," Andy joked, heading inside. "Man, what's that smell? You been cooking something?"

"Breakfast. Come here, man. Looking good!" The two men embraced. "C'mon upstairs. Hope you're hungry!"

Pancakes, bagels and a fruit salad covered the table. Both men helped themselves as Johnny talked about Larry's plea. Finally they were just drinking tea and picking at the fruit.

Andy had no idea just how far things had progressed. He had been too busy with his own life, with his family – Jacqui was pregnant with their second child – with Raymer Music Management. And yet he had never given up on Johnny.

All throughout the long period of inactivity, Andy had kept a flicker of faith that someday Johnny would return to his music. All that talent and likeability… it just seemed inevitable. But with the steady rejection of opportunities, Andy admittedly began losing hope.

There were a number of significant offers passed over. Among them: a multi-million dollar tour of Japan and Australia back in '95. With the *Poet* album enjoying a second wave of popularity off its international release, Andy was sure Johnny would head overseas and start anew in front of hungry audiences. But Johnny stood firm.

Andy plainly recognized that money would not be an enticement. Johnny's finances remained solid. Eventually, he grew tired of trying to discover the magic stimulant to revive his friend from artistic despondency. Not even the passage of time appeared to reverse the tide.

It had been months since Andy kept on top of Johnny's dwindling affairs. It was even longer since he last visited. But after taking the phone that early morning, Andy abruptly caught a glimpse of the comeback trail at the end of a seemingly eternal horizon. Suddenly, he was starting to feel vindicated.

"So, Johnny, should we discuss the concert in detail? It's not much time to decide."

"You finished? Let's go downstairs." Johnny gestured toward the basement staircase for Andy to follow.

Andy's recollection of the cellar was of an oversized dungeon with scattered boxes piled amid old pipes and a furnace. But as the lights came on with the touch of a switch, the transformation was truly astonishing.

Hung on the walls were many of the great memories Johnny had preserved from the height of his fame. Keepsakes tucked out of sight for too long had suddenly reappeared. Among them: framed magazine covers, ticket stubs, concert posters, a photo collage of live performances, gold records for sales achievement, and original lyric-sheets that once occupied a place in those beat-up spiral notebooks.

To Andy's right, a small, neglected kitchette had been converted into a snack bar with an old-time cotton candy maker, a popcorn machine, and an antique cash register. Along the sidewall were two rows of neatly folded metal chairs, though a few had been scattered throughout the room.

Elaborate track lighting in the ceiling faced a carpeted stoop in the far corner. On it stood three microphone stands, amplifiers, and a drum kit. The only thing missing were the musicians.

A rack near the stage held an impressive collection of acoustic and electric guitars. A second, larger platform to the left supported Johnny's prized baby grand piano – the very first delivery to the old apartment on Central Park West. Now, it served as the centerpiece of an amazing transformation.

"This is so cool!" Andy cried out, carefully studying this shrine-of-a-room to the best friend he'd ever known. "When did you do all this? And why'd you never mention a word of it?"

"So you like it?" Johnny had a wicked grin on his face.

"Like it? It's amazing! But what's this really all about? You been charging admission to your neighbors without giving your manager a cut? I just can't believe this!"

"Actually, it was all done in the last six months," Johnny said, looking around him. "I wanted a nice little home theater. Then it… just grew, I guess. No sense in turning my back on everything, right?"

"So no one else has been down here?" Andy gasped.

"Well, aside from my contractor and his crew, it's been my little secret. But, listen – this room isn't all I wanted you to see down here."

Johnny switched on a sound system with the touch of a button on a console. He then lifted a black six-string guitar off the rack. After stepping up on the mini-stage, he reached down and plugged a loose cord into the front of his instrument. "Make yourself comfy," he announced, while tuning the strings to his liking. "Welcome to my first live performance in one helluva long time."

As if on cue, Andy promptly applauded, offering a mock catcall from a folding chair in the center of the room.

Johnny tapped the mic twice. "So, when I was just starting out as a songwriter, I limited myself to thinking only toward the future; maybe one eye on the here and now. After all this time to reflect on my life, I've finally been able to delve into my past a bit."

Johnny began strumming a new song composition. One he called *Yearning For Childhood*.

> *Someone provide me direction*
> *Take me to that place I used to go*
> *Young minds are essential, unlimited potential*
> *And childhood friends I used to know*
> *I never wanted to leave there*
> *Wish I could have stayed but I had no choice*
> *As I grew much older, the world turned much colder*
> *and changed with the sound of my voice.*
>
> *(Chorus)*
> *Is it such a crime to turn back the hands of time*
> *when your childhood disappears so fast?*
> *I'll never understand why a boy must be a man*
> *And why our youthful days so soon have passed*
>
> *Someone map out where I'm going*
> *Take me to that playground of my youth*
> *On that roller coaster ride, I was never one to hide*
> *And the scars on my memory are proof*

Following an intricate guitar solo, Johnny repeated the first two verses, and a final rehash of the chorus. His hands moved easily up and down the frets. He stood silent while the last chord reverberated. Even he didn't know what he was waiting for.

Andy was choked up with emotion. He felt his throat tighten. "That was exquisite. Really among the best you've ever written. Your voice, it's much deeper than I remember it. And just when did you learn to play guitar?"

Johnny answered the flurry of questions by moving into an acoustic set; songs all written during his recent period of rediscovery. Titles included the irony-filled *Draw Your Own Conclusion*, and the biting *Vicarious Lives.* These folky compositions were as lyrically rich as any he'd previously put to paper. Though his voice cracked at times due to fatigue, the performance was filled with a renewed passion.

The two friends sat reminiscing for the remainder of the afternoon.

"So, Andy, if I do this gig, I want it to be a total shock to the audience; no expectations. I'm not the headliner, so even with a lousy showing, the crowd still can go home happy. Plus, no one knows the new material. They'll probably think I'm a no-name opener."

"John, if you can overcome the nerves and play like you just did… wow, an unannounced guest appearance! That's perfect! Great way to get you out there without any prior prejudice. It'll just be a man and his new music."

"But what about the old songs?" Johnny pointed to a framed concert poster from '92. "Think I can get away without playing 'em?"

"Truthfully, I don't think you need it. But you've got a couple of days if you wanna work up an oldie, you know, just to reinforce your identity. The choice is entirely up to you."

33

Hallucinations and Delusions

"**H**ere we are, Madison Square Garden," the driver announced, braking abruptly.

The limousine pulled up to the curb on 33rd Street, between 7th and 8th Avenues. Johnny could feel his anxiety mounting. He zipped his coat to brace for the cold, then slowly opened the door. He took one last contemplative breath before placing his feet firmly on the frozen ground. *So much for never coming back to the big town… the bright lights.*

He took it as a good omen when a young woman from the radio station appeared not to know who he was. "This way Mr. *Ellis*. Your dressing room's upstairs."

He had his guitar case slung over his left shoulder and was wearing his understated performing clothes: a white denim long-sleeved shirt, brown suede vest and a pair of comfortable black Levis. Understatement seemed fitting.

Johnny rode an elevator two flights up, then headed down a crowded corridor. No one shot him a second glance on the way. He ducked inside a small dressing room and briefly checked himself in the mirror. *Sure hope I'm up for this.* Seconds later, Larry knocked and entered. "Hey, is it really you?"

"Last I checked," Johnny said with a grin.

"Yeah, and it's great." Larry closed the door behind him. "You should know I've upheld every aspect of our deal. Guess you're still comfortable with it."

"Well, I'm here, aren't I?" Johnny sat down. "Can't say I missed all the insanity."

Larry laughed. "Funny, that's what everyone says after sitting an hour in cross-town traffic. But once a New York audience embraces you, you'll wish you never left."

Eight o'clock arrived. Johnny was deeply engaged in memorizing his newest lyrics, when a stagehand knocked on his door. "Mr. Elias, five minutes to showtime."

Johnny tossed his guitar strap over one shoulder. He took a final sip of water from a near-empty glass, then opened the door to face his uncertain future.

As he walked to the stage door, a thousand thoughts swirled through his mind, his heart fluttering in nervous anticipation. *What if they start booing? What if they're indifferent? Or what if they do remember me and want more than I'm prepared to play?*

Just beyond the stage curtain, Johnny caught a glimpse of Larry Jacobs dressed as one of Santa's elves, trying to fire-up the sold-out venue. "Ladies and gentleman, and all fans of rock and roll, WNYR is proud to once again bring you the finest holiday concert anywhere! So put your eggnog down; get on your feet. We've got a great show for you tonight, which'll be capped off later by Chrissie Hynde and the Pretenders. But first: a very special performance by a remarkably gifted singer-songwriter, who needs no introduction to this city. Ladies and gentleman… it is my distinct pleasure to welcome you all here tonight! Enjoy the show, and keep on rocking!"

The houselights went down. A slightly confused crowd took their seats. Larry passed Johnny in a narrow corridor on his way off the stage. "Anonymous enough for you?" he chuckled.

"Did you have to mention the singer-songwriter part?" Johnny smiled impishly.

A smattering of muffled clapping greeted Johnny's unannounced entrance. He plugged a cord from the amplifier into his Fender acoustic and stepped up to the microphone. *Should I say something clever, or ingratiating?* he wondered. Instead, he cleared his tightening throat away from the mic-stand, before stepping back into the streaming spotlight.

Johnny scanned the darkened audience for reaction while strumming the opening notes to *Yearning for Childhood.* During a mid-song instru-mental, he focused in on a random section to his right. Suddenly, his heart skipped a beat. The flowing strawberry-blonde hair. That petite figure. Sitting two rows up and three seats off the aisle, Johnny was sure he'd spot-ted Megan Price. He quickly turned away to the center rows and picked up the chorus a second too slow.

Polite applause followed the song. When he looked back to his right, he couldn't seem to locate her a second time. She was gone. Again.

Johnny had to be pleased by the generous reaction. Although he appeared notably different than the audience would have remem-bered, there was something familiar about the response to his music. It was almost as if he could read their lips: "Don't I know that guy from somewhere?"

The crowd grew warmer, more encouraging with each successive song. Most of Johnny's pre-performance jitters quickly dissipated with the rhyth-mic clapping on the third song, an upbeat yet satirical tune called *The Choreographer.* Before long, it hardly seemed important to the paying spec-tators that this apparent newcomer was playing entirely unfamiliar mate-rial. The obvious quality was plenty to keep them satisfied.

For the finale to his seven-song set, Johnny debuted the recently penned *Draw Your Own Conclusion,* an angry rant about a relationship gone bad, wrapped around a folkish, mid-tempo tune. To his delight, the spectators caught on quickly to the last line of every chorus, which was the song's title.

By the third time around, he simply held his microphone out to the audience. Obligingly, most responded.

Johnny left the stage to appreciative cheers. He set down his guitar just out of view from the audience. A stagehand provided a thirst-quenching cup of water, and a dry towel.

"That was brilliant." Larry Jacobs greeted him with a high-five. "And not a jeer to be heard. Told you these people never stopped loving your music. Just listen to 'em."

Johnny smiled. "Have to admit, this was better than anticipated! But certainly it isn't me they're clapping for. Must be the songs, or the way I played 'em."

"Come off it Johnny," Larry objected.

"Seriously, if you took a poll right now, I'd say ninety-five percent probably wouldn't guess who was behind the goatee and glasses."

"Don't be so sure," Larry shouted above the continued applause. "I think they want an encore. They're cheering for *you* out there, not a repeat of what you just played."

Johnny downed another cup of water near the stage door. The ringing from the applause hummed in his ears. Still, he had only prepared seven songs.

"Johnny, go take your encore," Larry insisted. "Grab your guitar and play something."

"But I don't have anything else. Can't just go out there and take a bow."

"What about an oldie? You must remember the words from your first album!"

"Aside from blowing my cover, those are mostly piano tunes. Don't have a guitar arrangement for any of 'em."

Larry huddled with one of the roadies. A flurry of activity followed. Three crewmembers carried out a stand-up keyboard and placed it near the center of the stage. With the houselights down and some of the crowd still buzzing, Larry approached Johnny once more.

"Just listen to that. You've already won them over. Now go out there.

Give the people what they want. I'm sure somewhere in there you have one song left."

Johnny nervously bent to touch his toes. "All right, I'll do it. But I gotta warn you, Larry, I'm entirely out of practice. If I screw up, it ain't my fault."

In spite of his words, he was feeling a familiar rush of excitement. Johnny walked out to an approving roar. He moved behind the keyboard and pressed a few notes in a brief warm-up. Uncertain as to whether his microphone was on, he tapped it twice. "I'm gonna try one I haven't played in years. An old Johnny Elias song." Subdued applause followed. He launched into a modest attempt at perhaps the least personal selection from his famous debut, the jazzy *More Than Friends, Less Than Lovers.*

The song – once also the centerpiece of a popular movie soundtrack – still registered with a fair portion of the crowd. Johnny's impromptu rendition gradually improved as he went along. He nearly got all the words right. And when he was finished, it was plainly evident from the affectionate cheering that his earlier fears no longer applied.

Johnny turned down Jacqui's invitation to stay overnight at the Raymer's apartment. Long before the Pretenders had completed their set, he was riding back to Connecticut, back to his other life.

Reflecting on his performance from the back seat, Johnny's thoughts kept returning to one particular moment. More than the warm reception, or Larry's promise kept, it was that one instant when he thought he'd spotted Megan among the audience that lingered. He had been unable to find her again despite repeated efforts, and he remained unsure if this vision had been real or just his mind playing tricks again.

Long before this night's performance Johnny's thoughts of Megan had grown fonder; more frequent. Her face had been regularly appearing in the most unusual places, only to disappear in the blink of an eye. In line at the supermarket. Walking on a crowded street…

In the early stages of this fixation, Johnny had himself convinced that Megan was shadowing him around his new neighborhood, keeping tabs. But as the phenomenon unfolded, he began to view these episodic delusions as his imagination's refusal to let her go.

Now, after "spotting" her in the audience, he realized finally that he couldn't keep watching for Megan everywhere. Some sort of closure was obviously needed.

Johnny stared out at the moving scenery. A deluge of fond memories came flooding back: Sunset strolls on the Brooklyn Promenade. Megan's flowing blonde hair being blown by the wind. Her loving gaze. That fragile smile. *But that was so long ago,* he reminded himself. So much time had elapsed. So much turbulence between them. Would she even take his call? Would a candid conversation shed light on unresolved issues, easing his burdened mind? Or would seeing Megan reopen old wounds that had yet to fully heal? No doubt, he found the uncertainty as troubling as any potential outcome.

Stretching in the backset of the limo, Johnny heard something rustling in his breast pocket. Curious, he pulled out a small piece of paper. His name was scribbled on it. Quickly, he unfolded the note and began to read familiar handwriting.

Johnny: Tonight was so uplifting. Best moment I've ever had in this house of horrors. I've always wished this hour would come.

My apologies for the interruption to our beautiful dance. Someday, you'll understand the joys of parenthood. Meanwhile, please accept this note as an open-ended raincheck to continue where we left off.

Love always -- Megan

Johnny's pulse pounded frantically. It only now occurred to him that the white shirt he had on was the same one he'd been wearing the last time he'd seen Megan. It hadn't left his closet since arriving in Connecticut. *She must've slipped it in there while saying goodnight.*

While saying goodnight six years ago.

Johnny roused himself. Even had he found this note that night, he was not convinced that things would have worked out differently. And yet... and yet. Reading Megan's sweet, simple words, he was even more certain that she could never have been capable of scheming to hurt him. And he had written her such a harsh note in return...

The limo pulled up into the driveway. Johnny headed straight for the basement, hitting the light switches as he went by. Sitting down at the piano, barely thinking, an inspired, anguished tune poured from his heart, guided by the lyrics waltzing in his head. By the time the sun came up, he had captured what he wanted to express.

I walk past a high-rise building and I see you on the twenty-third floor
I drive by a moving train and I see you waiting by the last car door
I jog on a crowded beach, you're a vision before too long
But the only place that I don't see your face – is right here where you belong
I walk out on stage and I can pull your face right out from the crowd
Your voice is what I hear best, even when the cheers are getting loud
You may not be here tonight, but you were there for me way back when
So I will not forget you from the day I met you – even if I never see you again

(Chorus)
Hallucinations bring you back to me – Though I know you're not around
Everywhere I turn, I see you there – although you can't be found
Photographs of you are fading – Still you haven't gone just yet
And living with your legacy – it's one I can't forget
I'm out on a busy street and it's your footsteps I'm hearing behind
The people are everywhere – But it's your smile I never fail to find

My phone's always ringing, but when I pick it up you're not there
I know you're not inclined to leave it all behind
So your forgetting me hardly seems very fair

I sit at my desk and I can see you when I open my top drawer
I reach in my pocket and I find a note you gave me once before
It didn't say much back then, but time's unbound that knot
Because we haven't spoke since the day it broke
And now it's much more than I've got
(Chorus repeats)

I turn on the TV screen – you're featured on the news at six o'clock
I open my window shade – Now I see you running round my block
I'm back on a crowded beach and you're drifting out at sea
It seems you're everywhere that my eyes can stare
except for being here with me
(Chorus – End)

34

That Old Chemistry

The Friday morning papers all seemed to miss the surprise appearance by Johnny Elias. All, that is, except the *New York Times*. In the Arts and Leisure section, a music columnist ran a review of the Pretenders performance, with a one-paragraph blurb tacked on to the end.

To the collective surprise of the audience, Johnny Elias energized the sold-out room with an unannounced opening acoustic set. The once-flourishing star returned to the stage after an absence of more than half a decade, looking trim and singing with conviction. If crowd reaction was any barometer, this new material might very well hold the promise of a long-awaited follow-up to his 1992 epic, Poet of the Wrong Generation.

Over the airwaves, Larry Jacobs continued touting Johnny's revival during his afternoon program. In between tracks from each of Johnny's albums, he lavishly heaped piles of verbal admiration, sparking a number of phone calls and further listener requests. Within days, Raymer Music Management received a wide array of proposals, including interview requests, recording deals and concert possibilities. There was even a query from Barbara Walters, offering Johnny to tell his side of the story on national TV. Andy was ecstatic by all the possibilities.

Up in Stamford, Johnny was responding differently than he had in the past. Not only did he seem receptive, he appeared tickled by the renewed interest in his career. Still, he continued to hold off on accepting anything, aside from one magazine interview: a feature on the art of songwriting. When pressed by Andy about the resumption of his career, Johnny pleaded for patience. Privately, he worked up a few independent ideas.

He was finally ready to capture more than a dozen new first-rate compositions in a formal session. But he had no record label, no producer, or even a band to work with. And even with his current state of musical proficiency, he knew that he couldn't attempt to do it all on his own.

Johnny could have easily accepted one of the deals being extended through Andy's office. A new label would surely have orchestrated the details for him. But with a bad taste still lingering from his Highpeak experience, Johnny's preference was to work independently. Whatever the out-of-pocket expense, he figured that once he had the finished product, he could use it as a bargaining chip to shop around in the hopes of a more lucrative and accommodating deal.

Having lost communication with his former bandmates – though never his appreciation for their talents – Johnny was determined to reach out to them.

He knew there was only one point man with the ability to track them all down.

On a weekday afternoon, Johnny sped southbound down I-95. He switched over to the Brooklyn-Queens Expressway, and headed back to his former neighborhood. The black Chevy he had bought years earlier for his friend sat in the driveway. He smiled. *Oh, good, he must be home.*

It had been nearly a year since Johnny had spoken with Howard Greffen, although he wasn't quite sure why. There was never any friction between them; no debate of any consequence. In fact, it was usually Howard who initiated most phone contact since Johnny had left the city.

Johnny knocked twice. It was not Howard who came to the door, but instead an attractive woman in her early forties.

"I'm looking for Howard Greffen." Johnny squinted at her in confusion. "Is he around?"

"Oh, my, you must be Johnny Elias! I recognize you from your photos. Please come in. Such a nice surprise."

Johnny stepped inside.

"I'm Marlene," the woman said, adjusting a red apron over a blue turtleneck. "Howie's out running errands. But he'll be so delighted when he gets back! If you aren't in a hurry, that is."

A great deal had changed inside the old house. For starters, the lingering musty smell had been replaced with the pleasing aroma of freshly baked bread. The main-level rooms all appeared so much brighter and tidier than he remembered.

Marlene excused herself and left him alone.

Inside Howard's piano parlor, Johnny was surprised to find the old dusty sofa replaced by a mint-green sectional with a new matching rug. Even the piano itself appeared to have been refurbished. "Wow, the place looks great!" he called out. "For the longest time I tried convincing him to modernize. Even offered to do it myself, but he always refused. What brought this on?"

"I suppose it needed a woman's touch." Marlene came back into the room, carrying a tray of sliced melon. She set it down on a new marble coffee table. "We needed to get the house cleaned up. At first I wasn't sure how he'd take it. But he went so far as to toss out much of the clutter on his own. Even felt good about it afterward."

Johnny was puzzled. "Hmm, I know it's been a while, but this doesn't sound at all like the Howard Greffen I know. And I take it that you guys are – um – together?"

"We met at school," Marlene said. "We're a long way from perfection, but Howie's always telling me that the journey is where you'll find the real gratification."

"Well, congratulations! No wonder he's been so preoccupied. I'd absolutely no idea that he was open to a new relationship."

"Well, it didn't hurt to have such a shared love of music," Marlene said, her eyes shining. "We always sit here in this room, singing our favorite duets. Don't laugh, but sometimes we even attempt a few of your songs. I'm sure you know how terribly fond of you he is." She paused, then added, a little awkwardly, "He credits you with saving his life; rejuvenating his very will to live."

"Did he really say that?" Johnny asked, clearly touched. "I always saw it the other way around. If it weren't for Howard, I'd probably still be scraping a living together somewhere on the streets of Brooklyn."

As almost if on cue, the sound of keys jingling was followed by footsteps from down the hall. "Hey, Marlene! Just went to park your car behind mine, but someone's truck is in the driveway. Do we have company?"

"We're in the music room, honey!" she shouted back. "I have a nice surprise for you."

Howard came in and caught sight of Johnny, his eyes immediately filling with tears. He hurried over to the couch with outstretched arms, taking Johnny by surprise. When he let go, he turned to Marlene, grinning. "Does he know yet?"

"I figured you'd want to be the one to tell him," Marlene whispered.

"Tell me what? You guys getting hitched or something?"

"I'll be right back." Howard displayed an intense smile, before swiftly exiting the room. Minutes later he returned, cradling a baby boy of about eighteen months. "So what d'ya think of my little guy?"

"No way, man! You had a kid and didn't tell me?" Johnny zoned in on Howard's face. "He kinda looks like you. This is… really amazing!"

"Actually, he's my grandson. Meet Jeremy Greffen. He and his daddy have been living with us about a year. Between caring for this precious boy and baby-proofing the old place, I'm sure you now understand what's kept me so busy."

"But… I don't… how…"

"Looks like you could use a seat again, kid. Why don't we get comfortable? I've got a whopper of a story to share."

Howard led Johnny back to the new couch, clutching the child on his chest. His version of everything that led to his current state of harmony caused Johnny to shake his head in amazement.

"I couldn't be happier for you. But where was Josh all this time? I mean, he just decided to come home after all these years?"

Howard leaned forward, placing his free hand on one knee. "Johnny, what I waited to tell you in person is: it was your recording of my song - our song - that got the ball rolling. I was sure you'd never believe it over the phone. But honestly, that's what started it."

"But how? And where in the world did he hear it? That album was recalled. Buried. The stations never played anything, other than *A Call To Action*."

"That's where you're wrong," Howard said, smiling. "Outside New York, your so-called scandals were hardly news. And most people really liked your second record. Radio played a few cuts, including *Tomorrow's Door*." Howard adjusted the squirming boy to his other shoulder. "Josh was at a bus station in San Diego. He just couldn't believe that it was *his* song on the radio. Remembered it from the time I first played it. Only this time, it had the coolness factor of it being sung by Johnny Elias, not his old man. A week later he heard it again at a pharmacy in Long Beach; realized he wasn't hallucinating."

"Coolness factor, eh?" Johnny waved a hand dismissively over his face, trying to conceal a budding smile. "So he was out west this whole time?"

"It's a long story. But yeah, been on the run for years. With only a backpack on his shoulders and fifty bucks in his pocket, Josh decided he'd had enough of living in a museum full of dusty tributes to his dead mother. Obviously, I was sending mixed messages, telling him to get on with his life, while I couldn't even throw out Suzy's old toothbrush. Depression, you know? In hindsight, I at least understand why he escaped."

"But you told me he never even called you," Johnny gasped. "Didn't he realize how much he hurt you by staying away?"

"Hey, you've gotta remember that he was a kid. Still is. In adolescence, they tend to only to think of themselves, and Josh was determined to prove he could make it on his own. So he hopped on a bus and went town-to-town, washing dishes, pumping gas – you know – anything to keep him in motion. At a garage near San Diego he learned to be an auto mechanic. Also met a girl out there; shacked up at some fleabag motel. Before long, she was nineteen, pregnant and terrified. Josh convinced her to keep the baby. But only six weeks after giving birth, she ran off one morning to get some diapers and… well, she bolted for good."

"Johnny wiped his brow. "Poor guy! Must've felt totally helpless! So I guess he turned to you in desperation?"

Howard sighed. "I think it was that, and the fact that he suddenly understood how it felt being on the other side. One runaway falling victim to another. And with no parental experience, he arrived at the door of the one person who he came to realize was best equipped to handle the job. Okay, so I wasn't the perfect dad. But I think it was hearing our song in his hour of desolation that really swayed him. So yeah, your little plan kinda worked after all."

Johnny shook his head, bemused. "I just can't believe it. So… can I meet him? Didn't you say he lived here?"

"He does. But I have him taking night-classes after he works a full-time day job. If I could get my diploma in my late-forties, no reason he can't do it at twenty-three. Plus, between him, Marlene, and me, little Jeremy is well cared for."

Johnny patted Howard on the back. "Sounds like you've finally reconnected with the family you never really had. If anyone deserved a shot at redemption... and now with Josh home, plus a grandson too! Must be so damn sweet!"

"You can't even imagine." Howard shrugged. "But really, this has nothing to do with being worthy. You know, sometimes life deals us a straight flush. Occasionally, it comes up all jokers. But as long as we do our best to play the cards we're dealt, we can never second guess. Mind you, I haven't always lived by that attitude. But I always knew that if I hung in long enough, eventually I'd be shuffled a decent hand. Hey, hand me that wipe, will you?"

Johnny passed Howard a cloth to absorb drool from the baby's chin. "Yeah, I've gotta admit: life has a way of kicking you in the gut, then patting you on the back later on. May not balance out, but it kinda makes us appreciate the good times all the more." Johnny coughed twice to clear his throat. "And keeping in the spirit of good news, I figured you'd want to know that I've rediscovered the songwriting itch again."

Howard bounced the fidgety little boy on his left knee. "No kidding! When did that happen?"

"While you've been preoccupied with your family, new and old, I've been rounding my skills into shape. Started just after I went back to finally wrap up my degree. The students, they really seemed to dig my old songs. A little youthful enthusiasm to restore my creative juices. Now I've probably got enough material for a double-album, if that concept even still exists."

"A double album?" Howard smiled playfully. "Quite an accomplishment, although I think that went out of style just after the birth of MTV." Suppressed laughter turned to encouragement. "But seriously, I'd love to hear what you've been working on. It's been way too long since you last played something new for me."

Johnny headed over to the old piano. "Hey, Howard, you, of all people should understand why I gave it up in the first place. When it all came crashing down on me – that door of creativity you used to talk about – it just slammed into the locked position. It was only in the last few months that I finally found a way to get back in."

"Ah, so I suppose that in finding new inspiration, you've also hit on the most common spark for greatness. If you don't mind me asking, what's her name?"

"Actually, not too lucky in love. Never have been," Johnny answered softly. "If anything, my muse is somebody I lost a long time ago. Who knows if I'll ever be able to fix the past?" He shrugged. "At least it makes for some heart-wrenching melodies."

Howard tugged gently on his graying goatee. "Ah, yes. The fantasy of what can never be. Always a choice theme in some of literature's greatest works. I believe one Billy Shakespeare once wrote a little ditty on the very subject. It's called *Romeo and Juliet*." He shook off the ironic tone. "If you're taking requests, maybe you can start with one of those?"

"No problem," Johnny acknowledged, placing his hands on the keys. "I've got some thirty new songs. I'll play 'em all if you like. But before I do, I'd like to ask a little favor."

"Okay, let's try this on three," Joe Rivera shouted. There was the sound of a guitar being tuned.

"Wait, I think I hear someone knocking." Ian banged twice on his drum.

"Maybe it's Johnny's crack dealer," Frank said, laughing. "Johnny, it's your place. Go get the door."

"No, wait," Ian snickered. "Might be a photographer too. Frank, maybe you should get it."

"Gentlemen, a little respect!" Howard glared disapprovingly.

"It's all right," Johnny cut in. "Let 'em joke… so long as our vocationally challenged friends remember who's signing their checks this time around."

They were all gathered together again in the basement of Johnny's Connecticut home: Frank Traber, a red Stratocaster in his calloused hands. Ian Klatt behind the drums. Howard Greffen on piano, and the rejuvenated composer on lead vocals. Joe Rivera sat at the portable recording console amid a slew of rented equipment. Only Art Tillman could not be located among the original participants. In his absence stood Gary Gaines, the young bass player who aided Johnny in recapturing his lost desire.

Seventeen consecutive days. That's how long the musicians spent inside Johnny's house, sleeping little and rehearsing often. The band recorded one song every day by noon and often a second by early evening. Johnny had guessed that, by working round-the-clock, most of the new material could be laid down before the resumption of Howard's teaching duties, and Gary's final college semester.

From the outset, the gathering felt something like a boys-school reunion. Through pranks, pizza deliveries and stories of the past, the six men spent every free interlude reliving the glory days and lamenting over what might have been.

By the tenth day, the band had recorded fourteen songs from the mini stage in the refurbished basement. Even a hardened music veteran like Joe Rivera was bubbling with praise during a group playback session.

"Boys, after a few days to work off the rust, it's thrilling to witness the old magic. I hate drawing comparisons to the past, but the unity down here... awfully impressive."

Even more rousing than the recordings was the band's chemistry. With Johnny's versatility, switching between piano and acoustic guitar, the capable lineup took on an added dimension. Instead of capturing each instrument independently, the band played every song in live takes. This method eliminated anyone from having to stand around, waiting his turn to play.

By the end of week three, Johnny overheard the not-so-subtle whispers about getting back on the road. He overheard a whole lot more through his screen door one night when Art and Ian went out for a smoke break on his back porch.

"Frankie, man, these tracks kick ass... some of the best we've ever done. But d'ya think it'll lead anywhere, aside from lining the boss man's pockets," Ian asked, scratching his head.

"Damn straight!" Frank exclaimed, lighting up his smoke. "I'm just waiting for Johnny to wig out again; leave us out in the cold. All those wasted years. All that wasted talent. Not just his, ours too. We coulda been rocking the masses all this time, instead of doing dishes for a living."

Ian laughed. "It's funny, man. Johnny asked the other day if I still wear the Rolex from the Poet tour. Didn't have the heart to tell him I pawned it a few years back to pay the rent. You still got yours?"

Frank coughed, then chuckled. "You kidding? Got ten grand on eBay for mine. Hard to stay sentimental when you got bills to pay." He took another drag and blew out a puffy nicotine cloud. "I mean, what can I say? Fingers crossed we make it out on tour this time around."

Johnny could feel his heart shrivel in his chest. Till now, he hadn't discussed a comeback tour with anyone. But he surely owed his bandmates this opportunity after essentially cutting them loose for six years. Still, he feared a conventional, well-publicized tour might make for easy prey to those who once sabotaged his life. There had to be a way to please everyone.

Between sessions, he sat compiling a list of promotional gimmicks. Quickly, he eliminated most ideas, knowing any major comeback couldn't be done halfway. No Brooklyn homecoming concert or college barnstorming tour would attract enough mainstream attention to win everyone back overnight. If only he could find a way to reconnect with most of his loyal following!

To the daring and improbable, Johnny next conjured up a short-list of outlandish publicity stunts: Grand Central Station. The Brooklyn Bridge. Liberty Island. Either the next stage was going to be colossal or it would be nothing at all.

Katherine Price sat in a circle of twenty strangers, staring uneasily at the faces. A hint of grey in her blonde hair and noticeable creases around her eyes made it clear that she'd aged at least twelve years in a period of half the time. Only today, her appearance hardly mattered; just her presence. "So tell me again how this works?" she asked the group leader. "It's my first time."

"Just introduce yourself," answered a white haired man in a green sweatshirt. "Then, tell us exactly why you're here."

"Well, okay, then." Katherine drew a deep breath. *Sure as hell isn't for the same reason they are,* she thought to herself. "My name is Katherine P. and I suppose I've become an alcoholic. Of course, not like my husband was years ago. But recently I've allowed drinking to get the better of me, both personally and professionally."

Katherine stared nervously at the group leader, awaiting his response. She found it odd to be feeling nervous, having spent years in front of TV cameras and much larger audiences.

"All right, Katherine. A good start. Care to tell the group how it began? And when did you realize that you had a problem?"

Katherine briefly looked down to the floor and coughed deliberately. She knew her real reason for being here had far less to do with overindulgence than her need to commiserate with a nonjudgmental audience. "Um, sure. I guess for many people, alcohol is the root of their problems. In my case, it was the other way around. I didn't start drinking until after I'd ruined my life."

The assembled gathering looked on in stony silence. Katherine continued.

"It's been almost twenty years since booze did in my husband. When he died, I swore I'd never touch another drop. And honestly, it was years before I even enjoyed a glass of champagne. But no matter, I was always in total control of my urges when it came to everything: Business. Diet. Family. Alcohol is only a recent side-effect."

"How so?" asked a woman across the way, probably in her late thirties. "Admitting your weakness *is* the first step to recovery. Sounds to me like you're somewhat in denial."

"About my drinking?" Katherine's eyebrows elevated. She smiled inwardly, knowing alcohol was hardly her downfall. "Well, I wouldn't be here if I didn't think I had a problem. But honestly, I didn't ruin my family with booze. I hurt them by trying too hard to perfect their lives. The drinking only began when I realized just how bad things got."

"So you drink out of depression, like I do?" asked a bearded man two seats to the left.

"I do it because it's an escape from the reality I've created," Katherine answered. "I once had it all. No, make that twice. Years ago I had a loving, successful husband and two adorable children. When that fairytale shattered, I picked up the pieces; built an incredible business. Life was good again. I was in total control. And then..." She paused to clear the bitterness from her throat. "Instead of perfection, I've alienated my daughter beyond repair. And my son's grown up a buffoon, instead of my successor. When I ran out of solutions, the bottle became my last resort."

"Well, no matter how you got here, you've come to the right place," the group leader chimed in. "Addictions come in many forms: Drinking. Gambling. Even power can be an unhealthy obsession. But if you're here to embrace the twelve step program and correct your personal defects, you've got a great opportunity to turn your life around."

Katherine nodded, as if to go along. A woman to her right patted her on the back for encouragement. Then the door to the room swung open and a latecomer strolled in. Katherine could swear she heard the strains of *A Call To Action* by Johnny Elias coming from down the hall. *If only it were that easy!* she told herself.

Up in Stamford, the dungeon sessions continued long after they were supposed to have wrapped. Johnny had hoped to have all songs recorded in a period of five weeks. However, with creative energies peaking, and new songs continuing to flow, that timeframe doubled.

Johnny sent the musicians home after a whopping twenty-nine tracks. He knew there was still a good deal of polishing to be done in Joe Rivera's studio, between sequencing, overdubs, and the addition of orchestration. Although both artist and his manager would have liked a finished project to shop around by springtime, it was becoming apparent that it wasn't going to be ready.

"Johnny, the window of opportunity is only so big," Andy lectured by phone. "Your mini resurgence'll only last so long without new product. Hate to pressure you, but we can't afford to be perfectionists."

"I want this as much as you do. I just didn't wanna lose any momentum with Joe and the guys. Like you said, the window of opportunity is only so —"

"Johnny, I know what I said. And I also don't hear the phone ringing for you like it did after the holiday concert, or when Highpeak rushed out that opportunistic greatest hits package. You really don't need a monster double-disc to demonstrate that you're back with a vengeance. Just split the tracks; have one conventional CD ready to go."

"I hear where you're coming from. But trust me: I've got something spectacular up my sleeve. I'll tell you the whole deal. Just waiting for the weather to warm up, while I organize how to pull this off."

"Pull what off?" Andy's paused. "Should I be afraid to ask?"

Johnny hesitated. He didn't mean to toy with Andy; the reality was that he was scared, and discussing big plans in person was always his preference. "Actually, I promised to meet Joe at his midtown studio for some editing next week. Why don't you fit me in on your calendar for Monday or Tuesday? And prepare to wear your goose-bump repellent, or maybe a straitjacket. Not really sure how you're gonna react."

35

Destiny Boils Over

The excitement of recording his new music had kept Johnny distracted from his inability to reach Megan. Then the musicians scattered. He tried her home number virtually every few hours, already planning what he would say, how he would apologize. And then one morning... *"We're sorry. The number you have dialed is no longer in service. No further information is available."*

Where could she be? Johnny wondered, feeling a little panic. Could Megan have moved?

Still, he had finally come to understand what had happened between them. Just before leaving for Manhattan, Johnny tucked the handwritten rain-check in an overnight bag, along with the printed lyrics to the song he'd recently composed for her. *Maybe I'll just turn up at her door while I'm in town,* he thought.

A stiff New York wind blew past Joe Rivera's studio on East 59th. After a productive morning session, Johnny had considerable time to fill. He stopped at FAO Schwartz on Fifth Avenue on his way over to the Raymer's apartment. Through a stream of jugglers, strollers and motorized scooters, he picked up a handful of preschool toys for young Julia.

But on this mild March afternoon, with ninety minutes left to occupy, he turned left, cutting through Central Park for the first time in years.

Johnny trekked down a winding path behind the zoo. A metal bottle cap lay on the pedestrian jogging path. He kicked at it and watched it skitter across the pavement before coming to a rest at the site of his fondest memory. It had been an oppressively cold winter. The brown turf and bare Spanish Oak trees appeared weeks away from turning green. Yet he could only envision a perfect summer day, filled with jubilant fans lying out on beach towels, waiting for the show to begin. Suddenly, he was back on Megan's green blanket, yards from the great stage. To his right: Andy and Jacqui laughing together again for the first time. Johnny could feel the crowd's electricity and the sun on his neck. He turned to stare over his shoulder at the mass of humanity. The aura of a bright summer afternoon when all was right with the world lingered.

The music played once again. Johnny knelt to the ground and lowered his shoulders, as if to let Megan climb up for a better view. But a poke from a passing sanitation worker brought this beautiful daydream to an abrupt end.

"Hey, buddy, you mind movin? I got trash to pick up here."

"Sorry." Johnny drew a deep breath and nodded, heading over to the Raymer's place. His spontaneous excursion had not only supplied a blast of his happiest memories; it solidified what he had been thinking about for weeks.

"Central Park, Andy. I'm gonna play a free show on the Great Lawn for all the world to see."

Andy laughed. "Surely you jest, John. You, the reluctant superstar, who refused to be introduced to a crowd of nine thousand, are now inviting half of New York to show up, after all this time away?"

Johnny stretched his arms across the back of the sofa. "Andy, I'm dead serious. This isn't something I've reached on a whim. For weeks I've been plotting this. I don't have it all figured out yet, but work with me here, okay?"

Andy's eyes lit up. "Man, you are serious!" He reached for a notepad on his table and began scribbling some thoughts. "Okay, then... Wow! Well I guess we should really talk about what's required for a show of this magnitude. We're talkin' permits from like a dozen city agencies. At least six months of lead time, maybe more. Oh, and targeted publicity. Lots of it. Obviously you want a massive crowd. If the park looks empty when you play, it could permanently mar your reputation. We're talking high stakes."

"Yeah, I know what's at stake," Johnny countered, leaning forward for emphasis.

"Do you?" Andy continued scribbling. "Well, before we go any further, let's talk dollars and cents. Obviously you remember Paul Simon's concert in '91?"

Johnny nodded. Andy continued his thought. "Well there's a good reason why there hasn't been another big show like that in eight years. Big bucks! Paul Simon had the backing of a major cable network... and a record company. Between sanitation crews for the cleanup, and cops working overtime, someone needs to cough up that dough. Not to mention the staging, a sound system, projection screens. We're talking at least two or three million. Might I remind you that you still don't have the support of a record label, let alone a lucrative TV arrangement?"

Impervious to Andy's overture, Johnny smiled calmly. "I've already been through most of this at least a hundred times in my mind. That's why I plan to do things a bit differently. Even if it all comes out of my own pocket."

"Out of your pocket? Are you aware of your up-to-date finances? Even with the spike in your old album sales, the royalties are miniscule compared to the old days. Plus, you just dropped some serious coin on these independent recordings. And then you've got that winter coat charity thing. It's very nice, but it hasn't come cheaply. Unless you're hiding monies somewhere, you don't have enough to your name for this kind of production. Not on your own, anyway!"

Johnny stood from the couch and began to pace the room. "Wait a second, Andy. Please, just hear me out. If there's anything six years has taught me, it's that I need to be ultra vigilant. And we have to be in total control, or it could all blow up in our faces... again. So listen, I'm pretty sure we can pull this off without incurring that kind of tab. Not to mention all the red tape it'll eliminate." Johnny spun in Andy's direction. "Simple as this may sound, I just plan to pick a date, show up in the park with the guys and start playing. However many people turn up'll be a bonus. But with no pre-expectations; no hype, I can simply —"

"Whoa! Johnny, you just can't do that!" Andy's glare intensified. "Without an outdoor sound system, hardly anyone'll hear you. And without a series of parks department permits, you have about zero chance of doing this without getting yourself arrested. Let's sit down, figure this out logically. Remember, I do this stuff for a living."

"They won't arrest me," Johnny answered, his face perfectly straight. "No one would dare pull the plug on a harmless performance, at least until it was over. There's gotta be a way to get a stage inside and enough audio to be heard. After that, well, you know how New Yorker's are? A large crowd gathers. Everyone stops to look. Just on curiosity I should be able to draw a decent number. Word has a way of filtering down. People'll call their friends. The media will eat it up. And I'll be standing up there, having stolen a free concert in Central Park!"

Andy excused himself from the living room for a moment. He returned in short order with a map of Central Park and laid it on out the coffee table. "Johnny, just look here a second." He pointed to the Great Lawn. "How do you plan to sneak a stage inside? You think the cops won't notice someone carrying all that gear? And assuming in the most far-fetched scenario that you get that far, do you honestly believe you're gonna be allowed to play a single note? The crowds won't be cheering when the cops dismantle the stage. And you and the guys'll certainly be arrested. Forget being the outlaw rock star. You could be hit with fifteen felonies."

Johnny remained eerily calm. "Call me crazy, but I don't have the same sense of dread as you do. Even without permits, I can't see how entertaining my fans is gonna get me locked up for life. It's not like I'd be hurting anyone. I'll even pay for the cops and cleanup when it's over. The notoriety from that show alone should pay me back to last a lifetime. Andy, I'm gonna find a way!"

Andy sat silently on his living room recliner, his head pounding. He could appreciate more than anyone, Johnny's enthusiasm. In some ways, it actually pained him to try and talk his friend down from this maverick idea. Yet, he was convinced that while a concert in the park could be the pinnacle of any career, it had to be done properly.

Of greater concern was the release of a new album to get Johnny back on the charts and the airwaves. Once a record label had made their best offer, he could even present the free concert as part of contractual requirements. Any shrewd company would surely recognize the promotional value of such a spectacle. Not wishing to dash Johnny's big hopes, Andy softened his stance.

"Listen, John. You don't need to convince me. I think your idea is pure genius, if not bordering on insanity. And in the right time, I know we can pull it off. But a bootlegged concert with no supervision… that's a recipe for disaster. You'll need one mega insurance policy to protect yourself from liability. In total chaos, anything can happen and probably will. All you need is one scraped knee to be party to a major lawsuit."

"Don't you think I realize this? I'm prepared to deal with the consequences. Hey, you were there with me for Paul Simon. This is the kind of event where New York always shows its best side. Other than t-shirt bootleggers and pot smokers, there were no arrests that night. And if I show up unannounced, we've eliminated the t-shirt problem."

"Johnny, come back down to earth buddy," Andy urged. "The reason Paul Simon's show was so successful: solid organization. That's what I'm here for, to manage things; make you look good. I mean, sure people might be on their best behavior. But with any big crowd, things happen. Spectators get knocked down. Some might even push to get inside the park. And how do you account for a crowd of thousands without a single bathroom for miles around? Let me make a few phone calls; see what's involved."

Johnny stared pensively out the living room window toward the East River. Andy had been so supportive up till now. And yet even he saw flaws in the plan that Johnny had fallen in love with.

"Andy!" he shouted, turning to face him. "You've gotta understand why this needs to be covert. If I work with the city, I'm putting myself back where I was six years ago. That can't happen again!" He quieted down. "When I dreamed this up, I envisioned Katherine Price looking out her window and seeing me in front of all those cheering fans. There I'd be, singing in her proverbial backyard. Only now, she and her cronies will be powerless to stop me."

"I know where you're coming from," Andy acknowledged with a nod. "But you just can't perform for free in the world's busiest park to avenge your past. Even if you played an authorized show, Katherine can't touch you now. The Dinkins era is over. Hey, I'd love nothing better than to see that woman squirm. But that doesn't justify doing something you'll probably regret."

Johnny resumed his pacing. "This isn't really about getting even. I could put Katherine in her place if I wanted to. Hey, it's not even about all those ball-busters who hung around my building, tearing through my garbage for a story. Andy, it's about doing this on my terms. I had too many enemies out there; don't wanna give anyone a chance to sabotage me ahead of time."

"So you're doing this as a big get-even for everyone who's ever wronged you? That's one helluva way to grab attention." Andy's frustration began to mount.

"Actually, it's much more than that," Johnny insisted. "I owe it to my band for their loyalty, for lost time and wages. And I'm doing it for the fans who've stuck with me. When I'm up onstage, looking out into the crowd, it'll be for them. It's always been for them. More than anything, I wanna feel that love, while giving 'em all I've got in return." He grinned. "Can you think of a more perfect setting to show them that I'm still that guy they remember?"

"You mean the poet of the wrong generation?" Andy adjusted the wire-rimmed glasses on the bridge of his nose. "It's all so perfect, the way you tell it. But as your voice of reason, I need to point out that even in the best-case scenario you'll win them over but you will go to jail. There'll be no post-concert celebration in Rikers. Just a cold cell and a warm bowl of mush, if you're lucky. Now there's one sparkling comeback!"

Johnny glared at him. "Thanks, man. Knew I could count on you for something. I just didn't realize it'd be bursting my bubble. Thanks for your encouragement." He grabbed his coat and overnight bag, heading for the door.

"I didn't say I wouldn't help you!" Andy shouted down the hall after him. "I just said we need to make it legal. Hey, if you didn't want my honesty, maybe you shouldn't have come here in the first place!"

The front door slammed in response.

Johnny had abandoned his plan of staying with the Raymers – it was pretty much impossible, after his dramatic exit. He checked into the nearest hotel, ordered up room service, then went to bed. The idea of popping in on Megan unannounced also seemed ill advised given his frame of mind. His negative mood won the day.

Johnny woke the next morning feeling bitter but determined. He grabbed a current calendar and flipped ahead to the warmer months. With no desire to wait until the height of summer and the notorious New York humidity, he circled Thursday, May 27th, 1999. This would be the evening just before the start of the Memorial Day weekend. *Yeah, people should be up for a party.*

He began outlining all his thoughts on paper: A concert set list. Transporting the instruments. Audio equipment rental. It was immediately clear that he couldn't do it on his own, and he reached for the phone. "Larry, it's Johnny Elias."

"Johnny! We haven't talked since you ducked out of the Garden with the Pretenders on stage. How the hell've you been?"

"Been a busy man," Johnny answered. "Gotten back to recording again. With a little luck, I'll be releasing something later this year."

"That's awesome!" Larry exclaimed. "So you're calling to give me an early preview?"

"Actually, I could use a favor. I'm hoping you might be able to hook me up with a few vendors. Might be needing some staging equipment."

Larry chuckled. "Staging? Like for a show? Smells like someone's cooking up a little stunt. I'm guessing you could also do with a bit of promotion behind whatever you've got going on."

"Truth-be-told, I wasn't gonna trouble you on that end. I mean, sure, I'll take all the help I can get. But this project, it's more than a little complicated."

"Long as it involves some kind of performance, I'm sure the station'll want our call-letters prominently on display. Just tell me where and when. After what you did for us back in December, we owe you big time."

"Larry, your enthusiasm's appreciated. It's just not that simple," Johnny said, rubbing his forehead. "I don't know what you have in mind, but I won't be playing some parking lot, or the Coney Island boardwalk. What I'm planning might not sit well with your suits. Is there a place we can talk in private?"

"Sure thing," Larry answered immediately. "It'd make it easier on me if you could come into the city. I mean, I could drive up to Connecticut, but —"

"Say no more," Johnny interrupted. "How soon?"

"Um, I guess it's just after twelve? I'm not on the air till three. Why don't we meet here at my office? I should have about an hour before picking the music for my show. Plus, you've never been to our new studios. I'll introduce you to —"

"I'm coming right over, Larry. But let's keep this discreet, okay? Not to ruin your fun, but it's probably best if we're not seen together."

Larry stood waiting upstairs in the eleventh-floor reception area. When Johnny arrived, he whisked him into a nearby conference room. Larry locked the door behind them. "Good to see you, man. So what is it you couldn't tell me about over the phone?"

"Well… it's a little comeback gig here in the city." Johnny sat down. "But, like I told you, it's a risky proposition."

Larry grinned. "Go on. Where and when? I hope it's somewhere that involves stopping traffic and a little rock-and-roll chaos. Lemme guess: a rooftop?"

"I don't know about the traffic part," Johnny said, laughing, "though I suspect we'll be drawing an awful lot of attention with this one. Here's the deal: I'm looking to sneak a stage into Central Park one night, right up there on the Great Lawn. Then I'll just show up the next day to play for whoever comes."

Larry fell back in his rolling chair, his grin growing wider. "Now there's something you don't see every day! A stolen free concert! And just who do ya plan to have for security: the Hell's Angels? Damn! That'll be a night nobody ever forgets!"

"So you like it?"

"Like it? Sheer insanity. I love it! Do I think you can do it? That's a whole other question." Larry lit a cigarette and took a drag. "But yeah, I'd say it ranks right up there with anything that's been done till now."

"Then you'll help me?" Johnny asked. "If you can get me a stage and some audio gear, I'd be immensely grateful. And I think I can take it from there."

Larry leaned forward and laughed. "So you're really serious about this?"

"Totally. One way or another, Larry, I'm gonna pull it off."

Larry coughed. He found himself thinking back to the zany radio stunts he'd attempted through the years – from sneaking into Mick Jagger's limo (for a surprisingly candid interview), to dressing like Elizabeth II to introduce an early performance by the band Queen – he thought he'd seen it all. And yet the prospect of this free concert had his imagination bubbling over… and his excitement didn't just have to do with Johnny.

"Hey, you're probably too young to remember the summer of '78. Back then I was lookin' to make a name for myself at an all-rock station at the height of the disco backlash. Led this little rally down in Washington Square Park."

Johnny smiled. Larry grinned and went on. "So I showed up one afternoon with a bullhorn; got people to start trashing their disco records. You shoulda seen it. Must've gotten like a thousand people stomping on vinyl, tearing up photos of the Village People, Donna Summer, all that crap."

Johnny was delighted. "Must've been a blast!"

"Oh, it was… for an hour, or so. Crowds were chanting *disco sucks*. It was inspired. But a few bonfires later – well, you get my drift. The cops had to come break it up. Luckily no one got seriously hurt. We got tons of free publicity. But I keep thinking had it been better thought out, man, coulda been an all-timer."

"So wait… are you suggesting I seek permission? What're you driving at?"

"I guess what I'm saying now is that you and I are gonna need to be more diligent when we firm up these classified arrangements," Larry said, unable to keep a straight face. "Thing is, if we can somehow keep this madness a secret, the key is going to be finding a way to draw the masses if no one knows to show up."

Johnny flashed a smile of gratitude. "I kinda figured with a big stage out on the lawn all afternoon – curiosity seekers will just hang there. Word gets around this city quickly. By the time I arrive that night, there should be a decent number. Why, what'd you have in mind?"

Johnny stood out on the terrace of his East Side hotel suite, waiting for the verdict. He knew that convincing the others to join him, sink-or-swim, was not going to be easy. From inside, he could hear Frank, Ian, Howard and Gary debating his proposal around the breakfast buffet he had ordered for them.

"I know you guys've all been itching to play live again," Howard reiterated. "This may not be the big tour some of us were hoping for, but potentially it could put us in front of the largest audience any of us will ever see."

"Bottom line, what's he paying us?" Ian asked, causing Frank to spit back his orange juice in a frosty glass. "Long as there are enough bucks in it, we still like paying gigs."

Howard leaned forward, placing both hands on the table. "Guys, you heard what the man said. He'll pay you for this one gig what you might normally get for a month on the road. Granted this one's risky. But I'd say the upside's just a little too good to ignore."

Gary put down his blueberry muffin and chimed in. "Guys, I know we might get busted and all. But we are talking Central Park! I mean, if this works out, isn't that the coolest gig ever?"

"The kid's gotta point." Ian nodded. "I'll never forget when Diana Ross played her show in the pouring rain. All those people singing along, getting soaked. It was awesome!"

"You're a closet Diana Ross fan?" Frank asked, giggling. "I'd never've guessed."

"What's wrong with Motown?" Ian defended. "The Supremes were goddesses. And everyone loves a free outdoor concert. But what happens to us if we get caught?"

"I think we go to jail," Frank noted with a distant gaze. "Trespassing. Disturbing the peace… something like that. We're looking at a few months behind bars. Maybe more. Is that really worth risking for the benefit of Mr. oversensitive out there?"

"Well, Johnny did promise to take all the heat if anything goes wrong," Gary reminded. "It's his name that everyone knows. Any negative fallout would be on his shoulders."

"But if it succeeds, you'll all hold a place in the upper reaches of rock and roll mythology," Howard interjected, quieting the murmurs. "Let's face it. The cops aren't pulling the plug in front of thousands, risking an all-out riot. At the very least, you'll all be part of an exclusive group who can say they pulled off the greatest renegade concert of all time."

"And what about you, Howard?" Frank pointed across the table. "You seem totally convinced that this is the greatest gig ever. But ain't it easy for you to preach, so long as you've got nothing at risk? Your mortgage is paid off!"

"Actually, Frank, I already accepted Johnny's invite. When he's out front, I'll sing harmony, play piano, whatever. And quite honestly, out of all of us, I may have the most to lose. But forget failure. This is the stuff legends are made of."

Howard adjusted his maroon glasses on the bridge of his nose and straightened his posture. "Remember: life isn't calculated in years and days. It's measured in moments. When you look back on it all some day, can you, as a musician, imagine anything cooler than having played for so many people in one place? And can you fathom the regret when you think back on what might've been if you say no?"

Frank and Ian headed off to a corner. Gary soon followed. Johnny remained outside on the terrace facing uptown. The sound of car horns blared from the street below. His heart was racing. So much depended on what they had to say...

Ian came to find him twenty minutes later. "How much again did you say we were getting paid for this lunacy?" He was smiling broadly.

A boisterous group huddle followed. Johnny offered one final thought. "Remember. Not a word of this gets out, or it'll jeopardize the whole plan. Not your friends, your family, or your next-door neighbors. We'll rehearse up at my place starting next week to keep out of sight. But if as much as a whisper gets beyond our little circle..."

Johnny was soon caught up in the intensity of planning and rehearsals. He had not spoken with Andy since the night of their heated exchange, and he had no idea when they would clear the air.

As for Megan, Johnny spent the majority of his limited free time trying to track her down. A trip up to her apartment on his last visit to the city had proved futile. The doorman confirmed that she still lived there, but that he hadn't seen her in weeks. A chain of phone calls finally led him to her volunteer job at the women's shelter. Now with just one week before the big day, he had at last gotten what he believed to be her new, unlisted number.

Johnny pulled out the lyric sheet of his haunting composition *Hallucinations*. He actually had his hand on the phone when it rang.

"Johnny, its Jacqui. You gotta minute?"

"Jacqui," he answered hesitantly, thinking immediately of Andy. "What's doin?"

"Well, since we haven't spoken in forever, I'm guessing you're probably hard at work on your plans to invade Central Park."

Johnny laughed. "So Andy told you about that! I figured since he had such a problem with the whole concept, he might've kept it to himself."

"So you're really going through with it?" she asked. "You know, I heard your whole conversation that night. And I thought I'd belatedly tell you: the idea is pure genius."

"Well, great! Thanks. Good to know I've at least got one of you in my corner. But right now, that's the least of my worries."

"So you mean you're not sure if you're actually going ahead?"

"Oh, we're doing it, all right. Been rehearsing 'round the clock! The thing is: I still need so much – a security team, sound engineers, a stage crew, and all of them discreet. If only I could stick to the creative end and have someone else tackle the logistical problems!"

"Sounds complicated," Jacqui agreed. "But actually, that's why I called. I may not be able to build a stage, or lug a drum kit. But working beside Andy all these years, I think I've learned a thing or two about promotion. So when did you say the big day was?"

"Actually, I didn't say. With Andy so convinced that I'll be jailed for life… all I need is to have him blow the whistle on me, just to prove his point."

"Oh c'mon, Johnny. Andy's the most loyal friend you've got. May not always agree with you, but he lives and dies with your every success and failure."

"Oh, really?" Johnny shook his head. "He's got an odd way of showing it lately."

"Listen, I agree he was a bit hard on you at our flat. But you're so close to a comeback. He still has a few record companies lined up to sign you. In his view, it'll be awfully hard for you to promote your new release from a prison cell."

"And what's your opinion, Jacqui?"

"Truth is, we both wanna help you. Only Andy still believes this show can't go on without going through the proper channels. But like you, I'm an artist first. Practicality takes a serious back seat to ingenuity. I reckon once everyone sees a harmless concert evolving, the cops'll cooperate."

"Thanks," said Johnny, relieved to hear someone else voicing his opinion. "Obviously that's how I see it. And you know, the risk is worth anything that could go wrong." Johnny switched ears with the phone and chuckled. "Like that Dylan song says, I ain't got nothing to lose. Forget my cost; the potential consequences. Been down before; I'll be down again. But there are these seldom moments when you believe your very fate lies in the balance. The chance – however remote – to reconnect, in the most spectacular venue imaginable..." Johnny grew quiet.

"So when again did you say this was happening?" Jacqui repeated. "I'd hate to miss my shot at a front-row seat."

Johnny sighed softly. "We're aiming for May 27th. It's a Thursday. If all goes right, we hope to be taking the stage just after eight."

"Wow! That soon! Well, I'll be keeping my digits crossed. And I hope to generate a little fanfare too. Must be a way to draw the biggest possible crowd without blowing your cover."

"So I can assume Andy'll be there with you, holding his breath?"

"C'mon, Johnny. I'm not getting into the middle of this, though I really do think you two should sit down and hash things out. But even if you don't, I know he'll be the one cheering the loudest."

Jacqui hung up the phone and turned to Andy, who had been waiting for her to finish the conversation.

He was anxious. "So, he still going ahead with it? Please tell me he's come to his senses?"

"One week, Andy. No sense puttering around. Time we roll up our sleeves; do what we can from behind the curtain. And if you want my opinion: I think somehow he's going to make it!"

36

FATE RINGS TWICE

It had been an eventful week for Megan Price. On Sunday, she called off a three-month fling with a forty-one-year-old veterinarian. New companionship had eluded her again.

On Monday, Megan and Alex caught a ballgame at Yankee Stadium. The company surely beat any of her recent dates. And it did get the two of them out of the house - a weeknight rarity.

On Tuesday after work, she dined at home with brother, Zach, who arrived bearing gifts for his enthusiastic nephew. Though Megan was generally wary of his periodic visits, it was one family concession she could stomach in bittersweet dosages.

Uncle Zach unabashedly sat wolfing down a plate of steaming linguini, as a giggling Alex attempted an imitation of the culinary demolition. Between bites, Zach mimicked a variety of farm animal noises.

The sight of Alex rolling on the floor in hysterics was cause for Megan to smile; but once her son went off to explore his new video game, Zach wasn't nearly as pleasant. "So whatever happened to that porker friend of yours? The chick from college you used to hang with?"

Megan grimaced. "Oh, you must mean Vera. Yeah, she's doing great.

You know, she got that stomach surgery; lost like eighty pounds. Last I heard, she ran off to live in some nudist colony in South Africa."

Zach laughed at the thought. "Geez. Guess she's no porker anymore. Good for her." He helped himself to another serving of pasta. "Oh, and what about that doggie doctor you were hanging with last we spoke? Doctor DiMarco, right?"

"Funny, I don't recall ever telling you about Barry, or any of the guys I've dated." Megan shrugged. "And given your track record of forgetfulness with your exes, I'm truly impressed that you could memorize one name I've never even mentioned."

Zach's faced flushed of color. "Okay, so maybe you didn't. But it's not like I don't care. Wanna be sure my big sis is being looked after. And you know I'm not the only one."

Megan tossed her linen napkin on her plate. "But that's exactly what concerns me, Zach. Even when I don't talk to anyone, her spying minions are still keeping tabs. Do you enjoy being her primary surveillance, sent to gather pieces of intelligence?"

"Oh, c'mon, Meg. I'm only here to hang with you and the little guy. I swear, no one put me up to it. And if by *her*, you mean Mom, don't you think it's time you gave her another shot? She's really mellowed. If only you knew how much this whole misunderstanding's killing her."

"Misunderstanding?" Megan couldn't help but raise her voice. "All right. It was really sweet of you to stop by and bring Alex those toys. Now it's probably best if you go before I start to lose it."

Megan felt torn over asking Zach to leave so abruptly. The uncharacteristic friction between them was particularly upsetting, though the attempt at deception was hardly shocking.

To no-one's surprise, Tuesday's feud proved only a prelude of things to come. Wednesday brought with it a desperate, late-night phone call from a voice Megan had hopped to have heard the last of some six years earlier.

"Sweetheart, I've missed you terribly. How've you been?"

Megan bit down hard on a wad of gum, trying to remain cool. At first, she was cordially conversational. But following the initial thawing out and small-talk, Katherine Price's predictable guilt-trip turned the discussion predictably sour. "Haven't I suffered on the sidelines long enough? All these years, and not a single call, nothing. Forget birthdays; Mother's Day cards, you haven't even sent one photo of your little boy. I could run into my only grandson on the street and I wouldn't even know what he looks like."

Megan twirled the phone cord around her pinky. "Funny, I could swear I've already told you where we stand. Guess the only thing that six years changed is your tainted memory."

"But Megan, I haven't forgotten. You made your anger perfectly clear. But you never did explain it. At least I deserve a chance to defend myself."

"Mother, stop playing the innocent victim! Doing this only explains what I've known all along: you got too powerful at work, and somehow you equated it to having the same dominance over your own flesh and blood. Look how many lives you've ruined!"

There was silence on the other end. Megan paused to clear a lump in her throat. "Instead of being with the one I love, I spend my nights singing lullabies to a child from a monster I should've never married. I have an ex-husband who required psychological help more than he needed a wife to torture. My six-year-old boy still can't understand why he's the only first grader who's never met his father. And dare I mention that somewhere in the world sits a talented man who lost everything, all because... because why? You needed to enforce your will? It's like you couldn't accept me being with him, and you couldn't stand seeing him prosper on his own."

"But, sweetheart, I swear, I never did anything to knowingly hurt you. Trust me: it would never have worked with you and Johnny. You cling to this fantasy that he was your dream partner. But he had problems, far worse than even Gerry. Plus, his motivation; it was always wrong. He only wanted to be with you in times of need. If he loved you so dearly, where's he been all this time since his career took off?"

Megan spit out her chewing gum. "This game's been over for ages, so give it up and stop pretending you don't know anything! It was you who planted all those nasty rumors. And it was you who smiled for the cameras on the night when he didn't show up. Clearly you rigged it so he wouldn't be there. Johnny would've never been so irresponsible."

"But Megan, I didn't do any of it. You've got to trust me. Maybe it was Sheila. She always had it in for Johnny. And she was the one who arranged that event. Must've been something from her music business days; I don't really know. But she doesn't answer to me anymore. And let's not forget: Johnny had a drug problem. I'm sure you must've seen where he ended up on the night he was supposed to play for those kids."

"You know what the worst part of this is?" Megan asked, now calm once again. "If you were calling to confess what you did; to genuinely ask forgiveness, I might've actually said yes. But all you do is compound your lies with more deceit. Sheila McLennan was always your puppet, and she failed on her own because she wasn't as shifty or manipulative as you. But what gets me the most is how you insist that Johnny had some kind of addiction. How dare you resort to using my name for the sake of sending him to that slum? And how'd two photographers just happen to stumble into that exact place to take his picture that night? Go ahead: tell me it was all coincidence. You probably figured I never knew about your sly little phone call."

Katherine paused to re-strategize. She sat quietly on her end of the line, carefully measuring her next words. "Megan. Sweetie. You've always been the brightest light in my life. I've only wanted the best for you. Maybe I overstepped my territory at times. And in hindsight, perhaps I made a few mistakes. But what single mother is perfect in raising her child? I'm sure you've had your regrets with Alex. Parenting is trial and error, just like the rest of life. For the mistakes I've made, I hope you can see it in your heart to forgive me. This is really all I ask."

Again seething, Megan wasted little time in offering a double-barreled reply. "Mother, forgetting to read a bedtime story, that's forgivable. Running the bath too cold is an accident. Even burning supper because you got side-tracked, fine, it happens. But there comes a point when every parent needs to let their kid make their own mistakes. What you did… you abused your authority, killed my self-confidence, destroyed people's lives. Even if I could somehow forgive you, it isn't my forgiveness you need to seek first."

"But there are some things that no one can change. How do you expect me to go back in time and correct the impossible?" Katherine countered.

"Well then, guess you better pray hard for Johnny Elias to find his way back to stardom, in spite of everything you've done. Maybe then you can track him down again and start scripting your apology speech. But until that day arrives, I don't ever wanna hear your voice again. And don't you dare come knocking on my door, or calling here even one moment sooner."

Thursday morning, after dropping Alex at school, a frazzled Megan headed to work, where she continued to counsel battered women – a fine distraction from the previous night's fireworks.

At a quarter to five, she went grocery shopping before a routine evening at home: dinner, laundry and math homework, all before seven-thirty.

With Alex asleep, Megan flicked on a countertop radio in the kitchen and began preparing Alex's lunch for the next day – a peanut butter sandwich with a smear of marshmallow fluff. She wrapped it in foil and tossed it in his plastic superhero lunchbox.

That's when the telephone suddenly rang.

Normally, Megan wouldn't have thought twice about answering. The voice of a friend, or a prospective blind date was generally welcome on her previously "private line." But on the heels of her mother's verbal assault, she had no desire to spar another round on an empty tank. Instead, she leaned against the counter, listening to her outgoing message. A new voice spoke into her answering machine. She stood frozen in stunned silence.

"Megan, you are one difficult person to get hold of! Forever on the run, unlisted numbers, constantly screening your calls! If I didn't know better, I'd guess you were in hiding."

"Johnny," she gasped, pulling the receiver to her face. "I… I don't believe it. How've you been? And… where have you been?"

"Wow! You can't imagine how hard it's been trying to get hold of you. I've tried calling for ages, coming by. You're never there, never answering your line, not accepting mail. Don't know what possessed you to pick up tonight, but please tell me I'm getting you at a decent hour. Didn't want to wake the baby."

"Oh, I see." She laughed nervously. "It's as good a time as any. Though I guess it *has* been ages. That baby you're talking about is now a first-grader! Still just the two of us."

"Ah, right. So, how've you been?" he asked eagerly. "I don't suppose you've been up in Stamford, Connecticut anytime recently."

"I knew it! So you did leave the city! And all this time… I called every radio station, record company, music journalist looking for a number, an address, an email. Even pestered Andy Raymer's office, only he was never around, and his staff insisted they no longer represented you. Wasn't sure I'd ever hear your voice again. But… why tonight? What made you call me now? I'd hate to think someone put you up to it, but —"

"Put me up to it?" Johnny interrupted. "I was coming home from a concert a few months ago and I found a note you must've stuck in my pocket. I never noticed it till now. But then there it was, sitting folded in my shirt, six years too late."

A note, what note? Flashing back to their last time at her apartment, it suddenly all came back to her. "You only just found it? That's incredible… but maybe not too late. It's just that people from my past are popping up from out of the blue these past few days. I suppose its all coincidence, so excuse me for being on edge. But about that note, you must mean the rain-check I tucked in your pocket on the night you were here."

"I guess," Johnny said. "Though I have no memory of you putting it there."

"Yeah, I scribbled that in Alex's room; slipped it in your shirt as you were leaving for that TV show. I was hoping you'd find it a lot sooner. But

I do believe it says something about being open-ended. That means it's still valid, no matter when it was found."

Johnny pinned the receiver in the crook of his neck. "Well, I probably should start by saying how sorry I am… sorry for actually believing that you were capable of wrecking my life; my career. I just… you know, the first time you betrayed me was pretty shattering. But it was the second time around that… that sent me running for cover. Only the pieces never seemed to fit, and I've spent all these years wondering, tortured by the uncertainty."

"So instead of confronting me, you send a scathing letter, accusing me of collaborating with my wicked excuse for a mother. And then you disappear off the face of the earth." Her voice was angry. "You never even gave me a chance to explain that I could never have made that call! Not even with a gun to my head! She orchestrated it all, with her publicity puppets. I'll bet she disguised her voice on the line to sound like mine. And the rest of the story you know."

"No, I don't know," Johnny said. "I wasn't supposed to play the children's benefit that night. Someone told Andy the week before that it was pushed off by a day. So I was at home when the phone rang. You – or whoever it was – told me that you and the baby were being held by your ex. Caller ID came up unavailable. I wasn't thinking straight; just ran to the place you… er, she identified. Next thing I know, two thugs are in my face, snapping pictures and running away."

Megan laid a hand over her heart. "What a helpless feeling that must've been. But why didn't you try calling me at home once you found out I wasn't there?"

"Meg, I was so worried. Even my initial instinct was to keep on searching, only I didn't know where to turn next. I figured going back to my place would be another trap. So, instead, I ran to Andy's office. Seemed the least likely place they'd find me. And then I picked up the phone and dialed your number. Your old number."

"You did? Did the machine pick up? I know you didn't leave a message."

"No, it was you on the other end. You sounded safe. Thank goodness!

And Alex was babbling in the background. Knowing you were both okay, I just hung up. In hindsight, yeah, probably a terrible mistake. But I kept thinking that somehow you must've made the original call from home, or a pay phone. I couldn't believe you'd set me up, but there I was, disgraced for abandoning a room full of blind children, with riots breaking out and cops rushing in. And it seemed that you were the bait who lured me from my apartment."

"But I swear I'd never do anything so dreadful. John, there was only one time I ever knowingly deceived you. And I paid for it dearly. Truth is: you've always been the only one I've wanted to spend my life with. I just couldn't hurt you anymore back then. So I lied and got burned for it. But you already know how sorry I was. Even blamed my marital problems on the pain I caused you. Poetic justice at its most distorted."

Megan paused to sneeze, then grabbed a tissue for her runny nose. Quickly, she filled a glass of water and downed an antihistamine in one gulp. "Then it seemed like we were on course to make things right. After losing you once, we were so close to finding a way back. Why in hell would I deceive you again; destroy not only us, but your career too? You certainly didn't need that little note in your pocket to feel my sincerity."

"Megan, all along I wanted to believe that it wasn't you who made that call. Never made any sense. But I couldn't seem to get your panicked voice out of my head." Johnny flipped through a pile of old photos. Megan's youthful face smiled back at him. "You know, I probably could've salvaged my reputation back then if I truly wanted to. A paparazzo's camera I confiscated had more than just shots of me in that crack house on the role. There were time-stamped pictures of your mother at a Dinkins event that same morning. She was chatting behind the mayor with a news photographer – the one who later got my pictures, then got away. Hell, she even had the good sense to distract Andy with theater tickets that night. Sheila's handwriting was on the envelope. I could've fought back if anyone cared to listen."

"So why didn't you? With your celebrity, *lots* of people would've listened. You know that! A counter-offensive. You could've reclaimed some dignity; a degree of revenge."

"Megan, I simply lost the will to fight on. The damage to my career; that was only part of it. But your betrayal yet again, your involvement… without motivation for rediscovering what was most important in my life, I felt as though I'd… emotionally evaporated."

Megan listened intently, trying to contain her emotions. Johnny had confirmed everything she'd hoped he had felt for her – in the past. But she still needed to find out why he had called. "You know, that letter you wrote me back then, cut me like a switchblade to my heart. But I want you to know: I used it as a springboard to reclaim my life. I always suspected my mother was involved; just never knew to what degree. John, that note some-how gave me the confidence, the courage I never had till then to finally take control; to banish her from my life."

"That's… that's so amazing, Meg. You did that because of me? I had no idea… no way of knowing."

"Johnny, till she called me just last night, I hadn't even heard her voice since '93."

"Six years. That's a long time… for all of us! Hey, I'm proud of you, ya know. Thought you'd never stand up to her. Couldn't have been easy, given that you have Alex."

"Yeah, her only grandchild!" Megan added empathically. "But some-one so calculating deserves no vicarious joy through me or my child. So I had to cut her off; bought a little place on Long Island a few years back. A place to run for cover anytime I suspected that she was about to hound me again. That's probably where I was when you were calling me, stopping by. In fact, the only reason I didn't sell this place and disappear altogether was the remote chance that you might someday come looking for me. In the back of my mind, I always clung to the hope that you and I would someday – I don't know – fit the pieces of our lives back together. Like the way we nearly managed to do it before it all came crashing down."

"Meg, what can I say? I mean, wow! I'm speechless. But I do hope you haven't placed your life on hold all this time because of me."

"Why'd you say that?" Megan asked, her stomach tightening. "Is it 'coz you've managed to move on? I suppose the news of you finding someone else would be bittersweet, but…"

There was a pause. "Listen, I can't say I haven't tried. But, you know, with this double-edged sword of stardom, I've always attracted people for all the wrong reasons. No one has ever… well, you know better than anyone that I could never settle for anything less than real. Less than what you and I had so long ago."

Megan rubbed her glistening eyes. "Johnny, it's been exactly the same for me. I've always tried too hard to convince myself that other guys were right for me. But I could never come to terms with who they weren't. And without closure, I kept thinking all those what-ifs, you know? I could never get too close to anyone because I just wanted you to walk back into my life."

Johnny digested her words carefully. Megan was still very much his… still waiting for him. And she had finally shed the one sinister obstacle that had twice stood between them. A sharp temptation began to grab hold. It was time to run and see her; to reclaim all these lost years of happiness… But then came the muffled music through the floorboards – the sound of his bandmates rehearsing in the basement. It was a subtle reminder of the other matter that was driving his life: a grandiose plan that required his every ounce of focus and energy. It could hardly be abandoned now.

Johnny took hold of the page in front of him, with the lyrics to the song *Hallucinations*. After clearing a lump in his throat, he recited each stanza, the words spilling out breathlessly. Megan was stunned. "Did you write that one for me?" she guessed, her voice quavering. "And does it have a melody?"

"It does," he answered, nervously folding the sheet of paper. "Megan Price: I've been haunted by your absence for six empty years. How ironic that my memories of the person who most inspired me through desolation has been the one thing that's kept me going." Johnny swallowed hard. "I wrote that one on the night when I discovered your note in my pocket. It's one of several I've recently recorded. I hope they'll re-ignite what I left behind, only this time on my own terms."

"That's fantastic; the best news of all!" Megan cried out, before remembering her surroundings. In a softer voice she added, "Half my pain during these years was the guilt I felt for costing you the chance to make music again. All selfish reasoning aside, I'd always kept a radio on, hoping someday I'd hear a new song with your voice. Just knowing you hadn't given up would've been a consolation. Please, will you sing that song you just read? I think it's the first you've written about me that didn't say goodbye!"

"I will. But not over the phone. That song, it portrays me as vulnerable. Don't want you to have that image of me, hearing it in this context. It's really more an affirmation of the feelings I could never let go of. Meg, you need to hear it properly to get the full impact."

"If not now, when?" Megan urged. "When can I finally hold you again... maybe finally run away somewhere like we once talked about? Please don't tell me it'll be *soon*, like last time. We both know how that turned out."

Johnny laughed. "I was gonna say that again. And honestly, I really meant it when I said it before." He paused at the sound of a crashing drum solo from below. "Meg, this time you really have my word. Hey, I'd drop everything, meet you tonight, if only I could. But please do trust me when I tell you there's something else – something enormous – I need to deal with first. Trust me. In a week it'll be over. I promise to see you then."

37

Precarious Implementation

At precisely eleven o'clock on the night of May 26th, a large red-and-white truck pulled out of the driveway at the Connecticut home of Johnny Elias. At the exact same moment, seven identical red-and-white trucks departed from various locations around the tri-state area, riding in synchronization toward Manhattan.

Johnny gazed apprehensively through the windshield, trying in vain to think of anything other than his fragile plan. He only occasionally glanced down at his clipboard to tick off a checklist item, or make a brief note. Soon they neared the southern tip of Connecticut. Johnny turned to the driver, breaking a prolonged silence. "You suppose we might make it there by a quarter past twelve? Every minute counts before sunrise."

"This is top speed," the driver responded, pinching his nose to stifle a sneeze. "Cargo back there's pretty damn heavy. Your four movers, a piano, all your gear: it's five times the weight of a coat delivery. Plus, this pollen count is killing me."

Two strenuous months of costly planning, rehearsing and wishing for the twenty-nine year-old musician had boiled down to a precious few hours. With the colossal assistance of Larry Jacobs, Johnny managed to obtain everything he needed, in a most unusual arrangement.

Unlike the massive stage used by Paul Simon in 1991, Larry rented one just a third of the size, based on the truck dimensions and assembly time. Even the audio system, while adequate for a large street fair, was only forty percent of what was required for this kind of production. But to Johnny, the concern wasn't how spectacular the show would sound. What mattered most was making it onto that stage, getting his opportunity to win back all that he had lost.

So many obstacles lay ahead. So much that could conceivably go wrong. Plus, Johnny now had further long-term concerns, making the success of this concert all the more vital. As Andy had pointed out weeks earlier, a once-hefty bank account was beginning to dwindle. He had blown a bundle on the home recording sessions; his charitable contributions; this enormously expensive undertaking. He'd even sprung for new instruments, responding to the band's concerns that theirs might be confiscated if the stage were seized. A new revenue source was desperately needed.

Johnny banked on this show to launch him to a new level of notoriety, if not popularity. This bootlegged concert would certainly create a spike in sales of the *Poet* album. At the very least, he hoped it would hold him over until a new recording deal could be secured.

With only the sounds of the radio to keep him calm, Johnny tried counting the red taillights of cars alongside the truck. A local weather forecast soon came on. He turned to the driver and broke another awkward silence. "Mind if I turn this up?"

"Your dime, your dance floor," the driver answered.

Johnny reached for the volume dial and adjusted it just in time to hear the recap.

Tonight: partly cloudy. Temperatures around seventy. Tomorrow, another beautiful spring day. Clear and sunny with a high of eighty-four. Tomorrow night: clear and warm with a low of seventy. No sign of precipitation throughout the Memorial Day weekend...

"At least Mother Nature's cooperating," Johnny mumbled optimistically. "Now let's see if everyone else is as accommodating."

Eight trucks reached Manhattan before midnight. Each lined up against the curb on Central Park West, near the pedestrian entrance at 86th Street. One by one the drivers got out. They huddled around a green park bench, where they were met by a solitary figure in a gray hooded sweatshirt.

"We enter one block down at 85th," Larry Jacobs reconfirmed, pointing to a detailed map of the Park. "When you've gone two blocks south, jump the curb and hang a left on the grass. It'll be bumpy; lots of trees. The park precinct is just north of us at 86th, so eyes open. Once off the road, it's just straight ahead. Headlights dark when you see the baseball diamonds. I have a crew of twenty in bright yellow shirts waiting to receive us. From there it's unload and go. No time for standing around."

Larry jumped into a waiting '76 Dodge Dart. The orange clunker sped away with surprising pickup. Each driver then climbed back behind the wheel of his vehicle. The eight men waited anxiously for their signal to restart and make the left-hand turn inside the park.

In itself, the sight of eight matching trucks, parked in a row at this late hour, had to appear peculiar – if not suspicious – to a casual onlooker. However, *The Coat Coalition* had become something of a fixture in aiding the city's homeless. Not even the most curious pair of civilian eyes offered a second glance.

Nonetheless, this parade of coat-distribution vehicles - on a day boasting a high temperature of 83 degrees - failed to elude the attention of Officer Michael Patrick from the nearby 20th Precinct. "Good evening," the patrolman said pleasantly, approaching the passenger window of the lead truck.

Stay calm, Johnny reminded himself, steadying a pair of trembling knees. "Good evening, sir," he answered back evenly. "How can I help you?"

"Couldn't help noticing your trucks out in full force tonight. Very admirable. Then again, it's almost June. What're you winter guys up to?"

"Well, Officer," Johnny improvised. "Early summer, that's the best time to collect old, bulky winter jackets, taking up precious closet space. There was a huge coat drive uptown. We're just heading to drop off the collection in our Brooklyn warehouse."

Officer Patrick shrugged. "Ah, makes sense, I guess. Mind if I have a peek around back?"

Johnny glanced at his watch. "You're welcome to sift through the old coats if you like. But my drivers are on overtime, and we're non-profit."

Officer Patrick's gaze lingered on Johnny's face as though he had recognized him from a past encounter. Unable to make a positive identification, he shrugged once more. "You guys do a bang-up job for the needy around here. Good luck with your collection."

Johnny exhaled.

Once the squad car drove off, the eight trucks were on the move. At a central location chosen for set-up, the hired staff quickly unpacked the cargo. Not another soul appeared within shouting distance. Sections of the wooden stage, audio towers and a covered soundboard began to take shape. The twenty-man crew used only the light of the moon and portable flashlights to erect the performance space.

Johnny posed as one of Larry's supervisors. Paraphernalia from WNYR's promotional closet had come in handy. He split his time keeping lookout and assisting with the physical labor through the wee hours. So many details remained unsettled. No time for much needed sleep.

Distant sirens, chirping crickets and echoes of faraway firecrackers provided the soundtrack of a tension-filled night. The closest call occurred when a trio of sanitation workers dragged a collection of trash bags along a nearby jogging path. Johnny held his breath. The work crew carried on as if they belonged. They were not disturbed.

Just after four o'clock, one of the red-and-white trucks unexpectedly returned to the area. A driver emerged from the cab and walked over to Johnny. "Hey buddy, last delivery! Get your guys over here."

"And what materials would those be?" Johnny asked, scanning the top page on his clipboard. "I thought everything we needed was already here."

"Check it out. Mr. J sent me back with some barricades. You know, for security. We kinda borrowed 'em from a construction site downtown."

"Borrowed?" Johnny flashed a puzzled look.

"Yeah, with the holiday weekend, he said no one would notice 'em gone till Tuesday."

Whoa! Johnny thought uneasily. *Larry's far more invested than he ever planned to be. Only my neck was supposed to be on the line.*

Morning's first light began to seep through the darkness. Johnny inspected the stage assembly. Four black speakers and a dark backdrop towered above the wooden platform, which stood approximately ten feet off the grass. *Not bad,* he thought looking out into the distance. *Good enough for what we've got planned.*

To his weary contentment, his cherished baby grand was soon raised by several workers and placed on the right hand side. It was 4:45am - time for Johnny to let his back-up team take over. He quickly made the rounds, wishing everyone good luck with a warm handshake and a crisp hundred-dollar bill.

Johnny soldiered toward the park exit at 85th Street on fumes of adrenaline. Along the way, he neared a pair of early morning joggers, who suddenly slowed to gaze at the activities on the lawn. Johnny unhurried his own pace to eavesdrop.

"That's odd," remarked a fortyish, red-bearded man, outfitted in a powder-blue tracksuit. "Did ya know there was a free concert tonight? I never miss the Philharmonic."

"Yeah, kinda strange," his much-younger female companion noted, out of breath. "Nothing was announced. Guess we'll just have to show up later, check it out."

Johnny smiled impulsively. *It's only a matter of time. Like the rest of this city, they'll all know our little secret soon enough.*

The streetlights on Central Park West lost their effectiveness at dawn. Through a sleep-deprived haze, Johnny searched for a dark green minivan along the sidewalk. After minutes of confusion, he heard Howard Greffen's voice from a rolled-down window between two parked cars. "Hop in, boss. Right on time."

Johnny climbed onto the second row seat. Marlene Harris reached back from the driver's seat for Johnny's clipboard, transitioning the reins of supervision. "So, has it all gone according to plan?"

"So far," Johnny smiled languidly, his voice growing weaker with each syllable. "No one seemed to recognize me. And the stage; much bigger than I thought. Too bad we don't get to play a soundcheck to test the audio capacity."

"Excellent," Marlene nodded confidently. "But your volume isn't sounding too terrific. Time for me to be your eyes and ears. Go rest that voice of yours." Marlene patted Johnny's knee, then spun around and kissed Howard on the cheek. "You too." She opened her door and took a step toward the park. Then turning back, she tapped on the windshield. "Howie, make sure he stays quiet; takes plenty of hot liquids. Unless he's in top form tonight, everything else'll be for naught."

Howard kept vigil in front of the television in an East Side hotel room. Johnny dozed briefly on the couch. His tranquility was not to last long.

In addition to blaring the local all-news channel, a fidgety Howard tuned into three different radio broadcasts. It took about ninety minutes and four cups of espresso, but at 7:40, the first mention of activity on the Great Lawn hit the airwaves.

"They just showed it!" Howard shouted, shaking Johnny from a short-lived slumber. "People are gathering. Might be a couple hundred in the overhead shot."

Johnny leaped to his feet and squinted at the flickering screen. The local CBS affiliate had dispatched a reporter to the scene. Excitedly, Johnny reached for the phone. "Larry! Looks like the cat's outta the bag! It's not even eight, the stage is still standing and we're already drawing a crowd!"

"Can't say I'm surprised," Larry Jacobs sighed. "I was over there incognito about an hour ago. It all looks quite professional. The crew did a miraculous job, getting that up in the dark."

"So what d'ya suppose the odds are that curiosity seekers will keep on coming?"

"Tell you what, Johnny. Have you got a radio where you are?"

Johnny glanced around the room, deciphering the sources of competing noise. "Yeah, we've got a few going. Why, what're you planning?"

"Just tune in to my station in about ten minutes. Now that our stage is public knowledge, there's no reason we can't fuel this fire with a little combustible speculation!"

Ramblin' Rob Martino had been the WNYR morning voice for fourteen years; a friendly alternative to shock jocks and AM gabfests. Now he began feeding public inquisitiveness in classic style.

It's ten past eight, on this Thursday morning in New York City and we've just been handed an interesting bulletin. It seems that overnight, a stage has been set up on the Great Lawn in Central Park. While we have nothing yet confirmed, rumors are swirling. One listener on the scene called in to say he heard it might be the Stones. A series of emails we've received suggest it could be anyone from The Grateful Dead to REM, or even a surviving Beatles reunion. Our staff is working the phones at this early hour. But as of now, what we do know is this: While New York slept last night, someone built a massive stage in the middle of Central Park apparently for a major free concert! We'll be bringing you the details as they're available to us!

"Andy, he's really doing it! It's on the news everywhere. Come see this!"

It was 8:20. Andy Raymer was finishing breakfast when Jacqui summoned him to their bedroom. Andy stood transfixed by the TV as live cameras captured the growing crowd near the makeshift platform.

"Don't know how he did it, but somehow he really got a stage in there." Jacqui smiled in awe. "Just how far along did you say you were in securing the permits he needs to pull this off?"

Andy shook his head. "Jacqui, I hate to say this, but Johnny's on his own with this stunt."

"So you're just going to stand idly by while he sticks his neck out tonight? Forget that you're his manager. You're his best friend. For ages you've wanted this… for him to pick up where he left off. Now he's attempting even more than you ever bargained for, on the grandest stage of all, and you plan to simply abandon him?"

"Look, it's like I've told you before. If I applied for permits under Johnny's name, there'd probably be a warrant out for his arrest by now! About the only thing I can do is round up the multitudes to see him play, then keep my fingers crossed. Otherwise, I'm powerless."

"But aren't these events profitable for the city?" Jacqui pressed on. "All those subway fares; concession sales near the park! I'll bet there must be some way we can appease the power's-that-be, now that it's come this far."

"Jacqui, the city only loves events where someone picks up the tab. We're talking upwards of four million dollars." Andy laughed. "Johnny actually mentioned that he'd foot the bill, but his pockets ain't that deep anymore. If he'd signed a new record deal —"

Jacqui posed with hands on her hips. "So get one done for him today. Put that money back in his pocket. Once a contract is signed, negotiate with the city. Offer to cover any expenses. If Johnny's really going through with this, he'll surely sign on as the logical next step. Your attitude should be more about whatever it takes, rather than whatever happens, happens."

By 9:15, three NYPD units were dispatched to the Great Lawn. Predictable disarray followed. With no one to arrest at a peaceful gathering, they simply stood by waiting for further instruction.

Meanwhile, city officials scrambled to determine if they'd mistakenly overlooked a planned event. At that hour, City Parks Commissioner Henry Stern – the man most responsible for managing these public events – was on a morning flight from JFK to the Bahamas, completely inaccessible. Many other administrators had already skipped town for the holiday weekend. Department bureaucrats frantically searched through a heap of date-books and permit applications, while the Police Commissioner awaited word on how to handle the steadily building crowd.

Word broadened throughout the city on this warm spring day. Hundreds of inquiring music fans entered the park, looking to secure the best vantage point for whatever lay ahead. Radios blared. Beach blankets were spread everywhere. Sunshine and camaraderie. The scene was beginning to resemble similar events held on this hallowed ground in years gone by. It almost didn't matter who would later be performing on that empty stage. If anything, the uncertainty only made for heightened anticipation. At least 15,000 revelers had gathered by 1pm. Countless others deliberated in offices around Manhattan if they too should soon join in. Lunchtime crowds seemed to swell, then lightly dissipate, due to the uncertain starting time for this unannounced performance. But by 3:30, while many got a jumpstart on the long weekend, thousands of the city's workforce made their way to the scene, wondering if this excitement would live up to mounting hype.

Johnny paced nervously in his hotel room, checking TV reports and communicating with his support team and bandmates. He was tickled by the wide-ranging rumors, particularly one erroneous report.

"Howard, MTV is saying that KISS is the only band brash enough to pull off this kind of stunt. Wonder if it's not too late to pick up some wild makeup, ya know, just in case." He laughed.

"Johnny, if you need to resort to trickery to win this crowd over, we're all screwed," Howard said. "You were always about the music, not gimmicks and pyrotechnics. That's the beauty of tonight. Your songs speak the language of the masses. When they recognize you up there and see that nothing's changed, they'll be delirious!"

Howard took a breath, then reached for his ringing mobile phone. "Hey, babe."

"Howie, it's getting wild out here," Marlene shouted. "Don't know if it's the warm weather, or all those crazy rumors. We've got everyone from Deadheads to those Jimmy Buffett fans in Hawaiian shirts."

"When you say wild, do you mean out of control?" Howard asked.

"No, no, everyone's on their best behavior. I mean it's a wild scene with all these people filing in. It's orderly, but things are getting exciting."

"And how 'bout the stage itself? How's our gear holding up?"

"So far, our security guys are holding their turf, although the cops have been pestering. I haven't been able to get close enough to hear their chatter since noontime, but I suspect it's more of the third degree like before. Who hired you? Where's your permit; that sorta thing."

From his East Side office, Andy and his staff continued to work the phones. Earlier in the day, with Johnny's best interests at heart, but without his authorization, Andy agreed in principle to a new recording contract with Marauder Records. The deal, which called for four new albums over nine years, would pay Johnny a twelve-million dollar advance.

Though the pact with Marauder had been on the table for months, Andy previously held off at Johnny's wishes, even costing him a few extra dollars in the process. And in truth, there had been more lucrative earlier offers. What Andy liked best about Marauder was their ability to market younger musicians and sustain their long-term popularity. In his heart, he knew it was a deal Johnny could feel good about… providing he had the opportunity to fulfill it.

Now prepared to negotiate from an enhanced position, he began calling the NYC Parks Commission, hoping it wasn't too late for a round of desperate negotiations.

Jacqui, meanwhile, worked the phones and the online chat rooms: anything within her capacity to recruit attendees for the "anonymous" performance that evening.

Frank Traber awoke in his Brooklyn bedroom just after 1:30. The lead guitarist switched on his television, then dialed Ian Klatt. "Hey, big guy, I suppose our services may be needed tonight, after all. That's your spankin' new drum kit I'm seeing onstage from overhead."

"Dude, you're just waking up to this?" Ian asked. "I could hardly sleep last night, not knowing what the hell was gonna happen. Since early this morning I've been glued to my set."

Frank yawned. "Well, to each his own, I suppose. So tell me: you spoken to Johnny yet? We still on for five? Regency lobby?"

"Uh, yeah, he sounds confident. Gary and Howard too. Everything's going our way. Just getting real nervous thinking about it, man. I don't know if it's 'cuz it's the biggest gig of our lives, or that we might not get to play it!"

"Well, no use getting all jittery over uncertainties," Frank noted, sounding carefree. "Even rehearsing these past few months, I never thought it'd get this far. But as long as we've still got a show to play..."

All day long, WNYR continued feeding the frenzy, with regular updates and a bevy of vague rumors. When a highly caffeinated Larry Jacobs took the airwaves at three o'clock, he immediately elevated matters to the next level of promotion.

Good afternoon, New York! On this glorious start to the big holiday weekend, it's looking like history in the making tonight in Central Park! Since early this morning, our station's been scrambling - along with the rest of the city - to determine just who'll be rocking the Great Lawn. We've all heard the rumors. And, I can assure you all that you don't want to miss what'll be going down! Everyone within the range of our signal: get on over to the park. And bring along your radios! WNYR will look to bring you a live simulcast. You've got picture-perfect weather, and what promises to be an unforgettable free con-cert. So make sure you don't miss the event everyone'll be talking about all summer long!

Within seconds of the opening notes to Steve Miller's *Fly Like An Eagle*, the switchboards at WNYR lit up like Rockefeller Center during holiday season. Most of callers sought to get a further scoop on the evening's festivi-ties. One in particular owned a more than curious interest.

"Mr. Jacobs, Detective Len Farcourt, NYPD. Just heard you touting tonight's unauthorized event in Central Park. Could you tell me just what involvement, if any, your station has in this stunt?"

Larry's grinning face turned instantly serious. "Ah, Detective, thanks for calling. To be perfectly honest, we here probably know a lot less than you do at this point."

"Really? Coulda fooled me with that rant of yours," the officer countered.

"Hey, man, this is exciting stuff. Our phones, we've been inundated all afternoon. Long as people are buzzing about it, and given that no one's called it off, I see no reason why we shouldn't have fun with it! Do you?"

Just feet from the metal barricade, Marlene Harris kept a watchful eye on the unfolding situation. An increased police presence around the stage became a growing concern. When she tried to get a closer view of the rear entry path, she was nudged back by a uniformed officer.

"Pardon me, ma'am. No one's allowed past this point."

"No problem." Marlene retreated innocently to her original position. "By the way, can you tell me what time the show's supposed to start?"

"Lady, hate to disappoint you, but this wasn't supposed to be here. Someone's probably gonna be arrested. Better you be going home before things turn ugly."

Once the patrolman was beyond an earshot, Marlene pulled her cell-phone from her belt clip. "Howard, the cops by the front barricades, they're not letting anyone near this stage. Looks pretty well surrounded from my vantage point."

"Hey, don't worry," Howard reassured her. "A plan's been thought up for everything. Long as they aren't confiscating our gear, we can still make this happen."

"Well, they haven't exactly pulled out bullhorns and told people to leave, but I sure hope your plan is foolproof! Tell me you're not planning to skydive."

Howard laughed, then turned to Johnny, who was glued to channel 2 news. "So what's the latest?"

"Well, the mayor's spokeswoman just announced that tonight's park event is *officially unauthorized*. She's spouting some rhetoric about the city's regrets over not being informed in advance, given their successful track record of shows they've hosted in the past, etcetera."

Howard's eyes lit up. "But they haven't told anyone to leave either. They're probably tryin' to keep a very large crowd from getting out of hand... or they aren't dead set against a peaceful performance, once they see who turns up. In my mind, nothing's changed."

"Same here," Johnny concurred. "Though I'd better check with Larry to make sure those vans and our sound engineers are good to go. Otherwise, we're toast."

At Raymer Music Management, Andy kept one eye on the news, while frantically phoning city agencies for an improbable, last-minute compromise. He spent most of his day trying to get anyone on the phone who would take him seriously.

Andy feared that a call to the disarrayed NYPD might only ensure Johnny's arrest – not to mention his own as a potential conspirator. Instead, he and his staff sat brainstorming on how to open the lines of dialog with the City of New York. He believed he exhausted all avenues, when a televised announcement from Mayor Giuliani's office provided one last, desperate idea.

If the mayor's so dead set against this stunt, why haven't we heard from the man himself?

Andy ran to hail a cab outside his office. From the curb, he turned back to Risa Sheppard, who had followed. "I'm off to City Hall to catch 'em before the close of business. If I'm not back by eight, just let Jacqui know where I went, before calling our lawyers. Could be a long night."

Five o'clock approached. Johnny received a familiar tap on the shoulder. "Kid, we've got fifteen minutes. Put down the herbal tea and go get dressed. Don't wanna keep the guys waiting."

Johnny reached for the hanger with his black linen jacket and ducked into the bathroom. *One last quiet moment before the brewing storm.* Calmly, he combed his hair in the mirror and took a final gander at his reflection. He drew a long, deep breath and held it. *Please give me the strength to sing, and the good fortune to pull this off.* He stared intently for a while. Then he closed his eyes and slowly exhaled.

On a crammed elevator, Johnny tried to avoid eye contact with a group of giggling bridesmaids in matching gowns and a curious groomsman, who seemed to stare excessively during the descending ride. When the double doors separated, the stranger straightened his bowtie and approached. "Hey, I'll bet you get this a lot, but don't I know you from somewhere?"

Johnny looked up and shrugged his shoulders.

"You're the guy who once had that huge record! Jimmy something, right?"

"Johnny Elias," he corrected, walking toward the hotel bar.

"That's right." The other man nodded. "You used to write some pretty cool stuff. If you don't mind my asking, whatever happened to you?"

Johnny tried to restrain his laughter. "Funny how often I've wondered the same thing. One day you're topping the charts; the next you're vilified.

Stardom's hardly an exact science." He accepted a pen on the move and scribbled his name on a cocktail napkin. "Hey, if you really wanna know what's become of me, you may wanna turn on the news tonight sometime after eleven. Just can't tell you how its all gonna turn out!"

As he reached the smoky bar area, Howard spotted Frank and Gary out of the corner of his eye. "So gentlemen, you ready for this?"

"I've got ice-water pumping through my veins," Frank announced, puling up a seat at the corner table. "The bigger, the better. Just bring it on!"

Howard smiled. "And how 'bout you, young master Gary? What a way to break into the concert business, eh? No butterflies, I hope?"

"Well, maybe one or two. But once we're onstage, I'll switch on my autopilot mode. Won't matter if we're playing to a hundred or a hundred thousand."

Johnny calmly pulled up a chair beside Howard and sat down unassumingly. He did his best to hide his jitters.

"Looking sharp, Johnny!" Frank raised a glass of club soda in his direction. "You're just a few pinstripes short of the perfect mug shot."

Johnny chuckled. "I haven't been photographed professionally in ages. Maybe I'll have 'em frame an eight by ten for you." Then detecting one notable absentee, he stared nervously. "Where's Ian? Wasn't he coming with you, Frank?"

"He did," Frank insisted. "A bit on edge right now; puking his guts up in the men's room. Otherwise, he should be fine."

A few tense moments passed before the drummer emerged from the washroom, flushed but otherwise presentable.

"So, did it come out all psychedelic?" Frank teased, lighting up a cigarette.

Ian took a bow, then gave Frank the finger. Johnny passed around laminated set lists and one last contingency. "Tuck 'em in your pockets. You can chuck 'em later when the show's done."

"What's this?" Gary gasped, staring at a linen business card.

"My lawyer's contact info," Johnny explained, his tone solemn. "I don't expect you'll need it, but Mr. Anson has been briefed on our little plan."

"So, like, if we get in trouble, we just give him a call?" Gary wiped the sweat off his forehead. "Where will he be during the show?"

"He and his associates will be sitting just a few feet from the stage, swaying to the music with the rest of the city." Johnny smiled. "And with any luck, without interruption."

38

To The Scene Of The Crime

Katherine Price sat typing a last-minute proposal in her office on lower Broadway. She hoped to have it completed before heading out to East Hampton for the four-day kick-off to summer.

An outline and the first three sections flickered on her screen. Katherine took a short break in the executive lounge for a can of chilled tomato juice. It was there she caught word of the unfolding events in the park. She raised the radio volume and suddenly broke into a smile.

Clever! she thought, her grin growing wider. *Talk about the perfect guerilla-marketing stunt… providing our mystery band can pull it off.*

Katherine kept one eye on the television in the corner of her cluttered office. No longer able to concentrate on the client presentation, she finally allowed her inquisitiveness to take hold. She popped out a computer disc and tucked it in a compartment of her soft leather case. "Now this, I've got to see first hand," she muttered, heading off to the elevator.

I'd like to thank you all for tuning in to another afternoon of great rock and roll! Those of you heading out to Central Park, remember: take your radios.

And let's be on our best behavior. Have an unforgettable time tonight! And please join me again tomorrow at three. I'll leave you with one from the Clash. Here's: Should I Stay Or Should I Go?

Larry Jacobs signed off at 6:30. He placed his headphones on the console and waited for the red light to go off. Stepping into the control room, he took the phone from his producer, Erin Monahan, and touched base with his crew in the park. "So what's doing out there?" Larry asked his late-night host, Rich Stevens. "Looks on the monitor like the place is jammed."

"It's incredible, Larry!" Rich shouted over an unmistakably excited crowd. "I've no idea what the estimate is, but we're talkin' tens of thousands. And everyone's partying kinda orderly. Fans, media, everyone."

"And what's going on around the stage? Cops still buzzing?"

"The men in blue have been really cool so far. There's still about a hundred in riot gear up front. But they haven't asked anyone to leave. From the looks of it, I think they just might let the show go on. Just wish you'd tell me already who'll be playing here tonight!"

Larry ignored the last remark. "It all sounds promising. But I can hardly hear you over that noise. I'm on my way over now with the simulcast equipment. Call Erin or me on the mobile if you need us. And remember your cue just in case."

Larry soon arrived at the lobby of the swanky East Side Regency, just blocks from the park. He immediately spotted Johnny at the bar and tiptoed up to him from behind. "Gotcha!" he whispered.

"Larry! Sonofabitch! Want me to have a coronary before we even get started?" Seeing the others doubled over, Johnny quickly broke into a smile. Then to Larry he whispered, "You sure did one helluva hype-job. I just hope they don't expect the blessed Beatles up there. You must have half this city believing they'll be seeing the second coming tonight."

"Indeed they will," Larry said, straight-faced. "And what a rush it'll be for them to watch their hero return to action on his home turf. Gives me goosebumps just thinking about it."

"I'm flattered," Johnny replied, trying not to get too caught up in the excitement. "But what about those barricades you *borrowed* last night? Just how deep into this are you? Not that I don't appreciate everything you've done."

"Let's not be naïve." Larry raised his eyebrows. "Long as we're waist-deep in felonious behavior, what're a few extra railings to keep the stage clear of fans? Besides, the hole in the ground they were guarding… even a blind man wouldn't miss it."

Johnny rolled his eyes in disbelief. He could think of no response. But then recalling one last critical element, he felt obliged to ask about the sound engineers and lighting team. "Without 'em, we're just a few dark, unplugged figures."

"Relax Johnny, I've got it all covered. The lighting is primitive in terms of effects. But it'll be plenty bright. And the soundboard: already plugged into the generators behind the backdrop. Should deliver enough juice till we get a secondary truck in the park."

"So how long do we have till the power goes off?" Johnny asked.

"The supply you have should last about an hour. And then we only need a few minutes to get plugged into the back-up unit, before they're ready for you again. Trust me, man, we got everything covered."

Andy heard the constant police sirens all the way up Madison Avenue. Over on Fifth, countless people were rushing toward the park's narrow entrance-ways. From the taxi's backseat, he quickly dialed Jacqui's mobile.

"Andy, where are you?" she gasped, stepping away from her large group of assembled friends, not far from the stage.

"I'm coming up from City Hall. Just got through with the mayor's people."

Jacqui struggled to hear Andy over the crowd. She raised the volume on her phone. "So tell me: when's showtime?"

"Actually, I think I'll start with the positive, since that's what you're waiting for." He took a deep breath. "So this meeting; talk about intimidating! I think I managed to get them to let the concert go on in exchange for a whopping fee, plus an assortment of penalties for cleanup and resodding the grass, etc. Only without Johnny being here, I had to personally lay out a huge chunk of change, which probably accounts for... oh, the net worth of our business."

"That's terrifyingly terrific." Jacqui pumped one fist in the air. "I know he'll repay you in a heartbeat, once he steps offstage."

"But that's not the full story," Andy said, as the taxi stopped for another red light. "We're not totally in the clear. Unfortunately, there's about fifteen hundred cops in the park right now. No aisles. No pathways. It's chaos in there! No one's been told yet that the show is on. Unless someone pushes through the crowds with the new orders, Johnny's never gonna get past them."

"But it's only half past seven! He told me he doesn't plan to start until after eight. By then, all the police should be aware of the situation."

"Let's hope so," Andy stated wishfully. "And no matter what, not a word of this should ever be told to him. If he pulls it off, I want him believing that he did it all on his own. Truth be told, even with my last-minute agreement, he needs a small miracle to fight through those crowds and the wall of cops."

Frank, Ian and Howard clustered around an overhead TV screen in the hotel's bar. A local news broadcast switched from coverage of the new *Star Wars* prequel to the breaking story in Central Park. With the sound barely audible, the only detail anyone could pick up on was the crowd's enormity and a mounting police presence.

Outside the hotel, Larry Jacobs led Johnny and Gary into a waiting blue cargo van. His assistant, Erin, escorted the others to an identical vehicle directly behind it. A third van, containing the supplementary power source and two sound engineers, waited behind, while a fourth emerged from a double-parked position and sped to the front.

They sat for several minutes. Larry barked out instructions to his team throughout the park. Johnny stared intently through a tinted-window. Countless people were hurrying into the park at East 65th Street. He could only wonder if Megan Price might be among them. *Megan...*

A golden springtime sun continued to shine over Manhattan. Johnny dwelled upon his decision to conceal his plans from her. Two police cycles roared by. Again, he recalled his excitement to see her when this was all over, and his unwillingness to burden her with his uncertain plight.

An abrupt tap on the shoulder brought him back to the present tense. "Johnny: a crazy thought. We gonna have a roadie up there with us? You know, in case someone pops a string?"

"Yeah, we're covered, Gary," Johnny answered, slightly startled. "This guy Neil Gordon; he and his son Geoff, are in the van with the sound guys. Old pros."

Seconds later, it was eight o'clock. Using a mobile phone rather than a walkie-talkie, to avoid a signal interception, Larry alerted the other drivers to "stand by for departure." The sound of helicopters whirled overhead.

At 8:03, Johnny spotted the lead van speed off en route to the West Side. Larry got word from one of his staffers. "Move out now!" he barked at his driver.

On Fifth Avenue, Johnny watched the van take a sharp right at 59th Street, where it became Central Park South. The Plaza Hotel flew by on his left. "Now hang another right," he heard Larry shout. They swerved onto a narrow road usually reserved for horse drawn carriages.

Four sleek blue vans zipped through the East Sixties along a winding path. Wollman Rink came and went on the right. To the left, the old Carousel and the elegant Tavern on the Green appeared in a blur. Normally, a ride to be taken in a slow gallop, this uptown jaunt left no time for sightseeing.

Each van slowed to a crawl near 79th Street. Larry took the next call on one ring. A string of profanities fell from his lips. He spun back in Johnny's direction, minus the steely determination he'd exhibited to this point. "Um, okay, boys, this is where we get off. Who's up to doing a bit of running?"

"Just a second." Johnny held up a hand like a crossing guard. "I thought we were driving right to the back of the stage, and jumping those four-foot barriers. What's with the running?"

"Johnny, you knew this plan had its share of holes. So now we've encountered our first serious crater. The lead truck just got stopped by the cops. Fortunately, that's our decoy van. So, anyway, they made him turn around. In about ten seconds, they should be heading our way."

Johnny grimaced as the lead blue van drove into view, just as Larry predicted. "So, if this first attempt is a failure, tell me again what Plan B is?"

Sensing uneasiness, Larry tried downplaying the negatives. "Just hang in there. We'll figure it out. No one thought we'd make it this far. And yet, you've got your stage; the big crowd. What're a few obstacles in the total picture?"

"Sorry. I wasn't panicking," Johnny assured, though his voice sounded otherwise. "Yeah, I knew it wouldn't all go according to form. But don't fault me for being a daydreamer."

"Certainly not." Larry smiled. "Let's not forget what got us here in the first place."

Larry stepped off the idle vehicle. Instantly, he switched to floor-general mode. He waved for Ian, Howard, Frank and Erin to join where he and the others stood. Soon they were met by the passengers of the lead van -- a throng of female college students he had hired for emergency decoys. Everyone assembled in a circular huddle on the grass near the East Drive. Larry knelt like a veteran quarterback, delivering the altered game plan.

"All right, listen up. This little glitch; nothing we didn't anticipate. So we won't be driving to the stage. Instead: how many of you remember playing freeze tag in the schoolyard as kids?"

Gary flashed a look of utter astonishment. "Are you kidding me?"

Frank dropped his head in apparent chagrin. "So I take it, the idea here is to simply run like a flock to the stage, hoping to outrun the cops? Man, this bites! How're a few of us musicians gonna overpower a squad of those ball-busters? I mean, come on!"

Larry wiped the sweat from his face. Sirens blared in the background.

"But that's not the whole deal," Howard interjected. "Must be more to it."

Larry shrugged. "You've got the basic gist. I'll have my guys do what they can up front for a distraction. And I'll run interference with one of the vans. But then it's up to you. For all we know, it may not be as hopeless as you think."

"And what if only some of us make it? We can't play a show without the full lineup!" Ian grumbled. "Sounds riskier by the minute. It sucks!"

Larry reached for his ringing mobile. Frank kicked at an empty soda can and started in the wrong direction. Ian followed. Police sirens blared ever nearer.

"Risky or not, it's the only chance we've got." Johnny took charge, sounding robust for the first time all day. "Whatever happened to chasing immortality? If the cops by the stage are the only roadblock, I, for one, won't let this derail everything we've worked for. Plus, it's already a quarter past eight. Just standing around and bickering can't be helping any! So who's with me?"

Frank and Ian stopped in their tracks. Johnny raised his voice.

"Listen, if any of you wanna walk away, fine, I won't hold it against you. But I personally hate to keep a big crowd waiting. And I know I've got a show to play."

Seeing the somewhat reluctant support of his bandmates – who had done a slow about-face – Johnny placed his hands out in what became the center of a huddle. The others gradually did the same. On the count of three, each pushed down on the pile. The quintet raised their arms in unison and let out a collective scream. Soon, they were in a running formation facing in the direction of the makeshift stage. Nine women surrounded them in a semi-circle. They waited for the signal.

With all eyes on Larry, a loud boom suddenly exploded above their heads, followed by the roar of the crowd. Everyone looked skyward.

"Fireworks!" Gary observed. "Someone's shooting off fireworks."

"And that's your cue," Larry screamed above the noise. "Now on the count of three. One, two…"

The sound of further explosions thundered above. Johnny and the group took off running westward. With hearts racing and adrenaline pumping, the musicians and their entourage sprinted to top speed. They disappeared beneath a section of trees, just beyond Larry's vantage point. Larry scurried back to the last of the trucks and hopped in the front passenger seat. "Floor it till I say stop!"

In addition to the pyrotechnic commotion, an organized group of forty fans, led by WNYR's Rich Stevens, burst through the barricades and began rushing the stage. Dozens of police abandoned their posts. Within seconds, more than sixty riot-geared officers were chasing the hoard back toward the railings over which which they had just jumped.

Much of the crowd *oohed* and *ahhed* at the exploding lightshow above. Johnny and the band reached within one hundred yards to the back of the stage. That's where they encountered their first line of resistance.

Nearly a dozen uniformed men sprang into action, forming a formidable human wall to intercept the onrushing hoard. But not slowing even one knot, the nine co-ed mercenaries slammed hard into the arms of the awaiting officers.

Now partially obscured from view of the police convoy, Johnny and the band made their move. Ian led the charge. He squared his shoulders, lowered his bald head, and ran straight at two helmeted patrolmen at full speed. Then came a wild spin maneuver. Breathlessly, he reached for the metal barricade. With one hand he pushed himself up and swung his legs over, until it was apparent he had made it.

Frank, meanwhile, never stood a chance. He was immediately surrounded by a blue trio and easily subdued, pinned down to the grass by a swarm of fists and nightsticks.

Gary took full advantage of being the slowest in the group. He waited until all the officers converged on the others before making his move. Running the most indirect route, the bass player managed to elude all but one policewoman. With a shifty fake to the left he then darted right, wriggled his leg from her outstretched arms and lifted himself over the cold steel railing.

Howard was feeling winded by the time he'd covered the difficult terrain. Though he did his best to keep up, the veteran musician was no match for three burly policemen. Sapped of his positive energy, Howard lay pinned to the ground, wishing it would swallow him whole. This was hardly the *destiny* he envisioned.

A pair of police choppers hovered overhead. Howard watched them circle the area. *Damn,* he lamented. *We shoulda landed one of those on stage. Talk about grand entrances!* He began to shiver at the thought of a missed opportunity. Then came an idea.

Four of the student decoys had momentarily broken free. A pair of detaining officers popped up to chase them. This left only one distracted detective now holding him down. Howard began flailing arms and legs vigorously. He'd even remembered to drool to make the seizure look authentic. While the frightened officer scurried off to get medical assistance, Howard got back on his feet and ran clear to the metal barrier. His clumsy plan had worked.

Johnny was an obvious attention magnet in his slick linen jacket and neatly styled hair. The beads of sweat from the long jaunt notwithstanding, he clearly stood out among the chaos. Looking the part was a lesson learned from Howard long ago. Carefully, he removed his jacket and slung it over one shoulder. He slowed his pace and held up his empty hands to display that he was harmless. While being frisked, he attempted pleading his case in his most convincing tone.

"Hey. Look at all those people waiting out there. Arrest me later if you have to, but please, you've gotta let me up there."

"That ain't happening," one detective snapped. "This area's unauthorized. No exceptions."

"C'mon, guys. We're only here to perform, not hurt anyone. Just a few songs."

One gray bearded officer nodded with some compassion. "Look: I don't know who you are, or what you sing, but not even Francis Albert Sinatra can just show up in the middle of Central Park 'cuz he feels like entertaining the masses. That's what we have concert halls for."

Johnny was led away to a waiting squad car. Turning back to face the rear of the stage, he caught a glimpse of Howard, Ian and Gary's glum faces, as they stood in confinement at the top of the wooden steps beyond the barrier.

Johnny dejectedly lowered his head as he was helped into the back of a dark sedan. The door was promptly closed behind him. He slumped down and pounded one fist on the back seat in disgust. Shortly thereafter, the officer behind the wheel struck up a bizarre conversation.

"So you're the one causing all this ruckus."

Johnny looked up but could not find the words to answer.

"You're Johnny Elias, aren't you?" the man asked. Seeing Johnny nod in the rearview mirror, he smirked. "Well if it isn't the Poet of the Wrong Generation, right here in this squad car? And I thought we'd never meet again!"

"Again?" Johnny's eyes popped wide open. "I've never been arrested before."

"I suppose I'll take your word on that. Though I'm awfully disappointed you don't recognize me. I mean, even if you hadn't hit the big time, I'd still remember that voice."

Johnny squinted through the partition. "Not sure I follow."

The officer chuckled and removed his cap. He peered through the grated metal divider. "We're practically on the very spot where we met. All these years and you never kept in touch. The name's Lieutenant Jim Penetti. But even these days, most of the guys call me Jimbo."

Johnny gasped. "Wait! You're… the guy I met at the Paul Simon concert? The one who told me about the *Lion's Gate* in the Village?"

"One and the same," the officer said, nodding.

"That's… just totally amazing! You know, that dungeon's actually the site of my first performance. As if any of this matters now."

Lieutenant Penetti shook his head. "But did you bother to invite me? And heaven forbid you should drop my name in an interview; give me some credit."

"Man, that was years ago! For what it's worth, I apologize fifty times over. But I'm sure you're probably aware of how insane life's been since then."

A blue van sped by the squad car, going toward the stage. The officer paused to hear a muffled announcement over the police frequency. "Copy that," he replied to the message. Then he looked up, grinning. "Of all the places to meet again... just incredible! So yeah, I followed your career. Caught your show at the Beacon while I was training at the Academy. Goes without saying that I own your album... and paid dearly for a bootleg of the second. I'm always telling friends about meeting you that day. None of 'em ever believe me."

"Wow! I don't know what to say," Johnny responded, leaning forward. "Hey, I'll happily sign your albums if you'll let me outta here. For your friends too!"

Jim Penetti laughed.

Johnny grew more determined. "So now you're a lawman trying to keep me from being the next big concert played in this park. Not that I blame you for doing your job. It's just... what an amazing paradox! It's like you own a share in both starting and finishing off my career."

Lieutenant Penetti ignored Johnny's observation. He took time to survey the unfolding scene. "Well, I can't see how holding a grudge'll benefit either of us. And you do have one helluva excuse to back it up."

Johnny's spirits perked up. The congenial officer turned forward and placed one hand on the steering wheel. With a foot on the accelerator and flashing lights on display, he put the car in drive and made an abrupt left turn. They pulled up directly adjacent to the rear barricade. Then turning back again to face Johnny, Penetti exhaled nervously. "Listen, I'm prepared to stick my neck out for you on one condition."

"Considering my less than ideal bargaining position, you can get me to do just about anything... providing I'm capable."

"Oh, it's within your grasp," the Lieutenant professed. "You've got a park full of people waiting to erupt. As a public service, I can't let you do it unless I know you'll be going up there to sing your ass off... even the old songs!"

The grinning officer hit a button on the dashboard, unlocking the door next to Johnny. "Now, before anyone notices, go get this party started. Just don't tell anyone old Jimbo sprung you!"

Johnny let out a sigh of reprieve. He was trembling. He pushed the open door up against the metal barricade, then ducked low, so as not to be noticed. After squeezing out, he straddled the gate and climbed over uncontested. "Now I really owe you!" he shouted, looking back into the squad car. He flashed a thumbs-up and a bewildered appreciative smile.

In the surrounding chaos, Johnny hardly noticed Neil Gordon, the stagehand, and his son Geoff unpacking equipment from a dark blue van. The pair mounted the six wooden steps to stage level, then hurriedly made their way around the thin black backdrop and out front, in full view of the large, eager gathering.

A huge roar went up for the father and son team. Many rose to their feet in anticipation. The Gordons nonchalantly plugged guitars, drums, piano and microphones into the amplifiers.

Backstage, Johnny embraced his bandmates. He did not need a head-count to realize that Frank was not among them. Still, four had gotten this far. There was no turning back.

"Guys, we obviously can't play this set minus our lead guitar. We could go acoustic. Or, I can try playing Frank's part if Howard'll cover for me on piano."

"I can handle keyboards, if you take lead," Howard nodded in agreement. "And I'm sure Gary can put down his bass to solo like we talked about. I just hope we don't come off sounding like a patchwork rehearsal."

"This totally blows!" Ian protested stomping around. "Frank's the power behind this band. Sure as hell we're not doin' this without him!"

Johnny tucked the set list into his back pocket, picked up a black six-string acoustic, then turned to Ian and Howard. "All right, here's the deal. See if you guys can try finding Frank in the general vicinity. Just don't wander too far. If he's not on this side of the barricade, we'll just have to improvise. Meanwhile, wish Gary and me a little luck. We're going out there to face the music."

"We are?" asked Gary, his voice quavering.

Johnny put his arm around Gary's shoulders. "For the moment, guess it's just us two. I have no idea how this'll sound, but there's a great song for our instruments that might work as a makeshift opening number."

Gary grimaced. "Man, this is messed up. But if you think it's worth a try…"

Johnny surveyed the landscape from a side curtain. Unsure as to the sound system's operational status, he took a deep breath and a calculated risk, hoping his grand entrance wouldn't fall literally upon deaf ears. The once self-proclaimed poet of the wrong generation nervously stepped out from behind six years of elective ambiguity. With no introduction or video projection to magnify his face, he emerged from the shadows of a drum kit to a mesmerizing sea of silhouettes – and a deafening eruption.

Was the ovation genuinely for him, or simply the result of a long-awaited performance by anyone? No matter, Johnny strummed a few chords as an unscientific test. By crowd reaction it became obvious that sound was in fact being amplified through the towering speakers. He lowered the center microphone stand with trembling hands and adjusted his guitar strap.

"Don't know if any of you can hear me, but good evening, people of New York City!"

The response was thunderous.

Johnny took another deep breath. "Here's an old song about new beginnings." On a count of three, the duo launched into an improvised but purposeful cover of the Beatles' *Dear Prudence*, punctuated by a forceful bass line and the lyrics, beckoning the masses to come out to play.

Much of the crowd rose to its collective feet, some singing along. The bright sunshine of a long spring day was slowly setting behind New York's fabled skyline, casting shadows on the emerald lawn. The stage lights had yet to take full effect. The lone singer emphasized the song's final chorus. It was a poignant greeting to those who waited all day.

Johnny soaked up the applause. Flashbulbs popped. Rows of TV cameramen squeezed near the front of the stage, shooting footage that would soon be broadcast across the nation.

Out in the crowd, a mere handful recognized their one-time hometown hero by his sweet, distinctive tenor. A good majority stood squinting, guessing aloud as to the performer's identity. Some men even hoisted girlfriends on their shoulders, hoping to provide a better view. They eagerly awaited the next song, in hopes of pinpointing the mystery headliner who dared to play on such hallowed ground.

Johnny sensed he had already reached a critical juncture. He knew he couldn't go on playing cover versions all night.

"Gary, we should probably do one from *Poet* to get 'em going. I just feel conflicted without the guys behind me."

"We can do one of yours; I'm flexible. I'll even play a BQE song, whatever."

The sky above Central Park was slowly darkening. Johnny looked up to the heavens. Failure was no option after all he'd been through. Fortunately, his plea would soon be answered.

An unexpected cheer went up in reaction to events unfolding onstage. Johnny turned back, fearing he'd find a cluster of angry policemen. Instead: the most reassuring sight imaginable.

Directly behind him, a ghostly pale Ian stepped up to his drum kit, followed by Howard, in a torn silk shirt, taking a seat at the piano. And finally Frank – with dry blood encrusted beneath his nostrils – strapping on his cherry-red Stratocaster. Before Johnny could soak it all in, Ian was tapping his drumsticks in time to a familiar rhythm. This was followed by Frank's wailing chords to the opening song on the set list in Johnny's back pocket.

Johnny spun back to the center microphone. He delivered the lines to the very first live rendition of his only song to top the singles chart.

"Terrorists in New York City. Unemployment on the rise..."

The veil of anonymity had been lifted to earsplitting approval.

On the streets nearby, normally mild traffic conditions were disrupted by thousands of latecomers, rushing to partake in the excitement. Two television stations broke into prime time programming with a news bulletin. Radio stations dispatched reporters to the scene. WNYR managed to pick up their simulcast through the soundboard by the third song. Word of Johnny Elias's revival spread quickly.

Onstage, Johnny mixed his newest compositions with a smattering of the past. The band performed with the precision of a skilled carpenter, building a solid foundation beneath Johnny's elaborate if slightly gruff vocals. The vibrations from the roar of the crowd could be felt onstage through the thin floorboards and trembling mic stands.

Several hundred yards away, Katherine Price stood frozen in disbelief. Like much of the vast assembly, she had initially applauded when the solitary vocalist took the stage. But as *A Call To Action* began playing through the sound system, Katherine gasped in bitter astonishment. Her longtime adversary had suddenly risen from the ashes before her eyes. Burning at her even more was the cleverness of his scheme, which had at first impressed her, but left no opportunity to thwart this re-ignition of a once-flourishing career.

Indirectly, Katherine once believed that Johnny's past success was her own doing. She considered his stardom a byproduct of her oblique challenge for him to make something of his life. And in that distorted conviction, her animosity only intensified when Johnny refused to take Megan back.

In her flawed sensibility, she attributed Johnny's outright hatred of her as the fuel that inspired his songs of mistrust and injustice. Katherine grew to hold him primarily accountable for all that had gone wrong in her own life. It was Johnny's face that she visualized each time she closed her eyes to conjure the image of her resentment.

Katherine scrambled through the Rolodex of her mind, seeking a number to call. After all, it wasn't long ago when she had a direct hotline to the mayor's office and the influence to make an impact. But this show, this crowd… too damn big to be halted by any one person. *Well, good for him,* she thought amid the wild cheering. *Maybe it's somehow for the best.* She bit down hard and shifted her focus to the one place where she could perhaps make a difference, make things right.

Megan, she thought suddenly. *Might this be the moment we've both been waiting for all these years?*

39

A Threshold To Cross

For Megan Price, May 27th began with an early alarm and breakfast for two. She dropped Alex off at school, then stopped by the salon for her once-a-month manicure – one of her few luxuries in an unpampered existence.

Megan stopped at the bank on her way to work. She used her safe-deposit key to retrieve a couple of items she had never intended to look at again. Around noon, she darted off on her lunch break to meet up with Ralph Cassalaro, the only man she trusted with the care of her valuables.

"And just how can I be of service, Ms. Price?" he asked fondly. "You seem rather motivated for someone dropping by for a cleaning or repair."

"Actually, Ralph, it's neither. What I want is for you to reconstruct a part of my past. Life's about to change for the better. Time to rid myself of all the old mementos."

Megan handed him a purple satchel containing her gold wedding band, diamond engagement ring, and a matching pair of earrings. "I was thinking maybe you could melt these down into a brooch or something. Something I can feel good about wearing going forward."

At a quarter to five, Megan zipped over to Alex's elementary school. It was a warm spring afternoon; her allergies were acting up. She took Alex for ice cream and watched him demolish a banana split with three scoops of his favorite flavors. *My, how quickly they grow up,* she found herself reflecting.

Later, at home, she quizzed Alex on two-syllable words in preparation for a spelling test. Francesca, the housekeeper, left for the night at half past six. A sneezy Megan saw her out to the elevator, entirely unaware of the drama unfolding just beyond her window. A lifelong city resident, she was conditioned to ignore the sirens and the like without so much as the mildest curiosity. And with the high pollen count, she was sure to keep the windows firmly shut.

By 7:30, Alex was in pajamas, requesting a bedtime story. Megan grabbed two Dr. Seuss books from the nearby shelf. Soon he would be fast asleep. She gently kissed his forehead and covered him with a favorite blue blanket before shutting the light.

Free to tend to her own matters, Megan checked her answering machine in hopes of a call from Johnny. It had been several days since their revealing conversation. She found herself constantly preoccupied with him. The message light flashed once. She eagerly hit play.

Hi, Meg. Just calling to let you know you've been on my mind. Hope to see you real soon… maybe sooner than you think. Sorry I missed you.

A glorious smile spread across Megan's face. She raced to her walk-in closet and pulled a dozen hangers off the rod. Ten summer outfits were modeled in front of a full-length mirror. Not wanting to appear overanxious, or overly conservative, she eventually settled on a sleek cream-colored dress with a matching lightweight blouse, adorned with rhinestones on quarter-length sleeves. "Perfect," she sighed.

A stack of recent mail-order catalogs were soon scattered across Megan's bedspread. She flipped through the pages, seeking the ideal gift to give Johnny when she saw him. A handsome leather folder with a replaceable interior notepad caught her eye. Fondly, she recalled how Johnny was always clutching a spiral notebook in their days together. Now she wanted him to have something equally useful for his future songwriting, yet symbolically more permanent.

Megan found nothing unusual about the absence of incoming calls. What she failed to realize was that she'd actually left the receiver off the hook after placing the catalog order. The silence afforded her an hour to soak in the tub. It was a soothing relief from the sneezing and watery eyes.

Just after nine, Megan dressed for bed and headed to the kitchen. She popped two antihistamine caplets and downed them with a swallow of tap water, then emptied the remainder of her cup into a vase of fading spring carnations on the windowsill. The generally serene view of Central Park appeared full of commotion. It was rare on even the busiest of days to see so many young people running about. And with the lateness of the hour, she found little explanation for this controlled mayhem.

Wait. What about Strawberry Fields? That was her first guess. These nearby musical pilgrimages marked John Lennon's birthday and the anniversary of his assassination. *Oh, but those are in October and December, not May.* She remained at a loss as to what was drawing all these people in. *Surely not Shakespeare in the Park!*

The living room window was the only one in Megan's apartment not covered by child safety bars. From this vantage point, she studied a trail of hundreds, pushing hurriedly a few blocks downtown.

Megan unlocked the glass door leading to her terrace. Her curiosity was going to be rewarded with a birds-eye view.

Andy Raymer rushed into the park just seconds prior to the opening number. A laminated tag dangled from his neck; a souvenir from the mayor's office. Skillfully, he navigated a course through spectators toward the stage. It took nearly a half an hour, but he eventually located a cheering circle of Jacqui's friends between two picnic blankets.

Andy took a second to catch his breath. Suddenly, he found himself on the receiving end of a near suffocating embrace.

"Is this insane, or what?" Jacqui gasped over the boisterous cheering.

Andy beamed triumphantly, pulling her closer. "Better than even Johnny could've imagined. It's unreal!"

Andy gazed up at the makeshift stage. He watched as Johnny paused between songs to peer out at the growing multitude. To the casual observer, it may have appeared that he was merely sizing up the enormity of the turnout. But Andy was close enough to recognize that his friend was seeking something, or someone. He followed Johnny with his eyes from the center microphone over to the piano, where he sat down on the matching wooden bench.

"This next one's dedicated to someone very special, somewhere out there in the crowd. A dear friend who'd better have brought along as many people as she promised." The opening piano notes to *Jacqui* sparked a roar of recognition.

As the tune played on, the couple – who had met on this very ground some eight years earlier – swayed to the sweet, familiar ballad. Two concerts had served as something of bookends to their enduring relationship, which now included one beautiful child and another on the way.

Dancing cheek-to-cheek with Andy, Jacqui leaned in just a little closer. "I've never been more proud of you than I am tonight. Thanks for doing what was right, no matter how crazy. Can't wait to see both your faces when he walks off that stage."

Onstage, Johnny kept the between-song banter to a minimum. He and the band clung tightly to the set list, comprised of more than thirty selections. Johnny overcame an early gruff voice, rolling out faithful live versions of the songs that once made him a star. And the standing spectators responded as though he'd never been away.

Throughout *Shadows of the Same Color*, countless faces, white and black, stood together, singing in unison. Many raised flickering lighters in an emotional show of accord. If this remarkable scene managed to stir exhilaration inside the poet, the next proved even more personally heartwarming.

Johnny stood to stretch from behind his black piano. A delicate breeze blew through his long dark hair. He addressed the crowd.

"Back in '93, I put out an album that enjoyed the shortest shelf-life in history. By a show of hands, how many have heard of the infamous, *A New Beginning*?" A good majority of the audience waved their arms, some whistling exuberantly. "Really? That many? Well then, I guess we're gonna have to play a few of 'em. This one's called *A View From The Top Of The World*. Kinda summarizes how I'm feeling about now."

While the song played up onstage, Howard tiptoed away from the backstage area. He easily spotted Marlene alongside the metal barrier at the front section of the crowd. And next to her, his son, Josh. Howard snuck up from the side, flashing a smile of pure joy. "So: enjoying the show?"

Marlene was speechless. Josh Greffen could hardly contain his giddiness. "Dad… aren't you supposed to be up there? My old man, the rock star!"

"Actually, I'm on insulin break." Howard pointed to a covered needle protruding from his pocket. "I really just stopped by to tell you guys something that couldn't wait."

"What is it?" Marlene asked, looking concerned. "You feeling okay?"

"Never better!" Howard assured her. "I just want both of you to know that as great as it is to be playing in the biggest gig of my life, it's even more meaningful to know the two of you got to finally see me onstage for the first time… and who knows when again."

"Better not be the last," Josh implored. "How cool is this? My first rock concert, and here's my Dad right up there in the middle. Guess I never thought of you like that before."

Larry Jacobs managed to win over the suddenly cooperative police. From a small folding table between the rear of the stage and the safety barricades, he successfully oversaw the second power source delivery, preventing an early shutdown of the show. Soon thereafter, he was doing some between songs radio commentary. He couldn't help coming across as the proudest man in the park.

You're listening live to the largest bootlegged concert ever attempted. Whether you're here on the Great Lawn, or somewhere within the range of our signal, I'm certain you can comprehend the magnitude of this great rock and roll caper; maybe the greatest of all time!

Larry's repeated request for fans to bring their radios was perhaps his greatest stroke of genius. Once the first third of the lawn had been jammed with people, the remainder wouldn't likely have been able to hear the performance, due to a less-than-adequate sound system. Instead, hundreds of portable radios made the show audible for concertgoers all the way up to 85th street – albeit on seven-second delay. Larry was aglow with pride. Witnessing Johnny's resurgence was the culmination of his rebellious vision.

Megan could faintly hear the decibel level of a growing audience as she stepped out onto her 23rd floor terrace. At the waist-high railing, she boosted herself up on an inverted terracotta planter in an effort to peek over the blooming maple trees. Bright lights shone alongside the large stage. Scores of people remained headed toward the immense gathering.

Skies were darkening; the music muffled. She could only deduce that it was not an orchestral performance. Strained guitar notes registered ever so weakly in her ears. Her curiosity was piqued. The antihistamines were dulling her senses. After trying unsuccessfully to make out the performer from her balcony, she ran inside to grab her binoculars for a better view.

In another time, Megan would surely have stripped off her pajamas, thrown on a pair of jeans, and run out to the park, no questions asked. But now with a sleeping first-grader down the hall, a closer investigation was hardly an option. Instead, Megan quickly flipped through a dozen channels on television seeking a report from the park. One local news station was in commercial. The networks were all into their primetime programming. *Like I've got the patience to channel-surf now!* Instinctively, she grabbed a brown leather case from the living room wall-unit and rushed back outside. On this warm, May evening, Megan was just one of several hundred curious spectators gazing from a terrace on either side of the park.

Just two floors above, a newlywed thirty-something couple sat outside watching the festivities. Despite the commotion below, Megan could make out every word.

"Wow, look at all those people," a female voice gasped in amazement. "Just staggering!"

"I'm not surprised," the man's voice responded assuredly. "This guy, he was once the prince of New York. And he hasn't performed in forever. There's gotta be what… a couple hundred-thousand out there for him?"

There was a brief pause in their conversation. Moments later, a radio was switched on. The dial was fiddled with, as though someone were seeking a particular frequency.

Megan got back up on the three-foot high inverted planter for a better vantage point. She adjusted her binoculars to a long-range setting. Staring two blocks downtown, she gradually made out some of the tiny faces in the crowd. She tried to distinguish anything taking place on the actual stage from her awkward, side-angle view. It all appeared to be happening in slow motion.

A slight southerly breeze blew past her building. Megan's hair was still damp from the bath. The gentle wind felt rather pleasant – almost liberating. For here at this moment, she could sense the winds of change blowing toward a happier time. One she had yearned for endlessly.

Megan held the binoculars in her left hand. She used her right index finger to push aside a long blonde strand that had blown across her face, briefly obscuring her hazy view. Her head grew heavier with each passing second. She was beginning to feel dizzy from the medicine, the muffled audio and the steady flow of people. Then the radio upstairs finally locked into a clear signal. Everything abruptly changed. Although the volume was not particularly loud, Megan had no trouble picking up the unmistakable sound of a cheering audience, followed by a voice she knew all too well.

I'd like to go all the way back to my very first song. This one was written believing someone very dear to me had deceived me; broken my heart. Perception: it's a funny thing. Tonight, I rededicate it to the person I wrote it for. This one's called Return To Me.

Megan's heart pounded like a frantic drum solo. She immediately synchronized the responsive cheering from the park with the seven-second radio delay. She trembled with elation and astonishment. Instinctively, she lurched forward beyond the waist-high railing, hoping to catch even a momentary glimpse of his face.

Megan's torso balanced delicately, one hand against the balcony rail. With the other, she pressed the binoculars against her face. The song played on. Tears of ecstasy sprang to her eyes. That was her man up onstage, recapturing all he'd left behind.

She was thinking back to their last phone conversation. Just before hanging up, he mentioned having *something important to do.* Now it made perfect sense. *What poetic justice! I'd have slept in the park a whole week if only he'd told me.*

Megan's thoughts raced to the future. Everything was feeling surreal. She shut her heavy eyelids and envisioned Johnny's arrival at her door. No doubt she'd be overcome by the greatest sense of joy as he kissed her face. She'd whisper congratulations in his ear, and attempt to lift him off the ground, if only she could. Suddenly, he'd topple down on her, bracing her for the fall, as they'd tumble to the ground in a loving embrace.

Another gentle breeze blew through her hair; Johnny's song played on hazily in the background. Megan could feel the warmth of his breath on her face, as he told her how he loved her once again. This time, there was nothing and no one to stand in their way.

Megan's eyes remained firmly closed. She held her hands out, as if to again receive Johnny's passion. She never even noticed the strap from the binoculars slide from around her wrist, sending them crashing into the darkness. She wasn't there anymore; she was somewhere else. Never had she experienced a more blissful moment.

Slowly, she swayed to the music in her heart. Confined to her pain for as far back as memories stretched, Megan unknowingly leaned inches forward. Suddenly, she was free. Floating through time, wrapped in the supportive embrace of the man she loved, she never once opened her eyes, as the wind's intensity increased…

Katherine Price tried desperately to leave the darkening park. After repeated attempts to reach Megan by phone, she had grown increasingly restless.

A score of latecomers persisted in their mission toward the Great Lawn, as word spread throughout the city. Katherine must have felt like a lone vehicle heading in the wrong direction up a busy one-way street. Each measly step became an immense struggle for the diminutive, fifty-six year old grandmother. Still, she remained undeterred.

Katherine forced her slender frame between the hurried masses. Many of them carried radios, backpacks and coolers. She was bruised and battered by swinging limbs and blunt objects alike. "Out of my way," she muttered helplessly, unable to sidestep the incoming horde. Even as she approached the pedestrian exit on West 85th, Katherine struggled to keep on her feet; the crush of fans seemingly endless.

Nearing the cobblestone entranceway, Katherine found herself on the losing end of a violent collision. The elbow of an oblivious, oversized policeman connected solidly to her forehead, knocking her senseless. Katherine took about a minute to come round. She brushed off her pinstriped pantsuit in a patch of knee-high bushes. Blood trickled from her nose. There was a sizeable tear in her left sleeve. But here in her state of urgency, vanity was irrelevant. Finally, Central Park West appeared. Katherine crossed the street at the corner of 85th. The arches of her feet ached as though she were running on the pointed end of her quarter-inch heels. At 83rd street,

Katherine removed her battered shoes on the run. She tucked them in her leather workbag – now scuffed and dangling by one strap – and reevaluated her surroundings. *Only two more blocks to go.*

That's when the flashing red and blue emergency lights caught her attention. The ominous sight left her with a feeling of dread.

By the time she arrived barefoot at the roped-off scene, she could do nothing more than shield her horrified eyes with trembling hands. A pair of binoculars lay shattered on the sidewalk. A set of ambulance doors slammed shut behind a collapsed stretcher. Katherine wanted to scream her daughter's name. Instead, she dropped to the ground, exhausted, bloodied, and having been rendered emotionally incapacitated.

Fatalistic intuition had firmly taken hold.

From behind his baby grand, Johnny sent the jam-packed audience into a joyous frenzy with his signature song. He used nearly all his remaining energy to give his most compelling performance of the night. Virtually all the spectators swayed from side-to-side, waving flickering lighters. Johnny felt like something of a symphony conductor, leading the masses in an epic sing-along.

Thousands of voices echoed across the park like a tabernacle choir through an open-air cathedral. This harmonious interlude was easily the emotional high point. The enthusiastic crowd refused to let it end long after the song was over. It was a moment wholly poignant, leaving the proud composer speechless and with eyes glazed over.

Johnny stood in pure elation, his body quivering. Finally, he allowed his eyes to wander off as far as they could see. Vociferous approval emanated from the Great Lawn. If there had been any doubt as to whether the audience would remember him, no longer was further validation required.

Once his composure returned, Johnny stepped up to the center microphone, his now-ragged voice summoning his bandmates back onstage for a series of well-deserved ovations.

Ian, Frank, Howard and Gary lined up with sweaty arms around each other in the center of the stage, for a triumphant, collective bow.

Of all the band members, perhaps Howard was most absorbed in the experience. His realization of playing to an immense audience now culminated with this staggering ovation. Years of torment and musical frustration now seemed a distant memory. For one night he was immortal.

Frank and Ian stood mesmerized. The longtime friends had gone from local club players to conquering heroes on the biggest stage imaginable. Their days of tossing picks and drumsticks into smoky aisles of sparsely populated pubs were over.

Johnny ducked behind the cloth backdrop and rounded the troops one last time. He embraced each in triumph. When he got to Frank, he held on extra tight. "Thought we'd lost you, dude! We'd have been totally screwed, ya know. How'd you ever find your way back?"

"Funny you should ask!" Frank shouted over the still roaring audience. "At one point, I was actually in cuffs, blinded by pepper spray, heading down to central booking. Next thing I knew, the car is turning around. Guess someone was listening when I told 'em I couldn't afford to miss the biggest payday of my life. You know how convincing I can be in desperation."

Johnny laughed, though he found Frank's explanation a bit curious. Howard tossed him a towel and a cold water bottle. "Time for you to go back out there; send 'em home happy. I noticed you omitted *We've Already Said Goodbye*. You saved it, didn't you? In case you got to play an encore?"

"Not a bad guess." Johnny raised his eyebrows. "Truth is, though, I've decided to retire that one. I mean, sure it was my first single. But no more singing goodbye to someone I wished I never had. If I'm gonna play an encore, I've got something just a little more fitting for the occasion."

Johnny shed his sweat-drenched jacket and wiped his glistening face. He tossed the towel aside and ducked back under the solid backdrop. Another boisterous reception followed. Shivers danced up his spine. He slowly stepped to the center microphone. Alone.

"Thank you all for coming tonight. Hope we haven't disappointed with our little surprise."

Humbled by the night's most extended roar, Johnny picked up an acoustic six-string from the rack and strapped it over his shoulder. A folded lyric sheet emerged from his shirt pocket.

"So how many of you were here back in '91 for Paul Simon?" A good many let out yet another majestic ovation.

"Anyway, back on that sweltering day, I was just a kid scribbling in a spiral notebook, right here in the Park. I wrote this little poem so my buddies and I would never forget the good times. Little did I know that someday I'd put those words to music and be standing up here, playing it for the first time tonight for you. I'd like to dedicate this one to Meg, Andy and Jacqui. Finally, here's that finished version I promised."

Johnny tuned out the mile of enthusiasm, adjusted the shaking microphone and began:

People gathered round upon the Great Lawn
The date arrived we'd waited for all summer
Blue skies were above us and the weather was so right
We sat there all day in anticipation
Short girls sat upon the tall boys shoulders
Blimps flew overhead with TV cameras
Banners waved and beach balls flew around us
On cable it was shown across the nation

And the hours passed – We had such a blast
Knowing someday in the future we would ask, "remember when?"
And the friends we made – we would never trade
Though we figured when we left we'd never see their face again

(Chorus)
But we danced and we sang and we whistled and screamed

And we left our voices behind
Still we knew this was all we would ever share somewhere in the back of our minds
So we traded life stories and craved precious shade
from the morning until it grew dark
But we swore in our lifetime we'd never forget
The Concert in Central Park

Tossing round the Frisbees and the footballs
Picnic blankets carpeted the grass
Some turned up their radios, while others bronzed their skin
And policemen got a well-deserved ovation
T-shirt vendors probably made a fortune
Though most of them were bootlegged and still drying
Many took a day from work, if only to be there
and share in summer's biggest celebration

And the atmosphere – drew the masses near
But the closeness we developed only lasted for the day
When that last chord played – we'd have loved to have stayed
Still the outside world continued and we'd all be on our way

(Chorus)

Raincoats and umbrellas weren't needed
The showers we were promised never did come
But even rain could not dampen our spirits
For this day just had too much in its favor
Many pushed along to score a prime spot
Crowds stretched out until they reached the sidewalks
Some were rude; most were kind, but all just blended in
The truest taste of New York City flavor

Then we saw the band – No room left to stand
And the crowd became electric in a fevered state of rage
Never dared to dream – with each cherished scream
That someday I would be the one, performing on this stage

But we danced and we sang and we whistled and screamed
And we left our voices behind
Still we knew this was all we would ever share somewhere in the
back of our minds
So we traded life stories and craved precious shade
from the morning until it grew dark
But we swore in our lifetime we'd never forget
The Concert in Central Park

40

Jilted Euphoria

Johnny Elias stepped behind the black curtain to a raucous ovation. He was physically, vocally and mentally spent after the nearly three-hour performance. But the unmatched feeling of stealing a concert in Central Park lifted him to emotional heights that not even he could've imagined.

Johnny climbed down from the back of the makeshift stage. A swarm of media and fans were being held back by police. Flashbulbs popped from every direction. He lowered his head and tried squeezing through the masses.

He was blindsided by a crushing embrace.

"Man, you really did it!" Andy was glowing. "I should've known if anyone were capable of pulling this off, it'd be my never-say-die visionary. Apologies for not making myself clearer!" He corralled Johnny's sweat-drenched torso even tighter. "So tell me, now that you've been up there, how does it feel to have actually stood in front of all those people?"

Johnny could not answer. He spun back in the direction of the crowd and marveled. Then recapturing composure, he replied gruffly, "Andy, you do mean *we* did it. Tonight never happens if it weren't for all you've done for me. And as for being up there... man, where to begin?"

Johnny spotted Larry Jacobs, sporting a wireless headset, no doubt still broadcasting live. Straight ahead, Carolyn Green chatted with the Coat Coalition drivers and a jubilant Jacqui Raymer. Just behind, Johnny caught a glimpse of Howard being mobbed by Marlene and Josh. To his left, Brian Quigley playfully bowed toward Gary, his onetime college bandmate, as he skipped down the narrow wooden staircase. It seemed that everywhere Johnny looked, here were the people who had been along for the journey.

And yet this improbable triumph still felt incomplete. Johnny continued to gaze in all directions. One face was noticeably missing from the celebration. The woman whose initial betrayal had placed him in touch with his musical soul, and with whom he now planned to soon reunite, was nowhere to be found.

Johnny tried unsuccessfully to locate her smiling face amid the officers, photographers and friends. *Damn. She's gotta be here somewhere, soaking this all in, cheering us on.*

Johnny was escorted to a waiting limousine by a team of Larry's hired bodyguards. At one point, he slowed to sign autographs for two delirious fans, but did so on the move.

Inside the shiny black car, Johnny could detect his aching feet touching the ground for the first time in hours. *Ah, tranquility*, he thought, even as muffled cheering was still audible from outside. All the anxiety leading up to this spectacle was emotionally fraying. It had been months since he enjoyed a moment uncompromised.

Lost in sweet reflection, Johnny was startled when the tinted glass divider began to roll down electronically. "Mr. Elias, my name's Dan: your driver for the party this evening."

"Party?" Johnny asked hoarsely. "Aren't you taking me home to Connecticut?"

"Mr. Jacobs left word to bring the guest of honor to the victory bash… if you weren't arrested tonight. Pier 17. The observation level. Fireworks and all!"

Larry thinks I have the stamina to party after this? Johnny wondered silently. *As if we haven't had enough fireworks already!* "I'll be lucky just to stay awake another ten minutes, but... so long as you don't mind one quick stop on the West Side."

The partition was still down as the car began moving in slow motion. Johnny noticed the driver listening softly to the all-news station. "Hey, can you please turn that up a sec?" he asked, knowing he'd almost certainly be part of the headlines. Unlike the last time his name got star-billing, Johnny now looked forward to the reports.

The driver raised the volume for the back speakers. It was exactly 11:30pm; the top stories were being updated.

In Central Park this evening: a startling comeback by one of New York's musical heroes. Johnny Elias, the self-proclaimed poet of the wrong generation, pulled the surprise of the year – a free, unannounced concert on the Great Lawn in front of a crowd estimated at more than three hundred thousand.

This unscheduled event initially drew the ire of city officials. It was permitted to go on after last-minute negotiations between City Hall and the singer's representatives. The concert, which ended only moments ago, saw a return to the stage by Elias after years of seclusion. Though chaotic, it seems to have occurred without incident. We now go to the park for reaction with our reporter on the scene, Irene Monaco. Irene, can you hear me?

I can barely hear you with all this delirium. But I can report that I've just witnessed one of the great music events this city has ever seen. No doubt, those lucky enough to be here will agree that this stunning comeback by Johnny Elias will go down as one of the wildest anyone's ever witnessed.

A handful of spontaneous interviews with overjoyed fans followed. Then the studio anchor returned:

Again, to recap: the NYPD estimate more than three hundred thousand were on-hand tonight for the unannounced performance by Johnny Elias – the first free rock concert in Central Park since 1991. More on this in just a few moments.

In an unrelated story we're following: an Upper West Side woman has reportedly fallen from an apartment balcony on Central Park West. Witnesses say the unidentified victim – said to be in her late twenties – apparently slipped

this evening, tumbling twenty-three floors, through the building's canopy in
what appears to be a tragic accident.

"Mr. Elias, she's in surgery up on the sixth floor. You're welcome to visit the waiting area. She may have some family already up there."

Johnny's remarkable triumph was remarkably short-lived. It took stops at four West-Side hospitals before discovering the right location. Now, as he stood in the lobby of Roosevelt hospital, he wondered if perhaps he was too late… if he should even be here at all.

Johnny paced by the elevator doors, the ringing in his ears having finally subsided. At last, a set of metal doors opened. He stepped inside and pressed the button. Throughout his frantic search that evening, the majority of Johnny's thoughts had been focused on seeing Megan again. To seeing her alive. To picking up the conversation they had shared in the days before his now astonishing comeback. To finding a way to make up for all the lost years.

Concurrently, his mind felt wracked with guilt. Had he never attempted this surprise publicity stunt, Megan surely would not have been out on her balcony that evening; would certainly not have taken this horrible fall. Now, as the elevator stopped on the fifth floor, the words of the front desk receptionist began to sink in. *Relatives.* Undoubtedly, this meant an inevitable encounter with Katherine Price.

Johnny adjusted his still-sweat-drenched shirt, then braced himself for what was to come.

The doors opened on the sixth floor. Johnny followed the signs to trauma unit, the last of his adrenaline fumes carrying his weary legs. An overhead clock read 2:33am. He pushed open a set of double doors at the end of a long hallway. The site of an equally disheveled, similarly worried Katherine Price sprawled out on a metal chair was both startling and oddly sympathetic.

Johnny made brief eye contact with the young man sitting to her left. It had been years since he had last seen Zach Price. His surprisingly long black hair covered much of the front of his vintage Grateful Dead t-shirt. Zach nodded in Johnny's direction, a hint of a smile forming at the corners of his mouth. "You were awesome," Zach mouthed silently, while pointing in Johnny's direction. Then he nudged his mother's shoulder, rousing her from her sorrowful meditation.

Johnny took a pair of steps toward them, but stopped cautiously short when Katherine lifted her head and scowled.

"You have some nerve showing up here like this. The conquering hero here to save the day, I presume?"

"I... I'm just–" Johnny was stammering, lost for any logical retort. He jammed his hands in the pockets of his pants and stared down at the cold tile floor.

"That's about right. The beloved poet of the people rendered fittingly mute." Katherine rose from her seat. She clenched her fists, gave out a sigh of anguish, then charged in Johnny's direction. "You selfish, unbelievable bastard! You did this to her! You ruined her life! Our lives! Why?" Katherine was wailing punches on Johnny's head, his chest, his shoulders. "Why couldn't you just stay down in whatever hole you were hiding?"

Johnny's instinct was to protect himself from the barrage of blows. But after freeing his hands from his pockets, he instead did the unthinkable. He wrapped his arms tightly around Katherine's torso, pulling her close in a firm embrace until the punches ceased.

Katherine let her arms dangle at her sides. Gradually, she lifted them and wrapped her arms around Johnny, tears spilling down her reddened face.

They stood together for several minutes, clinging to one another, breathing loudly. No words were exchanged.

Moments later, Zach approached and spoke in a low voice. "It's the doctor. I think he's got some kind of update."

Katherine opened her eyes, released her grip of Johnny's shirt, and looked up in Zach's direction. A bespectacled man with a green face mask and in matching hospital scrubs stood in the doorway between the surgical ward and the waiting area. Katherine walked hurriedly in his direction. "Please. What's the latest?"

Johnny walked slowly over to where Katherine and the surgeon were standing, eager for any positive developments on Megan's condition.

"From the height that she fell, and at that rate of speed… well, it's plainly miraculous that she wasn't killed on impact. That canvas canopy, it broke her fall; saved her life. She landed on her right side. There are a number of blunt trauma injuries. Broken ribs. A fractured right wrist and arm. Broken clavicle. She also has injuries from when she hit the pavement after she tore through the canvas. Torn knee ligaments, a displaced ankle."

"What about her head? Her brain?" Katherine was squeezing Zach's hand as she pushed out the words."

"Another miracle." The doctor brought his hands together and pressed them against his heart. "Neurologically speaking, she never lost consciousness. Her face is unblemished; eerily peaceful despite all the pain she must be feeling. Her right side took the brunt of the impact. We've managed to stop the internal bleeding. We've also stabilized the broken bones in her arm and legs. Not out of the woods by any means, but she's now in recovery. You can probably see her when she wakes from the anesthesia."

"So she's going to make it." Katherine released Zach's hand and pushed some tousled hair off her face. "She'll recover from this and lead a normal life?"

The surgeon drew a deep breath, then spoke in a soft, compassionate tone. "The next twenty-four hours are going to be critical. Beyond that, there will be further surgeries. Her body will need time to heal. Probably many months. No doubt she's going to need extensive rehab before she'll be able to do everyday things on her own." He patted Katherine gently on the shoulder. "But yes, it is possible that she may eventually resume a normal life… if all goes well."

When the surgeon departed, Katherine collapsed back into the waiting-room chair. She sobbed quietly with her head in her hands for several minutes. Zach sat down next to her, staring up at the ceiling. Soon, they both were overcome by the hour and their exhaustion.

Johnny collapsed in a corner of the room, reflecting on the spectrum of emotions he had experienced this night. The near disastrous encounter with the police blockade. The joyous insanity on the Great Lawn. The stunning news of Megan's fall. The hopeful words of her survival. Soon, the physical and mental exhaustion got the better of him as well.

Daylight spilled through the sixth floor window into the waiting room when Johnny awoke. A burly figure was standing above him, startling him from his slumber. Johnny rubbed his eyes with the sleeve of his shirt, then took a moment to re-acclimate his unfamiliar surroundings.

"Hey, she's asking for you. Mom's already been in to see her. They've got her doped up on serious meds, but she's alert; keeps calling your name." Zach Price held out a hand and helped pull Johnny up from the floor. "Don't keep her waiting."

Zach led Johnny up to the double-doors outside the recovery room. "She's in the last bed on the left. I'd go in with you, but I think you guys are gonna want your privacy."

"Thanks," Johnny uttered while patting Zach on the shoulder. "And where's your mother? Is she in with Megan?"

"Nah." He shook his head from side-to-side. "She's already been in there; had their first argument too. I think she's gone back home to freshen up, change her clothes. You know."

"Right." Johnny nodded in acknowledgement, then peeked through a glass window within the metal door. Some two dozen rolling cots were occupied by patients in varying degrees of pain and consciousness. A handful of nurses were making the rounds, analyzing clipboards and vital signs. Flashing monitors displayed blood pressure, oxygen and heart rate numbers. Intermittent beeping grew louder as Johnny entered the room.

He spotted Megan in the back, right where Zach had said she was. She was heavily bandaged from her neck down to her toes. A pulse monitor clamp was connected to the index finger on her left hand. Aside from an oxygen tube beneath her nose, her face was the only part of her body not obscured by dressings, or equipment.

Johnny stood over her, watching her labored breathing for several minutes. It greatly pained him to see her in this physical state. At least she was alive.

Megan's eyes opened slowly. An awkward smile spread across her pale face. "So you really did come," she spoke in a tone not much louder than a whisper. "Might be the first time in years that mother wasn't lying to me." A faint laugh ensued.

Johnny laughed too. He knelt down to one side of her bed and grasped her left hand gently in his. "Of course I'm here. I had to find you; to be here no matter what."

"The reunion we always dreamed of," she said, her eyes smiling at him. "Well, at least you held up your end of it. Sorry I had to kill it for the both of us."

Johnny stroked Megan's hand gently with his thumb. "You did no such thing. If anyone's to blame, it's probably me. If only I had let you in on my plans…"

Megan sighed softly, then squeezed Johnny's hand with her loose fingers. "So then I didn't dream this all up. It really happened. You played the park. For all those people." A lone tear trickled from the corner of Megan's eye. "You're back now. Bigger than ever."

Megan's heartbeat accelerated with excitement, setting off a beeping sound from a monitor above her bed. An attending nurse peered over in their direction until the sound faded.

"The show really happened. Yeah, somehow we pulled it off. That much is true."

"And now it can start all over again for you. The music. The concerts. The fanfare." Megan's eyes lit up at the thought.

"If I choose that path." Johnny squinted at Megan. "Okay, so I have a lot of new music to share with… whoever wants to hear it. It'll come out before long. If only that was the most important thing."

"After what you did; so spectacular. What could possibly be more important?" Megan's voice grew suddenly stronger, briefly setting off the beeping noise once again.

Johnny's eyes filled with tears, his heart fluttering ever faster. "Priorities, Meg. Ever since this music thing happened to me, to us, I've had it all wrong. I got… too caught up in feeding the beast of stardom. Clouded my judgment, my decisions. Made me lose sight of you. Of the one shining soul who makes me happy and whole."

Megan sighed once more, and slowly closed her eyes. "Johnny, if only…" Her eyes popped open and met his. "If only it wasn't too late."

"But it's not too late. Meg, you're still here. I'm still here. The doctors, they say you'll recover. Look, I made you a promise when we spoke the other night. I'm not going anywhere that takes me away from you. Not again."

"Johnny, I'm broken. My body is shattered. Just look at me. May never walk again; never be whole, or normal, or… I can't let you sacrifice your life to take care of me like this."

"Megan, I am looking at you." Johnny blinked back the tears. He slid a finger across her cheek. "I know its going to take time and hard work. But you will get better. I just know it. And even if you need to lean on me, rely on me, that's what I'm here for. For always."

Megan reached down deep, summoning the energy to slowly bend her left arm. She pointed to her fractured body. "Even if I manage to walk somehow, just look at me. I'm gonna be scarred and disfigured. Forever imperfect. Hardly the match for a musical superstar. I'll only be holding you back."

"As long as you'll be holding me…" Johnny let the words linger. He gently wiped the tears from Megan's face. "You talk about scars. I've got more than my share. You know that better than anyone. Perfection is a myth. It just doesn't exist, unless we accept each other for who we are and what we've been through. Love and understanding, it's the closest we'll come to reaching it."

Megan squeezed Johnny's hand with her fingers. She used her last remaining energy to pull him in her direction. Johnny leaned forward and kissed her forehead.

"I need a favor from you," Megan whispered.

"Anything." Johnny again stroked her free hand. "Just say the word."

"Alex," Megan muttered. "Can't let Mom raise him while I'm… like this. He's with my next-door neighbor now. I need you to look after him. Care for him, give him a good, stable life."

"Of course." Johnny nodded without hesitation. "He'll be in the best of hands while you recover. Even if I have to move back to the city to do it. I'll treat him like my own."

"Thank you." Megan exhaled, closing her eyes. "I already told Mom my wishes. She kinda stormed outta here earlier. But if I tell it to a lawyer…" Her tired voice trailed off.

"Just leave it all to me. I'll figure it out. Make it work."

Megan was fading. Her energy decreasing rapidly. She caressed Johnny's hand with her thumb, then gently let go.

A different monitor above her bed started to make intermittent sounds. A morphine drip had been activated, supplying another dose of powerful painkillers. A nurse walked over and tapped Johnny on the shoulder.

"Sir, time to let Ms. Price get her rest. She's going to need it. You can spend more time with her once she's in a private room."

Johnny stood up from his kneeling position and nodded in the nurse's direction. "Just let me say a proper goodbye." He leaned over Megan once more and tenderly kissed her cheek. Then moving his lips beside her ear, he whispered, "They're making me leave you for now. But I'll be back soon. Hang in there, Meg. I won't be long."

Johnny brushed a few blonde strands off Megan's face. He stood in place for a moment, watching her breathe. At last, he slowly backed away from her bed, his eyes on her all the while. But as he turned to depart the room, he saw Megan's eye's open slowly.

"Always running away from me, Johnny Elias," she uttered in a low voice, the hint of a smile lighting up her face.

Acknowledgements

Poet of the Wrong Generation was originally written as a screen treatment for professor, Terrance Ross at Adelphi University back in 1992. The 30-page original was radically different from this novel, though it did contain the basic story outline and most of the primary characters. Also interwoven into this eclectic school project were the lyrics to six song compositions, including the one from which the title was born.

The school draft merited an 'A' and opened a few eyes, though ultimately, it sat collecting dust in a dresser drawer for ten years. It wasn't until November of 2002, that I finally decided to revisit the project.

The years in between were not unproductive. I got married, had a child and launched a career in PR & Marketing. I always knew I had a story to tell, and would someday find a way to get it told. Giving up was never an option.

In July of 2002, my professional life took an unexpected turn -- a position promoting the literary career of the iconic novelist, Barbara Taylor Bradford. It was during the early months, while reading through a stack of Barbara's then 18 bestsellers, that I grew convinced of my ability to write a novel of my own. To date, I had written magazine articles, short stories, and an assortment of publicity materials. Surely the leap to composing a full-length saga couldn't be too difficult, I guessed. Plus, I did have this shell of a story sitting in a dresser drawer for over a decade.

It took four intense months of writing, researching, revamping and polishing. I'd spend every waking hour, either typing, or proofreading, when not earning a living, or seeing my family on rare occasion. It was a grueling process, but one I'd come to find as the most personally gratifying experience in my life to date.

Although the story of Johnny Elias and his musical poetry came from my imagination, there were many who provided extraordinary contributions along the way.

Firstly, I must acknowledge my wife, Simona, without whom this would never have been. Aside from her constant encouragement, 'Mo' was my virtual stand-in in all aspects of life while my mind was somewhere back in fictional 1992. I also must thank my daughter, Amber, who kept vigil by my computer desk, doing her best to borrow even a few minutes from her seriously distracted dad. My daughter, Casey, was not yet born during the writing of this work, but her constant encouragement to see my name on a "real book cover" helped push me to revisit this project long after it had been tabled for a third time.

I owe everything to my Mom and Dad who have made every conceivable sacrifice to ensure that my big break would eventually come. My brothers, Todd and Ryan, provided countless real-life inspiration, as did my in-laws, Judy & Jim, and my brother-in-law, Josh.

I've often told my editor, Jeannette de Beauvoir, that her contributions were like that of an Olympic coach, who could identify all my blind spots. Jeannette, in my quest for the gold, you've been a world class instructor – kind with praise, but never afraid to kick my butt where necessary!

My friend, Ben Wulfsohn, was my original story editor. He also helped give life to the immortal, Ron Neswick.

My heartfelt gratitude to Jan Brogan, an exceptional mystery writer who shared many clues in formatting and style on the roadmap to publication.

Thanks to all the early manuscript readers for your remarkable feedback – especially Judy, Josh, Carol, David P., Dean, Karen, Damian, Naomi and Rachel.

Thank you to my friend, Ann-Marie Nieves of GetRed PR and the folks at The Editorial Department for helping to bring this story to the masses. Hats off to Rob Sauber for his years of encouragement, and for his inventive execution of the cover design and interior layout.

Special thanks to my college English professor, William Hochman for pushing me to strive for written excellence.

And finally, thank you all for taking this fictional journey with me in reading this novel, which has been so many years in the making. I greatly look forward to your feedback and reviews.

CPSIA information can be obtained
at www.ICGtesting.com
Printed in the USA
BVOW08s0232091116
467325BV00001B/26/P